the COUNTRY COOKBOOK

Belinda Jeffery has shown herself to be the quiet achiever of the food industry. Renowned for her warm and reassuring style, she has garnered a strong following throughout her career as a chef, cafe proprietor, TV food presenter, radio personality and cooking teacher. From her home in northern New South Wales, Belinda now focuses on writing and teaching. She is a regular contributor to *delicious.* and other food and wine magazines, a restaurant reviewer for the *Sydney Morning Herald Good Food Guide*, and an experienced judge for a number of industry awards. Belinda's previous cookbooks include *Mix & Bake, Belinda Jeffery's 100 Favourite Recipes* and *Belinda Jeffery's Tried-and-True Recipes.*

for my darling Clive

the COUNTRY COOKBOOK

BELINDA JEFFERY

photography by Rodney Weidland

LANTERN
an imprint of
PENGUIN BOOKS

CONTENTS

INTRODUCTION: A Life in the Country

Looking over the pages of my journal that chronicle our move to the country in December 2002 brings it all flooding back to me.

'Who would have thought it! That somehow things would finally come together and we would find ourselves packing our belongings into the back of a truck and heading off to a new life. We had talked about it for years but somehow it seemed to be a carrot that always dangled just beyond our reach, something that other people did. What finally tipped the scales and sent us on our way? I suspect a number of things coming in fairly quick succession.

We had all but decided towards the end of 2001 that, if we were ever going to move, now was the time. We weren't retiring (we are a long way off being able to do that) but we really wanted our lives to change. Clive travels a lot with his work as an industrial auctioneer and valuer, but his head office is in Sydney, and he was taking longer and longer (often up to three hours a day) to do the return journey and it was slowly taking its toll. I had given up my television career the year before, much to everyone's surprise, and was hoping to make a living from writing and teaching. We both found the pace, noise and just the sheer numbers of people in the city were starting to overwhelm us, and we were longing for something quieter, more peaceful. To help us decide, we set off on a trip up the coast to revisit some places we hadn't been to in years and stumbled into what for us was paradise . . . Paradise Mullum(bimby).

We returned to Sydney all fired up to get things under way, but as is so often the case, we both got bogged down in our work again and tended to put things on hold for a bit. I was finishing my second book; Clive was busier than ever at work. Slowly, but inexorably, time was slipping past. On the weekends we looked at houses and land on the internet, yet still felt unable to commit to the Big Move. It was always *next week, next month*.

We were both brought up short when, in May 2002, I was diagnosed with the early stages of breast cancer. (It's the first time I've written those words, and seeing them on the page makes my stomach feel quite hollow.) I was fortunate that it was picked up very early so although I had surgery and radiation treatment, I didn't have to undergo the gruelling rounds of chemotherapy. The cancer diagnosis wasn't the reason for our move, as we had long before decided to go. However it is one of those events in life that really does focus your attention on what you are doing and where you are going, and we realised we didn't want to put things off any longer.

That was June. By the beginning of December we had sold our house; Clive had resigned from work; we had sadly farewelled our family and friends, and were heading up the highway to who knows what?

That's a scary, yet exciting, feeling. For the first time since our twenties, when we had travelled around Europe in a Kombi van, we had no real ties anywhere. All our worldly goods were in the back of a truck and it would be a few days before we could move into our rented home. It was actually rather wonderful, a no-man's land where anything seemed possible.

That first night we stayed in a motel at Brunswick Heads and walked up the road by the river to have dinner in the beer garden of the lovely old Brunnie pub. It was a warm evening and, as we sat underneath the blossoming poinciana and frangipani trees watching the sun dip behind the hills, we toasted each other and, with some awe, said the words we've repeated over and over since then, 'We live here now'.

And so began our new life.'

Extract from Belinda's journal, which first appeared in *Scorched: Penguin Australian Summer Stories* (2004)

It's hard to believe that I wrote those words seven years ago. So much has changed in that time. As I write this now it's early morning, and I have to pinch myself when I look out onto the hills and hear the cows in the distance, remembering that in our city life I would have quite probably been stuck in a traffic jam on Military Road at this hour – and feeling ever so grateful that I'm not.

I really don't know what on earth possessed me when I proposed writing this book. I guess it seemed like a good idea at the time! However, I can only conclude that I must have been of unsound mind when I suggested it, since what I thought was going to be a small book about living here has grown like Topsy into the rather large volume you hold in your hands.

In my defence, I so love the area we've moved to, and our life here, that it just seemed as natural as breathing to write about it. But now, as I read my words about birds and bees, flowers and food, people and places, I do wonder if anyone will be remotely interested. But then again, if I think of the regular phone calls we get and the questions we are asked about our move, I figure that many of our friends and colleagues are feeling much the same as we were seven years ago and wondering what a move to the country may mean.

Truth be told, like everything we do in this life, moves like ours have their highs and lows. The 'ups' for us have far outweighed the 'downs', but it hasn't all been one easy ride, and our initial struggles to survive financially put a big strain on us. Fortunately, I can write about that in retrospect now (at least I hope so!), however for the first few years it was really hard and many times we wondered if we would be forced to sell our home and perhaps even return to the city to get by. I'm happy to say that to date this hasn't been necessary.

In many ways I find it difficult to answer the question: how is life in the country (or perhaps more truthfully worded, away from the city)? For I can feel the yearning and hopes behind it; the hope that we will say, yes it's true that life in the country is more peaceful and calm, people are more friendly, there is more time. However, it's not really possible to give such a simple answer, for it's not that straightforward. Life here is just different. Certainly not quieter (oh goodness, now there's an understatement!); richer – yes, I think so; more closely linked to the environment – a resounding yes; peaceful – well, that's definitely stretching things a bit; kinder – yes, perhaps that's the best way to put it. For us, life here is kinder, simpler and more how we hoped to live our lives. Perhaps that's the biggest difference of all: we both feel in our bones a contentment that we didn't have before.

So although this is fundamentally a book about food and cooking, it also goes far beyond that. For me it is a celebration of, and a grateful thank you for, the life we have here.

And so to the food around which much of our lives revolve . . .

INGREDIENTS & COOKWARE

I try to avoid being too prescriptive about what you should use in recipes, or what equipment you should have in your kitchen, but there are some things I'd find it hard to do without. The following really add to the pleasure I get from cooking, and so I'd like to share them with you.

Ingredients

CAPERS

Lots of capers come pickled in vinegar and/or brine but perhaps the nicest tasting of all are salted capers. These are preserved in salt only and sold in small jars. You need to rinse them in a few changes of cold water to remove the excess salt but the flavour is much less sharp and more complex than the vinegared ones.

CULTURED (CONTINENTAL) UNSALTED BUTTER

In all the recipes here I recommend using unsalted butter. Regular unsalted butter is fine, however if you can find cultured unsalted butter (it's also called continental butter) then give it a whirl. This butter has a culture added to it, in much the same way as milk has to make yoghurt, or cream to make sour cream. It gives the butter a superb, slightly tangy flavour and lovely clean finish that is particularly delicious. There are lots of different sorts around, ranging from costly French imports to local supermarket brands. The French ones are divine and look beautiful in their rather special packaging, but quite honestly for everyday use I stick with the middle of the road ones and they're very good.

DUTCH PROCESSED COCOA POWDER

There are a few types of cocoa powder on the market but I nearly always use brands that have been 'Dutch processed' – all this means is that the cocoa has gone through a process that removes some of its acidity. It gives the cocoa a softer, smoother flavour, richer colour and it tends to dissolve more easily. This style of 'Dutched' cocoa is usually available in good delis, speciality food shops and larger supermarkets.

EGGS

All these recipes were made with 60 g eggs at cool room temperature (unless I have specified otherwise). As to the eggs themselves, by all means use regular eggs, they'll work just fine. However, I prefer to use free-range eggs for both ethical and taste reasons – the chooks lead a more normal, scratching-about kind of life and the eggs usually have a lot more flavour. You can also buy free-range organic eggs; if you see some I really recommend that you give them a try, especially if you're an egg sort of person. You'll find that they're a revelation . . . they taste wonderful, just how you hope an egg will, and make the best omelettes, poached eggs and simple soft-boiled eggs.

MAPLE SYRUP

Maple syrup is magical stuff, with an intense woody flavour and a fragrance that nothing else can duplicate. The trouble is, there are a lot of syrups around that appear to be maple syrup, but they're not. Always check the label to make sure you're getting the real McCoy; you want pure maple syrup, not maple-flavoured syrup. It's also important to remember that once you've opened the syrup it must be stored in the fridge, as it's highly perishable at room temperature.

PURE VANILLA EXTRACT

This may be a bit hard to find but it is worth pursuing. It's a gorgeous, dark sticky syrup made from vanilla beans and has the most wonderfully intense vanilla flavour. It's expensive but a little goes a long way. Look for it in speciality food shops, some delis and cookware stores. And if you can't find it, don't despair – if vanilla essence is all you can get, that will be fine, just increase the quantity specified in the recipe by half again to help give it a good vanilla flavour. Alternatively you can make a pretty good version yourself. To do this, dissolve a tablespoonful of sugar in a litre of white rum or brandy. Add 10–12 split vanilla beans, seal the bottle tightly, then leave it for at least three weeks, shaking it now and then, before using it.

RICE FOR RISOTTO

The best varieties of rice to use for risotto are carnaroli, vialone nano or arborio. They are all plump, large-grained rices (although vialone nano is a little stubbier than the other two) that give off a good amount of starch to thicken the risotto, but at the same time absorb the stock without disintegrating so they retain a slightly chewy firmness.

SAFFRON

Saffron gives food a wonderful warm spicy fragrance with a slight hint of bitterness and a glorious golden glow. It's actually the tiny golden stamens from a particular type of crocus flower – each flower has only three stamens and roughly 20,000 of these equate to just 125 g of saffron and it's all hand picked! Which is why it's so expensive. If you have the choice, buy the threads rather than ground saffron as the flavour is far more intense. To get the best colour and flavour out of them, crush them and then infuse them for ten minutes in a little of the cooking liquid from the recipe you are making.

SMOKED PAPRIKA

Smoked paprika is made from peppers that are dried over smouldering oak fires for about two weeks before they're cooled and ground. This gives the paprika the most wonderful rich, smoky flavour but it is quite intense so it's a good idea to add a bit less, rather than more initially and then go from there, otherwise its flavour can be overwhelming. There are at least three styles available: sweet, bittersweet and hot, so just use whichever you prefer.

STOCK

Ideally, when I mention stock in a recipe, I am referring to homemade stock (see, for example, the chicken stock recipe on page 210). However, I realise that we don't all have it on hand all of the time, and there is nothing more frustrating than being admonished by a recipe that insists you must use homemade stock or nothing. Sometimes I think it really does matter – in risottos, certain soups and some sauces – but not always. I certainly get caught out from time to time, and when I do (and I don't wish this to sound like an advertisement), I make up some Marigold vegetable stock and it works really well. It's certainly the best commercial stock powder I've ever tried.

Cookware

KUGELHOPFS, BUNDTS AND OTHER SUCH THINGS

Many people's eyes glaze over when they hear the terms 'bundt', 'kugelhopf' (or gugelhupf if you prefer!) and 'fluted ring' tins. They are basically similar in that they're fluted cake tins with a central hole, much like an elaborate deeper version of a regular ring tin. You can quite often swap one for the other when you make big cakes but a bundt is only ever a large tin while a kugelhopf or fluted ring tin can come in many sizes. If you sit the three of them side by side, the kugelhopf is taller with a central funnel and quite an elaborate two-tiered pattern on the outside. The fluted ring tin has long swirling flutes from top to bottom and the bundt has a less elaborate pattern with a wider central tube and broader fluting with alternating wide and small raised ribs. They tend to be measured by the volume of liquid they can hold (that is, you can buy 6, 8,10 and 12 cup kugelhopf tins).

LE CREUSET CASSEROLES

Oh, how I wish I had more of them! I only have the one – a deep, medium-sized dish that is perfect for a casserole for four. However, I have to confess I covet one of the larger, slightly shallower dishes that is perfect for cooking for up to eight people. Yes, they're expensive, but I figure that any I have will outlast me so that's got to be a good investment! I love the way they go from cooktop to oven to table, so you don't have to swap pans and dishes and generally create more mess.

MANDOLIN

I promise this is the one bit of exotica that I'll mention but it is just so useful that I couldn't leave it out. It is the fastest way to shred and slice anything perfectly. They range considerably in price from expensive restaurant-quality ones to plastic Japanese ones (which is what I use) that are half the price, although still not cheap. However, if you do a lot of cooking I can't recommend them highly enough.

OVEN TEMPERATURES

The oven temperatures given throughout the book are for conventional ovens; if you have a fan-forced oven, you may need to reduce the temperature by 10–20°C, depending on your oven.

PRESERVING PANS

These large, wide, heavy-based pans are designed to allow excess water in the fruit mixture to evaporate as quickly as possible. Traditionally they were made from thick beaten copper and these beautiful pans are still available (although they're hideously expensive). There are also some very good stainless steel ones with off-set handles and lips for easy pouring. These are somewhat cheaper, and if you are going to make jam and/or marmalade regularly then it's probably worth investing in one. I've had mine for years and I love it as it's burnished with age and so wonderfully functional.

SPICE MILL

I don't want to rave on about it, but if you use spices regularly in your cooking then it's really worthwhile buying a little electric spice mill to grind them yourself as the flavour is so much fresher and brighter. Small quantities are fine to grind in a mortar and pestle, but I'd have to say my mill has been worth its weight in gold over the years and saved me an awful lot of elbow grease. A small electric coffee grinder is another option – they're fantastic for grinding whole spices to a powder in no time. Just don't use the same grinder for coffee beans or you'll have a very interesting brew!

WIDE-MOUTHED FUNNEL

One of the best cooking utensils I have ever bought myself is an inexpensive, wide-mouthed preserving funnel. They are fabulous things if you are one of my mob and like your preserving, as they enable you to funnel the mixture easily into the jars without it dripping everywhere. Before I would have marmalade or chutney all over the sides of the jars and the bench, but now, thank goodness, it tends to go where I want it!

DECEMBER

1st December

It is the first day of summer and it somehow feels appropriate that I start here, as it is the anniversary of the day we first arrived in Mullumbimby. Back then a cruel drought was in full swing, wreaking havoc everywhere, and in our very small way we too were affected, as we had to cart water to the few herbs we'd planted in the garden to help them survive.

It's hard to believe that today. As I write this I can look out my window to the herb garden and see tall heads of parsley nodding in the breeze, and mint running rampant (I know it should be in a pot but I rather love the way it pops up willy-nilly, and every so often I do have a blitz on it to get it under control). Straight spires of rosemary shoot out of their pot; thyme, both my favourite sweet thyme for cooking and its more picturesque cousin, lemon thyme, sprawl across the bed. The chives, with their delicate mauve flowers, are flourishing, and the neighbouring garlic chives are totally out of control! Basil is springing up all over the garden because I shake the long seed heads out when I cut them and let the seeds find a home where they will; and the oregano has taken off under the pavers, which I know isn't a good idea, but I must say the perfume that wafts up when we walk on them is delicious. Along with these staples, at different times of year dill and coriander flourish, and various other herbs make an appearance in their own season.

I love them all and, having lived in an apartment for many years, being able to pad across the lawn barefoot to pick them always feels like a huge privilege.

But if I had to pick a favourite it would probably be the most common of them all – parsley (or more truthfully, flat-leaf or continental parsley, as I can't abide the scratchy texture of curly parsley). I never used to like it – as a child I loathed its intense 'green' taste but, as is the case with lots of foods we take an early disliking to, I sort of grew into it. Funnily enough, the same thing happened with tea – I couldn't bear it at one stage, then slowly but surely it won me over, and now the thought of a day without a cup of tea leaves me feeling less optimistic about the world around me. And now I can't imagine life without parsley either. I scatter seedlings throughout the garden and delight in the emerald-green clumps that form. I also love the flowers and invariably let a few plants go to seed so they form their impossibly lacy, umbrella-like heads that dust me with pollen as I garden beneath them.

I have just picked a huge bunch to make some pesto to go with roasted tomatoes. The parsley makes a greener, slightly sharper version of traditional basil pesto and, for want of a better name, the rather wonderful resulting parsley sauce-cum-dip is known affectionately in the family as 'gloop'.

But before I give you the recipe I must mention the tomatoes. I was smiling to myself as I unpacked the shopping this morning, for in amongst it all were my 'classical' tomatoes. Only in Mullumbimby! They look beautiful – as plump as plump and bright red. The farmer who grows them lives just over the hill from us, and has classical music piped into his greenhouses to help his plants grow (hence the name), and I have to tell you, they taste wonderful! How could they not with all that TLC and the Brandenburg Concertos playing in the background?

Roasted Tomatoes with Parsley & Macadamia Pesto

SERVES 6

You won't use up all the pesto on the tomatoes in this recipe, however it's so delicious that I always make the full quantity – about 2 cups (600 g). Leftovers are lovely stirred through cooked green beans, or spooned into roast mushrooms during their last few minutes in the oven; we've also blobbed it onto carrot soup (the colours are stunning) and mixed it into pasta with a good handful of grated parmesan (rather fabulous, particularly if you add some chopped roasted tomatoes too). It also makes a delicious dip when mixed into soft goat's curd or marinated goat's cheese – the proportions are about ½ cup pesto to 150 g goat's cheese. It freezes well, but if you're doing this, don't add the lemon juice or mayonnaise until you are going to use it. This way, you'll retain the brilliant green colour.

10 nice smallish red tomatoes, halved
2–3 tablespoons extra virgin olive oil
sugar, to taste
sea salt flakes, to taste
200 g goat's cheese marinated in olive oil
tiny parsley sprigs or leaves, to garnish

PARSLEY AND MACADAMIA PESTO

large bunch of flat-leaf parsley (about 200 g), coarsely chopped
2 cloves garlic, coarsely chopped
140 g roasted macadamias (or almonds)
1½ teaspoons sea salt flakes
½ cup (125 ml) extra virgin olive oil
2 tablespoons lemon juice
⅓ cup (100 g) good-quality mayonnaise
2 tablespoons freshly grated parmesan, or more to taste
olive oil, for storing

- Preheat your oven to 160°C and line a shallow baking tray with baking paper. If you're using oval roma tomatoes, slice them lengthways and make a very shallow V-shaped cut to remove the core from each half. If you're using round tomatoes, halve them horizontally but leave the core intact. Sit the halves, cut-side up, on the baking tray.
- Drizzle a little olive oil evenly over the halves, then sprinkle a tiny pinch of sugar and salt onto each one. Put the tray in the oven and roast the tomatoes for about 1½ hours. The time will vary a bit depending on their size – they should look somewhat crinkly but still moist.
- While the tomatoes are cooking, make the pesto. Put the parsley and garlic in a food processor and whiz them together for about 10 seconds. Add the nuts and salt and whiz for another 10 seconds or so. With the motor running, drizzle the oil through the feed tube and process until the pesto is as fine as you would like it. Finally, add the lemon juice, mayonnaise and parmesan and process until just combined. Scrape the pesto out of the food processor into a container (use one with a tightly fitting lid or your fridge will reek of garlic!). Smooth the top of the pesto and pour a thin film of olive oil over the surface to seal it. Store it, tightly covered, in the fridge, where it will keep well for a couple of weeks, or you can freeze the pesto base (without the lemon juice, mayonnaise and parmesan) for 4 weeks, adding these ingredients after it has defrosted. ›

- When the tomatoes are ready, remove them from the oven. Sit a little goat's cheese on each tomato half, then return them to the oven for a minute or so to soften the cheese slightly. Carefully transfer them to a platter, scoop some pesto on top of the cheese and finish off with a tiny sprig or leaf of parsley. They are lovely as part of an antipasto spread, and go particularly well with barbecued fish, lamb and chicken.

PIG TAILS . . .

If you want pretty, curly 'pig' tails on the parsley leaves (like those in the photograph below), pull the tiny leaves gently off their stalks, trying to bring a thin string of stalk with them. Pop them into a small bowl and cover them with iced water. Store them in the fridge for 30 minutes or so and their little tails should be nicely curled!

3rd December

We have been eating outside most nights, in the hope of catching what little breeze might be around as it is just too oppressive indoors. Tonight, as we sat in the cool listening to the frogs start up, we both caught the exquisite fragrance of the night-blooming jessamine. It is the most unprepossessing, straggly-looking shrub with tiny trumpet-shaped green and cream flowers, which in the daytime have no scent whatsoever, but once night falls they open up to release one of the all-time great perfumes. The air was positively heady with it and we sat quietly talking, bathed in its extraordinary scent. I must admit that despite the heat I treasure these evenings, as there is something so restful and soothing about being out under the stars, listening to the night sounds. Eventually our conversation stops and we just sit gazing up in wonder at the night sky.

5th December

Oh gosh, it's sticky today. It has been unbelievably soggy here this past month, and the dreaded black mould that I was warned about when we first arrived has finally made its appearance. I nearly wept when, in a fit of pre-Christmas cleaning, I pulled my shoes and favourite leather jacket out of the cupboard only to find them streaked with mould. I have now bought every closet camel within cooee and decided that I should invest in some of the company's shares as I've no doubt there will be a run on them this summer. However, the plus side of all this is that the fields are knee-deep in lush grass, the dams are full, and creeks that haven't run for years are actually starting to. Whoopee!

By the way, if you are wondering what on earth closet camels are, you are not alone. I'd never heard of them until we moved here, and for ages I wondered what everyone was talking about. Basically they are little pots of moisture-absorbing beads that you put in cupboards to help prevent the aforementioned mould. Although they need regular replacing, they're worth their weight in gold – otherwise I suspect our wardrobes would be fertile ground for growing mushrooms!

Speaking of mushrooms, these little chaps sprang up overnight on an old piece of timber that was outside the back door. They looked so cheeky and perfect that we couldn't resist photographing them.

The rain has also given the trees a new lease of life – I can't remember ever seeing the poincianas look as magnificent as they do this summer. They are a blaze of colour, with great garlands of vivid red and crimson flowers cascading down the branches, which, in turn, dip almost to the ground, creating pools of shade that always make me want to stop and lean against the trunks.

We have a small-ish one (relatively speaking, as they grow to quite massive proportions) in our garden, and in summer we set up a table and chairs underneath. It's our favourite spot to sit with a cup of tea when we've been gardening. From its shade we watch the finches and wrens splash and swoop in and out of the birdbath.

The brown kurrajongs are flowering too, and I love the way the creamy white clusters of blossom make the trees look as though somebody has dusted them with icing sugar. Much like me at this time of year! I find myself almost permanently swathed in a cloud of it as I do my Christmas baking – a job I love and only wish I had more time for.

Shortbread & Fruit Mince 'Pie'

SERVES 8–12

2 cups (300 g) plain flour
1 teaspoon baking powder
pinch of salt
250 g unsalted butter, at cool room temperature
1 cup (220 g) caster sugar
2 egg yolks
2 teaspoons vanilla extract
1 cup (about 300 g) fruit mince
icing sugar, for dusting

What's that saying about the path to heaven being paved with good intentions? Well, hopefully my Christmas good intentions will help pave my way! For I always resolve to make mince pies for Christmas, as they are one of my favourite things, but time invariably gets away from me and I rarely end up doing them. Having said that, I have been known to stay up on Christmas Eve baking batch after batch as gifts, but this really is cutting things a bit fine, and you need it like a hole in the head with all the other cooking to be done.

So last Christmas I decided I would have to do something (anything!) to get my mince pie fix, and this recipe is the result. It is soooo easy to make and tastes wonderful: crisp, buttery shortbread encasing a lovely, boozy fruit-mince filling. Ideally the fruit mince would be homemade, but there is nothing wrong with using a good bought one – I do, and usually doctor it with a bit more brandy. And although the end result may not look quite as whimsical as bite-sized mince pies, it does look very pretty and Christmassy in its own way, with its lacy shortbread top and dusting of icing sugar.

- Put the flour, baking powder and salt into the bowl of a food processor and whiz them together so they're thoroughly mixed. Tip them into a bowl.
- Cut the butter into rough chunks and put it in the food processor along with the caster sugar. Whiz for about 40 seconds until the mixture is pale and creamy (you may need to stop the machine and scrape down the sides once or twice). Add the egg yolks and vanilla, then process again for 15 seconds until well combined.
- Now add the flour mixture to the butter mixture and pulse the machine in short bursts until a ball of dough forms around the blade (try not to over-do this mixing or the shortbread may be a bit tough).
- Turn the dough out onto a very lightly floured board and shape it into a log (if the dough seems too soft to do this, chill it for a little while first so it firms up enough to handle comfortably). Divide it in half and wrap each piece in plastic film. Put the dough logs in the fridge and chill them for at least 3 hours (or you can leave them overnight) until they are really firm.
- Preheat your oven to 180°C and very lightly butter a 25 cm loose-based tart tin. Remove one of the dough logs from the fridge. Use the side of a box grater with the largest holes to grate the dough onto a plate. I tend to do this in batches as the grater fills quite quickly and the dough strands will squash if they become too compacted. As you finish each batch carefully transfer the grated dough to the prepared tin. When you have finished grating it, gently pat the dough strands out evenly over the base of the tin, trying not to squash them down too much.

- Now dollop the fruit mince evenly over the grated dough, then smooth it out thinly as best you can with a palette knife, leaving a 1 cm border all the way around the edge. Grate the remaining log of dough the same way as before and sprinkle it over the fruit mince. Give it the lightest pat down to even it out.
- Carefully transfer the tin to the oven (watch out you don't 'pop' the base up – I have been known to do this!) and bake the pie for about 35 minutes, or until it's golden brown. Remove it from the oven and leave it to cool completely in the tin on a rack.
- To serve, gently remove the pie from the tin, dust it with icing sugar and cut it into wedges. It's equally lovely served simply with a cup of tea, as a dessert with a spoonful of double thick cream or, to be really Christmassy, a little brandy or rum butter.

10th December

I discovered the most beautiful bundles of fat organic asparagus spears at the market this week. They're grown by two friends of ours who have planted out a number of beds and laughingly call them their superannuation – on their reckoning, by the time they retire asparagus will cost a fortune. And it's not hard to imagine they're right! It's wonderful asparagus: brilliant green and so tender that as I snap off the bases I end up eating them raw – no peeling needed with this little lot. I know it may sound a bit odd to peel the spears, but the skin on some asparagus is very coarse and it's best to strip it off with a sharp peeler, peeling from the base to just below the tip. It also looks rather beautiful when it's cooked, as the peeled stems turn a glorious translucent green in contrast to the vivid tops. By the way, if you're lucky enough to come across some white asparagus, just remember it must always be peeled as the skin is very tough. It is worth the work as the flavour is exquisite – mellow and buttery without the need for butter, although I have been known to gild the lily from time to time.

Along with the asparagus I also managed to snaffle half a dozen blowsy 'rouge de marmande' tomatoes. They're such whimsical-looking things; the kind of tomato I used to draw when I was young – slightly squashed and knobbly with mottled crimson skin that tapers to green at the top, with a jaunty little stalk sunk like a belly button into the folds. They're not made for travelling as the skins are delicate, so I carefully sat them on the back seat of the car for the journey home. They usually take a few days to ripen and when they have, I can do no more than combine them with some tender mouthfuls of bocconcini, basil leaves and lots of good olive oil and freshly ground black pepper.

Fortunately we don't have to wait for the asparagus, so I shall cook some tonight in a classic dish of asparagus mimosa. It looks wonderful mounded up on a simple white platter, and all you really need is some good wheaty brown bread and butter to go with it. A simpler version still, and one we eat a lot, is just to poach some eggs and sit these on top of the bundles of warm asparagus, along with a good dose of melted butter and squeeze of lemon juice – there is nothing finer.

Asparagus Mimosa with Mustard Vinaigrette

SERVES 2

This is such an appealing-looking dish, with the jade-green asparagus spears contrasting with the gold and white of the eggs. I know it may seem a little odd to grate the eggs, but in fact it gives them a lovely fluffy texture and they look much prettier than when they are chopped. Honeycup mustard is a terrific slightly hot, sweet mustard available from delis and food stores. I also mention the possibility of using Dijonnaise – this rather fabulous invention is a combination of Dijon mustard and mayonnaise. I always make sure I have a jar in the fridge as it adds the perfect little jolt of piquancy to all sorts of sandwiches and salads . . . and I have been known to slather it over lamb chops. Just don't blame me if you get hooked on the stuff!

about 20 nice fat spears of asparagus
2 hard-boiled eggs, finely grated
a few chives, snipped, to garnish (or some chopped parsley)

DRESSING

¼–⅓ cup (60–80 ml) extra virgin olive oil
3 teaspoons lemon juice
1 teaspoon white wine vinegar
2 teaspoons Honeycup or Dijon mustard (or Dijonnaise), optional
sea salt flakes, to taste

- First, make the dressing. To do this, put all the dressing ingredients into a bowl and whisk them together until the mustard has thoroughly dissolved. Taste it and adjust the flavours to suit you. I know I bang on about tasting things but it's so important – ingredients vary all the time and I am forever tweaking recipes to make them just right. I don't think I've ever made the same salad dressing twice!

- Meanwhile, fill a large frying pan with water and bring it to the boil. Trim the bases of the asparagus and peel them if you like. Lay the spears in the water and adjust the heat so the water bubbles gently around them (if you don't have a large pan, use two smaller pans or cook the asparagus in batches). Cook for 2–3 minutes or until just tender – the cooking time will vary quite a bit, depending on the thickness of the spears. To check, pierce the thickest part of one stalk with a fine skewer; it should 'give' quite easily. As soon as they're ready, lift them out of the water onto a thick tea towel and wrap them up to keep them warm. (Or if you want to serve the asparagus cool, tumble it into a bowl of ice and water to stop it cooking and set the colour, then drain and dry it.)

- To serve, thoroughly combine the spears with some of the dressing in a large bowl and pile them onto a platter. Drizzle the remaining dressing over the top. Sprinkle the grated egg over the spears, leaving the tips and bases exposed, and scatter with the snipped chives or parsley.

12th December

What a sight for sore eyes! Rodney is up for a few weeks so we can take more photographs for the book, and as it is so hot we've been starting early in the morning in a bid to beat the heat and avoid everything melting before we can shoot it. Well, this morning as Rodney, Clive and I had our breakfast outside (at 6 a.m., God help us!), we could hear much excited chittering in the bushes and next minute, two dear little blue fairy wrens appeared. They were obviously courting, and so absorbed in each other that they were totally oblivious to us. Usually they are constantly on the move, but much to our delight these two sat for ages, quietly grooming each other – it was a wonderful sight.

13th December

We are having our annual Christmas street drinks party tonight. It's always a very relaxed affair where we set up a table on the verge of the road overlooking the hills, and everyone brings chairs, something to drink and a plate of food. It's fun for one and all – adults, kids, dogs, even the odd cat joins in – and so laid-back. We sit about talking and laughing, watching the sun go down and the stars appear, and generally enjoying time out from what can feel like the headlong rush towards Christmas.

For my part, I have just made a tray of parmesan crisps (see page 24) and four batches of these unbelievably more-ish macadamias (see recipe overleaf). It was a no-brainer for me to decide what to bring, as my neighbours informed me that I *had* to make both of these!

Sweet & Salty Toffeed Macadamias

MAKES ABOUT 2 CUPS (300 G)

- **1–2 tablespoons macadamia oil (or light olive oil)**
- **280 g shelled macadamias (whole or halves are fine)**
- **½ cup (110 g) caster sugar**
- **1½ teaspoons regular salt**
- **2 teaspoons freshly ground cumin seeds**
- **¾ teaspoon freshly ground coriander seeds**
- **1 tablespoon caster sugar, extra**
- **1 teaspoon sea salt flakes**

This must be one of my most asked-for recipes – these nuts are so simple to make and incredibly addictive. We usually have them with a drink before dinner, and I've had friends beg me to take the bowl away as they can't stop eating them. I think what does it is that fantastic blend of sweet, spicy and salty flavours that works so well, especially when combined with the crisp crunch of the toffee-coated nuts. I've always loved this sweet/salt combination of flavours – even when I was a littlie I would dip slices of apple into salt before eating them, or munch on pears with slices of cheddar. As a grown-up I've simply graduated to a wider repertoire of combinations: I love cheese served with sweet quince or plum paste; or a creamy, salty gorgonzola dolcelatte with honey drizzled over the top.

By the way, if you want to double this recipe, it's best to make two single batches in separate pans. I know it seems a bit of a hassle, but if you lob them all in together the nuts tend not to caramelise properly.

- Line a large baking tray with baking paper and set it aside.
- Heat the oil in a large, heavy-based frying pan over medium–low heat. When it's warm, tip in the macadamias and shake the pan about to coat them with the oil. Reduce the heat to fairly low and sprinkle the ½ cup of caster sugar evenly over the nuts. Now, cook the nuts, stirring constantly so they don't burn, until they're golden brown and the sugar has caramelised to form a darkish toffee. You need to watch the nuts like a hawk as once the sugar starts to colour, it can go from golden to burnt rather rapidly; I find I usually have to adjust the heat a bit too. Although I say cook them until they're golden brown, don't worry if some are darker than others – it's nigh on impossible to get them evenly browned (I certainly never do) and the darker ones taste just as delicious as their lighter counterparts.
- While the nuts are cooking, mix together the regular salt, cumin, coriander and extra tablespoon of caster sugar in a large heatproof bowl. As soon as the nuts are ready, add them to the spice mixture and toss them about so they are thoroughly coated in it.
- Now scrape them out of the bowl onto the prepared tray and separate them as best you can with a wooden spoon, as they tend to stick together. Sprinkle them evenly with the sea salt and leave them to cool and set.
- Once they are completely cool put them into a jar and seal tightly, then squirrel them away where no one can find them too easily!

BY THE WAY . . .

Ideally it is best to grind the cumin and coriander seeds yourself; second best is to use the freshest ground spices you can buy. Give any open packets you may have lurking in the cupboard a good sniff before you use them, to make sure they still have lots of fragrance, as ground spices tend to lose their oomph quite rapidly.

One thing I have noticed when making this recipe is that if the macadamias are very fresh they tend to release quite a lot of oil as you heat them in the pan. The first time this happened to me, I was a bit taken aback at the amount of oil they gave out. However, I sopped up the excess and they still tasted delicious. If this happens to you (and it's good news if it does, as it means the nuts are very fresh), just let the nuts set, then pat them with paper towel to absorb the excess oil.

Parmesan Crisps with Avocado, Lime & Chilli

MAKES ABOUT 16 CRISPS

about 50 g finely grated parmesan (or grana)
herb leaves and flowers, or fine shreds of chilli and tiny mint leaves, to garnish

AVOCADO AND LIME

1 very large, just-ripe avocado
1 tablespoon lime juice, or more to taste
½ teaspoon finely chopped red chilli, or more to taste
2 packed teaspoons finely chopped chives
2 packed teaspoons finely chopped mint
sea salt flakes, to taste

It's rare for me to do what I think of as 'fiddly' food, as most things I cook tend to be a bit more robust and rustic, however just occasionally (and Christmas is one such occasion) I do make these little parmesan shells with their rather scrumptious avocado filling. They look so festive and pretty, and they tend to disappear like hot cakes. What I like about them is that although they look as if they may be quite a lot of work, they're not at all – you can whip up a batch remarkably quickly, which is a real plus in amongst all the busy-ness of Christmas.

As lots of my herbs were flowering when we photographed these, I couldn't resist using the tiny flowers and leaves as a garnish. Obviously this is not essential – they look really lovely and very Christmassy if you top them off with a few tiny shreds of chilli and wee mint leaves. (BTW, you may well have thought of it already, but guacamole is terrific in the crisps too.)

- Preheat your oven to 180°C.
- Line a baking tray with baking paper and sit an egg ring or scone-cutter, about 6 cm in diameter, on top. Sprinkle 1 tablespoon of parmesan evenly inside the ring, and press down on it gently. Lift off the ring and use the back of a spoon to tap the parmesan out very slightly. Make two more rounds, leaving a gap of a few centimetres between each round as they spread a little.
- Bake them for 5–6 minutes, or until they're pale golden and lacy-looking. When they're ready, remove the tray from the oven. Working *very* quickly (this is crucial as the cheese sets again quite rapidly), use a fine palette knife or something similar to transfer a crisp to a non-stick, mini muffin tin, lightly pressing it into one of the muffin cups to shape it. Repeat this with remaining crisps. As soon as they have set, transfer the crisps to a cooling rack. Going back a few steps, I find the first few crisps are always a bit of a learning curve as you work out just how much time you have to shape them before they set. This is why I only bake three at a time – any more than this and they've started to harden before I get to them. If you do find they have stiffened, try putting the tray back in the oven briefly and the crisps may well soften again. I usually figure on losing a few at this 'trial and error' stage (and to me popping at least another two into my mouth!).

- Continue making more crisps with the remaining parmesan. Cool the baking tray between each batch – I usually run it under cold water then dry it, or alternate between two trays. Wipe off any oil that's come out of the parmesan from the baking paper before re-using it. When all the crisps are cool, store them in tightly sealed airtight containers. They keep well for up to 5 days, which is rather a boon as you can make them well ahead of when you need them.
- Just before serving the crisps, make the avocado and lime filling. To do this, halve the avocado, remove the stone, and scoop the flesh into a bowl. Add the lime juice and mash them together until the mixture is fairly smooth. Mix in the chopped chilli, chives, mint and salt, then taste and adjust the flavours to suit you.
- Sit the crisps on a serving platter and gently scoop a heaped teaspoonful of avocado mixture into each one. Garnish with herb sprigs or chilli shreds and mint leaves. Serve them immediately, as they will soften as they sit.

18th December

The garden is a mad tangle at the moment and looks more like a jungle each day as everything runs riot in the heat. As they do every year, the gloriosa lilies have sprung up out of nowhere and surreptitiously wound their way through the pink grevilleas, only to reveal themselves now as they burst into flower. The two look stunning together.

20th December

I am at the stage of pulling out all my tried-and-true recipes to help ease the way into Christmas, for I tend to blithely ask friends around for a bite to eat (which, I hasten to add, I love to do) and then wonder how I am going to find the time to cook something. A case in point is that we have some friends coming for dinner on Christmas Eve, so in amongst writing this book, baking cakes, sending the last of the Christmas cards and cooking batch after batch of the aforementioned macadamias to give as gifts, I have just, with considerable relief, stuck a tub of honey semi-freddo in the freezer to have for dessert. At least we shall have that to eat, if nothing else! I have wonderful cook and food writer Ruth Pretty to thank for this, as the recipe is based on one of hers. All of Ruth's recipes work beautifully, as this one shows.

Honey Semi-Freddo

SERVES 6–8

⅔ cup (230 g) mild honey
8 egg yolks
300 ml thickened cream
300 ml sour cream
2 teaspoons vanilla extract

A WORD ABOUT HONEY

I tend to use a fairly light honey – more often than not, macadamia flower or white mahogany honey. However, if you prefer something with a bit more punch, you could try it with one of the darker, stronger honeys; if you are a Tasmanian leatherwood fan, I imagine it would be terrific in this.

This is a recipe that I come back to again and again as it is such a delightful dessert and takes very little time and effort to make. Although it's lovely plain, it really comes into its own when it's served with lightly cooked stone fruit of some sort or other . . . like the poached nectarines on page 40 or the roasted plums on page 113 (my favourite, as the slight tartness of the plums is perfect with the fragrant honey, and the colours are gorgeous together).

Occasionally I stir in about 80 g of coarsely chopped honeycomb just before I put it in the freezer – the little chunks add a terrific texture, although they tend to soften over time. You could also sprinkle them over the top just before you serve the semi-freddo so they stay nice and crunchy.

- Bring the honey to the boil in a small saucepan over medium heat. Leave it to boil for 2 minutes, keeping an eye on it so the honey doesn't scorch around the sides of the pan.
- Meanwhile, put the egg yolks in a large bowl (preferably stainless steel, as it will help the mixture to cool faster). With a hand-held electric beater on high speed, start beating the egg yolks. When the honey is ready, slowly pour the boiling honey onto the yolks, beating all the while so it is quickly incorporated. Keep beating the mixture for 6–8 minutes until it is pale, thick and cool. I tend to pick up the bowl as I do this to allow air to circulate around it, which helps cool the mixture down. You can make it faster still if you carefully sit the bowl with the honey mixture in a larger one that contains ice and a little water, so as you beat the icy slush cools the mixture rapidly.
- When the honey mixture is ready, set it aside for a moment. In a separate bowl whisk the thickened and sour cream with the vanilla until it is very softly whipped. Gently fold this vanilla cream into the honey mixture – if you want to add any honeycomb chunks, now is the time to do it.
- Pour the semi-freddo mixture into a freezer container, seal it tightly and freeze overnight. (It keeps well for a couple of weeks so you can make it well ahead of time if you like.)
- As I nearly always serve it with fruit, I usually just pile balls of semi-freddo into a chilled bowl and serve it family style at the table so everyone can help themselves.

Stout & Mustard Glazed Ham

MAKES 1 BAKED HAM

Like most people, I suspect, I rarely cook a whole leg of ham, however I wanted something simple and special for our Christmas Eve dinner . . . and so it was. It somehow seems so grand, sitting there in all its glazed glory, and we all felt very spoilt to be able to enjoy such a treat. I have my friend and very good cook Emma Duncan to thank for this wonderful recipe.

1 medium-sized leg of ham (about 8 kg)
1½ cups (375 ml) stout
1 cup (220 g) brown sugar
2 teaspoons ground ginger
1 heaped teaspoon freshly ground cardamom seeds
2 teaspoons English mustard powder
2–3 tablespoons stout, extra
sprigs of fresh bay leaves, to garnish
your choice of mustards and chutneys, to serve

- If you have a standard-size oven you will probably have to juggle the shelves around a bit so the ham can fit comfortably. I usually sit one shelf towards the bottom of the oven and remove the shelves above it so there is plenty of room. Once you've done that, preheat the oven to 150°C. Make sure your roasting tin is large enough to fit the ham, then line it with baking paper.
- Make a fine cut in the brown skin all the way around the shank end of the ham. Now run a finger under the edge of the rind, just underneath the skin, to loosen it from the creamy white fat beneath. Start carefully pulling the skin away from the fat. As you pull more away, hook your fingers under the skin to get a better grip. Just take it slowly and steadily so you don't tear into the fat, for ideally you want a nice, smooth layer of fat over the ham. (If the skin just won't budge in parts, use a fine knife with its blade pressed well against the skin, to loosen it from the fat.)
- Sit the ham in the roasting tin, fat-side up. Drizzle the stout over the fat, rubbing it in with your fingers as you go. Put the ham in the oven and bake it for 2 hours, basting it every 30 minutes or so with the juices that collect in the bottom of the tin.
- Meanwhile, thoroughly mix together the brown sugar, ginger, cardamom and mustard powder in a bowl.
- When the ham is ready, take it out of the oven and increase the temperature to 190°C. Now use a knife with a fine, sharp tip to score the ham, taking care to make shallow incisions into the fat only – deep ones tend to open up too much and don't look all that great once the ham is cooked. Traditionally ham is scored in a diamond pattern, but don't feel bound to this. I sometimes do wavy lines across the ham, which look rather smart, as do zigzags.
- Mix enough of the extra stout into the brown sugar mixture to form a thickish paste. Spread this evenly over the scored fat. (I usually slip on food-preparation gloves for this, as I find it easier to do with my hands rather than a spatula.)
- Return the ham to the oven and bake it for another 30 minutes. It's a good idea to check it and rotate the tin if it is browning unevenly. When it's a gorgeous deep, glossy mahogany, remove the ham from the oven and leave it to settle for at least 20 minutes before carving it. ›

- In an ideal world the ham is best sat on a ham stand to serve – they look wonderful and steady the ham, which makes it much easier to carve. Much as I have lusted after one over the years, I keep thinking it's too extravagant to buy if it's only to be used once or twice a year. What I do instead is cut a thin sliver from the base of the ham to steady it before sitting it on a large platter and decorating it with clusters of bay sprigs from our tree – the deep green leaves look beautiful against the pinks and browns of the ham.
- I always get a bit anxious about carving as it's really not my strong point, but as far as carving goes, a ham is the least difficult of meats to slice. The key is to use a good, sharp knife – if you have one, a ham knife, with its long, thin flexible blade, is ideal.
- So to the carving: use a carving fork to steady the meat and make the first cut a V-shaped one to the bone near the shank end. Remove the small wedge of ham from this cut, and then continue to slice down towards the bone, at a slight angle, steadily moving up to the thicker part of the ham with each slice. As you go, the slices will be larger and you will need to take longer sweeps with the knife. Once they get too big to manage, you can carve ham from the sides as well. I usually partly slice the ham, then put it on the table so we can all admire it as we munch. Inevitably, I rummage through the pantry for some good robust chutney and hot English mustard to go with it.
- As to any leftover ham, you can store it in a ham bag or clean cotton pillowcase. First rinse the pillowcase or bag in a solution of 2 cups of cool water mixed with 1 tablespoon of white vinegar and wring it out so it's barely damp. Cover any cut surfaces of the ham with baking paper, then slip it into the bag. Store it in the fridge. Change the paper and bag every 2 days and it should stay moist and fresh for at least a week.

My Last-Minute Christmas Cake

MAKES 1 LARGE CAKE

300 g unsalted butter
420 g dark brown sugar
1–1.2 kg mixed dried fruits (such as raisins, pitted prunes and dates, sultanas, currants and lovely smoky sun-dried apricots – use whatever you have in your pantry)
2 teaspoons bicarbonate of soda
1 cup (250 ml) rum, port or muscat
½ cup (125 ml) water
½ cup (125 ml) cognac
2 teaspoons freshly grated nutmeg
2 heaped teaspoons ground cinnamon
4 eggs, lightly beaten
2½ cups (400 g) stone-ground wholemeal plain flour
about 150 g pecan halves and 120 g whole blanched almonds, for decorating
apricot glaze (see note overleaf), optional

Although I published a version of this recipe in my last book, *Mix & Bake*, I couldn't leave it out here as I invariably end up making it every Christmas. Truth be known, I make it all year round as fruitcake is my favourite cake of all, and this one is lovely and dense, chock-a-block with fruit and fragrant with spices. However, I would have to say that each time I bake it, it's slightly different as I am forever varying the dried fruits and liquids that I use in it. One thing that doesn't vary, however, is that you won't find one scrap of mixed peel within cooee of it. I can't bear the stuff; never could, actually. Much to my mum's despair, I would pick out every piece of mixed peel in her Christmas cake before I ate it . . . although the fact that I persisted with such a finicky task should tell you something about my love of fruitcake.

When I was finishing off the cake, I couldn't resist gilding the lily with some gum blossoms from the flowering red gum on the corner of our street – they just seemed so perfect and appropriate.

- Place the butter in a saucepan large enough to eventually hold all the cake ingredients and melt over medium heat. Add the sugar and stir to partially dissolve it so it's wet and slushy.
- Meanwhile, slice any large pieces of dried fruit (such as prunes and dates) into two or three pieces.
- Now, tip all the dried fruit, the bicarbonate of soda, rum, port or muscat, water and cognac into the pan with the sugar mixture. Increase the heat to high and keep stirring until the sugar has dissolved. Stop stirring and bring the mixture to the boil, then reduce the heat and let it simmer for 4 minutes. You need to keep an eye on it and adjust the heat at this stage, as it froths up considerably because of the bicarbonate of soda. When it's ready, turn off the heat and leave the mixture to cool in the pan. I often make this in the evening and leave it to cool overnight. However, if you do this, cover it well – I once left the lid slightly askew and woke to find an army of very inebriated ants weaving their way to and from the pan!
- Preheat your oven to 150°C. Butter a 23 cm × 23 cm × 8 cm square cake tin and line the base and sides with a double thickness of buttered baking paper.
- Add the nutmeg, cinnamon and egg to the dried-fruit mixture and stir them in well. Mix in the flour, then leave the batter to sit for a few minutes. Scrape it into the prepared tin and give it a gentle shake to level the top. ›

APRICOT GLAZE . . .
IS EASY TO MAKE

Boil about ½ cup of apricot jam or conserve with 1½ tablespoons of water for 5 minutes or so until the mixture becomes thick and syrupy (keep an eye on it and stir it regularly so it doesn't catch and burn on the bottom of the pan). Pour it through a fine sieve into a bowl to remove any bits of apricot skin that may be in it, then brush the hot glaze over the cake and leave it to set.

- Now comes one of the most enjoyable things to do: decorating the top of the cake. I love doing this as you can create all sorts of different patterns by marching alternating bands of pecans and almonds across the top, curving them into waves, or creating smaller and smaller squares.
- Bake the cake for 2¼–2½ hours or until it feels firm-ish in the centre when lightly pressed and a fine skewer inserted in the middle comes out clean. After an hour or so, it's a good idea to check the top; if it's a good rich brown, cover it loosely with a sheet of foil to stop it getting darker.
- Leave the cake to cool completely in the tin on a rack, then remove it from the tin, wrap it tightly in plastic film or foil, and store it in the fridge where it will keep well for up to 6 weeks.
- Just before serving the cake, I usually brush a little warm apricot glaze over the top, but this is not essential.
- P.S. I rarely bake just the one cake as I like to give little cakes as gifts, so I make up a few batches of the cake mixture and divide it among smaller tins. As a guide, this recipe makes one large cake or three smaller (13 cm × 13 cm × 8 cm) cakes.

Christmas Day

We have woken to a perfect Australian Christmas morning. The dawn light is golden and prisms through the gossamer strands of the spiders' webs. In the early-morning stillness, I see perhaps the most beautiful and exotic Christmas tree of all – the flowering red gum on the corner. With its clusters of deep-pink flowers it looks like some kind of exotic Christmas tree, festooned as it is with a squabble of busily feeding, brilliantly-hued rosellas, blue-faced honeyeaters, brush wattlebirds and more – all hanging upside down to catch the nectar. It is a truly glorious sight and quite takes my breath away.

It is one of our traditions to go to the beach for an early-morning swim on Christmas day. This morning it was absolutely glorious, with one of those high Christmas tides making the water crystal-clear and cold as cold. We've come back refreshed and ravenous, and I am on a promise to cook scrambled eggs for breakfast so I had best get to it, for there is much to do before the day is out – including making little Thai prawn cakes (see recipe overleaf). They are a family favourite and I shall be in trouble if they're not on the menu later!

Boxing Day

We had such a lovely day yesterday . . . gentle and happy, spent with dear friends, which was just what the doctor ordered. The afternoon clouded over and turned into one of our beautiful soft, grey days, which was just perfect for what turned out to be a veritable feast.

Each of us cooked one course and we ended up with the most beautiful, simple meal. Our friends grow all their own produce and are wonderful cooks, and we feasted on fragrant Middle Eastern lamb, succulent poached chicken spiked with home-pickled lemons, a riot of salad greens from the garden, basmati rice and a honey-sweet carrot salad. Oh, how I love to eat!

My contribution was honey semi-freddo (see page 28) with poached white nectarines (see page 40) and shortbread (see page 86) which somehow, after we had all tangoed around the kitchen doing the dishes, we managed to make room for!

Fragrant Thai Prawn Cakes

MAKES 30–35

750 g uncooked prawn meat
1 clove garlic, finely chopped
inner heart of 1 large stalk lemongrass, very finely chopped
1 tablespoon finely chopped ginger
1 large spring onion, finely chopped
1 small red chilli, finely chopped
2 large handfuls finely shredded coriander

continued next page

These tender little prawn cakes are the most wonderful morsels to have with a drink: sweet, salty, hot and sour all at once. If you can find betel leaves, the cakes look gorgeous sitting on them – and there's no need for plates or cutlery, as you can pick up and eat the cakes, leaf and all.

I suggest red curry paste in the recipe but I tend to use whatever I have in the fridge, so there is no need to buy a jar if you have another curry paste on hand. And you may already know this, but green prawn meat is available frozen. It is terribly handy to use as you don't have to peel or devein the prawns (for which I am very grateful as it's one of my least favourite jobs!).

- Finely chop the prawn meat and scrape it into a medium-sized bowl. (Tempting as it is to do this chopping in a food processor, it's best not to as it tends to whiz the prawns to a paste, which means you don't get the nice nubbly texture that hand-chopping gives.) Thoroughly mix in the remaining ingredients, except the

oil, leaves and lime wedges. The mixture will be quite wet and sloppy – this is fine, it just needs to hold together. At this stage, you can cover the mixture tightly and keep it in the fridge for a couple of hours if you like.

- When you're ready to cook the prawn cakes, pour enough oil into a large frying pan to make a layer 1–2 mm deep. Heat the oil over low-ish heat. When it's hot, drop heaped dessertspoonfuls of the prawn mixture into the pan, flattening each mound slightly with the back of the spoon so the cakes are about 1 cm thick. (If you would rather something a bit neater, you can scoop the mixture into your hand and shape it – it's a bit awkward as it's quite sloppy, but it does work.) Cook the prawn cakes for about 4 minutes on each side, or until they're golden and cooked through – just be a little careful as you turn them as they are quite delicate. Keep an eye on the oil and make sure it doesn't get too hot because the coconut cream in the mixture tends to make the cakes brown quickly. As the cakes are ready, transfer them to paper towels or crumpled greaseproof paper to drain. Continue with the remaining mixture. When all the prawn cakes are done, sit them on a platter (on betel leaves if you are using them) and press a coriander leaf onto each cake. Serve with lime wedges.

1 kaffir lime leaf, very, very finely chopped
1 large handful finely shredded basil
3 teaspoons caster sugar
1 tablespoon sweet chilli sauce
2 tablespoons fish sauce
1 teaspoon red curry paste (or your favourite curry paste)
2 tablespoons coconut cream
3 egg whites
light olive oil, for frying
betel leaves, coriander leaves and lime wedges, to serve, optional

KAFFIR LIMES AND LEAVES

These funny-looking knobbly limes, with their distinctive double leaves, are much more readily available than they used to be. The limes themselves can be quite seedy and a bit dry but the zest is incredibly fragrant and terrific for flavouring everything from curries to cakes and desserts. The leaves have an intensely floral lime aroma and can be added whole to soups and curries, or chopped *really* finely (they're very tough), and used in dishes like these prawn cakes.

Poached White Nectarines

SERVES 6

300 g caster sugar
600 ml water
1 vanilla bean
12 just-ripe white nectarines, thoroughly washed

Every time I look at this photo I am reminded yet again of how exquisitely beautiful food is and why people spend a lifetime creating still-life paintings of fruit and vegetables. I just wish I could paint myself – it must be wonderful to be able to capture such beauty. But then again I am blessed that Rodney is here and is such an extraordinary photographer, with a love and respect for food that matches my own. As I look through the shots in this book, I am filled with admiration for his ability to capture the essence of each dish so beautifully – none more so than these rose-blushed nectarines, perhaps one of my favourite photographs of all.

But enough of my waffling. More prosaically, I don't think a week goes by in summer when I don't cook a batch of these nectarines – they make such an exquisite dessert and are so easy to do. As I mentioned earlier, we ate them last night with the honey semi-freddo (and I must say they were really lovely together) but they are equally delicious with a scoop of thick yoghurt, cream or vanilla ice-cream.

- Combine the sugar and water in a large wide saucepan that will hold the nectarines in one layer. Put the pan over high heat and stir until the sugar has dissolved, then stop stirring and bring the syrup to the boil. Add the vanilla bean. (You can slit it if you like, which adds considerably more flavour, however the tiny black seeds will escape and dot themselves all over the nectarines. If it's just for us, I do this as the vanilla flavour is stronger, but if I want them to look pristine I leave the bean whole.)

- Once the syrup is bubbling, add the nectarines. Cover the pan and return the syrup to a gentle bubble, then adjust the heat to maintain this. Poach the nectarines until they are tender, rolling them around gently in the syrup every now and then so each side is cooked. The time will vary somewhat, but should be in the vicinity of 10–12 minutes. When you are rolling them about, do it with a wooden spoon as they are quite fragile and metal spoons can easily gouge the tender flesh. When the nectarines are ready, carefully scoop them out of the syrup into a bowl or container. Now, increase the heat under the remaining syrup and bring to the boil. Let it boil until it is reduced by a third to a half, then remove the pan from the heat.

- If you are serving the nectarines fairly soon, gently slip the skins off before covering the fruit in the syrup. If you are not serving them for a while, leave the skins on until just before serving them, as the skins help colour the syrup and give the nectarines their rosy blush.

- They look most beautiful of all simply served in a white bowl surrounded by their syrup and topped with the vanilla bean.

New Year's Eve

It's a soft, dreamy morning with gentle grey skies and wisps of mist flowing languidly over the hills. As I sit outside looking across to Mount Chincogan, I find it hard to believe the year is finishing – how can it have happened so quickly? One minute it seems as though it stretched ahead as far as the eye could see, yet now we are at the end. Still, it's all relative, and I guess a year is really as long or as short as we wish to make it – or is it simply a man-made concept that doesn't exist at all? Oh dear, I don't know that I can cope with all this philosophising before my first cup of tea!

One cup of tea later . . . well, that's improved the situation somewhat. My feet are more firmly on the ground now, which is just as well as I need to get weaving and make some cheese biscuits for a get-together we are going to later. There really is nothing like a crisp, buttery cheese biscuit to munch on with a glass of champagne – the two were just made for each other; and as we are sure to be bringing in the New Year with a glass of bubbles, I had better make plenty.

Delicious Crisp Cheese Biscuits

MAKES 70–80

I invariably keep a stock of these more-ish little biscuits in the freezer – or more correctly, I should say that I keep a couple of rolls of the frozen biscuit dough on hand so I can bake a batch at short notice. They are very buttery and crisp, with just the right amount of 'bite' from the cheese and chillies.

250 g plain flour
1 teaspoon salt
½–¾ teaspoon medium-hot dried chilli flakes
250 g good extra-tasty cheese, grated
250 g cool unsalted butter, cut into small chunks
nigella seeds or sesame seeds (black or white), for sprinkling

- Put the flour, salt and chilli flakes into a food processor and whiz them together until well combined. Add the cheese and blend everything together again until the cheese is thoroughly mixed in. Add the butter and let the processor run until the mixture forms a ball of dough around the blade – don't be alarmed if this takes a minute or two.
- Lay a large sheet of foil on a bench and cover it with a sheet of baking paper. Knead half the dough lightly to bring it into a ball, then shape it into a log about the diameter of a 50 cent piece. Sit the log along one side of the baking paper and roll it up in the paper. Next, roll it in the foil. Twist the ends tightly in opposite directions so you end up with something that looks like a very long bonbon. Do the same again with the remaining piece of dough. (Or if you would rather, you can divide the mixture into thirds or quarters and make smaller rolls to freeze.) If you're baking the biscuits the same day, chill the logs for 2–3 hours in the fridge until they're firm enough to slice. Alternatively, at this stage you can freeze the logs until you need them. They will keep for about 5 weeks – just defrost them in the fridge before slicing and baking.
- Preheat your oven to 180°C and line a couple of baking trays with baking paper. Cut the logs into 5–6 mm thick slices and sit them on the baking trays, leaving a little gap between each one to allow for spreading. Press some nigella or sesame seeds on top and bake for 12–15 minutes, or until the biscuits are golden. (I often ease one or two up with a small palette knife to check the bottoms are cooked too.) Remove them from the oven and leave the biscuits on the trays for 1 minute, then transfer them to a wire rack to cool completely. Store in airtight jars – they keep well for up to a week.

JANUARY

New Year's Day

New Year's Day and there is water everywhere – dripping from trees and bushes, running down the escarpment, filling the ditches by the side of the road, frothing through the downpipes and falling out of the sky as though it will never stop. The seas are gigantic and we were nearly blown off our feet when we walked along the beach, struggling to carry on a conversation as the wind roared in our ears.

We ventured out for a walk across the fields a while ago as we were starting to go stir-crazy, and everything is saturated, the ground sucking and squelching beneath our feet. Clumps of mushrooms just like miniature minarets are popping up everywhere and the frogs are having a field day in these near-perfect frog conditions.

It's wonderful to step into the calm of the house, and as the rain tumbles down outside it seems a day made in heaven to play in the kitchen. And I know exactly what I am going to play with, as I have been dying to try the next recipe for ages. I read about it some years ago and tucked the article away in a folder which I finally unearthed last week. I can't believe I leave things so long, but I do eventually get around to them – it just may take a year or three!

Pastel de Tres Leches (South American Three-Milk Cake)

SERVES 10–12

1 cup (150 g) plain flour
2 teaspoons baking powder
3 eggs, separated
pinch of salt
1 cup (220 g) caster sugar
¼ cup (60 ml) milk
1½ teaspoons vanilla extract
1–2 punnets strawberries, hulled and sliced lengthways
icing sugar and softly whipped cream, to serve

TOPPING

225 ml condensed milk
180 ml cream
280 ml evaporated milk
1½ teaspoons vanilla extract

Although it may sound as if it will be impossibly sweet and rich, this classic custardy South American cake is truly delicious. But before you start making it I should probably sound a note of warning: it's not the most beautiful-looking cake in the world, but for me its exquisite flavour more than makes up for this. Basically, it's a sponge with a rich vanilla-scented milk mixture poured over it while it's still warm. This gradually trickles down into the cake and the melding of the two is quite wonderful – the cake retains some of its texture but is imbued with the milky mixture so it becomes a sort of a cross between a trifle and a cake . . . 'squidgy' is the word that springs to mind. Traditionally it has a meringue topping, but I thought that might make it a bit too sweet; left as is, with some sliced strawberries to add a tangy counterpoint to the creamy richness of the cake, it's perfect. Raspberries, blood plums or any other slightly sharp fruits would also be terrific.

I turned it out onto a cake stand – which, I would have to say, was a fairly nerve-racking experience, but as it was a birthday cake I needed to make it look a bit more special. I'm delighted to say that it did work, however if you're contemplating doing the same, know that it wasn't easy. I had to keep loosening around the cake while it was upside-down in the dish, which is somewhat awkward, to say the least. However, it did finally plop out and once the top was covered with swirls of softly whipped cream, roasted flaked almonds and a mass of candles, it did indeed look very special.

- Preheat your oven to 160°C. Lightly butter a 25 cm round Pyrex dish that's about 6 cm deep (or similar glass or ceramic baking dish) and set it aside.
- Use a balloon whisk to whisk the flour and baking powder thoroughly together in a small bowl. Put the egg whites and salt into a separate clean, dry bowl and beat them with a hand-held electric beater on medium speed until they're softly fluffy. Beat in the caster sugar, a little at a time, until the mixture is thick, white and glossy – all up, this takes about 5–6 minutes. Now beat in the egg yolks, one at a time. Add a third of the flour mixture to the egg mixture and half-fold, half-stir it in. Fold in the remaining flour mixture in two batches along with the milk and vanilla (I usually mix the vanilla into the milk first). I find that the folding-in process is just a little awkward as the milk tends to run over the mixture initially and not want to mix in, but with a bit of gentle persistence it will.
- Spread the batter evenly into the prepared dish and bake for 30–35 minutes until the top feels firm-ish and a fine skewer inserted in the centre of the cake comes out clean. Remove it to a rack to cool in the dish.
- While the cake is baking, thoroughly mix together all the topping ingredients. Pour this mixture into a jug and set it aside.
- When the cake has cooled a little (but is still warm) use a fine skewer or toothpick to prick the top all over at roughly 3 cm intervals. Give the topping mixture a good stir then drizzle it evenly over the cake (ease around the sides of the cake with a fine spatula so the mixture seeps down the sides too). Leave the cake to cool completely, then cover the dish and pop it in the fridge for at least 4 hours, or preferably overnight (it keeps surprisingly well for up to 5 days).
- As I said earlier, this isn't the most beautiful-looking cake you will ever see, but you can dress it up a bit. If you are serving it whole in the dish, swirl a little whipped cream over it, then decorate the top with sliced strawberries (or other fruit). Or to do individual serves, slice the cake in the dish, then lever out a wedge and carefully invert it onto a plate. Overlap the strawberry slices on top, letting a few tumble onto the plate. Dust it with a little icing sugar and serve it with cream.

3rd January

We have started the New Year quietly, in many ways relieved to see the end of what has been quite a difficult year. I must be getting older and (I hope) wiser, as peace, good health and kindness are my major wishes for us and our loved ones in this coming year.

It's still pouring today and everything is sodden. The poor little birds are looking woefully bedraggled and even Gus, our neighbourhood dog, has given up coming to the back door as he has to squelch his way through mud. There was an almighty thump on the front door this morning to let us know he was there instead.

It's high time I properly introduced Gus, the wonder dog, whom we love and adore and spoil far too much. He is not our dog at all, but our neighbour's; however, from the day we arrived here, he adopted us and we are now his surrogate family (I should add that his owners are the loveliest people and he is much loved by them too). He's a big sook and a real Leo, who loves to be the centre of adoration and attention – and fully expects to be!

5th January

And even more rain is forecast . . . We sat this morning watching huge rain clouds roll in from the coast. The weather seems to be coming almost directly from the east, as there is a cyclone in the Coral Sea driving the winds down the eastern seaboard. It really is quite extraordinary, and soooo sodden. I slipped and slid around the garden earlier and everywhere I trod, water oozed into my boot prints. It's certainly going to take a while to dry out.

In spite of the rain, some things are thriving – especially the Lebanese cucumbers. The vines are covered in them and although I picked an armful only a few days ago, when I checked this morning there are at least another dozen or so ready to eat. In fact one is gi-*normous*. I find they tend to hide under their leaves and if we miss a couple (which we invariably do), they grow to alarming proportions in the space of just a few days.

I can't tell you the great delight I get from picking something from the garden and eating it straight away. I have just rinsed two cucumbers under the hose and ducked inside to give one to Clive – they're crisp as crisp, and almost sweet. I'm not sure yet what I'll do with the rest, but I expect cucumber salad will feature heavily on the menu over the next few weeks.

I've tried not to include too many recipes here from my previous books, but I'm making an exception for this refreshing salad which we eat again and again over summer. It goes with so many things and is wonderfully sprightly and cooling at the same time – just the thing for jaded summer appetites.

Cucumber, Chilli & Roasted Macadamia Salad

SERVES 4

6 Lebanese or other small cucumbers, peeled
1–2 small red chillies, finely chopped
good handful finely chopped coriander or mint
about ½ cup (70 g) roasted macadamias, coarsely chopped

DRESSING

¼ cup (60 ml) lime juice, or more to taste
¼ cup (60 ml) rice vinegar
¼ cup (55 g) caster sugar or palm sugar
1½ tablespoons fish sauce, or more to taste

This easy salad is terrific: crunchy and cool, with a lovely prickle of chilli and the tart sweetness of fresh lime juice and sugar. It's superb with simply cooked fish or chicken and a bowl of jasmine rice – so good, in fact, that I often double or triple the recipe as we eat rather a lot of it.

- To make the dressing, whisk together the lime juice, vinegar, sugar and fish sauce in a large bowl until the sugar has dissolved. Taste and adjust if necessary to give a good balance of sweet, sour and salty flavours.
- Halve the cucumbers lengthways, then scoop out and discard the seeds with the tip of a teaspoon. Slice the halves thinly on the diagonal into crescents. Add them to the dressing in the bowl, along with the chilli and coriander – don't mix them in at this stage; just leave them sitting on top. Now, cover the bowl and put it in the fridge to chill.
- Just before serving the salad, add half the macadamias and mix everything together. Scoop it into a shallow serving bowl, then sprinkle on the remaining nuts.
- You can easily prepare the salad ahead of time as long as you keep the dressing and salad ingredients separate, otherwise the cucumber becomes a bit soggy and the coriander loses its colour. What I do is mix the salad ingredients in one bowl, make the dressing in another bowl and chill them separately, then mix them together just before serving.

A LOVE–HATE RELATIONSHIP

Fish sauce straight from the bottle can be *extremely* pungent. But, like anchovies, used judiciously it can be sensational, setting up complex depths of salty flavour that nothing else can duplicate. As with all these things, it's about finding a brand you like – some are mellower than others, while some are too salty or bitter. It takes a bit of trial and error, and I've had to throw out more than one bottle, but once you settle on one you like, you'll find it's fantastic for adding an elusive 'Asian' flavour and fragrance to so many dishes.

8th January

This morning our road was flooded, which always causes great excitement. There is an awful lot of to-ing and fro-ing of neighbours kitted out in gumboots, Driza-Bones and brollies to marvel at the lake that has magically appeared overnight where the road should be. It's alive with ducks and waterbirds, all splashing about happily as if it has always been there.

Clive has made a quick run into town to stock up on milk and bread as it's likely we shall be flooded in for a few days. Living as close to the coast as we do, the flooding is directly related to the tides, and high tide will probably cause enough water to back-up to make the road impassable. It always feels very exciting and a bit scary when this happens.

On my splosh back home from visiting this latest water feature, I noticed that the fields are full of mushrooms, and when I looked by my feet I saw I was standing right by a perfect fairy ring of them; the only thing missing was an elf sitting on one.

With the weather closed in and the mountains completely obliterated by rain, it seems the perfect time to do some cooking as long as the power stays on. It's so easy to forget how reliant we are on all these utilities, and I would have to admit that it is only since we've lived here that I've become far more mindful of them. In fact, I shall make some chickpea patties, for if the power does go off I can still cook them, as we use bottled gas.

There is a bit of a story behind this recipe. The area we live in is often referred to, rather fondly, as 'hippie heaven', and I certainly relate to that – my first visit here was back in my hippie days when I had flowers in my hair and an amazing range of tie-dyed velvet clothes in my backpack! I fell in love with the place then so it was no real surprise to family and friends that we were drawn back here when we decided to leave the city. But I digress. As you can imagine from the 'hippie' moniker, just about every cafe and restaurant has an amazing range of menu choices: vegetarian, organic, vegan, gluten-free, dairy-free and sugar-free – you name it and you can find it. Having eaten at lots of these places, I've tried more than my fair share of veggie burgers. Some are terrific, but others really do hark back to the 1970s 'nut cutlet and lentil' style of cooking – heavy, solid, undoubtedly healthy and, truth be known, boring as all-get-out (something I clearly remember from my days living in a yurt in Nimbin with 20 of my closest friends – yes, truly!). I find this really disappointing because I know they don't have to be like that, so over time I've fiddled about trying variations on the 'burger' theme to see what I can come up with, and this recipe is the result.

Middle Eastern Chickpea & Hummus Patties

MAKES 8

These gently spicy patties are surprisingly light and dead-easy to make (I usually whip them up in about 20 minutes, and that includes the washing up). And they're versatile too: you can serve them just as they are with a rocket, tomato and olive salad; go down the classic burger track with tomato, onion, beetroot and all the trimmings; tuck them into warm pide bread that has been slathered with baba ganoush; or, if you have a bit more time, try them with some warm sautéed or barbecued eggplant (my favourite) – it's a fabulous combination.

- 2 × 400 g cans chickpeas, rinsed and thoroughly drained
- 1 cup (70 g) fresh soft sourdough breadcrumbs (or other country-style bread)
- ¾ cup (190 g) good-quality hummus
- 2½ tablespoons tahini
- ½ teaspoon ground cumin
- paler parts of 3 spring onions, finely chopped
- 1 small red chilli, finely chopped
- 1 clove garlic, finely chopped
- 2 tablespoons chopped coriander
- 1 tablespoon lemon or lime juice
- sea salt flakes
- olive oil, for frying
- 1 tablespoon sesame seeds
- 1½ tablespoons fine dried breadcrumbs
- 1 cup (280 g) thick Greek-style plain yoghurt
- 2–3 tablespoons finely chopped mint or coriander
- 1½–2 tablespoons extra virgin olive oil
- coriander sprigs and lime wedges, to serve

- Put half the chickpeas into the bowl of a food processor with the fresh breadcrumbs, hummus, tahini, cumin, spring onion, chilli, garlic, coriander, lemon or lime juice and 1 teaspoon of salt. Whiz them together until the mixture forms a thick, coarse paste around the blade. Scrape this paste into a bowl and mix in the remaining whole chickpeas – I use my hands for this as the mixture is quite stiff. Shape the mixture into eight even-sized patties and sit them in a single layer on a large plate lined with baking paper. At this stage you can cook the patties straight away or chill them, lightly covered, for up to 8 hours.
- When you're ready to cook the patties, glug enough olive oil into a large frying pan to form a 3 mm layer over the base. Heat it gently over low heat.
- Meanwhile, mix the sesame seeds and dried breadcrumbs together in a shallow bowl. Lightly coat the patties in the crumb mixture, then add them to the pan and cook over a low-ish heat for 4–5 minutes each side until they're golden. (Just be careful not to have the heat too high as the sesame seeds have a tendency to catch and burn.) When they're ready, scoop them out of the pan and onto paper towels to drain.
- While the patties are cooking, mix together the yoghurt, mint or coriander, olive oil and salt to taste. Scrape it into a small bowl and serve with the hot patties, garnished with coriander sprigs and lime wedges.

DRESS THEM UP OR DOWN . . .

You can serve the patties in any of the ways suggested above, with the herbed yoghurt dolloped on top or on the side. To dress them up a bit, when I serve them with sautéed eggplant, I usually sit two slices of eggplant on each plate, top each slice with a patty, then a scoop of the yoghurt and some coriander leaves or tiny sprigs. The finishing touch is a wedge of lime on the side.

10th January

I must say it really does feel as though two giant hands have picked up this whole far-north-coast region and set us down fair and square on the equator. The sound of water is everywhere – from a gentle pitter-patter to a savage pounding on the roof; dripping from leaves; trickling over rocks; rushing down gullies, tearing through culverts, pouring down the river and then finally like a huge brown serpent, snaking out to sea. The air is so moist and thick that you feel you could wring it out. I must admit I feel as if mushrooms will start sprouting on my skin if it continues much longer. In fact, mushrooms are one of the few things not affected by the terrible flooding we've had. The fields are absolutely full of them at present, and I am waiting for an old friend of mine (who is an expert mushroom forager) to arrive so we can go out picking. I don't dare do it on my own as I don't know enough about them.

Surprisingly too, in amongst all this wetness the gingers and heliconias are flourishing. Our ornamental ginger plants have sent up delicate spikes of creamy flowers and the other gingers are happy little campers too . . . the extraordinary-looking beehive gingers are sprouting their perfect little honey pots and the blue ginger is ready to flower. But, best of all, our snail vine is covered with exquisite clusters of purple and cream flowers whose fragrance is so haunting that it stops us in our tracks whenever we get a waft of it. It always surprises me that such a beautiful flower has such a prosaic name.

14th January

It is now the middle of January, and still it rains. We've become more accepting of the big wet and realise that things will be as they will be, and fretting about it doesn't change a thing. Unfortunately, though, the humidity has set in with a vengeance. Our skin is constantly bathed in a fine film of moisture and although we long to get back into the sea, that is a long way off yet as the beaches are unswimmable due not only to the huge seas, but also to the hazardous foam that has formed on many of them. With the amount of rain we've had, there's been a huge leaching of the soil and subsequent wash out to sea, and sadly, along with the debris and trees, a lot of agricultural chemicals have been washed out too. Combined with other elements, these chemicals have formed toxic foam – it's positively scary, isn't it?

Despite the heat, I find that I'm itching to get into the kitchen and, as the rain poured down over the weekend, I happily cooked to my heart's content. The two dishes we enjoyed most were a chilled roasted summer vegetable soup (see overleaf), which is so good I can't stop dipping my spoon into it, and a lovely light, orange-scented ricotta cheesecake (see page 60) – an unusual duo, but delicious nonetheless.

However, before I go any further, I must just mention the soup in particular as I know it's not the first dish that springs to mind at this time of year. I realise it's not everybody's cup of tea either, but if I can twist your arm to try this one, you may become a convert. It's just so light, refreshing and wholesome in the best possible way. I can happily eat bowlful after bowlful on a hot day and we'll often make a meal of it with some good bread. Interestingly, as rustic as this soup sounds, it can also look pretty special too – more than once I've served tiny bowls of it as a prelude to our Christmas dinner. And I've always thought it would be divine in shot glasses at a cocktail party . . . not that I've been to such a thing for a very long time; I rather suspect my little black dress is full of moth holes by now!

Roasted Summer Vegetable Soup

MAKES 8–10 SMALL SERVES

- 2 medium-sized eggplants (aubergines) – about 800 g in total – halved lengthways
- 1 large red onion, skin on, quartered
- 100 ml extra virgin olive oil
- 3 large red capsicums (peppers), quartered and cored
- 3 large ripe tomatoes, cored and halved
- 2 large cloves garlic, unpeeled but pricked with a fine skewer
- 1½ tablespoons extra virgin olive oil, extra
- leaves from 5 large thyme sprigs
- 1 small red chilli, finely chopped
- about 1 litre cool water, to cover
- 3 teaspoons sea salt flakes, or more to taste
- about ¼ cup (60 ml) lemon juice, or more to taste

If we are making a meal of this I often sit torn rocket leaves in the bottom of the bowls to add a bit of 'green' to the proceedings. There is no end of ways to garnish it, depending on how sophisticated or simple you would like it to be. I like to finish with a slice of avocado and a scattering of tiny basil leaves, and occasionally I crumble goat's cheese over the soup (a few chunks in the bottom of the bowls are good too).

- Preheat your oven to 200°C. Line two large baking trays with baking paper.
- Put the eggplant and onion into a large bowl and mix them with 50 ml of the olive oil so they're lightly coated in it. Sit the eggplant halves, cut-side down, on one baking tray and strew the onion quarters around them.
- Now combine the capsicum, tomato, garlic and remaining olive oil in the bowl and mix well. Spread this mixture on the other tray, sitting the capsicum pieces skin-side up, and the tomatoes cut-side up.
- Pop both trays in the oven and roast the vegetables for about 30 minutes, or until they're tender and wrinkled-looking. Remove them from the oven and let them cool down a bit. As soon as they are cool enough to handle, peel away as much skin as you can from the eggplant, onion, capsicum and tomato – it may not all come away easily but most will. Gently squeeze the skins of the garlic cloves to pop out the buttery flesh. (I do all the peeling and squeezing over the trays to catch any juices from the veggies.) Set aside three pieces of capsicum for garnishing.
- Warm the extra 1½ tablespoons of olive oil in a large saucepan over medium heat, then stir in the thyme and chilli. Scrape the skinned vegetables into the pan, along with any of their juices, and stir well to coat them in the oil and herbs. Add about 1 litre of cool water (enough to cover) and 3 teaspoons of salt. Bring the mixture to the boil, then reduce the heat and simmer for 30 minutes.
- Leave the soup to cool slightly, then purée it in batches in a blender (or use a stick blender, which is much easier). Pour the soup into a large bowl, taste it, then add enough lemon juice to sharpen it slightly, and more salt if it needs it – I find it usually does to bring out the flavours of the vegetables. Cover it tightly and chill it for an hour or two. (It actually keeps really well for 5 days or so in the fridge – just let it warm up a bit at room temperature before serving it.) As cold can mute the flavour, it's a good idea to taste the soup again before you serve it in case it needs a bit more seasoning.
- To serve the soup, ladle it into small bowls. Slice the reserved pieces of roasted capsicum into fine strips and sprinkle some over the top of each bowl.

16th January

I am beating a very wary path to the clothes line as Clive saw a rather large brown snake there yesterday. Oh, it gives me the heebies when I know snakes are around. I've become more used to having them about the garden, and to date they've been relatively harmless ones, but the browns make my blood run cold. I must look as though I am doing some kind of mad dance as I stomp my way across the lawn in my boots, setting up as much vibration as I can, so that any self-respecting snake will take off before I see it.

To settle my nerves, I've just polished off the last slice of the cheesecake I made on the weekend – what better excuse does a girl need to eat cake than snakes in the garden? I realised I haven't given you the recipe for it yet and must do so before I forget. It's a super warm-weather dessert as it's much lighter and less cloying than a regular cheesecake, and it goes beautifully with all sorts of summer fruits.

Orange-Scented Baked Ricotta Cheesecake with Summer Fruits

SERVES 10–12

900 g ricotta
100 ml cream
⅔ cup (150 g) caster sugar
⅓ cup (50 g) plain flour
¼ teaspoon salt
3 teaspoons finely grated orange zest
¼ cup (60 ml) orange liqueur
2 teaspoons vanilla extract
6 eggs
½ cup (40 g) flaked almonds, very lightly roasted, optional
icing sugar, for dusting, optional
summer fruits and softly whipped cream, to serve, optional

This simple baked ricotta cake is very easy to make, as the mixture is just whizzed up in a food processor and scraped into the tin – no crust, no fuss. Just so you know, it is rather rustic-looking (there, that covers a multitude of sins!): the top cracks a little and the sides sink in a bit as it cools, but for me that's all part of its charm. The texture is a little grainy due to the ricotta and it has a delicate orange flavour, which works beautifully with all sorts of fruits. In summer I often serve it with poached white nectarines (see page 40) or, and this looks especially beautiful, fresh lychees mixed with fine crescents of white nectarines and raspberries. In winter, it is more likely to be with caramelised oranges (see page 348), which is a truly glorious combination.

- Preheat your oven to 150°C (or 140°C if you are using a dark, non-stick tin). Line the base and sides of a 23 cm springform cake tin with lightly buttered baking paper. Dust the tin with flour and tap out the excess.
- I should precede the next instructions by saying they are for a large food processor; if yours is on the small side, it is best to do the mixing in two batches. Put the ricotta into the bowl of a food processor and whiz it around, stopping and scraping down the sides occasionally. (It's important to do this thoroughly so the ricotta is as smooth as possible.) Now add the cream, sugar, flour and salt, and process everything for 10 seconds until well combined. Add the zest, orange liqueur and vanilla extract and briefly whiz again. Break the eggs into a jug then, with the processor going, slowly pour them through the feed tube. Whiz the mixture for 30–40 seconds until it is smooth and creamy, stopping and scraping down the sides occasionally. ›

AN ASIDE . . .

Much as I love this with the lychees and nectarines, when I don't have heaps of time, I often just serve it with a selection of summer fruits. Rather than using too many flavours and colours, I rather like sticking to tones of gold and pink by gently combining fine crescents of mango, yellow peaches and pink papaya, with a little passionfruit scooped over the top; or a mixture of summer berries.

- Scrape the ricotta mixture into the prepared tin and shake the tin gently to level the surface. Sprinkle the almonds evenly over the top, if you are using them. Bake the cake for about 1 hour, or until it is pale golden and feels set when you lightly rest the palm of your hand on the surface and gently wobble it. Transfer it to a rack and leave it to cool in the tin. It will sink somewhat as it does, so don't be alarmed.
- The taste and texture of the ricotta are best if it is served a little warm or at room temperature. To turn it out, release and remove the sides of the tin. Carefully invert the cake onto a flat plate, then sit a serving platter on top and invert it again onto this so it is almond-side up. Dust it with icing sugar if liked, and serve it with a scoop of summer fruits and cream. Store leftovers in the fridge but warm them gently (a microwave works well) before serving them.

18th January

I can't believe that the rain is still pouring down. It feels as though the gods have turned on a giant sprinkler and then all gone off to bed and forgotten to turn it off. There will be nothing left of the garden at this rate. In between showers, I have squelched through the mud to see what remains of the herbs – and the answer is . . . not much. The snails, slugs and grasshoppers have had a field day, but I have managed to salvage some basil, mint and thyme, which feels like some kind of achievement. I also picked the first limes from our very thorny golden lime tree; the thorns are positively lethal, but the limes themselves are incredibly fragrant.

The kaffir lime tree is covered in fruit too, and I can never resist scrunching the leaves as I brush past them so they give off their wonderfully exotic fragrance. Although it is the leaves that are used most in cooking, I find I use the fruit as well, for despite reading many times that the flesh is dry, our limes are fat with juice and I love combining it with regular lime juice when I'm cooking. If you do have access to kaffir limes, try using a little of the juice and zest in the salmon dish below to reinforce the lovely floral fragrance of the leaf.

Fragrant Coconut Salmon in Banana Leaves

SERVES 4

This dish is an absolute stunner – perfect for when you want a real knock-'em-in-the-aisles little number. It does require rather a lot of chopping, but gosh it's worth it. The salmon tastes wonderful, imbued as it is with spices and coconut, and looks sensational nestled in its banana-leaf wrapping. When I serve this I invariably accompany it with pineapple oil and curry leaf pickle (see page 67), a bowl of perfect jasmine rice (see page 70) and cucumber, chilli and roasted macadamia salad (see page 50).

Please don't abandon this recipe if you can't lay your hands on banana leaves – it's much too good for that. The salmon can be parcelled up in baking paper then a layer of foil instead of the leaves, then cooked in the same way but for a bit less time (about 10–12 minutes).

4 salmon fillets, skin on or off
4 pieces fresh banana leaf (see note overleaf), cut into 24 cm × 22 cm rectangles (or use baking paper and foil)
12 thick wooden toothpicks
fresh banana leaves, optional, to serve
lime wedges or cheeks, to serve
½ kaffir lime leaf, cut into the finest threads

continued next page

- The first thing you need to do is remove the pin bones from the salmon. These are the small curved bones that sit in a ridge through the thickest part of the salmon fillets – sometimes the fishmonger removes them, but it's always a good idea to check. You will feel them if you run a finger over the thickest part of the salmon. If they are still intact, use a clean pair of pliers (I keep a pair just for the kitchen) or salmon tweezers to remove them. Once that's done, line an airtight container with a large snap-lock bag and slip the fillets into it. ›

MARINADE

2 large cloves garlic, finely chopped
1 tablespoon finely chopped fresh ginger
2 large spring onions, finely chopped
3 teaspoons freshly ground cumin seeds
2 teaspoons sweet Hungarian paprika
sticky black seeds from 8 cardamom pods, crushed
2 small red chillies, finely chopped
juice of 1 large lime
sea salt flakes, to taste
large handful finely chopped fresh coriander
1 very, very finely chopped kaffir lime leaf
1 cup (250 ml) coconut cream

- Now put all the marinade ingredients into a bowl and thoroughly mix them together. Carefully pour the marinade into the bag over the salmon. Squeeze as much air as possible from the bag; seal it, then squish it around gently to coat the salmon in the marinade. Put the bag back into the container, cover it tightly and chill the salmon for 2–3 hours, squishing it around occasionally. (I have left it all day by mistake and although I thought the lime juice might 'cook' the salmon, it didn't, and the dish was every bit as good.)
- Just prior to cooking the salmon, preheat your oven to 220°C and line a baking tray with baking paper.
- Soften the banana-leaf pieces by very carefully passing them back and forth over an open flame (I use the smallest burner on my gas stovetop) for a few seconds until they're pliable. Or if that seems a bit daunting, put them into a large bowl and cover them with boiling water. Leave them to soften for about 5 minutes then pat them dry.
- Lay a rectangle of banana leaf, shiny-side down, on the benchtop. Sit a salmon fillet in the centre and spoon a quarter of the marinade over the top. Wrap the leaf around the salmon as though you were wrapping a present, then secure it with toothpicks. Sit the parcel, toothpick-side up, on the baking tray and wrap the remaining fillets the same way. (If you're using baking paper and foil, there's no need to use toothpicks – just fold and crimp the parcels to seal them well.) When they're all done, put the tray in the oven and bake the parcels for 15–18 minutes (the timing rather depends on their thickness).
- When they're ready, remove the tray from the oven. There are a number of ways you can serve this. I sometimes just sit the bundles on each plate and let everyone unwrap their own, or open them up slightly so you can see the salmon. Occasionally I take the salmon out of its wrapping and sit each fillet on a strip of fresh banana leaf with a spoonful of pineapple oil and curry leaf pickle and a lime wedge on the side – this looks particularly lovely as the soft pink of the spice-speckled salmon contrasts with the golden oil of the pickle and bright-green lime wedges. Serve with lime wedges or cheeks and a few threads of kaffir lime leaf on top.

A FEW TIPS ON BANANA LEAVES . . .

Lots of backyards still sport a cluster of banana trees as, like lemons, they were planted in many gardens in the 1950s and 60s. If you're fortunate enough to still have some, then your banana-leaf problems for this recipe are solved. If not, see if you can beg or borrow two large leaves from a neighbour, or ask your local greengrocer or Asian food shop if they can get them for you. I wipe down the leaves with a damp cloth before cutting them with a sharp knife. It's also a good idea to get a few more leaves than you need as they tend to tear easily. You can cut the leaves well ahead of time as long as you store them in a tightly sealed plastic bag in the fridge – they will be fine for 4–5 days.

19th January

I'm a preserver at heart and am never happier than when I'm pottering around in the kitchen preparing a batch of something-or-other to tuck away. It almost doesn't matter what it is, it's the whole process that I love: from chopping the fruits and vegetables, grinding the spices and washing the jars in lots of hot, sudsy water, to seeing my big jam pan bubbling away on the stovetop. It always makes me feel very contended and calm. And of course, the results are wonderful: my pantry shelves are laden with jar after jar of marmalade, salted lemons, deep-crimson strawberry jam, peach and nectarine chutney and all sorts of pickles – fiery brinjal, spicy green mango, old-fashioned bread-and-butter cucumbers, and my all-time favourite, pineapple oil and curry leaf pickle (see recipe overleaf).

I'm thrilled to bits to say that the curry leaves in the photo are from a tree I planted last year. It struggled initially, but has finally taken hold and these are the first leaves I've picked from it. They have an extraordinary fragrance – a cross between the crisp, dry scent of freshly laundered washing and that of toasted nuts. I'm told the trees are very hardy (they need to be with me!), and I know they're beautiful as a friend has one as the centrepiece of his veggie garden. It is really exquisite – almost like a large bonsai with its twisted branches and tapered green leaves drooping softly over the ranks of garlic and onions planted beneath it.

Pineapple Oil & Curry Leaf Pickle

MAKES 6–8 MEDIUM-SIZED JARS

It's rare that we don't have a jar of this pickle squirrelled away somewhere (I feel far too insecure if I don't!). I'm as happy to spoon it over a bowl of rice with a few steamed or stir-fried vegetables, as I am to serve it with the salmon in the previous recipe. It's also very good with coconut chicken with spicy cucumber ribbons (see page 360) and coconut and cardamom chicken with glazed pumpkin (see page 176).

2½ cups (625 ml) white wine vinegar
2 teaspoons fenugreek seeds
2 very large, very sweet pineapples
6 very large or 10 medium-sized cloves garlic, peeled
½ cup (about 120 g) finely chopped ginger
½ cup (55 g) cumin seeds, freshly ground
½ cup (40 g) coriander seeds, freshly ground
2½ cups (625 ml) light olive oil
2 tablespoons black or brown mustard seeds
2 tablespoons (about 36) fresh curry leaves
1½ tablespoons fennel seeds
1 tablespoon ground turmeric
1 tablespoon medium-hot chilli flakes
350 g caster sugar
3–4 small red chillies (or more if you like it hot), finely chopped
1½ tablespoons sea salt flakes, or more to taste

- Pour the vinegar into a blender and stir in the fenugreek seeds. Set the blender aside while you prepare the pineapple.
- To do this, sit a large colander over a bowl. Now, peel and core the pineapples then chop them finely, scooping the chunks into the colander as you go. When it's all done, balance a plate on top of the pineapple chunks and sit two or three cans on top of this to weigh down the chunks. Leave it for 30 minutes or so, pressing down gently on the cans every so often. Quite a lot of juice will have dripped into the bowl by this point (the juice is lovely, but you don't need it for the recipe so I usually pour it into a glass with a few ice cubes and drink it as I go).
- Now add the garlic, ginger, cumin and coriander to the vinegar mixture, and blend everything together until it is well puréed. Set the mixture aside. (If you only have a small blender, do this in batches or it may spurt out the top.)
- You need a good-sized stainless steel (or other non-reactive) pan to cook the pickle, as there is quite a lot of mixture. Heat the oil in the pan over medium–high heat. When it's hot, mix in the mustard seeds, curry leaves, fennel seeds, turmeric and chilli flakes – stand back a bit as there will be an amazing burst of fragrance as they hit the hot oil and the mustard seeds will start to pop. Carefully pour the puréed vinegar mixture into the pan – again you need to be careful as steam shoots up when it hits the oil (I usually trickle it down the sides of the pan so it mixes in slowly). Cook the mixture for a couple of minutes, stirring constantly. Now, scrape in the drained pineapple, sugar, chopped chilli and salt. Increase the heat and bring the mixture to the boil, then reduce the heat and let it bubble gently and steadily for about 30 minutes, stirring occasionally, until the oil is floating on top and it smells utterly delicious. At this stage, I usually scoop a little out into a cup, let it cool then taste it to see if it needs more salt.
- Once it is as you like it, remove the pan from the heat and immediately ladle the pickle into hot, sterilised jars (see page 165.) Make sure the oil covers the top of the pineapple in each jar. Cover the jars loosely with a sheet of baking paper and leave them to cool. Once they are completely cool, seal the jars tightly then label and date them.

LIQUID GOLD

Just be aware of the 'oil' part of the name, for the exquisite sunny oil that floats on the surface of the pickle is very much part of it, and should be spooned up and eaten with the pickle. The pickle keeps well in the fridge for 6 months or more and only gets better with time.

CURRY LEAF
$2

Perfect Jasmine Rice

SERVES 2–3

1 cup (200 g) jasmine rice
sea salt flakes, to taste
1½ cups (375 ml) cold water
1 fresh bay leaf, cardamom leaf or piece of pandanus leaf, optional

I have a real soft spot for jasmine rice. I am just as happy to eat a bowlful of it plain, with a touch of soy sauce or squeeze of lemon juice and a sprinkle of sea salt, as I am to do something to it or serve it with something. You'll notice I mention it time and again in this book as its distinctive fragrance goes so beautifully with so many dishes. This method of cooking it is terrific as it results in lovely tender, but separate grains.

You can easily double this recipe, however if you do it's important that you don't quite double the water content: for example, 2 cups of rice only needs 2¾ cups of water, not 3. It's also a good idea to increase the size of the pan as you increase the quantities, so that the rice cooks evenly.

- Tip the rice into a medium-sized saucepan with a tight-fitting lid, sprinkle in a little salt to taste and put the pan over high heat. Stir it well for a minute or two until the rice is hot and smells ever-so-slightly toasty. Pour in the water (watch out as it may hiss and spit a bit), then add your choice of leaf, if using, and stir well. Bring the water to the boil and, as soon as it's bubbling rapidly, cover the pan with the lid. Reduce the heat to the lowest possible setting and leave the rice to cook, covered, for exactly 12 minutes without stirring or disturbing it in any way.
- Now, turn off the heat and lay a folded tea towel between the lid and the saucepan, wedging the lid on firmly so no steam escapes. Leave the rice to sit for at least 10 minutes before serving it. (If you don't want to serve the rice straight away, just leave it covered with the tea towel and lid, and it will stay hot for up to half an hour.)

SCENTED RICE . . .

I have a bay tree planted in a pot just near the kitchen so I tend to pick big bunches of its glossy green leaves and keep them in a jug on the windowsill – mainly because they look so lovely. And because they are right there, I often pinch off one or two leaves and add them to all sorts of dishes as I cook. It was purely by accident I tossed one in with some rice: it was raining that particular day and I didn't want to get wet going out to pick some cardamom leaves (which, if you can lay your hands on some, are exquisitely scented and superb in rice). I decided to use a bay leaf off the bunch instead – I scrunched it up a bit first to release its fragrance then buried it in the pan. The taste was subtle but definitely there and rather lovely, so I now tend to do this more often than not. If by any chance you have access to pandanus leaves, just a small piece adds a smoky, toasty flavour to the rice.

20th January

Early Sunday morning is one of my favourite times to be out in the garden. Winter or summer you'll find me there, unless the rain is just so torrential it's not possible. I don't know how the ritual developed but I do so love it and it sets me up for the day and week ahead. I usually slip out of bed and into my boots at dawn, and for the next few hours I lose myself in the rhythm of gardening . . . pulling out weeds here, pruning back branches there, dead-heading flowers. It's like a meditation for me, and I find that if I'm worried or upset about something, within a short time I'm so lost in what I'm doing that the problem has somehow miraculously receded into a calmer, more peaceful place. In fact, it's only the increasingly loud growling of my tummy that brings me back inside, as it has this morning.

It may sound a bit funny, but I look forward all week to that first Sunday-morning cup of tea, *and* the toast with homemade marmalade that follows it. I have the tea so hot that it's almost scalding – I know it's not meant to be a good way to drink it, but it seems I follow in my mother's footsteps in this regard and can't bear lukewarm tea. If possible I sit outside in the stillness, watching the steam curl from my cup, savouring the sharp tang of the marmalade, and just enjoying 'being'.

There is rarely a plan, and this morning I found myself tidying up the chillies and clipping the flower heads off the basil to help it bush out. I always feel a bit mean doing this, as the bees love the nectar and need it more than ever – after months of drought we've almost instantly been transported to the Big Wet and they're struggling to find enough. So I have struck a compromise and left one plant entirely alone to flower its little heart out and hopefully provide enough nectar for them.

The basil finds its way into everything – salads, marinades, pestos, pasta, stuffed tomatoes, zucchini pies . . . even ice-cream. Our favourite way to have it (and I won't write a proper recipe as I suspect many of you will have your own version) is to fold it through a tomato salad. There's nothing difficult about this and the only thing to be mindful of is to use the best ingredients you can find. Ours usually consists of wedges of whatever tomatoes are ripe, plenty of good olive oil, a little sea salt, occasionally a splash of balsamic vinegar, and roughly torn chunks of milky bocconcini. Depending upon my whim, it might also include sharp little black olives, slivers of red onion or grilled capsicum.

Oh gosh, would you believe it's the end of the day and we've both been out in the garden since I wrote the words above early this morning! As always after a day of digging, pruning and carting barrow-loads of mulch, we're tired and famished – dinner will have to be something easy and filling for I don't have much oomph left in me. I think a carbohydrate boost might be in order, and as there's always pasta in the pantry I shall cook that, along with some spinach and a few of the chillies I picked earlier this morning. It will do perfectly – it's quick too, which is just as well, for I suspect we shall both be tucked up in bed before nine!

Penne with Spinach, Ricotta, Chilli & Pine Nuts

SERVES 2

This recipe makes plenty for two hungry people, and is easily doubled for more. However if you do this, you will probably have to wilt the spinach in two batches as there will be a small mountain of it when it's raw, which is unlikely to fit into the pan all at once. All you need to do when both batches of spinach are cooked and vastly reduced in volume, is combine them and continue with the recipe. I know I suggest using penne for this, but on the day we took the photograph I was given some filei calabresi (slim hand-rolled pasta twists), which were so gorgeous I couldn't resist using them.

- 350 g baby spinach leaves
- 150 g ricotta
- 60 g soft goat's cheese marinated in olive oil, or more to taste
- 20 g freshly grated parmesan
- 50 ml extra virgin olive oil
- 1 large clove garlic, finely chopped
- 1–2 small red chillies, finely chopped
- 250 g penne (or any other small hollow pasta)
- sea salt flakes and freshly ground black pepper
- splash of lemon juice, optional
- small handful of roasted pine nuts, mixed with a smidgen of olive oil
- a chunk of parmesan, to serve, optional

- Give the spinach leaves a thorough wash and leave them to drain in a colander. Mash the ricotta, goat's cheese and parmesan together and set them aside.
- Heat the oil in a good-sized frying pan over low heat. Add the garlic and chilli and cook gently for 3–4 minutes, stirring now and again, until they're tender but still quite pale (if the garlic browns, it tends to taste bitter). Turn off the heat and leave them in the pan.
- Meanwhile, stir the penne into a large pan of rapidly boiling salted water and cook it until it's al dente. I find the only way to check this is to fish a bit out of the pan and bite it – it should still have a bit of firmness to it. When it's ready, drain the penne in a colander, reserving a little of the cooking water in case you need it to thin the pasta sauce later.
- While the penne is cooking, turn the heat back on to high under the frying pan. When the oil mixture is hot, but before the garlic browns much, add the spinach. Cover the pan and cook the spinach for a couple of minutes, stirring occasionally, until it has greatly reduced in volume and is wilted but still bright green (there will be a bit of liquid in the pan too which is fine as it helps create the 'sauce'). Scoop out a spoonful of leaves and set them aside for garnishing.
- When the spinach is ready, stir the ricotta mixture into it. Taste it and add salt and lemon juice if you think it needs it. Turn off the heat and mix in the drained penne so it's thoroughly coated in the spinach mixture. Dribble in a little of the reserved cooking water if it seems a bit gluggy.
- Scoop the pasta into warm pasta bowls. Scatter the reserved spinach leaves here and there and sprinkle with the pine nuts and ground black pepper. Shave a few long strips of parmesan over the top, if you like.

21st January

I never realised that there was such a thing as a green-barked gum tree but I'm delighted to find that such a tree exists. Over the last few weeks of heat and wet, some of the gums have started to shed their bark to the most extraordinary effect. For as the strips peel away, they're revealing beautiful pearly green limbs with the texture of smooth skin, even down to the folds and wrinkles that form where each bough meets the trunk – I've never seen anything quite like it. They really are a sight to behold.

I must admit, prior to moving here we had always lived in apartments or townhouses, so it's only recently that I've discovered the utter delight of compost. Never did I imagine that something so simple and earthy could bring so much satisfaction to my heart.

As I peel, chop, dice and slice my way through our meals all the scraps are swept into the compost bucket, which I then (with great glee) tip into the compost bin. Every so often I sprinkle in some lime to sweeten it, and add a spadeful or two of horse manure. The result is the most wonderful piece of alchemy ever – even more magical than cooking – for all the potato peelings, banana skins, apple cores, tough outer salad leaves and garden clippings are transformed by air, worms, warmth and gazillions of tiny insects and bacteria into the most beautiful rich, dark, earthy-smelling, alive soil ever. I lavish it where I can in the garden and can almost hear the plants saying 'thank you' as they soak up its promise of life and health. What a gift!

24th January

I never tire of mangoes. Frankly, I can eat them until the cows come home, and we've been doing just that these past few weeks, making real little pigs of ourselves. I remember my dad saying that they should only be eaten in a bathtub, and I well understand why – these are so luscious that the juice leaves sticky trails down our arms as we munch on them, but they are oh-so-good! I could quite happily go on ad infinitum eating them just as they are. However, as we're having friends for dinner, I'm going to make some little mango tartlets for dessert. It's a simple recipe . . . no pastry, just a biscuit-crumb crust, delicate passionfruit cream and slices of those gorgeous mangoes.

Mango & Passionfruit Tartlets

MAKES 6

You can make the tartlet crusts a day ahead if you like and store them in an airtight container (just make sure it is airtight, otherwise they will soften rapidly in summer's humidity). The passionfruit cream can also be made a few hours ahead, which really only leaves the mangoes to be sliced and the passionfruit seeds to be scooped out of their leathery skins onto the tartlets just before you serve them.

- 2 large ripe mangoes, peeled and thinly sliced
- seeds from 1–2 passionfruit
- tiny mint leaves, to garnish, optional

BISCUIT CRUST

- 250 g digestive or ginger biscuits (I love the subtle flavour of Swedish ginger biscuits), finely crushed
- 125 g unsalted butter, melted and cooled

PASSIONFRUIT CREAM

- 4 large or 8 medium-sized passionfruit
- 1 cup (250 ml) sour cream
- 300 ml double thick cream
- ½ cup (80 g) icing sugar

- Preheat your oven to 180°C. Line six 11 cm tartlet tins with foil, leaving a small overhang all the way around. Use a folded cloth to press the foil down snugly to ensure it follows the contours of the tins. (I often sit one tin in another and press down lightly on it to make quite sure it is as snug as possible.) Sit the tins on a baking tray and set them aside.
- To make the biscuit crust, tip the crushed biscuits into a bowl and pour in the melted butter, then stir the two together until the mixture is crumbly. Divide this evenly among the tartlet tins. Now press the crust mixture firmly and evenly onto the sides and base of each tin. I hate to say it, but this is easier said than done. I start off using a spoon to spread it evenly, then my fingers to press it into the sides of the tin, and finally I use a small tumbler to press the mixture firmly onto the base to compact the crumbs.
- Put the tray with the tartlets into the oven and bake them for about 12 minutes until the crumb mixture is slightly darker. Remove the tray from the oven and transfer the tins to a cooling rack. The mixture may well have puffed up and slipped down the sides of the tins a bit at this stage. To remedy this, hold one tin at a time in a thick cloth to protect your fingers from the heat and use the back of a spoon to push the mixture back up the sides. Leave the crusts to cool completely in the tins. ›

- Meanwhile, make the passionfruit cream. To do this, halve all the passionfruit then scoop the pulp into a fine sieve sitting over a measuring jug or bowl. Use the back of a spoon to work the pulp against the sieve to extract as much juice as possible – you need ⅓ cup (80 ml) all up (if you have any left over it makes a lovely drink, mixed into some fresh pineapple or orange juice). Set the juice aside and discard the seeds.

- Spoon the sour cream and double thick cream into a chilled bowl. Sift in the icing sugar and, using a balloon whisk, gently whip the mixture until it is softly thick but not stiff. Pour in the passionfruit juice and stir it gently with the whisk – the mixture may thin a bit initially, but will thicken again quickly. Cover the bowl and store it in the fridge.

- When you are ready to serve the tartlets, use the overhanging foil to help you gently ease the crusts from the tartlet tins. Peel away the foil – the crusts are very fragile at the edges, so be careful – then sit a tart crust on each dessert plate. Divide the passionfruit cream evenly among them. Lay the mango slices decoratively over each one, then spoon a few passionfruit seeds on top. If you are using the mint leaves, scatter some over each tartlet and serve.

26th January – Australia Day

. . . and it couldn't have been a more beautiful Aussie dawn – a clear blue sky tinged with pink, the sugar-cane fields golden in the first light, and a quiet hum settling over the bush. We've already been down for a swim in the river as the king tides are with us again and the water is so clear we can see the ripple lines in the sand and schools of whiting drifting leisurely on the tide. I love swimming here, it's such a beautiful spot and just so Australian – casuarinas sway by the rock wall, flotillas of cormorants hunt in the channel, early fishing boats make their way through the river entrance (blessedly calm today), surfers trailing their boards on push bikes teeter along the break-wall to check out the waves; and big fat pelicans fly ponderously overhead only to splash down not far from where we swim to scoop up a bill-full of fish. It's magical.

Our day will be low-key, but tonight we're having a get-together. Everyone is bringing a dish and mine's going to be prawns with capsicums and beans. It just doesn't seem quite like Australia Day if we don't eat prawns, and there are some terrific local ones at the Fishermen's Co-op at the moment. I have bought a couple of kilos as a treat – half to eat for lunch with a squeeze of lemon juice and some wholemeal bread and butter (there's nothing nicer, is there?) and the rest for this vivid salad (see overleaf).

28th January

Well, the sun has continued to shine for a few days now and it's as if all of nature is celebrating and out in force. There are butterflies everywhere; birds singing, trilling and cooing (the butcher birds in particular, with their exquisite silvery song, are egging each other on to greater and greater feats of musical prowess); bees are flitting busily from flower to flower; and to cap it off, while I've been sitting outside having a cup of tea, the dearest young blue-tongue lizard has crept out onto a rock near my feet and quietly and trustingly settled down for a sunbathe. How good is that!

Warm Salad of Prawns, Grilled Capsicum & Beans

SERVES 4

3 large red capsicums (peppers)
200 g baby green beans
2 × 300 g cans butter beans, drained and rinsed
2 cloves garlic, finely chopped
¼ large red onion, very finely sliced
big squeeze of lemon juice, to taste (or use fig vinegar, if you have some)
sea salt flakes and freshly ground black pepper
2 tablespoons finely shredded basil
½ cup (125 ml) extra virgin olive oil
80 g cultured unsalted butter (see page 3)
1 kg uncooked prawns, peeled and deveined, tails left on
1 small red chilli, finely chopped
¼–½ teaspoon smoked paprika

You may well notice as you read through this book that capsicums turn up in many guises – more often than not grilled, as I love the way grilling concentrates their flavour and brings out their inherent sweetness. Over the years I've experimented with all sorts of ways to use them: puréed in soups and sauces, tossed in salads, slow-cooked with tomatoes, and combined with all sorts of seafood. But I would have to say that, of all the seafood I've eaten with them, there is nothing quite like the synergy between grilled capsicums and prawns. I think it's to do with the sweetness of the capsicums complementing the briny sweetness of the prawns. This gorgeous summer salad is a prime example – the only thing I ever serve with it are chunks of chewy baguette to blot up every last skerrick of the juices.

- Preheat the grill to high and line the grill tray with foil.

- Slice the capsicums down their natural contour lines into large pieces, then remove the cores, seeds and white ribs. Sit the pieces of capsicum, skin-side up, in a single layer on the prepared grill tray. Slide the tray under the grill and cook the capsicums until the skins blister and blacken. As soon as they do, remove the tray and cover the capsicums completely with a heavy tea towel (you can also transfer them to a plate and cover them tightly with plastic film). Leave the capsicums to sweat for a few minutes. As soon as they're cool enough to handle, peel away and discard the skins. Slice a third of the pieces into fine strips and very finely chop the rest.

- Trim the stalks only from the green beans – I always leave the curly tails intact as I think the beans look much nicer with them on. Cook the beans in a large saucepan of rapidly boiling, salted water until they're still nice and green but cooked through – I find the only way to check properly is to scoop one out, blow on it like crazy for a few moments and then take a bite. As soon as they're ready, drain them and immediately plunge them into iced water to set their bright green colour. When they're cool, wrap them in a tea towel to dry.

- Now make a salad with the butter beans by mixing them with the garlic, onion slices, lemon juice, salt, pepper, basil, ¼ cup (60 ml) of the extra virgin olive oil and the capsicum that you cut into strips. Set the salad aside while you cook the prawns.

- Heat the butter and remaining oil in a wide, heavy-based frying pan over high heat. Add the prawns and sauté them for a couple of minutes until they're just cooked. Stir in the chilli, smoked paprika and reserved chopped capsicum, warm them through, then remove the pan from the heat. Taste the mixture and add more salt or a splash of lemon juice, if needed.
- To serve, sit a small pile of the green beans on each plate and spoon some of the bean salad over the top. Keep adding a few more beans, then a bit more salad until they are both used up. Scoop the prawn and capsicum mixture over the top and serve the salad straight away.

FEBRUARY

3rd February

Gus has just come for his morning visit. Having retriever genes, he never arrives without a little gift of some sort. Dreamer that I am, I like to think they're tokens of affection, but I suspect there is a far more pragmatic reason – to pave the way for a possible treat. Did I mention he is smart too?

Occasionally his gifts have been a little more than we bargained for, like the time he arrived with mouth bulging, looking terribly pleased with himself, and proceeded to do victory laps around the outdoor table. Initially he refused to drop his gift, but eventually he very gently let it go into my hand.

Our 'gift' turned out to be a wee double-barred finch, which must have knocked himself out on one of the windows. Gus, ever on the alert, found him and no doubt thought a wounded bird would make a very good impression indeed, possibly earning him an even bigger treat than usual. He is a wonder, though – for, as retrievers do, he has a 'soft' mouth and the bird, although covered in saliva and more than a little shocked, was very much alive and after a few minutes flew off completely unharmed. Needless to say, Gus was lavished with many hugs, pats and the odd Schmacko or two.

4th February

Oh no, it's raining again! We've been in Sydney for a few days and have arrived back, somewhat incredulously, to near-floods. We were lucky to get back at all actually, as we had two failed landing attempts at Ballina airport. Fortunately, the pilot tried one more time and the cloud cleared just enough for us to duck underneath it – we were the first and last plane to do so all day. I must say it was a bit wild, so much so that everyone cheered when we drew to a halt. It was certainly a good feeling to be back on terra firma, even if it is under a few centimetres of water.

Despite the wet, the birds still beat a constant path to the birdbath, and as I write these words a brown honeyeater is having a ball swooping in and out of the water . . .

6th February

It has become somewhat of a ritual for me as I write this book to have a tea break each afternoon. I invariably make myself a pot of Ceylon tea, and put it on a tray along with my favourite cup and saucer and two plump fingers of shortbread. I usually take it out into the garden and sit watching the birds and listening to the wind. It's lovely just to do nothing for a short time and rest my eyes, which are more often than not bleary from some hours spent on the computer. I find these small pleasures add immeasurably to my days.

Funnily enough, this custom of stopping for afternoon tea takes me back to my teens, when I was staying in Sabah with a family whose patriarch was the most delightful Scotsman. Every afternoon on the dot of four, usually after the first monsoonal downpour, a 'proper' afternoon tea would be served on one of the wide verandas that surrounded the bungalow. Being the home of a proud Scot, it invariably included Dundee cake and an embossed red and gold tin of shortbread biscuits which he ordered especially from Scotland. These were ceremoniously handed out, along with a slice of the cake, and we would sit munching on them while we discussed the day that had been and the night that was to come. It was all terribly civilised and I remember feeling I needed to pinch myself to make sure I hadn't been transported back to colonial times.

As I look back, I realise that since then I seem to have been on an unintended quest to make the best shortbread I possibly can, perhaps in a bid to recapture such a special time. I've tried it every which way: using a little rice flour instead of all plain flour (this tends to make for a crisper, 'shorter', biscuit); varying the proportions of butter and flour; baking it at different temperatures; and even including slivers of crystallised ginger in the dough, which is probably nothing short of heresy to a true Scot!

My Classic Shortbread

MAKES 10–12 WEDGES OR FINGERS

225 g unsalted butter, at cool room temperature (preferably cultured unsalted butter – see page 3)
½ cup (110 g) caster sugar
2 teaspoons vanilla extract
2 cups (300 g) plain flour
½ teaspoon salt
a little white granulated sugar, for sprinkling

GIVING . . .

I love making gifts for Christmas, although more often than not my good intentions go out the window as it gets closer to the time and everything seems to become ridiculously busy. However, last Christmas I did manage to cook some of these shortbread rounds as gifts and I can't tell you what a hit they were. I bought half a dozen tart tins to bake them in, and gave the tins as part of the gift too, leaving the shortbread in them. They looked rather fabulous all wrapped up and finished off with fat tartan bows.

KEEPING . . .

One of the really nice things about shortbread is that as long as the container is airtight it will keep well for up to a month.

This is the shortbread recipe I return to again and again – it's wonderfully 'short' and buttery. Marvellous as is with a cuppa, it also makes a delicious dessert served with poached or roasted fruit. At this time of year, almost invariably for us the fruit is a bowl of rosy poached white nectarines (see page 40) or sticky roasted plums (see page 113).

- The first thing to do is to put a 24 cm round fluted, loose-based tart tin in the fridge to chill. You can also make the shortbread in a rectangular loose-based band tin (approximately 35 cm × 11 cm × 2.5 cm), which I did for the photograph – it makes a thicker, softer shortbread.
- Now put the butter and caster sugar into the bowl of an electric mixer (or you can use a regular bowl and a hand-held electric beater). Beat them together on medium speed for 4 minutes, until the mixture looks light and creamy. It's best not to over-do the beating as it may incorporate too much air into the mixture, which will affect the shortbread's texture. Reduce the speed and mix in the vanilla.
- Turn off the beater and add the flour and salt. Mix them in on low speed (if the beater is going too fast you will discover, as I have more than once, that you'll end up covered in a fine coating of flour!). Mix only until the flour is incorporated, stopping and scraping down the sides as you need to, to make sure it is evenly mixed. Press the dough into the chilled tart tin, patting it down gently to get it as even as possible. I usually finish off by rolling a small tumbler or jar over the top to smooth the surface.
- Make a decorative border by pressing the tines of a fork all around the edge of the shortbread (or use a finger instead of the fork, to give a more scalloped effect). Now rest a ruler across the top of the tin and use it as a guide to cut the round into 12 even wedges (or 10–12 bars, if you are using a band tin). Finally, prick each wedge or bar a few times with a fork. Cover the tin and chill the shortbread for at least 2 hours (or up to a day ahead of baking it).
- Preheat your oven to 155°C. Sprinkle the shortbread with a couple of teaspoons of granulated sugar, then bake it for about 1¼ hours, or until it is pale golden and smells delicious (if you're using a band tin, it may take a bit longer as the dough is thicker). Remove the tin from the oven and place it on a rack. Let the shortbread cool for 8 minutes then, with the ruler as a guide, use a fine pointed knife to carefully cut along the score marks right down through the shortbread. Leave it to cool completely in the tin.
- Store the wedges or bars in a tightly sealed, airtight container.

CAKES

9th February

We've been blessed these past weeks, as a friend has been experimenting growing various sorts of melons, and we're the lucky recipients of his largesse. To me, a ripe, sweetly fragrant melon is an absolute joy to eat; however, they're not always the easiest things to come by here (and, I rather suspect, elsewhere too), so it has been a real treat for us. Apart from eating them as is – and I have to fess up that I actually demolished a whole rocky at a single sitting – we've been making this lovely salad, which is so simple and refreshing on a steamy day.

Honeydew Melon, Prosciutto, Goat's Cheese & Black Olive Salad

SERVES 1

1 handful of mizuna, elk-horn lettuce or watercress sprigs, plus extra to garnish
1 good-sized slice of ripe honeydew melon
30–40 g goat's curd or goat's feta
3 slices prosciutto
freshly ground black pepper
7–8 smallish black olives (niçoise or ligurian are ideal)
extra virgin olive oil, to taste
2 teaspoons pine nuts

MIZUNA

Mizuna is such a pretty salad green with its slender white stalks and pale to deep green lacy leaves. It has a lovely delicate mustard flavour which is terrific in salads, however as it becomes older it gets hotter and a little coarse. When it reaches this point, it's best stir-fried with that holy trinity of Asian cooking – garlic, ginger and chilli.

I published a version of this exquisite recipe in my first book (*Belinda Jeffery's 100 Favourite Recipes*), however I really felt I should include it here, as we eat it again and again in the dog days of February, when it's so humid that even the thought of cooking anything is enough to make me break into a sweat. It has a wonderful play of sweet and salty flavours and is beautiful to look at – the cool jade greens of the mizuna and melon are punctuated by the rosy-pink prosciutto with its ruffle of white fat and the jet-black olives. As far as quantities go, please just use those included here as a guide as I tend to just put it all together until it looks right. This makes enough for one serve, so increase the quantities to match the number of eaters.

- Before I start making the salad I usually pop some bread in the oven to warm through, so it will be ready when the salad is.
- Wash whichever salad green you are using really well and shake it dry. Pick off sprigs and put a small pile in the middle of each plate. (It looks prettiest if you point the stalks to the middle so the leaves are facing out.)
- Remove the rind from the melon and cut the flesh into small chunks. Pile these up on top of the greens. Now dab little bits of goat's cheese over the melon, or if you're using feta, crumble it on top.
- Halve the prosciutto slices then roll them up to form loose rosettes. Tuck these here and there into the pile of melon as best you can. Now grind a little black pepper on top and scatter the olives over everything.
- Heat a splash of olive oil in a small frying pan over medium heat. Add the pine nuts and cook them, tossing them about, until they become golden and fragrant. Take them off the heat and sprinkle them over the salad. To finish, put a mizuna or watercress sprig on top and drizzle a little olive oil over the lot.

11th February

I grew up in an era where virtually every home had a lemon tree in the backyard, and we were no exception. I used to love going out with my mum to pick an apron-full of them, trying carefully to avoid the lethal thorns that inevitably grazed our arms as we plucked lemon after lemon. She would then scrub them and get me to grate the zest before making her lemon cordial – a drink we lived on over summer. They also went into all sorts of other dishes, and as I've grown older I well understand why, as never a day goes by that I don't use lemons in my cooking in some way. In fact, we go through so many of them that we've recently planted another three trees – a Meyer, a Eureka and a Lisbon – just to keep up with the supply! I love the way they add tang and balance to both sweet and savoury dishes, and it never ceases to surprise me how a simple squeeze of lemon juice can lift a dish from being just nice to something really special. A prime example of this is the roasted bean dish that follows – it's most unusual and utterly delicious, and it really is that final splash of lemon juice that makes all the difference.

Roasted Green Beans with Lemon & Anchovies

SERVES 4

I nearly didn't write the word 'anchovies' in the name of this dish as I know that many people will pretty much automatically by-pass any recipe that has anchovies in it. It's such a shame, because they add a depth of flavour and intriguing background note that is perfectly delicious without being at all fishy. If you're one of my mob and love them, or even if you're an anchovy sceptic, but are feeling adventurous, then do give this recipe a try – it's such a simple dish yet full of flavour. I sometimes add a chopped red chilli to give it a bit more oomph too. These beans are terrific with any sort of grilled meat or fish, but a particular favourite of mine is to serve them with barbecued tuna and a little dish of anchovy-flavoured mayonnaise. Oh, there is one more thing I should say: this isn't the most beautiful dish to look at, as the fierce heat of the oven dulls the colour of the beans, but to me their flavour more than makes up for this.

550 g medium-sized green beans
¼ cup (60 ml) extra virgin olive oil
2 large cloves garlic, squashed and halved
3 thyme sprigs, broken into small pieces
sea salt flakes and freshly ground black pepper
2–3 anchovies, to taste
3 teaspoons lemon juice, or more to taste
1 tablespoon finely chopped flat-leaf parsley

- Preheat your oven to 220°C. Line a large baking tray with baking paper.
- Trim the stem end of the beans if necessary but leave the tips intact. Wash them well, then roll them in a tea towel to dry them off.
- Spread the beans onto the baking tray then drizzle them with the olive oil. Add the garlic, thyme sprigs, salt and pepper then swizzle the beans about so they are well coated in the mixture. Slip the tray into the oven. Roast the beans, turning them once or twice, for about 15 minutes until they are tender and brown in patches.
- Meanwhile, put the anchovies into a large bowl and mash them with the back of a spoon or fork so they disintegrate into a paste. Mix in the lemon juice. (If you want to add a little chopped red chilli, do this now too.)
- When the beans are ready, tip them into the bowl with the anchovy mixture and toss them about so they are well coated. At this stage, it's a good idea to taste one to see if the dressing needs any tweaking – I sometimes add a bit more salt or lemon juice. You can serve the beans straight away, or leave them to cool to room temperature. Mix in the parsley just prior to serving, so it keeps its bright green colour.

13th February

We've been to see our friends who live up the valley today. The drive there is a joy, as the road twists and turns as it climbs the escarpment, and when we look down the steep slopes they're carpeted in a dense green mat of banana trees. How the farmers work these slopes is beyond me – it must be back-breaking carting the massive bunches to and fro.

Once we reach the top, the road plunges down, then up again; one minute flanked by a dense mass of overhanging gums, the next running by the side of the creek, which is quite swollen and rushing furiously after the last few months of rain. The further we drive the narrower and higher the valley walls become, and plumes of water tumble off the distant cliffs, disappearing into gullies below. More often than not on these visits, a python or rock wallaby will appear on the road. The wallabies leap into the bush in a flurry of bounds, however the pythons are more sanguine, stopping dead-still to sense what's happening – they're a truly spectacular sight with their exquisite diamond markings. Often they stay a while, but once they know the coast is clear, they glide into the undergrowth. I always think of my niece when I see one, as the first time we brought her here she couldn't believe her eyes at the sight of a 3-metre python coiled on the road. You've never seen a car window wound up so quickly in your life! We all ended up hooting with laughter, but I well remember my first few encounters with snakes and I know just how she felt.

We get the most beautiful organic vegetables from our friends, and amazing almost orange-yolked eggs from their 'girls', a clutch of very happy hens who are much loved and cared for, and spend their days foraging about the garden and forest. Although I shouldn't just say 'girls', as there's also a magnificent rooster – he is quite a sight in the sunlight, which picks out every colour in his extraordinary plumage and makes him gleam as though he were made of metal.

We've come back not only full of tea, cake and happy conversation, but also laden with bits from the garden and a dozen beautiful fresh eggs, half of which I've already ear-marked for a cheese roulade for dinner tonight.

Cheese Roulade with Herbed Goat's Cheese & Grilled Red Capsicum

SERVES 6–8

I know at first glance this recipe might seem a bit complicated, but it's surprisingly easy to do and rather special and beautiful. Think of it as a cheese sauce bolstered with egg yolks, lightened with egg whites and then baked. The capsicums for the filling can be prepared several days ahead; the filling itself is dead-easy as it's whizzed up in a food processor – and the whole thing can be assembled up to a day ahead. I tend to decorate it with whatever herbs I happen to have in the garden. When we took the photo my parsley had started to flower, and as I love the look of the tiny little umbrellas it forms, I used these with small Greek basil leaves.

60 g unsalted butter
55 g plain flour
1¾ cups (440 ml) cold milk
6 eggs, separated
60 g finely grated parmesan
sea salt flakes, to taste
herb sprigs, to garnish

FILLING

1½ large red capsicums (peppers)
250 g cream cheese, at room temperature
150 g goat's or ewe's milk feta marinated in oil (I use Meredith goat's feta for this)
1 heaped tablespoon finely chopped chives
1 heaped tablespoon finely chopped flat-leaf parsley
1 tablespoon good-quality mayonnaise
sea salt flakes
2–3 tablespoons small parsley leaves
about 6 large basil leaves, torn (or the equivalent in tiny basil leaves)

- Preheat your oven to 180°C. Lightly butter a shallow baking tin (40 cm × 26 cm × 3 cm) and line the base and sides with a large sheet of baking paper.
- Melt the butter in a large saucepan over medium–low heat. Stir in the flour and cook, stirring regularly, for about 3 minutes until the mixture looks sandy – a sauce whisk is ideal for stirring this, as its flat base gets into the corners of the pan. Increase the heat slightly and whisk in the cold milk. Bring the mixture to a gentle bubble, then reduce the heat so the bubbles just plop slowly and cook the sauce, whisking regularly, for 5 minutes or so until it's smooth and thick.
- Remove from the heat and whisk in the egg yolks, one at a time, making sure each one is well incorporated before adding the next. Stir in the parmesan and salt and, once the parmesan has melted, set the sauce aside.
- Tip the egg whites into a clean, dry mixing bowl and whip them with a pinch of salt until they form smooth soft peaks when you lift the beaters out of the bowl. Gently mix a quarter of the beaten whites into the cheese sauce to lighten it, then add this mixture to the remaining whites in the bowl and gently fold the two together. Try to use as gentle a touch as possible for this to keep the roulade light – it's better to have a few streaks of white showing than to over-mix it and risk deflating the mixture.
- Spread the cheese mixture evenly into the prepared tin, making sure it reaches into the corners. Bake it for about 17 minutes, or until the roulade feels springy and firm in the centre when you press on it gently. ›

BY THE WAY . . .

This is rather lovely warm too. To heat it, cover the roulade loosely with foil and put it into a preheated 180°C oven for 15–20 minutes (don't leave it any longer, though, or the filling will melt).

- While the roulade is baking, slightly overlap two large sheets of baking paper on your benchtop. When the roulade is ready, remove it from the oven and, taking your courage in both hands, quickly invert it onto the sheets of baking paper. I know this sounds a bit precarious, but it does work! Remove the tin and leave the roulade to cool for 20 minutes or so. (If the baking paper lining from the tin sticks to the roulade, just leave it there until you come to roll the roulade.)

- Meanwhile, to make the filling, cut the capsicums along their natural contour lines into large pieces. Remove the cores, seeds and white ribs then run them under a hot grill, shiny-side up, until the skins blister and blacken. Take them out and cover them with a thick tea towel. As soon as they're cool enough to handle, peel away the skins and finely chop the flesh. (The grilled and peeled capsicums can be stored, covered in olive oil, for up to 5 days in the fridge.)

- Put the cream cheese and feta into a food processor and whiz them together, stopping and scraping down the sides occasionally, until the mixture is smooth. Add the chopped chives, parsley, mayonnaise and salt to taste, then whiz everything together again to thoroughly combine them.

- When the roulade is just cool, use a long palette knife to spread the cream cheese mixture evenly over it. Scatter the chopped capsicum, parsley leaves and torn basil all over the top. Next it needs to be rolled up to enclose the filling. I find the easiest way to do this is to roll it from the long side nearest you, using the paper to help you shape it into a log. (Start the roll with as tight a fold as you can, to avoid leaving a gap in the centre of the roulade.) This may sound a bit awkward but it isn't that hard to do, as the roulade is quite flexible. Once it's rolled, wrap the paper tightly around the roulade to help keep its shape, and carefully transfer it to a baking tray using that long palette knife again or a couple of wide spatulas. Don't worry if it loses its shape a bit as you do this, just pat it back with your hands then put the tray with the roulade into the fridge. Chill it for at least 45 minutes to help firm everything up (it's much easier to handle when it is cold). At this stage, you can serve the roulade immediately, or cover it loosely and leave it overnight.

- About 20 minutes before you are ready to serve it, take the roulade out of the fridge to warm it up a little. Remove the paper and carefully slide it onto a long serving platter. Sprinkle it with herb leaves and flowers.

Green Beans with Pesto Dressing & Pine Nuts

SERVES 6–8

750 g small green beans, stalks trimmed
handful of roasted pine nuts, tossed in a smidgen of olive oil to make them shine
tiny basil leaves, to serve, optional

DRESSING

½ cup (125 ml) extra virgin olive oil
1–1½ tablespoons white wine vinegar
2 heaped tablespoons pesto (see note), or more to taste
sea salt flakes, to taste

We have a plethora of beans at the moment as all the bush bean seedlings I planted have shot up at a rate of knots and are now producing so many beans we're harvesting them every day in an effort to keep up. The basil is rampant as well and as the two go so well together we've been eating bowlfuls of this delicious salad. It's particularly good at this time of year, for although we love leafy green salads, the salad greens themselves are pretty thin on the ground at the moment and rot quickly in the humidity, so this more robust dish is a terrific alternative.

- Drop the beans into a large saucepan of rapidly boiling salted water. Boil them until they're cooked through but still a good bright-green colour (a pet hate of mine is under-cooked green beans – I don't find the flavour nearly as delicious as when they're cooked through). I know they look lovely when they are really bright green, and there is certainly no need to cook them until they're dull, but it's a matter of finding just the right time to take them off the heat. Check by fishing one out and taking a bite.
- As soon as the beans are ready, drain them in a colander. Now, tip them into a big bowl of ice and water to stop them cooking and set their colour. Once they're cool, wrap them in a tea towel to dry. (You can store them in the fridge like this for a few hours – just slip the whole bundle into a plastic bag and seal it.)
- Make the dressing just before serving the salad so the pesto keeps its bright-green colour. Whisk all the ingredients together in a big bowl, then add the beans and toss them in the dressing so they're thoroughly coated. Pile the beans into a shallow bowl and sprinkle with the pine nuts and basil leaves, if using.

PESTO

Lots of delis sell pesto, but if you want to whip up a batch of your own it's very quick and easy. Just put 100 g of basil leaves, 2 crushed cloves of garlic, a little sea salt, 25 g of pine nuts and ½ cup (125 ml) of extra virgin olive oil into a blender. Whiz them together on high speed then scrape the paste out of the blender and stir in 75 g of freshly grated parmesan. Spoon it into a container and cover the surface with a thin film of oil. Store it in the fridge for up to a week. If you want to freeze the pesto, leave out the parmesan, then add it after you've defrosted it. A neat way to package this up for the freezer is to put a couple of tablespoons of the pesto into little snap-lock bags. Smooth the pesto out so it forms a thin layer, then seal the bags. When you want to use it, just pull out a bag or two, let them defrost and stir in the parmesan. This is such a treat in winter, when basil is thin on the ground: I just pop open a bag or two and drop the pesto, still frozen, into whatever I'm cooking – more often than not a casserole or pot of soup – to give it a little taste of summer sunshine.

BANGA

FEDERAL
LISMORE
EUREKA
SPORTSGROUND

17th February

This morning started with not one but *three* blessings. I was heading out into the garden early to do some work before the heat of the day set in. The first thing I saw when I opened the blinds was a young, brilliantly plumed male king parrot sitting peacefully on the pergola, munching on seed we had left out for the finches. They're a rare sight out in the open like this but each time we see them a similar scene unfolds, as they're the most inquisitive of birds and instead of flying away when they see us, they're incredibly curious. As I peered up at him (for he was above my head) he craned his neck down to fix me with an intensely interested, unblinking gaze. Each time I moved slightly out of his line of vision, he would walk along the pergola until he could see me more clearly, to the point of almost falling off in his desire to get as good a look as possible. This continued for about five minutes, until startled by another bird landing, he finally flew away. They're magnificent birds and it was breathtaking to see one so close up, with the saturated greens, blues, oranges and reds of his feathers. I often think when I see the plumage on king parrots (and so many of the birds that visit) that if you painted one, and someone who saw the painting had never seen the bird before, they would think that you were grossly exaggerating the colours.

So that was blessing number one. Five minutes later, blessing number two arrived in the shape of the dearest little green tree frog, absolutely perfect and so tiny that he could have fitted on my thumbnail. He'd somehow wandered into the garage and couldn't find his way out. Fortunately I managed to trap him under a glass and, with a bit of judicious handling, gently restore him to a more hospitable home in a clump of papyrus outside my office window where I know a family of similar frogs resides. Occasionally as I sit and write this journal, one climbs up a papyrus stalk and if my eyes are tuned in I can watch as it shelters under the umbrella of leaves at the top – they always make me feel so happy.

And much later still, blessing number three appeared. We were sitting quietly having a cup of tea and eating the last of Clive's birthday cake when we heard an almighty thump on the window. We both realised what it was – a bird had flown into the glass and knocked itself unconscious. It's always upsetting when this happens, but not uncommon, so we immediately swung into our 'recovery' routine. This involves covering the bird with an up-turned shoe-box, the front of which has been cut out so the bird is protected from any larger birds or animals, is in shade and relative dark, yet can see out and fly away (hopefully) once it's over the shock. We both thought the bird was a blue fairy wren, but when we got closer we realised that it was in fact a sacred kingfisher.

The dear little soul was stunned, but managed to fly onto the outside table, where it perched for at least 10 minutes while we sat almost within touching distance of it. It was truly extraordinary. I've only seen kingfishers on a few occasions down by the creek, where they're no more than swift flashes of iridescent blue that dart across the water. None of those encounters have ever been anything like as close as this one, but even so they've felt truly magical, for they're the most exquisite of birds. The colours, which we could now see in all their glory, are a brilliant array of turquoise and rich, deep blues with a creamy-orange breast, but its beak is the real surprise as it's nearly as long as the bird itself. We sat spell-bound, until with a fleeting glance at us both, it shook its head and darted away in a streak of blue.

Speaking of birthdays, we have a bit of a tradition in the family that was started by my mum. When we were children she would let us each choose what we wanted for our birthday dinner and cake, and so it has continued to this day. Clive's birthday dinner was no exception – we had crisp parmesan-coated lamb cutlets with slow-cooked red capsicums and tomatoes, watercress and avocado salad, a bowl of his favourite crunchy roasted potatoes (see page 145) and finished off with a banana upside-down cake (see page 399). Not exactly the most balanced meal in the world, but nor does it have to be – it's all about the food we love.

Crisp Cheese & Prosciutto-Stuffed Lamb Cutlets

SERVES 4

I'm a sucker for lamb cutlets. Whenever I cook them I think of my mum, and remember standing next to her in the kitchen as she set out bowls of flour, beaten eggs and breadcrumbs to coat them. I loved helping her do this – even back then I found something very soothing and pleasing about the dipping, shaking and dunking that went on. And of course, I loved the results: crisp, golden little cutlets that went perfectly with the mashed potatoes and peas she always served with them. Coming from a family of enthusiastic carnivores, the best part was nibbling on the bones, which we all did with great gusto! This is a variation on my mum's cutlets, but I've no doubt she would have relished them as she loved anything with cheese in it. If I'm in a hurry I don't always stuff them, I just coat them with the parmesan and crumbs, fry them and eat them with a simple tomato salad and some greens.

12 small lamb cutlets (ask your butcher not to flatten them as they are going to be stuffed)
50 g fontina or gruyère, sliced into fine slivers
6 slices prosciutto, halved
about 30 g finely grated parmesan
2 eggs, lightly beaten
120 g fine dried breadcrumbs, plus a little extra for sprinkling
olive oil, for cooking
herb sprigs, to garnish (I use whatever is in the garden – oregano looks particularly lovely)
lemon wedges, to serve

- Sit the cutlets flat on a chopping board. Use the tip of a sharp knife to cut a small pocket in the fleshy side of each one. Gently work the knife from side to side to widen the pocket a little. Now push a couple of slivers of cheese inside each one, then roll up the strips of prosciutto and push those in too (if the prosciutto slices are very large, you may not need them all). Press the edges of the meat together to seal in the stuffing; then press down gently on the cutlets with the palm of your hand to flatten them out slightly. ›

CRUMBS . . .
As far as the dried breadcrumbs for this go, I keep a jar of homemade crumbs (see page 156) in the pantry to use. I don't mean that to sound quite as smug as it may – it's just that they taste so much better than bought ones as they don't have all the added flavourings, and they brown so beautifully. They are easy as pie to make if you're pottering about in the kitchen, and keep for months.

- Put the parmesan, beaten egg and breadcrumbs into three separate shallow bowls. Line a large baking tray with baking paper and sprinkle with a fine layer of breadcrumbs. One at a time, press each cutlet firmly into the parmesan to coat both sides. Now dip it into the beaten egg, holding the cutlet over the bowl briefly to allow any excess egg to drip back in. Lastly, press the cutlet into the breadcrumbs so it's completely coated in them. Sit the cutlet on the prepared tray. Repeat this dipping and crumbing with the remaining cutlets and place them on the tray, taking care not to overlap them or they may become soggy. Pop the tray into the fridge, uncovered, and chill the cutlets for an hour or two so the coating dries out a little and firms up.
- You need to cook the cutlets in a decent amount of oil, otherwise the crumbs tend to burn, so pour olive oil into a large frying pan to a depth of 5 mm or so. Heat the oil over low–medium heat. Add the cutlets to the pan in a single layer (do this in batches, if necessary) and fry them for 3–4 minutes on one side, then turn and cook the other side for 2–3 minutes or until they're crisp and golden on both sides (thicker cutlets will take a little longer). You may find you need to reduce the heat as they cook, because the crumb coating can burn quite easily. Be a little careful as you turn the cutlets for the crust is quite fragile and easily torn. When they're done, sit them on paper towel to drain.
- To serve the cutlets, put them on a warm platter or individual plates and garnish with herbs and lemon wedges.

Slow-Cooked Red Capsicums & Tomatoes

SERVES 6 AS A SIDE DISH

4 very large or 5 medium-sized deep-red capsicums (peppers)
90 ml extra virgin olive oil
8 large cloves garlic, peeled and left whole
1 tablespoon thyme leaves
750 g ripe tomatoes, cut into 2 cm chunks (or the equivalent in halved cherry tomatoes)
1½ teaspoons sea salt flakes, or more to taste
freshly ground black pepper

I make this simple dish of capsicums and tomatoes throughout the summer, as it tastes so good and keeps so well. The long, slow cooking causes the capsicums and tomatoes to become really unctuous, and although there is rather a lot of garlic it becomes sweet and mellow over the cooking time.

It's one of those dead-easy, wonderfully versatile dishes that goes with an amazing range of things. We eat it with herb-roasted chicken, barbecued butterflied lamb, seared salmon fillets, even spooned over polenta with a scatter of parmesan or little nuggets of soft goat's cheese, and of course Clive's lamb cutlets! However I'm just as likely to make a meal of it as is, sometimes with tiny balls of cherry bocconcini, and always with chunks of good country-style bread to sop up the lovely, oily juices.

- Preheat your oven to 160°C. It's best to use a large enamelled cast-iron casserole for cooking this, as it can go from stovetop to oven. If you don't have one, it's fine to use a large frying pan for the stovetop cooking, then transfer everything to a casserole dish to go in the oven.
- Cut the capsicums into quarters then remove the seeds and any white ribs. Slice each quarter in half lengthways.
- Now, heat the oil over medium heat in a large-ish enamelled cast-iron casserole. Add the capsicum slices, garlic cloves and thyme and stir them so they are well coated in the oil. Thoroughly mix in the tomatoes, salt and pepper. Warm the mixture for a couple of minutes then cover it with a lid and transfer the dish to the oven. Cook the capsicums and tomatoes for 2 hours, stirring them gently once or twice during that time. Remove the lid and cook the mixture for another 30 minutes (they smell wonderful as they cook).
- When they're ready, remove the casserole from the oven and leave it to cool to room temperature. Sometimes the capsicum skins have pulled away from the flesh a bit – I generally leave them on, but if you think they look a bit naff, just gently pull them away.
- To serve, spoon the capsicums and tomatoes into a bowl (white looks gorgeous with the brilliant reds) and trickle the herby juices over the top.

18th February

We've now had more than seven weeks of rain and there's no sign of it abating. The flooding has been widespread, and I feel so sorry for people in low-lying areas as we're due for more downpours in the next few days. It must be terrible – they've only just mopped up from the last floods around Christmas and now it looks as if there will be more. Fortunately for us, even though we do get flooded in and the water covers the road below us, our house is up on a hill so we're high and dry. God help everyone if it comes up this far – a second Noah's Ark will definitely be needed!

We're both hard at work today. Me writing this book and enjoying it greatly (but, truth be known, feeling somewhat daunted as I realise the magnitude of what I've committed to), and Clive out working locally. Well, relatively locally – I tend to think in country miles now, so anything within about three hours' drive is local!

19th February

The garden is full of baby blue-tongue lizards at the moment, and they're as cute as buttons, tumbling through the undergrowth and following the trail of snails and slugs that we leave out for them. And there's certainly no lack of *those* at the moment, as they, along with the caterpillars, are having a field day in the wet, slowly and methodically munching their way through anything in their path. In fact, one of my neighbours has just given me a couple of beautiful eggplants, which were just about all she could rescue from her crop. When she went out this morning, nearly every last one had been feasted on by caterpillars overnight and she was determined not to let them have the whole lot.

I'm so glad she did, as I was wondering what we were going to have for dinner tonight. We have some cold lamb cutlets leftover from Clive's birthday (I do love leftover lamb, don't you?), and now I shall make up a batch of sweet-and-sour eggplant to go with them. In a way, the cutlets and eggplant are a version of that classic combination of leftover roast lamb and pickles, but with a bit more of an Italian leaning.

Sicilian-Style Eggplant, Pear & Tomatoes

SERVES 4 AS A SIDE DISH

- 1 medium-sized eggplant (aubergine), cut into 2 cm dice
- salt, for sprinkling
- 90 ml extra virgin olive oil
- 1 onion, diced
- 2 cloves garlic, finely chopped
- 1½ tablespoons capers, rinsed and drained
- 2 × 400 g cans crushed or diced tomatoes
- 2 ripe pears, peeled, cored and cut into small chunks (or you could use canned pears in natural juice)
- ¼ cup (40 g) currants
- 2 teaspoons caster sugar
- 2 teaspoons balsamic vinegar
- sea salt flakes and freshly ground black pepper
- ¼ cup (40 g) pine nuts, lightly roasted

This eggplant dish is typically Sicilian in flavour and has a terrific sweet–sour balance that goes with so many things. It's wonderful tossed through spaghetti with a little parmesan and fresh basil; roast or barbecued lamb is all the better for a scoop or two; it's spectacularly good with seared tuna; it makes a delicious salad if you sit it on a bed of watercress and spoon marinated feta or goat's curd over the top; and it's great spread onto good bread, topped with a little rocket and goat's cheese then flashed under the grill just until the cheese melts (my latest lunchtime treat) . . . and that's just for starters. It also keeps really well in the fridge, which is always an added bonus for me as I've been known to indulge in the odd midnight snack or two, and more than once have been sprung eating it straight out of its container!

- Layer the diced eggplant in a colander, sprinkling a little salt over each layer. Sit the colander on a plate and leave the eggplant to drain for 30 minutes. When that's done, rinse it under cool water and tumble it out into a clean tea towel to pat it dry.
- Now heat ¼ cup (60 ml) of the oil in a large frying pan over medium heat. Add the eggplant chunks and sauté them until they're golden all over, then scoop them out into a bowl.
- Return the pan to the heat and warm the remaining oil in it. Add the onion and garlic and cook them gently for 8–10 minutes, until they're tender. Stir in the cooked eggplant, capers and tomatoes and their juices and cook for another 10 minutes, stirring now and then. Now gently mix in the pears, currants, sugar, vinegar and salt and pepper. Cook the mixture for another 10 minutes, stirring regularly, then turn off the heat.
- Leave the mixture to cool a little, then taste it and adjust the flavour if you think it needs it by adding a little more salt, vinegar or sugar – what you are after is a good sweet–sharp balance. Stir in half the pine nuts.
- If you are not eating the mixture straight away, pop it in a container with a tight-fitting lid and store it in the fridge. About half an hour before you are ready to serve it, remove it from the fridge to bring it back to room temperature (the flavour is always more rounded when it has warmed up a bit). Spoon it into a serving bowl and scatter the remaining pine nuts over the top.

23rd February

For the second day in a row I've woken feeling vaguely uneasy, as though something is missing – and it is. I realise that I've become so acclimatised to the sound of rain that its absence feels strange! But I'm not sorry. It's the most beautiful morning, and going by the dreamy golden mist that's filling the valley, it's going to be a scorcher.

Rarely a day passes that I don't walk in the early morning – it nourishes me in ways that it's hard to quantify. I love the stillness and the peace; the dawn chorus from the birds and the way the butcher birds let me walk right up to them before calmly side-stepping to let me pass (always with a tilt of the head as though letting me know that they're doing *me* a favour). In summer these walks are often punctuated by the deep-throated 'whoosh . . . whoosh . . . ' of hot-air balloons firing up as they take off on their scenic flights across the valleys. They look amazing and I love the way that everybody waves and smiles as they soar overhead. We call them 'dragons in the sky', because of all their huffing and puffing and the burst of flame that lights up their canopies as they rise higher.

I'm regularly joined by various dogs that are out sniffing the morning air; and on one memorable occasion by a dear little echidna, who trundled happily along beside me as I tried to escort him off the road. I see them quite often up by the cemetery; they usually scuttle into the bush as they hear my footsteps, but this little lad was obviously made of sterner stuff.

This morning I noticed that somehow in all the wet and grey of the past weeks, the seasons are still turning in their inexorable cycle – something I find almost magical. I don't think I noticed it so much in the city, but here, where I regularly walk through fields or drive through the surrounding countryside, these small changes seem so noticeable. Despite today's heat, the Hottentot trees are surrounded by a carpet of fallen leaves. And when I look up, the crimson flowering spokes of the umbrella trees are at their most brilliant, as they are in those few weeks before they start to brown and droop.

It's really far too hot to cook, but we're off to friends for dinner and I promised that I would take dessert. I must admit I've fallen back on my old standby – a round of buttery shortbread (see page 86), accompanied by some maple and vanilla roasted plums. To go with it, I'm making a concoction of yoghurt mixed with a little brown sugar and very lightly whipped cream. It's such a simple dessert and just perfect for a sultry February evening. It's the sort of dessert I pull out when I've asked people for dinner on the spur of the moment (or said I would bring a 'plate', as I have tonight), forgetting just how hot and humid it gets at this time of year, and then wondered what on earth I am going to make that doesn't involve too much work. I know this sounds a bit churlish, but I think heat can dampen even the most enthusiastic cook's ardour. It certainly has that effect on me!

I made the shortbread dough yesterday, and as I was making it I thought what a wonderful standby recipe it is. It takes all of 20 minutes, maybe 25 at the most, to measure it out, make it *and* clean up, and it tastes so homely and delicious – definitely my sort of recipe. Plus, the unbaked shortbread can stay in the fridge overnight, which is exactly what mine has done. I shall bake it now and pop the plums in afterwards before it gets any hotter and I can't bear to turn on the oven.

Roasted Maple Syrup & Vanilla Plums with Brown Sugar Yoghurt & Sugared Almonds

SERVES 4–6

Although somewhat squashy-looking and wrinkled ('rustic' is probably a kinder word), these plums and their juices are the most glorious deep-crimson colour and have a wonderful, sharp–sweet flavour, which I love. They take only a few minutes to put together to roast, and the brown sugar yoghurt that goes with them doesn't take much longer, so they are a terrific, quick dessert to make when plums are about. Recently I tried a few leftover plums with the honey semi-freddo on page 28; it was a wonderful combination and looked rather fabulous too, with the vivid plums in stark contrast to the honey-gold semi-freddo.

The glazed almonds are optional. If you do decide to make them, you can do this a couple of days ahead of time, as long as you store them in a tightly sealed jar.

- 10–12 medium-sized just-ripe plums (or the equivalent in smaller plums – about 700 g)
- ½–⅔ cup (125–170 ml) pure maple syrup
- 1 teaspoon vanilla extract
- icing sugar, for dusting, optional

BROWN SUGAR YOGHURT

- ½ cup (120 g) sour cream, stirred
- 1 tablespoon soft brown sugar
- ½ cup (140 g) thick Greek-style yoghurt
- a few drops of vanilla extract, optional

continued next page

- Preheat your oven to 240°C. Wash and dry the plums. Use a sharp knife to cut them in half right through to the stone. Hold each half in your hands and twist them in the opposite directions to pull them apart – sometimes this is easy, other times the stone clings rather stubbornly to the flesh of one half. If this happens, cut carefully around the stone as best you can to loosen it and pull it free of the flesh (it's a bit difficult to do this neatly, but don't fret about it as once the plums are cooked it's hard to tell the difference). ›

TOASTED GLAZED ALMONDS
100 g flaked almonds
30 g caster sugar
about 3 teaspoons amaretto

PLUM PERFECT . . .
I have made this dish with quite a few different varieties of plums, all of which worked well. However, if you have a choice, I think blood plums look and taste best of all.

- Sit the plums, cut-side up, in a single layer in a shallow ceramic baking dish or gratin dish so they fit snugly. Stir the maple syrup and vanilla together then drizzle this mixture evenly over the plums. Put the dish in the oven and roast the plums for 12–15 minutes, or until they're tender. To check if they're ready, insert a fine metal skewer into one – it should slip in easily.
- Remove them from the oven and leave them to cool in the dish. Now and again as they cool, gently spoon some of the juices that have accumulated in the dish over them. You will find the amount of juice the plums give out will vary somewhat depending on the variety of plums you use – blood plums seem to release copious amounts. If there doesn't seem to be enough, drizzle on a little more maple syrup.
- Once the plums are cool, carefully transfer them with their juice to a shallow container, seal them tightly and store them in the fridge. Looks-wise, they are best in the first couple of days, but they will keep well in their syrupy juices for up to a week, and make a rather wonderful addition to breakfast with a little yoghurt (or, my favourite, spooned over Bircher muesli).
- For the brown sugar yoghurt, combine the sour cream and brown sugar in a cool bowl and whisk with a balloon whisk until soft peaks form. Stir the yoghurt to loosen it, then gently whisk it into the cream, along with the vanilla. Cover the bowl with plastic film and store it in the fridge until you need it.
- If you are making the almonds, preheat your oven to 150°C and line a baking tray with baking paper.
- Toss the almonds and sugar with enough amaretto to lightly moisten them, then spread the mixture as best you can in a single layer on the prepared tray. Sit the tray in the oven and cook the almonds, turning them frequently, for 20 minutes or so until they are golden. Remove them from the oven and let them cool and crisp up on the tray. Store them in an airtight container until you need them. They keep well for a couple of days and are really delicious on all sorts of things – I even find myself eating them straight out of the jar when I'm in need of a little 'something' sweet. Surprisingly, they freeze quite well for a month or more too.
- To serve, spoon three or four plum halves into a small bowl or glass. Dollop some of the yoghurt cream on top, then finish off with a scattering of almonds. Dust with a little icing sugar, if you like.

25th February

As you must have realised by now, we're mad about our native birds and delight in their comings and goings. I can't begin to tell you how thrilled I was when I bowled out the front door a few minutes ago with a basket of washing, ducked under the grevilleas to get to the clothes line, and there less than an arm's length away sat the most beautiful spangled drongo, totally absorbed in feeding from the brushes. It looked extraordinary – glistening black with a metallic blue sheen to the feathers around its head. And I could finally see why it gets the name 'spangled', as around its neck there is a necklace of feathers sprinkled with tiny white dots. I'm still totally bewildered about the origin of the second half of its name, though – I can't begin to imagine, but I do so love it. Only in Australia could a bird actually be called a spangled drongo! But perhaps what I love most about them is their beautiful mermaid's tails, which you can see in the photograph.

He's now just landed in the bird bath and is having a ball, splashing and spraying water all over the shop . . . the photo here was taken a few minutes later, as he was puffing and preening to dry off – he looks like some kind of punk-rocker bird, doesn't he?

Speaking of punk rockers, the real 'bovver' boys of the bird world are the black cockatoos. They're *enormous*, and they literally crash-land into trees, sending smaller birds flying and causing the branches to almost bend in half under the force of their impact. They then proceed to rip off seed pods and leaves and generally leave a swathe of destruction behind them. That said, I think they're fantastic. We often watch trios of them (for some reason there is nearly always three) beating a steady path above the valley in the early morning. They have one of the most plaintive bird cries I've ever heard – it's sad and haunting, as though they've witnessed too many terrible things. It always leaves me feeling slightly ruffled and I have to almost physically shake my head to help the feeling pass.

26th February

We're having duck with peaches for dinner tonight – a rare treat, but we have an old friend visiting and duck is his most favourite thing in the entire world, so I promised to cook it for him. I'm pleased to say the duck I'm using is local and organic to boot, and although I sometimes have to pull out the odd pin feather or two it's a small price to pay for such a find.

The peaches are local too and the last of the late-season's crop, which surprises many visitors. For although much of the fruit grown here is tropical (in summer we've so many mangoes we can't give them away – my friends who live in the city nearly weep when I tell them this!), there are also flourishing stone-fruit orchards around Bangalow, and the peaches are to-die-for – sweet and juicy, with just a hint of sharpness. Perfect, in fact, for duck.

Duck Breasts with Honey-Pickled Peaches (or Peach & Mint Salsa)

SERVES 4

I'm not all that much of a fan of meat and fruit together but in some cases it works perfectly and this is a case in point. I've given you two different accompaniments for the duck breasts as I make both regularly and they each go beautifully with the sweet honey glaze on the duck. If you have some to hand, use Honeycup mustard for the marinade – it has a terrific slightly hot, sweet flavour and is available from delis and good food stores.

The salsa needs to be made not long before you serve it, so if you're looking for a 'do-ahead' accompaniment, then go for the pickled peaches. You can make them a few days before you need them and keep them in the fridge. I quite often make a batch at Christmas time as they're also terrific with glazed ham.

4 × 200 g duck breast fillets, skin on

DUCK MARINADE

90 ml clear honey
2 tablespoons Honeycup or Dijon mustard
25 ml fresh orange juice
25 ml tablespoons olive oil
1 tablespoon white wine vinegar
3 teaspoons chopped ginger
sea salt flakes, to taste

HONEY-PICKLED PEACHES

220 ml clear honey
180 ml white wine vinegar
8 whole cloves
1 cinnamon stick, broken in half
6 thin slices ginger
4–6 just-ripe small slipstone peaches, washed, halved and stones removed

continued next page

- Line a container that will fit the duck breasts with a large sturdy plastic bag. Score very fine cuts across the skin and into the fat of each breast then sit them in the bag. Now, whisk all the marinade ingredients together until the honey has dissolved, then pour the marinade over the duck. Tie a knot in the top of the bag to seal it then squish it about so the duck is well coated in the marinade. Put the bag back into the container, cover it tightly and pop it into the fridge for at least 3 hours or, better still, overnight.
- If you're serving the honey-pickled peaches with the duck, now is the time to cook them. Put the honey, vinegar, cloves, cinnamon and ginger in a large-ish saucepan over medium heat and stir to dissolve the honey. Once it has dissolved, bring the syrup to the boil, then reduce the heat and let it simmer for 3 minutes. ›

PEACH AND MINT SALSA

- 5 medium-sized ripe peaches, very finely chopped
- 1 small red chilli, finely chopped
- finely grated zest of 1 lime
- 2 tablespoons lime juice
- 1 teaspoon finely chopped ginger
- 2 teaspoons sugar, or more to taste
- 2 tablespoons very finely shredded mint
- sea salt flakes
- very fine threads of chilli soaked in iced water for 1 hour, tiny mint leaves and lime wedges, to serve, optional

Slip the peach halves into the syrup and cook them gently for 5 minutes or so until they're just tender – to check, slide a fine skewer into one. As soon as they're ready, remove the pan from the heat. Gently transfer the peaches and their syrup to a bowl and let them cool slightly. Once they're cool enough to touch, peel the peaches then return them to the syrup. It's a good idea to taste the syrup and see if the balance of vinegar and honey is right – I quite often add a little more honey, depending on how acidic the vinegar is. If you're making this ahead of time, remove the cinnamon stick or its flavour will become too overpowering.

- If you're serving the salsa, make it just before you're ready to cook the duck. It's really simple to do – just put the peaches, chilli, lime zest and juice, ginger and sugar into a bowl and gently stir them together. Cover the bowl tightly and pop it in the fridge. Just before you're ready to serve the salsa, stir in the mint and a little salt. Taste it and adjust the sweet/sour/salty balance if necessary.

- To cook the duck, remove it from the marinade, pat the fillets dry and sprinkle the skin with salt. Heat a heavy-based, non-stick frying pan over medium heat until it's hot. Add the duck breasts to the pan, skin-side down, and cook them, undisturbed, for 6 minutes (don't be alarmed that the skin looks charred – it won't taste burnt). Turn the breasts over and cook them for another 8 minutes – this gives you pink, not rare, duck. When they're ready, remove the breasts to a plate, cover them loosely with foil, and let them rest in a warm spot for 5 minutes.

- To serve the duck, slice the breasts thickly and sit the slices on four dinner plates. If you're using the honey-pickled peaches, spoon two or three peach halves and some syrup onto each plate. If it's the salsa, scoop a spoonful onto each plate, then garnish with chilli threads and tiny mint leaves, if desired. Serve with any remaining salsa and lime wedges on the side, if you're using them.

CHILLI THREADS . . .

These make a terrific garnish without adding too much heat. To make them, halve small red chillies lengthways, then scrape away the seeds and any white membranes. Using the sharpest knife you have, slice the chillies into fine, fine shreds. Scoop these into a small tub of ice and water, cover them and put them in the fridge for an hour or two. By the time you take them out, the threads will have rolled up to form pretty curls and the soaking will have softened the heat of the chillies.

27th February

Wonder of wonders, a dry wind, which is like a balm after the humidity of the past few months, is blowing its way up the valley, whipping up a frenzy in the treetops and causing the palms to rattle their spikes like sabres. It's enough to send me scuttling indoors as, just like my mum, I find really strong wind makes me feel scratchy and vaguely troubled, so I have firmly shut the door on it and turned to the kitchen for solace instead.

It's the sort of day that awakens all my baking instincts and I've just put the finishing touches to a pie to use up the last of the peaches. I must admit, I don't make pies all that often, but it seems just the thing today. And it appears everybody else thinks so too, as the fragrance of it baking is drawing everyone into the kitchen to enquire if it will be ready soon.

Late-Summer Peach Pie

SERVES 6

I find it fascinating that despite there being so many beautiful and sophisticated desserts around, everyone seems to love a good old-fashioned pie. I can't begin to tell you just how many times I'm asked to make one if I offer to bring dessert to a get-together. And this lovely simple peach pie is a classic that needs nothing more to go with it than a drizzle of cream or scoop of good vanilla ice-cream.

You may think it a bit odd that there is tapioca in the pie filling, and I admit it is a little unusual, but it's a trick I learnt from my mum: what it does is absorb some of the peach juices as the pie bakes, adding a bit more body to the filling. It is available in some supermarkets and health-food stores – you may well see it called 'seed tapioca'.

2¼ cups (335 g) plain flour
¼ teaspoon salt
185 g cold unsalted butter, cut into small chunks
90 ml iced water
1 egg yolk mixed with 2 teaspoons water, for glazing
granulated sugar, for sprinkling
cream or good vanilla ice-cream, to serve

PEACH FILLING

⅔ cup (150 g) caster sugar
⅓ cup (75 g) soft brown sugar
2½ tablespoons tapioca
½ teaspoon ground cinnamon
1.25 kg medium-sized just-ripe slipstone peaches
1½ teaspoons vanilla extract

- For the pastry, put the flour and salt into a food processor and whiz them together. Add the butter and whiz everything again until the mixture resembles coarse breadcrumbs. With the motor running, pour in the iced water and process only until the pastry forms a ball around the blade. The time for this varies a bit depending on the weather – when it's warm it seems to come together faster.
- Tip the pastry out onto a board and shape it into two balls – about two-thirds of the quantity for the pie base and one third for the lid. Flatten the balls into discs, and wrap them tightly in plastic film. Chill for about 40 minutes or until the pastry is firm but supple enough to roll. (By the way, you can make the pastry ahead as it keeps well in the fridge for up to 3 days, however it will be too firm to roll out straight from the fridge, so let it warm up a bit at room temperature until it's pliable.) ›

- To make the filling, thoroughly mix together the sugars, tapioca and cinnamon in a small bowl, and set it aside. Now peel the peaches – if the skins don't slip off easily, dip each peach into boiling water for 10–20 seconds to loosen the skins, dunk them briefly into cool water, then peel them. Cut each peach into quarters, discarding the stones as you go. Put the quarters into a large bowl then gently mix in the sugar mixture, along with the vanilla. Leave them to stand for 15 minutes, stirring occasionally (you will find that as the peach juices mingle with the sugars a caramel-coloured syrup forms).
- Preheat your oven to 220°C.
- Roll the largest pastry disc out thinly on a lightly floured board so it's big enough to completely line a 22–23 cm pie tin. Line the tin with the rolled pastry, gently easing it into the corners and leaving a little pastry hanging over the edge. Chill the tin briefly while you roll out the remaining pastry to make a lid that will cover the pie. Carefully transfer it to another baking tray and put it in a cool (not cold) spot.
- Remove the pie tin from the fridge and sit it on a baking sheet. Put a layer of peaches, cheek-by-jowl and cut-side up, all over the pastry base – they need to be tightly packed. Drizzle half the syrupy tapioca mixture over this layer. Now, settle the remaining peaches, cut-side down, over the top of this first layer and spoon the remaining syrupy mixture over them.
- To finish off, dampen the edges of the pastry case with a little water, and drape the pastry lid gently on top. Using your fingers, press the lid and base together to seal the edges. Use a sharp knife to trim away all but 2 cm of the overhanging pastry. Roll this overhanging pastry in to form a rim for the pie, and pinch it decoratively to seal it. Cut eight 2 cm slits in a spoke-like pattern around the lid, so steam can escape as the pie bakes. I also love the look of pastry leaves on top and usually roll out the scraps of trimmed pastry and cut some leaves out from it – if you mark the veins with a blunt knife they look really lovely. Dampen the bottom of the leaves with a little water then sit them on the pie. Brush the lot with the egg yolk and water glaze, then sprinkle a little sugar over the top.
- Put the pie in the oven to bake. After 10 minutes reduce the heat to 180°C and cook it for about 35 minutes more or until the crust is golden and the filling is starting to bubble up through the slits. Transfer the tin to a cooling rack. Leave the pie to cool until it is barely warm, then serve straight from the tin with a jug of cream or bowl of vanilla ice-cream.

MARCH

Sweet
Potato $2.50/
Kg

1st March

It's the first day of March, and it feels as if somebody has flicked a switch and autumn has arrived, for there is a distinct coolness in the air and the dry wind of the past few days has freshened even more to become a bracing southerly. We woke up in the night to hear the blinds rattling and to feel great gusts of cool air blowing in through the windows. I pulled on a blanket for the first time in weeks and drifted back to sleep. When we opened our eyes this morning there was a real nip in the air and the countryside looks beautiful. After all that rain the skies have finally cleared, and everything looks as though it has been washed and polished to within an inch of its life.

We're absolutely pooped, having spent the whole day working in the garden – it's the first time for ages it's been dry enough and cool enough to do so. We've pruned, weeded, fertilised and mulched ourselves to a complete and utter standstill! And that's only covered the tiniest amount of what needs doing. However, they say a garden is forever a work in progress, and I can see that ours certainly will be.

The best job of all was planting out some more citrus trees. We now have kaffir limes, Tahitian and golden limes, Meyer lemons, mandarins, a navel orange and a blood orange. There's also a tangelo; however, we ran out of steam before digging that in, so it will have to wait. I know when I say we've planted all those trees that it sounds as though our garden is huge, but it's not – it's a bit over the classic quarter-acre block, and it has been both a constant joy and nightmare with its awkward slopes and underlying layer of clay.

2nd March

It's the monthly Brunswick Heads market today and we're up and off bright and early as it's one of our favourites, as much as anything for its setting, which is right by the river with pines towering overhead. The tide is high this morning too so the water will be clear as crystal; it's such a lovely sight and I pinch myself every time I see it and realise this is where we live.

As always, I have my trusty shopping trolley in tow, which has become a source of great amusement to some of my visiting friends who can't believe I use it. It's not particularly smart (unlike some I've seen), it's more like one I remember my gran having, although it does have a rather swish black and red colour scheme with what Clive cheekily calls 'racing stripes' down the sides. I'm inordinately fond of it and find it's wonderful for carting all my purchases around – it saves lots of to-ing and fro-ing to the car, as we always end up buying more than we mean to.

I inevitably make a bee-line for the fruit stall. I love this stall as Phil, the owner, seems to know every farmer and orchardist within cooee who has a few old fruit trees tucked at the end of a field or behind the chook house, and it's from these trees that he garners as much as he can. Today the trestle tables are piled high with ruby and gold plums, peaches and new season's apples. Many are old-fashioned varieties that have all but disappeared, for they don't travel well and don't fit supermarket requirements for sturdy fruit that will last the distance (more often than not too long a distance, if you ask me). Often there is only a box or two of these fruit, as picking them is usually hard work and the trees don't yield much – but what they do yield is wonderful. I'd forgotten just how good a plum can taste. There are three varieties this week and they're all superb. The blood plums are small and slightly sharp; the drier-fleshed sugar plums sweet as sweet; and there is a small box of greengages that glow like baubles from a Christmas

All Citrus
3 for $1
noney box
n the right
Thanks
Welcome
This Food is brought to you with
hard work + Love from US
Please Show your Support
by respecting our prices

tree and taste superb. As is always the way, I end up buying all three plus a big bag of organic apples that are just perfect for baking. It looks as though I have rather a lot of cooking coming up!

As befitting the first days of autumn, there is also a stall of pumpkins with a real liquorice allsorts selection – in the end we settle on a couple of hefty butternuts and a beautiful two-toned Kent pumpkin that I know I'll end up just admiring for a time before I can face surrendering it to the pot.

It's usually about now that the siren call of freshly ground coffee is more than either of us can bear and we head to the food stalls to see what's what. I love cruising up and down here. At one end the brilliantly painted fresh juice van – which looks like something out of a fairy tale – sells everything from mango smoothies and carrot juice to shot-size cups of juiced wheat grass (I always feel as if I grow a centimetre or two after drinking one). The highlight here is that the juicer is pedal-powered, so if you order a fresh juice the owner hops onto what looks like a fixed bicycle, pedals furiously and out spurts the juice. You've got to love it! There are also vans selling samosas, spicy fish with beans and rice, big wedges of organic pizza and addictive little sugar-dusted Dutch pancakes called *poffertjes*. Then there's my all-time favourite: sugary, organic cinnamon doughnuts . . . yum. We inevitably sample a bit of everything (God help our stomachs) and polish it all off with a cup of local coffee, which is thick and rich.

I've not mentioned the people yet (my mind is always firmly fixed on food first), but this would have to be the best people-watching place I know. What I love is that there's such a vast range of people. Exotic-looking women walk by, hair in dreadlocks, navels and faces pierced, and their bodies swathed in all sorts of wonderful and improbable clothes. Tatts are everywhere and on every age group; farmers wear wide-brimmed hats, checked shirts, shorts and boots; children whiz around underfoot; and the church ladies at their stall are always as neat as pins in their matching aprons. (I haven't mentioned their stall yet, have I? The table groans under the weight of homemade banana cakes, coconut tarts, Anzac biscuits, tray after tray of slices, eggs from their chooks and an array of jams, relishes and chutneys, a jar or two of which always ends up in the trolley.)

About the only thing everyone has in common are the colours they wear. After life in the city where, for a working girl, black, white, grey and brown are virtually de rigueur, the sight of a veritable rainbow of colours is quite startling . . . and wonderful. It makes me happy just to see it. The colours range from day-glo pink and green (big in the hair department) to great starbursts of purple and blue and nearly every shade in-between, tie-dyed onto just about anything that moves. After years of wearing neutrals with the odd splash of colour, I find myself heading the same way and am gradually acquiring a somewhat eclectic collection of brilliantly hued clothes. Whenever I return to the city now I'm conscious that I tend to stand out like the proverbial sore thumb!

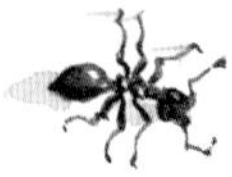

3rd March

I had every intention of digging out my basil bushes today, however when I ventured down to the bottom of the garden where they thrive amidst the grevilleas, I saw that they have decided to have a final growing flush and are absolutely bursting with leaves and flowers. The bees are having a ball and I can't bring myself to pull them out. Instead, I've cut them back where I can and have now ended up with an armful of basil to make some pesto. I'll also make a pumpkin salad for lunch – it's one of our favourites and as it's liberally spiked with basil, I can use up some of this little lot.

Crisp Haloumi, Pumpkin & Red Capsicum Salad with Basil Dressing

SERVES 4

This vibrant, colourful salad is great in cooler weather as it's quite hefty and satisfying, needing only a loaf of good bread to mop up the dressing. I'm especially chuffed with the one in the pic as I used one of the pumpkins I bought at the market yesterday and it was beautiful. The flesh was an incredibly deep orange, which is ideal for this salad – especially once it's been roasted to concentrate its sweetness and give it lovely crisp edges.

- 1 kg butternut or Kent pumpkin, cut into smallish pieces (I usually make them about the size of my little finger)
- 2 tablespoons olive oil
- sea salt flakes and freshly ground black pepper
- 350 g haloumi, sliced into little-finger-sized pieces
- olive oil, for frying
- 1 small bunch rocket (about 4 handfuls)
- 2 red capsicums (peppers), grilled, peeled and cut into strips (see page 80)
- fine slivers of red onion, to garnish, optional

BASIL DRESSING

- ½ small clove garlic, finely chopped
- 1 cup (250 ml) extra virgin olive oil
- 1–1½ tablespoons white wine vinegar
- sea salt flakes, to taste
- 2 big handfuls of basil

- Preheat your oven to 220°C and line a large baking tray with baking paper.
- Sit the pumpkin pieces on the prepared tray. Drizzle the oil over them and sprinkle on a little salt, then toss everything together. Put the tray in the oven and roast the pumpkin, turning the pieces occasionally, for 30–40 minutes until it's just cooked through and deep golden with crisp edges.
- For the dressing, put all the dressing ingredients in a blender and whiz them together until they form a lovely deep-green dressing (don't make this too far ahead as it loses its bright colour quite rapidly). Taste it and adjust the flavours to suit you – I find I always have to do a bit of balancing out, as oils and vinegars vary so much. Just be careful not to make it too vinegary.
- When the pumpkin is ready, remove it from the oven. Pat the haloumi fingers as dry as possible with paper towels. Quickly heat a little oil in a large frying pan over medium heat. Add the haloumi fingers and cook them, turning regularly, until they're golden all over – this should only take a few minutes as they brown rapidly. Drain them on paper towels.
- To put the salad together, first toss the rocket with enough of the dressing to lightly coat it. Now sit a pile of rocket on each plate, top this with some pumpkin pieces, capsicum strips and haloumi fingers, splotching a little more dressing here and there as you go. Repeat the layering until you have a nice pile of salad on the plate; finish with a leaf or two of rocket and a sprinkle of onion slivers, if using. Give each salad a good grinding of pepper and serve them straight away. Serve any remaining dressing separately.

5th March

Ah, the first quinces have arrived – they're still covered in fluffy grey down and are incredibly fragrant. When I smell quinces like this I can understand why they were used in the past to perfume linen cupboards. Unfortunately, I suspect that were I to do that here every insect within cooee would end up in the cupboard after them! However, I shall let these ones sit out for a few days so I can enjoy the perfume just a little longer before I cook them.

I must say that whenever I cook quinces it seems somehow magical to me that their hard, creamy-coloured flesh is transformed by the alchemy of long, slow cooking and a liberal dose of sugar into tender, rosy-pink slices.

Slow-Cooked Vanilla Quinces

SERVES 6–8

3 large or 4 medium-sized quinces
juice of 1 lemon
about 1 litre cold water
2 cups (440 g) caster sugar
long spiral of lemon zest
long spiral of mandarin or orange zest
1 vanilla bean, split

I suspect quinces are available for quite a while further south; however, the quince season here is fleeting so we make the most of them while we can. This is a lovely recipe – I make batch after batch of these quinces and keep them in the fridge for a quick dessert or to eat as a breakfast treat with a splodge of yoghurt. And you can use them in other ways too. I sometimes chop up half a dozen slices and add them to an apple crumble – their fragrance permeates the apples and makes this homely pudding nothing short of wonderful. They're also divine in tarts (try nestling them into an almond frangipane filling) or baked into a simple pound cake – it only needs a sprinkle of icing sugar to be quite perfect.

- Give the quinces a really good scrub in cool water to remove any greyish fuzz from the skin, then pat them dry. Just a gentle reminder before you start peeling: quinces are *very* hard (similar to pumpkin to handle), so you need to be really careful when you are working with them.
- Squeeze the juice from the lemon into a large bowl of cold water and sit it nearby. Cut each quince into quarters. Peel and core each quarter, letting the skins and cores drop into a big stainless steel or enamelled saucepan. Slice the quince quarters in half lengthways, and put them into the bowl of lemon water. Don't worry if the quince slices become quite oxidised and brownish – the lemon water prevents this to some extent, but once they're cooked it disappears anyway.
- Pour about a litre of cold water over the skins and cores in the pan. Bring them to the boil over high heat, then reduce the heat to low and simmer for 30 minutes. After this time, strain the mixture through a fine sieve into a bowl, reserving the liquid and discarding the rest. Rinse out the pan. Measure out 3 cups (750 ml) of the ›

quince peelings liquid, pour it back into the saucepan and place it over medium heat. Add the sugar, zests and vanilla bean to the saucepan and stir constantly until the sugar has completely dissolved.

- Drain the quinces and rinse them under cool water. Add them to the pan and bring the liquid to the boil, then reduce the heat to very low. Simmer the quinces, covered, for about 3 hours or until they're rosy and tender, carefully turning the top ones once or twice during the cooking time so they cook evenly.
- When they're ready, remove the pan from the heat and leave them to cool in their syrup. Carefully transfer the quinces and syrup to a container with a tight-fitting lid. Seal it and store the quinces in the fridge. They will keep well for at least 3 weeks.
- To serve, spoon the quinces into a serving bowl and ladle the syrup over the top. They are lovely with double thick cream and shortbread (see page 86).

7th March

It's not just quinces that have put in an appearance; the tamarillos are back with a vengeance too. The season starts in February, but what only a few weeks ago was a trickle of tamarillos given to us by friends has turned into a torrent and we're absolutely swamped with them. Everybody is trying to give them away while they're still fresh.

I do love these tart yet sweet fruits, but hadn't really used them much prior to living here. However, as they thrive locally I've become quite hooked on them. The trees aren't particularly notable – somewhat scrawny-looking, with thin trunks and a sparse canopy of large leaves with the egg-shaped fruits dangling beneath. And the mottled garnet fruit on these local trees are smaller than the ones I've seen in shops, but looks can be deceiving as they're intensely flavoured.

Much of the time we just eat them raw for breakfast – peeled, sliced and sugared then left for a bit to let their juices flow. They're really lovely with some thick Greek yoghurt (a little brown sugar sprinkled over the top and allowed to melt in to make a sort of caramel sauce is even better). However, there are only so many we can eat like this and we haven't made much of a dent in the somewhat daunting number we have. Fortunately, they keep rather well once they've been cooked so I'm about to gently poach some in a red wine and vanilla syrup perfumed with star anise, a spice that enhances their musky fragrance.

Tamarillos in Star Anise & Red Wine Syrup

SERVES 4

Served with an exotic chai-scented cream, these tamarillos make a stunning dessert and are just perfect after a spicy Asian meal. If I really want to pull out all the stops I make shortbread studded with glacé ginger to go with them.

- 1 cup (220 g) caster sugar
- 2 cups (500 ml) shiraz or merlot
- 2 whole star anise
- 1 vanilla bean, split
- 1 cinnamon stick
- 8–10 medium-sized tamarillos
- 1–2 teaspoons rosewater, optional
- chai-scented cream (see page 136), to serve

- First off, find a saucepan that will hold the tamarillos in a single layer. Put the sugar, wine and star anise into the pan and sit it over medium–high heat. Stir to dissolve the sugar, then stop stirring and bring the mixture to the boil. Add the vanilla bean and cinnamon stick.
- Meanwhile, score a small, shallow cross into the pointy end of each tamarillo. As soon as the syrup is boiling, add the tamarillos to it. Reduce the heat so the liquid bubbles very, very gently, and cook the tamarillos until they are just tender, rolling them over occasionally so they cook evenly. You will find the cooking time varies a bit, depending on how ripe they are – a just-ripe, slightly firm tamarillo usually takes about 10 minutes. To check, slip a fine skewer through the skin into the centre of the tamarillo; if the flesh feels soft, it's ready.
- When the tamarillos are cooked, use a slotted spoon to carefully transfer them to a shallow container – preferably one where they can sit in a single layer, as they tend to get squashed if piled on top of each other. ›

- Increase the heat under the pan and bring the syrup to the boil. Boil rapidly until it has reduced by about half and is the consistency of maple syrup. Remove the pan from the heat, let the syrup cool slightly then add a little rosewater if you are using it. It's a good idea to taste the syrup at this stage: if the cinnamon flavour is as you like it, remove the cinnamon stick as the flavour will become stronger over time (if you decide to leave it in, it's worth checking the syrup again in a day or two). Pour the syrup over the tamarillos and leave them to cool, then cover them tightly and store them in the fridge . . . they keep well for at least 10 days.
- To serve, carefully peel away the skins. This can be a bit fiddly – if they are too awkward to handle, just split them open and let everyone scoop out the pulp themselves. Drizzle with some of the red-wine syrup and serve with a spoonful of chai-scented cream.

Chai-Scented Cream

SERVES 4–6

300 ml thickened cream
2 tablespoons caster sugar
2 heaped teaspoons chai
splash of vanilla extract

I don't think any two blends of chai (or masala chai, as it's known in its homeland) are quite the same. Basically it's an aromatic, spice-scented black tea that is heated with water, milk and sugar before serving. As you can imagine, the combinations of tea and spices are endless, and many families make their own mixture, but most include the lovely warmth of cardamom, ginger, cinnamon, cloves and nutmeg.

I've always loved the taste of chai, and have tried it in all sorts of ways with desserts, which is how I ended up with this cream; the flavour is delicate but fragrant, and beautiful with the tamarillos above.

- Put the cream, sugar and chai into a small saucepan over low heat. Mix them together, then very slowly bring the mixture to just below the boil, stirring occasionally to dissolve the sugar. When the cream is steaming but not bubbling, turn it off. Cover the pan and leave the cream to sit so it becomes infused with the chai. After an hour or so, strain it through a very fine sieve into a bowl. Use a spoon to press down on the chai mixture so you extract as much cream as possible. Drizzle in a little vanilla to taste, then cover the container and chill the cream. Just before serving, whisk it until it forms soft peaks.

8th March

Our day started with three beautiful hot-air balloons swooping low over the house before floating effortlessly off up the valley. As I write this they're still there, sitting almost still as though suspended from a spider's thread, and looking quite wonderful as the early-morning light bounces off their rainbow canopies.

Speaking of rainbows, for a region that prides itself on them (we're even known as the Rainbow Region in travel brochures), they've been in remarkably short supply this summer. Thankfully, yesterday the most glorious one arced across the sky.

11th March

This past week I've heard a lot of billing and coo-ing as I've walked past the scrap of rainforest at the bottom of the hill, and the perpetrators of these sounds have finally come out into the open. They are two white-headed pigeons and what lovely birds they are, with their small snow-white heads and large tapered grey bodies. They sit like sentinels on the telephone wires, watching the comings and goings in the early morning – I call them sentinels, but really they're almost like angels, with their beautiful long wings and majestic presence.

I've just stopped mid-sentence as I've heard the call of a bird that shouldn't be in our garden. In fact, it's not just one bird, but two. And there they go again, with their distinctive long whoop and crack. I keep a set of binoculars on my desk, but try as I might, I can't see the birds; they're famously shy and I haven't ever seen one, despite the fact that their calls often punctuate my walks. They've certainly strayed a bit too far if they're in our garden, and hopefully will find their way back to a safer haven.

What I had started to write, before my unexpected visitors stopped me, was how I find it so wonderful that even now, after years of cooking, I can still be surprised and delighted by ingredients. I've never been a big fan of snake beans, often finding them tough and relatively tasteless. But as they're one of the few vegetables that are flourishing in our ongoing monsoonal weather, I've been forced to take another long look at them. And I'm so glad I have! The beans I cooked last night were truly delicious, and I was really chuffed with the result.

A Simple Asian-Flavoured Dish of Purple Snake Beans & Green Beans

SERVES 2–4

This is a bit of a Clayton's stir-fry – that is, the stir-fry you have when you're not having a stir-fry! I've no doubt that more purist Asian cooks than me will be appalled by this recipe, but it's perfectly delicious and makes a lot less mess than a regular stir-fry. Most of the time I'm happy to make a mess, but just occasionally the thought of cleaning the whole cooktop (which seems to be inevitable when I stir-fry) is a bit daunting. By the way, I regularly make this with green snake beans (and often use all snake beans, rather than a mix of green and snake), but it just so happens that some dear friends of ours grow these beautiful purple ones, and it's such a treat to be able to use them.

350 g purple or green snake beans (as young and fine as possible)
150 g green beans
1½ tablespoons light olive oil
4 spring onions, pale green and white parts only, finely chopped
1 packed tablespoon finely chopped ginger
1 large clove garlic, finely chopped
1 small red chilli, finely chopped
2 teaspoons sesame oil
sea salt flakes

- Wash both lots of beans thoroughly. Slice them on the diagonal into 3–4 cm pieces and set them aside. Put a large saucepan of water over high heat and bring the water to the boil.
- Add the beans and cook them until they are just tender – I usually fish out a bean and bite into it to see how they are going. When they're ready, drain them well and set them aside.
- Return the saucepan to the stove over low heat. Gently warm the olive oil in the pan, then add the spring onion, ginger, garlic and chilli and cook, stirring regularly, for 3–4 minutes until they have softened but not coloured.
- Now add the drained beans and sesame oil to the pan and increase the heat to medium. Cook for a couple of minutes, tossing the beans about constantly so they are well coated in the ginger mixture. When they are ready, sprinkle in a little salt then tip them into a warm bowl and serve them straight away.

THE COLOUR PURPLE . . .

The very nice thing about purple snake beans is that, unlike many other purple-hued vegetables which turn a funny khaki-green after cooking, these retain their deep colour which looks rather fabulous in the finished dish.

Star Anise Chicken

SERVES 4–6

8 free-range chicken chops (partly boned leg and thigh portions)
lime cheeks, to serve

CHICKEN BRAISING LIQUID

1 cup (250 ml) kecap manis (sweet Indonesian soy sauce)
1 cup (250 ml) soy sauce
1 cup (250 ml) water
⅓ cup (55 g) brown sugar
2 whole star anise
2 tablespoons sherry
2 cloves garlic, lightly crushed
2 slices ginger

BY THE WAY . . .

One of the great things about this dish is that you can keep recycling the braising liquid. To do this, strain it through a fine sieve, then pour it into a clean container with a tight-fitting lid and store it in the fridge. It sets like jelly and the fat from the chicken floats to the surface and seals it (just scoop this off before you use it). You can keep cooking with it again and again, as long as you boil it every 4 weeks or so. However, you will find that the taste does weaken over time and you may need to adjust the flavours somewhat – I quite often add a bit more of each of the ingredients to keep it lively.

This is one of my most well-used recipes. I never tire of its smoky, almost haunting flavour. When we were photographing the chicken I served it on a bed of purple snake beans and green beans (see page 139) as the two dishes go beautifully together. We often eat it like this with fragrant jasmine rice (see page 70), however it goes well with all sorts of Asian-style salads and stir-fried vegetables too.

- Preheat your oven to 170°C.
- Put all the ingredients for the chicken braising liquid into a large flameproof casserole dish over medium heat. Stir to dissolve the sugar then increase the heat to high and bring the liquid to the boil. Slip the chicken pieces, skin-side down, into the liquid; it splashes up a bit as you do this so take care – I have washed more than my fair share of soy-splattered tee-shirts over the years! As soon as the liquid returns to the boil, cover the dish and put it into the oven for 30 minutes.
- Remove the dish from the oven and leave the chicken to cool in the liquid for 20 minutes, then carefully transfer the pieces to a serving platter. If you like, you can put a little of the braising liquid into a small saucepan and boil it down over high heat until it forms a syrupy glaze to brush over the chicken. (Keep any remaining braising liquid in an airtight container in the fridge – see note, left.)
- Brush the chicken pieces with some of the syrupy glaze, if you are using it, and finish off with a pile of lime cheeks. Serve warm or at room temperature.

14th March

I've just ducked out to pick some herbs for tonight but was stopped in my tracks as two beautiful eastern rosellas are sitting on the bird-feeder, delicately eating seeds. The young male is absolutely resplendent: I've never seen clearer, more intense colours on a bird before. Honestly, I look at these birds and think that whoever made the universe must have been going through a psychedelic phase at the time they were created – they really are most extraordinary.

As you can see, the world easily distracts me from my tasks, however I must hot foot it to the kitchen as we have friends coming for an early dinner and I've loads to do before they arrive. It's an all-vegetable meal tonight as the produce in the market was so good yesterday that I've bought far too much and now have the enjoyable task of deciding what to do with it. I suspect we're going to end up with a heap of antipasti, no main course as such and a dessert. The eggplant torta overleaf will be the pièce de résistance – it's ideal, as it's quite substantial and I can work the other dishes around it.

I often serve dinners like this – something which I guess comes down to my background in the restaurant business. The place that I loved most, and probably one of the best known in food circles, was Taylors in Surry Hills, which won many awards for its simple, beautifully cooked Italian dishes. The owners, Anne Taylor and Ian McCulloch, were always so generous with their knowledge, and I learnt so much from them both – about friendship as well as food.

The restaurant was renowned for its antipasti and I loved preparing it, combining all the different flavours and textures to make each plate. So much so, that I find when I entertain now I often just put out five or six antipasti dishes as the whole meal, letting everybody mix and match to their heart's content. It's always a hit, and is such an easy way to entertain as pretty much everything is best served at room temperature, so there's no last-minute cooking. The food is invariably eaten with great gusto, which is always a joy to see.

Eggplant, Mozzarella & Parmesan Torta

SERVES 6–8 AS PART OF AN ANTIPASTI SPREAD

about 1.8 kg firm, fresh eggplants (aubergines), peeled
1 heaped tablespoon salt
100 ml olive oil, for cooking (or more as necessary)
4–5 large oregano sprigs, leaves finely chopped, plus extra sprigs to garnish
300 g mozzarella, grated
120 g freshly grated parmesan

I tend to barbecue the eggplant for this as I find it the easiest option and the one that uses the least oil, however it's also fine to grill it under an overhead grill or fry it. If you're frying you will probably need more oil than the recipe specifies – the torta is particularly delicious when the eggplant is fried as it's more luscious, but considerably richer too. I sometimes make a larger, deeper torta when I've got more people coming – if you want to do this, increase the recipe by half again and bake it in a deep 24–25 cm dish.

- Cut the eggplants lengthways into 4 mm thick slices. Layer the slices in a large colander, sprinkling a little salt between each layer. Leave them to sit for 20 minutes to release a bit of their liquid. After this time, rinse them under cold water and pat them dry – as there are rather a lot of slices, I usually layer them in an old but clean bath towel to dry them off.
- Preheat your barbecue or chargrill pan to medium–high. Brush both sides of the eggplant slices sparingly with oil, then cook them in batches on the barbecue. As the slices are so thin, they only take a couple of minutes per side, so keep an eye on them. When they're ready, transfer them to a plate. (If you are frying the slices, they will need to be drained on paper towels to absorb any excess oil.)
- Preheat your oven to 220°C. Line a 20 cm springform tin tightly with foil, then line the base and sides with buttered baking paper. (You can also use an ovenproof dish of a similar size and shape – I use a Pyrex one. If you are using something similar, dispense with the foil and just use the buttered paper.)
- Mix the oregano and grated mozzarella together. Arrange a single layer of eggplant slices decoratively over the base of the tin. Sprinkle them with a little each of the grated parmesan and the mozzarella and oregano mixture. Continue layering the eggplant and cheeses until they are all gone, pressing down very lightly on each layer and finishing with a layer of eggplant.
- If you are using a springform tin, sit it on a baking tray. Put the torta in the oven and bake for 25–30 minutes. When it's ready, remove it from the oven and leave it to cool in the tin until it's tepid or at room temperature. Carefully invert the torta onto a serving plate and gently remove the tin, paper and foil. Decorate the plate with oregano sprigs. (You can also slide it out of the tin onto the plate, which is a little more awkward to do, but it means the more golden top is uppermost.)

- When it comes to slicing the torta, I use a sharp serrated knife as it tends to cut through the layers more neatly than a regular knife. And if you are wondering whether you can serve it warm, you can and I have done this – just be mindful that it's a little more difficult to slice neatly as the cheese hasn't firmed up.
- The torta keeps well in the fridge for about 5 days, but remember to bring it to room temperature before serving it. I have been known to stick a slice or two in the microwave to warm, and it works a treat.

Tiny Capsicums Stuffed with Peperonata

SERVES 8

8 small red capsicums (peppers), for stuffing – the ones I used were rather squat and about 5 cm in diameter
oregano or small basil leaves, to garnish

PEPERONATA

2 tablespoons extra virgin olive oil
2 red onions, finely diced
2 cloves garlic, finely chopped
1 small red chilli, chopped
2 red capsicums (peppers), diced
2 really ripe tomatoes, seeded and chopped
1 tablespoon sun-dried tomato pesto
½ teaspoon sugar
1–2 tablespoons wine vinegar (preferably red)
sea salt flakes and freshly ground black pepper
1 tablespoon shredded oregano or basil

I hadn't actually planned to serve the eggplant torta (see page 142) with these little stuffed capsicums for the photo. It just happened that at the time we photographed it, I had some cute-as-a-button capsicums on hand *and* some leftover peperonata in the fridge – it didn't take me long to put two and two together and stuff the capsicums with the peperonata. They looked divine and went beautifully with the torta, along with a few snowy chunks of goat's cheese drizzled with extra virgin olive oil.

The peperonata is also lovely on its own, and is terrific to have in the fridge. It's great with pasta or polenta, along with some black olives and goat's cheese, or as a vegetable salad to go with just about any simply cooked meat or fish – if I'm serving it like this, I quite often add a handful of roasted pine nuts.

- Preheat your oven to 180°C and line a baking tray with baking paper.
- Sit the capsicums on the baking tray, then use a fine skewer to prick them two or three times around the stalk end. Pop the tray in the oven and cook the capsicums for about 20 minutes, or until they have softened and are quite tender but not collapsing.
- While the capsicums are cooking, make the peperonata. To do this, heat the oil in a large frying pan over medium heat. Add the onion and cook, stirring occasionally, for about 8 minutes until softened and slightly translucent but not brown. Add the garlic and chilli and cook, stirring, for a couple more minutes. Now increase the heat, tip in the diced capsicum and cook, tossing constantly, for a few more minutes. Add the tomato, sun-dried tomato pesto, sugar and half the vinegar and thoroughly mix it all together. Now reduce the heat to low, cover the pan and cook the mixture until the capsicum is tender – this will take about 12–15 minutes. When it's ready, taste the peperonata and add a splash more vinegar if it needs it, and salt and pepper to taste. Stir in the oregano, then let the peperonata cool a bit (it always tastes better at room temperature).
- Remove the capsicums from the oven and, when they're cool enough to handle, slice off the tops and scoop out the seeds. Spoon some of the peperonata into the capsicums, piling it up a little. Sit a small herb sprig jauntily on top and set them out on a platter. Store any leftover peperonata in the fridge, where it will keep for several days.

15th March

Sadly our gardening activities were cut short this afternoon when we broke a water outlet pipe while trying to dig out some very recalcitrant palms. Fortunately only the top is broken so it's not too bad; however, Clive is now doing a 'bush' fix-it job with wire, a piece of old plumbing pipe and a pile of bricks – don't ask!

In fact, I've decided that discretion is the better part of valour, and beaten a hasty retreat inside to cook something nice for dinner, as I suspect it will be needed. It's nothing too flash: lamb chops marinated in a bit of olive oil and lemon juice with a few herbs and crunchy rosemary potatoes. (Clive's a potato man from way back, and quite honestly I don't think it matters how they're cooked.)

Crunchy Rosemary Potatoes

SERVES 6

Without a shadow of a doubt, these potatoes would have to be one of the most popular dishes I cook. When we have friends over I invariably get a request to make some of 'those lovely crunchy potatoes with the herbs'. It's almost become a catch-cry now, and I'm sure I would miss it if I wasn't asked! They go with many, many things and are just so scrumptious and ridiculously easy to make.

1.5 kg potatoes (desiree or nicolas are good), peeled and cut into 3–4 cm chunks
needles from 3 large rosemary sprigs
extra virgin olive oil, for coating
sea salt flakes
rosemary sprig, extra, optional

- Preheat your oven to 220°C.
- Line a large shallow baking tray with foil then cover with a sheet of baking paper. Spread the potatoes over the tray in a single layer. Scatter the rosemary needles over them, then add a decent 'slurp' of olive oil. Mix everything together so the potatoes are thoroughly coated in oil. Cover with a sheet of foil, but only tuck it under loosely on the long sides of the tray.
- Put the potatoes in the oven. Roast them for 20 minutes, then remove the foil and turn the heat down to 210°C. Continue cooking them for another 35–40 minutes, turning them once or twice, until they're a gorgeous golden brown with crisp edges. When they're ready, remove them from the oven and sprinkle them with sea salt. Toss to coat them in the salt, then using the foil and paper to help, lift them off the tray and slide them into a bowl. Garnish with a rosemary sprig if liked.

16th March

At this time each year the apples from Stanthorpe arrive in the market and they're just so good – sweet with an ever-so-slightly sharp edge, gloriously crunchy and as juicy as anything. Of course, being my usual self, I've ended up with half a truckload (or thereabouts) of them, but they're such a treat I'm sure they won't go amiss. In fact the first kilo is already accounted for, as we're off for a late afternoon-tea-cum-early-dinner with friends (I wish there was a name for such a meal; after all, we have brunch, so I feel there should be an early-dinner equivalent), and I've promised to bring dessert, which will be an apple crostata. Crostatas are such gorgeous-looking things and perfect if you're a bit wary of pastry, for they're terribly forgiving and can be easily patched up. And as they are meant to be rustic, any wibbles or wobbles just look like part of the scenery!

A Delicious Apple & Cinnamon Crostata

SERVES 8–10

icing sugar, for dusting
double thick cream or vanilla bean ice-cream, to serve

SHORTCRUST PASTRY

1½ cups (225 g) plain flour
¼ teaspoon salt
125 g cold unsalted butter, cut into small chunks
¼ cup (60 ml) iced water

As you can see from the photos, I don't worry about arranging the apples in perfect rows over the pastry as I rather love the higgledy-piggledy look of the slices if they're just tumbled into the crust. Sweet apples – such as gala, fuji or pink ladies – are ideal for this as they hold their shape when they're cooked and don't collapse into a mush.

- To make the pastry, put the flour and salt into a food processor and whiz them together. Add the butter and process everything until the mixture resembles coarse breadcrumbs. With the processor running, pour in the iced water and process until the dough forms a ball around the blade.
- Tip the dough out onto a board and form it into a ball. Flatten it into a disc and wrap it tightly in plastic film. Chill it for 40–50 minutes, or until it's firm but supple enough to roll out. (I often make the pastry a day or two ahead of baking the crostata so I only have to roll it out when I need it; just remember to let it soften up a bit at room temperature first.)
- Preheat your oven to 200°C. Line a large round pizza tin (approximately 30 cm in diameter) or a baking tray with a sheet of baking paper, then set it aside.
- For the filling, crush the biscuits and mix them with the 1½ tablespoons of caster sugar, cinnamon and flour – or whiz them all together in the food processor. Set the mixture aside.
- Peel, halve and core all the apples except one, and cut them crossways into thin slices. Peel the one remaining apple and cut it crossways into rounds, then remove any seeds – I love the look of apples sliced like this as the seed holes form perfect

little stars in the centre of the slices. Put all the apple slices in a large bowl and sprinkle them with the ⅔ cup (150 g) caster sugar. Mix together the vanilla and melted butter, drizzle it over the apple and toss everything together. Leave this bowl aside while you roll the pastry.

- On a floured board, roll the pastry out thinly into a round that is a bit larger than the prepared pizza tin. Drape it over the tin, leaving an overhang all around (this overhang eventually forms a border for the crostata) and pressing it very gently into the sides. Spread the biscuit mixture evenly over the base. (If you're making the crostata on a baking tray, centre the rolled-out pastry on the baking paper. Sprinkle the biscuit mixture evenly over the pastry, leaving a 5–6 cm border all around so you can flip this over to form the rim of the crostata.) Strew the apple slices (but not the rounds) higgledy-piggledy over the biscuit mixture. Now tuck the reserved apple rounds here and there over the top. Gently fold the overhanging dough over the fruit, pleating and pressing it gently to seal it and form a pastry rim. Sprinkle the extra 2 teaspoons of sugar over the pastry rim.
- Bake the crostata for 35–40 minutes or until the pastry is crisp and golden brown. Remove from the oven and place the tin on a cooling rack. Dust the apples with a little icing sugar (it melts with the heat and gives them a lovely sheen) and leave the crostata to cool in the tin for at least 40 minutes so the filling firms up.
- With the help of the baking paper underneath, gently slide the crostata out of the tin onto a large, flat serving plate. Dust it lightly with a little more icing sugar and serve it with cream or vanilla bean ice-cream.

FILLING

120 g digestive biscuits (preferably McVities)
1½ tablespoons caster sugar
1½ teaspoons ground cinnamon
2 tablespoons plain flour
1 kg small or medium-sized sweet apples
⅔ cup (150 g) caster sugar
2–3 teaspoons vanilla extract
40 g unsalted butter, melted and cooled
2 teaspoons caster or granulated sugar, extra

BY THE WAY . . .

The crostata keeps quite well so you can bake it a few hours before you need it. Store any leftovers in the fridge – I'm always surprised that even a couple of days later the pastry is still relatively crisp.

17th March

I must admit I love the way homemade food and home-grown produce circulates around our community of friends and neighbours. It has been one of the deep pleasures of living here, a welcome reminder of generosity of spirit and of the wonderful produce we share.

In fact, even as I wrote that last sentence there was a knock on the door and a friend who lives up the valley was standing there with a huge bag of windfall limes and crimson tamarillos from his trees. They're so fresh they're nearly leaping out of their box, and I can see I shall have to increase my tamarillo repertoire as we can't possibly eat them all before they start to soften. But what a joy it is to be part of this giving cycle!

Here's a good example of how it works: when I visit my acupuncturist for an appointment, I invariably arrive with a carton of eggs from my friends who have the chooks, and maybe some cake or biscuits from a recipe I've been trying (especially as he and his partner are dear friends and an important part of my greatly valued taste-testing team!). In return I'm given a bundle of exquisite purple snake beans and spiky ivory cucumbers or whatever else may be thriving in their veggie garden. I might make a pickle from them and give a jar to my neighbours, who will at some stage leave a bagful of chillies or just-picked corn cobs on my doorstep, and so the wheel keeps turning . . .

18th March

With all my talk of rain, I realise that something I haven't mentioned is the sound of the rain as it arrives. I never noticed it before we lived here, but now I can always hear it coming. The only explanation I can think of for this is that it's so much quieter here – there isn't a lot of ambient noise except for the twittering of the birds and the varied hums of the insects. Sometimes the rain roars up the valley, and in the 20 seconds or so before it starts it sounds like a train charging along its track. At other times, it's quieter and I almost can't tell if I'm really hearing it, then with a soft plop that grows steadily louder the first drops plonk onto my umbrella. I absolutely love it.

Of course, speak of the devil, I can hear a squall coming up the valley now, so I must stop writing and go out and pick some thyme before it gets too heavy, otherwise I'll get soaked. The thyme is to go into what I hope will be a rather delicious onion and goat's cheese tart – I've been meaning to make it for ages, and have finally got around to it. I made and rolled the pastry yesterday and blind-baked the shell earlier, so it's sitting waiting for its cargo of caramelised onions and creamy marinated goat's cheese. All that remains is for a little nutmeg-scented savoury custard to be trickled over the top and into the oven it goes. And, as you can see from the photo overleaf, out it comes 40 minutes later, looking golden and gorgeous.

Caramelised Onion, Thyme & Goat's Cheese Tart

SERVES 6

1 pre-baked 25–26 cm tart shell, in its tin (see page 371)

FILLING

2½ tablespoons extra virgin olive oil
5 large brown onions, finely sliced
1½ tablespoons brown sugar
1 tablespoon balsamic vinegar
2 teaspoons thyme leaves
sea salt flakes and freshly ground black pepper
3 eggs
½ cup (125 ml) cream
¾ cup (180 ml) milk
freshly grated nutmeg, to taste
200 g goat's cheese marinated in olive oil, well drained
2 tablespoons freshly grated parmesan
tiny thyme sprigs, for scattering

I'm pleased to report that this tastes every bit as good as it looks – luscious as only caramelised onions can be, with their sweetness offset by the slightly salty goat's cheese and crisp pastry. My favourite cheese for this is Meredith Dairy's goat's cheese marinated in extra virgin olive oil with garlic and herbs, which is available in jars at supermarkets and delis.

I shall write the recipe down at once before I lose track of it. This is something I've finally learnt to do early in the piece, for I jot down things as I cook but they're in my own cook's shorthand and unless I decipher them fairly quickly I'm often left wondering what on earth all the little squiggles and arrows actually mean!

- To make the filling, heat the oil in a large frying pan over low heat. Add the onion and cook, stirring regularly, for 20–25 minutes until it has collapsed and softened. Now add the brown sugar and vinegar and cook for 5 minutes, stirring frequently to make sure the onion doesn't stick to the pan – by now it should be a gorgeous, glossy pale-toffee colour. Turn off the heat, sprinkle in the thyme leaves and add salt to taste, then set aside to cool.
- Preheat your oven to 180°C and sit the tart shell in the tin on a baking sheet.
- In a bowl, whisk the eggs to break them up then whisk in the cream and milk, and a little salt, pepper and nutmeg to taste.
- Spread the onion mixture evenly over the base of the tart shell. Now break the goat's cheese up with your fingers and dab it around evenly as best you can (it's a bit soft and oily). Give the egg mixture another quick whisk in case it has settled, then drizzle it over the top. Finish with a sprinkling of parmesan and thyme sprigs.
- Put the tart in the oven and bake it for 35–40 minutes, or until it's a glorious golden colour and lightly set. To check, insert the tip of a fine knife into the middle and gently press the sides of the cut apart. The filling should be softly set with no liquid running into the cut. Remove it from the oven and leave it to cool and settle for at least 10 minutes before serving. Then just slip off the outer ring of the tin, and gently slide the tart onto a serving plate.

20th March

We're having a blissfully quiet Easter, but even so I have this ridiculous urge to stock up on food. Goodness knows why – the shops will be open over the break, yet I always get a slightly panicky feeling that we might somehow run out! I know it's silly but it seems to be hard-wired in me. I wonder if this is just a cook's thing, or do we all do it?

In fact, I tell a lie: *not* all the shops will be open, and I must say it's one of the pleasures of living in our small town that many shops do close at 1 o'clock on Saturday and don't re-open until Monday morning. I love that the shopkeepers also get to have a weekend – it takes me back to my childhood and shopping with my mum at the bakery on a Saturday morning. There was always a lovely bustling feel to it, with people getting ready for their weekend. The bakers' shelves would be laden with buns, breads, pies and cakes that looked and smelt wonderful. We would buy baguettes (to go with Mum's homemade chicken liver pâté) and wonderful apple strudel. The bakers were Austrian and the strudel was exquisite: delicate, buttery layers of pastry wrapped around an astonishing amount of cinnamon-scented apples. Eaten warm, with vanilla ice-cream melting in a puddle around it, it was my 13-year-old self's idea of heaven.

This morning we're heading out bright and early – not to the bakery, but to buy hot cross buns at the market. It's always extra busy at this time of year as the town is full of people going to the huge Bluesfest music festival at Byron Bay that runs right through Easter.

And busy it is, but in an exciting holiday kind of way as people get ready for the break. The stall-holders have really gone to town and there's beautiful produce every which way. It's hard to know where to begin, but a waft of cinnamon leads us straight to Faith, the market's wonderful baker. She has been up all night baking hot cross buns and her table is overflowing with sticky piles of them. Even this early a queue is forming but we're happy to wait. As always, along with our purchases we have a chat and there is her bright, if somewhat weary smile this morning, to send us on our way to our next stop: a cup of locally grown coffee. Thus fuelled, we feel more than ready to join the throng of shoppers.

25th March

As I sit writing this, doors flung open to catch the breeze, Clive is mowing, and as he does so the glorious perfume of basil and mint is floating in. They've both well and truly escaped their beds and are popping up through the lawn so with each run of the mower yet another burst of fragrance wafts in – it's exquisite. I have always wanted a chamomile lawn . . . well now I have my very own mint and basil one!

31st March

We have just been sitting outside having a cup of tea and looked up to see the most enormous eagle wheeling over the valley. I swear that its wing-span would be as great as the distance between my palms if I stretched my arms out wide. It couldn't possibly be looking for prey from such a height, and as it manoeuvred its way effortlessly up and down the air currents, we felt it was doing it more for pleasure than anything else. I've no doubt a farmer would tell us we're being hopelessly romantic, but that's not such a bad thing to be.

It's hard to believe it's the last day of March: it's a clear, balmy 28°C and everything is sparkling after a gentle shower of rain last night. It's so beautiful that I'm finding it very difficult to stay inside, and I'm fighting the urge to go out into the garden and check on how everything is growing . . . which, of course, having little willpower in these things, I have just done for the third time this morning! But, to make myself feel a bit less guilty for skiving off from my writing, my excursions have solved the question of what's for dinner tonight. There are masses of chillies on the bush, the parsley has shot up in the few days we've been away and I've just picked the first lemon from the Meyer lemon tree – all in all, the perfect makings for a quick bowl of pasta.

A Satisfying Pasta Supper

SERVES 4 AS A STARTER OR 3 HEARTY EATERS AS A MAIN

- 170 ml extra virgin olive oil
- 2 large cloves garlic, 1 halved, 1 very finely sliced
- 1 cup (70 g) breadcrumbs, grated from a stale loaf of good country-style bread (sourdough is great)
- salt, for cooking pasta
- 400 g spaghettini or spaghetti
- 2 anchovy fillets
- large handful of chopped flat-leaf parsley
- 2 small red chillies, finely chopped
- 2 tablespoons small capers, or more to taste
- 2 tablespoons lemon juice, or a little more to taste
- 180 g freshly grated parmesan, plus extra to serve, optional
- sea salt flakes, to taste
- 3 tablespoons nice small parsley leaves, extra, to serve

BREADCRUMBS . . .

Rather than drag out my food processor to make these, as long as the bread is pretty dry, I find the easiest way to make the crumbs is to grate the bread on the coarse side of a box grater. You have to push it firmly against the cutting surface, but it works a treat and gives you a really good mix of crumb sizes.

This is one of those classic dishes that is so much more than the sum of its parts. It makes a supremely satisfying meal at the end of a long, busy day when you want something delicious to eat that doesn't take too much brain power or work. Although simple, the combination of crunchy breadcrumbs and garlic with the clean, cool parsley, fiery chillies, bite of capers and lemon, and good olive oil leaves you almost startled at just how good it is.

- The first step in this recipe is to prepare all the ingredients, so once you start cooking you can just roll along from one stage to the next. While you are doing this prep work, bring a large saucepan of water to the boil over high heat.
- Warm 2 tablespoons oil and the halved clove of garlic in a large frying pan over medium heat. When it's fairly hot, remove the garlic then add the breadcrumbs and cook them, stirring constantly, until they're golden brown and crunchy. Tip them onto a plate to cool. Wipe out the pan and set it aside.
- Once the water in the pan is boiling, salt it liberally (I operate on 2–3 teaspoons of salt per litre of water). When it returns to the boil, add the spaghettini and cook until it is al dente, stirring once or twice initially to keep the strands separate.
- While the spaghettini is cooking, heat the remaining olive oil in the frying pan and cook the sliced garlic gently over very low heat, stirring occasionally, until it smells fragrant but has only very faintly coloured. Add the anchovy fillets and crush them with a spoon so they dissolve into the oil. Turn off the heat. When the pasta is close to ready (the best way to check is to fish a strand out and bite it), add the chopped parsley, chilli and capers to the anchovy mixture in the pan and warm them through.
- Drain the spaghettini well, shaking out any excess water, and add it to the frying pan with the lemon juice. Give it a quick mix, then add the parmesan and sea salt. Toss everything together and add most of the small parsley leaves. Scoop the spaghettini into warm bowls and sprinkle with the crisp breadcrumbs and remaining parsley leaves. Serve with grated or shaved parmesan, if liked.

APRIL

April Fools' Day

What a lovely start to a month. I was just out filling one of the bird baths from the watering can, and lo and behold, along with the rush of water, out plopped two rather startled green frogs. I'm not quite sure who was more surprised – them or me! They're now very happily doing laps, but I shall have to take them back to their home behind the water tank as they're too exposed where they are. They're such amazing creatures and it's wonderful to know they're thriving in the garden. I can see I shall have to take a daily check of the can before I start to pour . . .

2nd April

We've just come home from walking around the back-streets of Bangalow, our pockets filled with windfall pecans that have dropped off the trees that line the streets. They're unbelievably sweet and nutty, and easy to open as they're so fresh – we can just squeeze two nuts together, cracking the thin shells enough to prise out the kernels.

Although they're not as prevalent as macadamias (there are macca orchards as far as the eye can see up here in the hinterland) pecans grow very well too, and the nuts are so delicious and reasonably priced that I cook with them more and more, and always have roasted ones in the freezer ready to toss into cakes, salads and biscuits. This afternoon, however, I'm making a batch of blue cheese and pecan 'snails' to go with some soup. Now the weather is cooling down, soup will become our staple food, and we often make a meal of it with bread and salad.

Blue Cheese & Pecan 'Snails'

MAKES ABOUT 14

These first came about when I was making blue cheese scone dough and decided that rather than incorporating the cheese and nuts into it, I would pat the dough out and spread the cheese and pecans over the top, then roll it up and cut it into slices. They worked a treat and, because of their curvy shape, have become affectionately known as 'snails'.

- 2 cups (300 g) self-raising flour
- ½ teaspoon salt
- 1 teaspoon caster sugar
- 75 g cold unsalted butter, cut into little chunks
- ¾–1 cup (185–250 ml) milk
- 100 g roasted pecans, fairly finely chopped (you can do this in a food processor)
- 1 egg yolk, whisked with 2 teaspoons water to make an egg wash

BLUE CHEESE BUTTER

- 70 g unsalted butter, at room temperature
- 90 g blue cheese (a mixture of a strong blue cheese and a milder, creamy one is ideal)
- 45 g finely grated parmesan

- Put the flour, salt and sugar in the bowl of a food processor and whiz them together to combine. Add the butter and process the mixture until it resembles fine breadcrumbs, then tip it into a bowl. (You can also do this by hand in a large bowl: simply rub the butter chunks into the flour mixture with your fingertips.) Pour in the milk and mix it in lightly with a fork. You will have to adjust the milk a little – you need just enough to make a soft, slightly flaky dough.
- Turn the dough out onto a floured board and knead it gently until it's fairly smooth. Then roll the dough (or pat it out with your hands) into a rectangle about 35 cm × 20 cm.
- For the blue cheese butter, put all the ingredients in a food processor and whiz them together until they're thoroughly mixed. Otherwise, you can just cream them together in a bowl with a wooden spoon. Spread the blue cheese butter evenly over the dough, leaving a 1 cm wide strip uncovered on the long side that is ›

furthest away from you. Sprinkle the chopped pecans evenly over the top and press down on them gently to embed them in the butter.

- Line a baking tray with baking paper. Brush a thin layer of egg wash on the strip of dough that is uncovered. Starting at the long side nearest you, roll the dough up like a jam roll, pressing down gently on the final roll to help seal the egg-washed edge to the roll. Carefully transfer the log to the tray and chill it for at least an hour (you can safely leave it for 2–3 hours, if you like).
- Preheat your oven to 200°C.
- Remove the tray from the fridge and gently transfer the log to a cutting board. Use a lightly floured knife to cut the roll into 2 cm thick slices. (The dough may be a little squashy to cut but I find if you use a serrated knife and a gentle sawing motion it works well.)
- Sit the resulting snails, cut-side down, on the lined tray, leaving a gap between each one to allow them to spread.
- Just before putting the snails in the oven, brush very lightly around the sides and over the top of each one with the egg wash to give them a golden glaze as they bake. Bake them for 13–18 minutes or until they're golden.
- When they're ready, remove them from the oven and sit them in a serving basket lined with a clean cloth or tea towel to keep them warm. Serve them straight away with butter, if you like, although they are very good as is.

3rd April

The farmers' market is the best indicator of the steadily turning wheel of the seasons and despite it being quite hot still, today we noticed there is a dwindling supply of summer produce and those things that like cool feet are beginning to appear. We came back with lovely firm okra pods, big hands of pink-tipped ginger with bright green stalks, fat orange fuyu fruit, crisp fuji apples and all sorts of beans. However, the biggest treat of all was a bagful of beautiful crimson rosellas. They really are the most remarkable-looking things and seeing them has reminded me that I've been meaning to plant some bushes – they're quite lovely with their burgundy stems, delicate creamy-yellow flowers with dark red centres, and narrow sage-green leaves.

I've just finished making some rosella jelly with this lot and can't wait for it to cool enough for me to try. It's the most extraordinarily clear, deep-ruby colour and has a slightly exotic berry-ish fragrance, almost as though there is a background note of rose. In fact a few drops of rosewater might be lovely in it – I shall try that next time I make it.

Rosella Jelly

MAKES 4–5 MEDIUM JARS

2 large lemons
about 1 kg rosellas
2 apples, washed and chopped (including the cores)
2 litres cold water
about 1.5 kg granulated sugar

I wish you were with me now and I could share a jar of this with you. I have just plopped a spoonful onto a warm scone with a dollop of cream and I can't begin to tell you what a wonderful combination it is. The jelly is the most exquisite colour and I can see I shall have to hide it away or it will be gone in no time.

If and when you make it, something to be aware of is that you do need a very large saucepan to cook it in, as the jelly froths up rather alarmingly as it cooks. If you don't have one, either divide the mixture between two pans or make a half quantity.

- Squeeze the juice from the lemons, reserving any pips. Set the juice aside then make a bundle of the pips in a small piece of muslin and put that aside for the moment too. (Make sure it's knotted tightly or the pips will escape as they cook.)
- Rinse the rosellas well. The first job is to separate the fleshy burgundy part (or calyx as it's technically known) from the green seed pod (you need both for the jelly). It takes a little while, but is one of those pleasingly mindless jobs, so I usually set myself up at the outside table and watch the birds come and go as I peel . . . and if I'm very lucky, somebody will bring me a cup of tea!
- Put the seed pods, chopped apple and bundle of lemon pips in a very large saucepan. Pour in 1.5 litres of the water, bring the mixture to the boil then immediately reduce the heat and let it bubble very, very gently. After 40 minutes, add the reserved calyxes along with the remaining 2 cups (500 ml) of water. Increase the heat so the mixture boils again, then reduce it and simmer for another 20 minutes.
- Now you need to rig up some kind of a jelly bag. I usually line a very large fine sieve with two thicknesses of fine clean muslin, leaving a big overhang all the way around. Secure the muslin to the edges of the sieve with some clothes pegs to help keep it in place when you pour in the rosella mixture. Sit the sieve over a large deep bowl. It needs to be deep enough so that once the rosella liquid has flowed through it, the bottom of the sieve won't touch the surface.
- Or, you can improvise an excellent jelly bag if you have a small stool. To do this, turn it upside down, brush off any dust, then firmly tie or knot a corner of the muslin (you will need at least four thicknesses to hold the weight of the fruit) to the tips of each of the four legs to make a deep bag. Sit a large bowl under the muslin on the base of the stool and you have the perfect jelly bag!
- Carefully pour or ladle the hot rosella mixture into the muslin. Cover it loosely with a sheet of plastic film and leave it to drain for at least 6 hours, or overnight if the weather is cool. Don't be tempted to press down on the rosella mixture as this will extract some of the pulp and make the jelly cloudy.

- When you are ready to finish the jelly, scoop some of the calyxes out of the drained pulp and set them aside (you don't need masses, just enough to have a few pieces floating in each jar). Discard the rest. Measure out the rosella liquid, to work out how many cups of liquid you have, then pour it into the saucepan. Add the reserved calyxes and lemon juice. For every cup of rosella liquid, add an equal amount of sugar.
- Put the pan over low–medium heat and warm the mixture, stirring gently until the sugar has dissolved. Now, clip a sugar thermometer to the side of the pan (this is helpful but not essential, so don't worry if you don't have one). Increase the heat to very high and let the liquid boil rapidly for 20–30 minutes until it reaches setting point, stirring it regularly to make sure it isn't catching on the bottom. I'll explain what setting point means in a moment, but just before I do, it's important to be mindful that when jelly is close to setting point it bubbles up in the pan, so you need to keep an eye on it and adjust the temperature so it doesn't boil over (you may well need to do this a few times).
- Back to the setting point; there are a few ways to check this. First, if you're using a thermometer, check the temperature has reached 105°C, which is a good indication it's close. The next thing to do is to dip a wooden spoon into the boiling jelly, then lift it up high above the pan, turn it sideways and let the jelly on it drip back in. What you're hoping to see is those last few drops looking quite thick and syrupy, and ideally, running together and joining up then falling as more of a 'sheet' than individual drops (however, long fine tails on them will do nicely!). You can also spoon a little jelly onto an ice-cold saucer and put it in the freezer. After a couple of minutes push your finger through the jelly: if the surface wrinkles up a little, it's ready. I tend to do all three just to be sure!
- Keep testing the jelly every minute or so, and as soon as it's ready, take it off the heat and let it settle for a few minutes. Use a metal spoon to remove any pink froth from the jelly's surface. Ladle the jelly into hot, sterilised glass jars (see note, right), cover them with a sheet of baking paper to protect them, and leave them to cool completely. When they're ready, remove the paper and seal the jars tightly. Label and date them, and store them in a cool, dry, dark place for up to 4 months.

STERILISING JARS . . .

This jelly recipe begs the question of how to sterilise the jars. But just before I go into that, it's important to remember that the jars must be hot when you fill them with the hot jelly, otherwise they may crack, so you need to get your timing somewhat in sync with the jelly when you sterilise them.

There are a few ways to sterilise jars, but the two I mainly use are these:

- Wash the jars in warm soapy water, rinse them thoroughly then sit them and their lids (as long as the lids aren't plastic or won't melt) on a baking tray. Put the tray with the jars into a cold oven then turn the heat to 130°C. Leave the jars for 30 minutes, then carefully take them out and cover them with a sheet of greaseproof paper until you're ready to use them. (Or you can just switch off the oven and leave them in to stay hot if the jelly isn't quite ready.)
- The other way, if you have a dishwasher, is to put the jars and their lids through the hottest cycle, and leave them in once the cycle has finished, so they stay hot until you fill them. Just make sure they are dry before you do, or the jelly may become mouldy over time.

8th April

These last few days have whizzed by as Rodney, my photographer and very dear friend, has been up all week and we've begun photographing this book. It's been a lot of work, but a very happy time too. It's such a relief to be under way, for up until now the book has been very much in my head and felt rather like an amorphous mass that I've been trying to catch hold of and shape, but now that I'm seeing the images coming to life I'm feeling vastly relieved and think it will actually work after all!

We both went to the markets early, which I know from past visits with him is a very dangerous thing to do, as we keep finding things to shoot and between the two of us end up absolutely laden with produce. This time was no exception. Just as we were leaving and I had vowed not to buy one more thing, I spotted the first of the season's radishes and couldn't resist buying them to make this delicately hued salad.

Bocconcini, Celery, Prosciutto & Radish Salad with Mint Dressing

SERVES 6–8

The pastel colours of this salad are so beguiling and the jolt of mint makes it wonderfully refreshing. It's great with things like grilled or barbecued fish, chicken or lamb. Just remember to slice the celery and radishes as finely as possible as it gives them a lovely translucency (a mandolin slicer is ideal for doing this, if you happen to have one). If you are wondering what the Dijonnaise is in the recipe, it's a luscious combination of Dijon mustard and mayonnaise – I've made it optional in the dressing, as it is delicious with or without it.

12 radishes, very finely sliced
6 celery stalks, finely sliced on the diagonal
2 handfuls of small pale green and yellow inner celery leaves
12 bocconcini, thinly sliced
18 kalamata olives (the purple-coloured ones look best)
6 large or 12 small slices prosciutto, torn into strips, then rolled
tiny mint leaves, to garnish

DRESSING

¾ cup (180 ml) extra virgin olive oil
1½ tablespoons white wine vinegar
¾ teaspoon caster sugar
1½ tablespoons Dijonnaise, optional
sea salt flakes, to taste
handful of finely shredded or torn mint

- To make the dressing, whisk all the ingredients except the mint together thoroughly, then set it aside. It's best to slice the mint and add it just before serving, so it keeps its vivid green colour.
- To make the salad, in a large bowl gently mix together the sliced radishes, celery, celery leaves and bocconcini. Just before you are ready to serve, add the dressing and olives (reserving a few for garnishing) and gently mix them all together.
- Sit a small pile of salad on each plate (or scoop it into a shallow bowl), tucking little curls of prosciutto here and there as you go. Scatter the reserved olives and tiny mint leaves on top.

Pumpkin Vine Stems with Olive, Lemon & Chilli

SERVES 2–3

1 bunch (about 700 g) pumpkin vine shoots and leaves, well washed
extra virgin olive oil, to taste
2 cloves garlic, finely chopped
1 small chilli, finely chopped
sea salt flakes
lemon juice, to taste

While we were at the market, I was standing looking quizzically at bundles of vaguely familiar, soft green leaves with delicate tendrils (which I had just realised were pumpkin leaves) when an Italian friend of mine came up behind me and pounced on them with a cry of delight. He was terribly excited to see them and waxed lyrical about the way his nonna used to cook them. He then went on to show me how to trim the tender shoots and carefully strip away the fuzzy skin so they're ready to cook. With his enthusiastic endorsements ringing in my ears we came home and did just that . . . and this is the delicious result.

Although we're not so familiar here with eating pumpkin vine stems, I've since done a bit of research and discovered they're widely used as a vegetable in a surprisingly diverse range of countries – everywhere from Laos to Italy. I imagine eating them is born from hard times and frugality, when nothing is wasted and every bit of an animal, fruit or vegetable is used in some way.

The stems have a delicate 'green' flavour and taste like a cross between silver-beet stems and zucchini. It's a labour of love to prepare them as peeling away the fine, fuzzy skin is fiddly (although a few friends armed with sharp knives and plenty to chat about would strip them back in no time), but they are delicious, and I am now eyeing my newly planted pumpkin vines in a totally different light.

It is a bit hard to give quantities for this recipe, as the size of the bunches of leaves you're likely to find will vary considerably. However, from a bunch weighing 700 g I trimmed enough shoots to serve two to three people.

- Use a sharp paring knife to peel away the celery-like strings from the most tender pumpkin shoots – as you do this, the prickly skin peels away too. Cut the stems into 5–6 cm lengths. You can also use the smallest, most tender leaves: just rub them gently to remove as many of the tiny hairs as possible, then give them a good rinse. (I usually leave a few of the long curly tendrils attached to the stalks too as they look so beautiful, though they are chewy to eat.)

- Quickly steam the pumpkin shoots in a large saucepan until they are just tender and still nice and green. Drain them and set them aside. Return the saucepan to the stove over medium heat. Add a good slosh of oil and warm it through. Now add the garlic and chilli and cook, stirring constantly, for a couple of minutes. Tip the drained pumpkin shoots back into the pan and toss them about in the garlic oil mixture so they are well coated. Add salt and a big squeeze of lemon juice to taste, then scoop them out into a bowl. They are a refreshing change as a green vegetable with simply cooked fish, chicken or pork.

BRIDGE
Reach for the sky

10th April

The delicate lilac flowers in this photograph are society garlic blossoms – a wonderful name, isn't it? They look delightful scattered over a salad and pack a surprisingly robust garlic punch. And, thankfully for this not very experienced gardener (I don't have a particularly green thumb and gardening for me is very much a matter of trial and error, but, I hasten to add, also a great joy), these hardy plants seem to grow happily despite everything.

My mum was a wonderful gardener and at times I surprise myself by the things I unwittingly learnt from her. I can be walking down a street and see a tree and think, 'Oh, that's a weigela, or an Indian hawthorn', despite having not seen one since my childhood. It's amazing how these things stick, isn't it?

In fact, the first thing I remember planting when I was four or five was a small veggie patch, for which my mum wisely gave me carrot, radish and pumpkin seeds, knowing I would need things that grew rapidly. Every morning I would rush down to the seeds, willing them to send up leaves, until one morning to my great joy, instead of bare soil there was a pale green fuzz of new shoots. I probably loved them to death and how they continued to flourish I don't know, but flourish they did until the red-letter day when I pulled my first carrots out of the ground. (Although truth be told, I had checked on them many times, pulling them up then carefully re-planting them when I saw they were far too tiny to eat. It's amazing any at all survived!)

To this day, I have a soft spot for all three of these vegetables and cook with them regularly – particularly pumpkin, for which I have a bottomless appetite. I love it every which way, as you will probably notice as you read this book. In summer I tend to use it in salads (such as the pumpkin and haloumi salad on page 129), but come the cooler weather I'll put it in just about anything – soups, cakes, muffins, bread, and the supremely satisfying chicken dish overleaf.

Spiced Coconut & Cardamom Chicken with Glazed Pumpkin

SERVES 4

2 large cloves garlic, finely chopped
2 heaped teaspoons cumin seeds, ground
2 heaped teaspoons coriander seeds, ground
1½ teaspoons fennel seeds, ground
½ teaspoon cayenne pepper
sticky black seeds from 3–4 cardamom pods, coarsely ground
1½ tablespoons finely chopped ginger
3 teaspoons curry paste
sea salt flakes
8 smallish chicken chops (partly boned leg and thigh portions) or skin-on chicken thighs
1.2 kg butternut pumpkin (you need 1 kg after trimming), cut into 2.5 cm chunks
1 whole lemon
1 × 400 g can diced or crushed tomatoes
2½ tablespoons brown sugar
2 tablespoons sun-dried tomato pesto
140 ml light coconut cream
1 cinnamon stick, snapped in half
lemon or lime juice, to taste
lemon or lime wedges, to serve
coriander sprigs, to garnish, optional

I love this. It is not the most beautiful-looking dish in the world and takes a while to prepare but it is *soooo* delicious – the pumpkin and chicken become imbued with the spicy coconut sauce and are wonderfully succulent. I tend to serve it with rice to soak up any excess sauce, and something green, fresh and sprightly to balance the spices and coconut, usually a watercress or cucumber salad. Just about any curry paste will work here, but I tend to use Patak's Tikka Masala (coriander and lemon) curry paste – it's medium-hot and perfect in this dish.

- In a large bowl stir together the garlic, cumin, coriander, fennel, cayenne pepper, cardamom, ginger, curry paste and a little salt. You will need to squash the curry paste in a bit with the back of a spoon so it's thoroughly mixed with everything else. Add the chicken, one piece at a time, and rub all over with the spice mixture so it is well coated. I wear prep gloves for this as it's somewhat messy and tends to leave your hands a rather remarkable (and remarked on!) shade of yellow.
- As they are done, put the chicken pieces into a large snap-lock bag. Once you have finished coating them all, seal the bag and squish it around in your hands a bit. Now pop the bag into a container, seal it tightly and put it in the fridge for at least a few hours but preferably overnight. Every so often, when you remember, take the bag out and squish the chicken again.
- When you're ready to cook the chicken, preheat your oven to 180°C.
- Scatter the pumpkin pieces over the bottom of a large roasting tin (36 cm × 26 cm is ideal for this amount) in a single layer. Nestle the chicken in amongst the pumpkin chunks as best you can.
- Peel the lemon, making sure you remove all the white pith. Cut the flesh into little chunks, removing any seeds as you go. Tip the chunks into a bowl and thoroughly mix in the tomatoes, sugar, pesto, coconut cream and cinnamon. Scrape this mixture over the chicken and pumpkin. Now use your hands to thoroughly coat the chicken and pumpkin pieces in the coconut mixture (it's a good idea to don those prep gloves again for this). Make sure the chicken is sitting skin-side up in the tin.

- Pop the tin in the oven and bake the chicken, uncovered, for about 1–1¼ hours (depending on the size of the thighs), carefully turning everything around after 40 minutes. When the chicken is ready transfer it to a plate, then sit it in a warm spot and tent it loosely with foil to keep it warm. Increase the oven temperature to 210°C and return the pumpkin to the oven. Cook it for another 20 minutes or so until the edges of the chunks are crisp and the sauce around them is thick.
- Take the pumpkin out of the oven. There may be a thin film of oil from the coconut cream on the sauce – if there is just blot it up with paper towels. Taste the sauce and add more salt or a squeeze of lemon or lime juice if needed.
- To serve, put a little mound of pumpkin and sauce on each plate, then prop the chicken alongside it. Serve with lemon or lime wedges and garnish with coriander sprigs if you like.

CARDAMOM

Cardamom seeds have a haunting flavour, a bit like a cross between citrus and camphor. When they're freshly ground, they're incredibly fragrant and almost heady in their intensity. To get the sticky black seeds out of the cardamom pods, just sit the pods on a chopping board and press down very firmly with the flat side of a heavy knife or sharpening steel to split the pods open.

12th April

A family of white-cheeked honeyeaters has just arrived in the garden from their summer feeding grounds. They're the most exquisite birds, with their black and white striped breasts, vivid yellow-splashed wings and delicate curved beaks. They forage all day amongst the grevilleas and callistemons and are spellbinding to watch. They also adore water and the minute I fill the bird baths, even if I've only taken a few steps away, they're in, splashing and whirring their wings – it's a sight to behold. They do this even if it's pouring with rain! You would think they were wet enough already, but it seems there is no such thing as being too wet in bird-land.

I've just been wondering what on earth to cook for dinner tonight. The cupboard is relatively bare but I've managed to find some brown onions and I know there's a jar of goat's cheese in the fridge, so we shall have roasted onions for dinner with whatever salad greens I can find. Because of what I do people often imagine that I whip up fabulous meals every night, but more often than not we have very simple meals indeed – these onions being a prime example (see page 181).

Roast Onions with Goat's Cheese & Thyme

SERVES 4

I rarely mention brands, but make an exception for Meredith Dairy's goat's cheese marinated in olive oil. The soft cubes of snow-white cheese have the most wonderful voluptuous texture and taste scrumptious with their subtle hints of garlic, herbs and olive oil. I always keep a jar or two in the fridge, ready to add a bit of pizzazz to dishes like these roast onions, which have become a great favourite of ours. They show the very real affinity between goat's cheese and the onion family at its simplest and most delicious. (Try them with the crunchy herb-crusted racks of lamb on page 383 – they're fabulous together.)

8 brown onions
extra virgin olive oil, for drizzling
1½–2 tablespoons thyme leaves, plus some tiny sprigs
100 g goat's cheese marinated in olive oil, or more to taste
freshly ground black pepper
a few extra thyme sprigs, to serve

- Preheat your oven to 200°C. (I should let you know here that I have cooked these onions at all sorts of temperatures, depending on what else I'm cooking at the same time. If there is a roast of some sort under way I just adjust the timing for the onions – and cover them with a bit of foil if they start to look too brown. The recipe is really very forgiving, so it's not a problem.)
- Cut the tip and base off each of the onions. Carefully peel away the brown skin and the layer of onion directly beneath it. Try not to cut into the onion layer below this one if possible – it's no big deal if you do, but it can cause the onions to split open as they roast so they don't look quite as appealing.
- Line a small roasting tin with baking paper (ideally the onions should just fit snugly in a single layer) then pop the onions in the tin. Drizzle some olive oil over each one then roll them around so they are well coated in it. Sit them back up on their bases and sprinkle about ½ teaspoon of thyme leaves over each onion, then scatter a few sprigs of thyme on top.
- Slip the dish into the oven and roast the onions for about an hour, or until they are tender when pierced with a fine skewer and have lovely crisp brown edges and flecks. Cover them loosely with foil once they are as dark as you would like. When the onions are ready, remove them from the oven. Gently squash some goat's cheese onto each one and return them briefly to the oven for the cheese to soften (2–3 minutes should do it). Transfer them to a warm serving dish and finish off with a good grinding of pepper and a few extra thyme sprigs, if liked.

14th April

It's clear and cool today with a very blustery wind blowing. Clive has gone to the market in a tee-shirt, which will no doubt elicit the usual comments about the 'mad Pommie' – he's the only person I know that gets around all winter in one.

Hopefully he will come back with lots of fruit: apples, quinces and maybe the first of the mandarins. There are also some beautiful Pink's mammoth custard apples around now, which are wonderful – creamy and delicate with barely a seed. Such a treat.

I know it's not quite the done thing these days, but throughout my childhood we always had a 'pudding' of some sort to finish dinner; it just wasn't considered complete without one. And they were such wonderful puddings too: mulberries from our neighbour's tree with cream and a dusting of icing sugar, golden syrup steamed pudding studded with raisins, lovely eggy baked custards, and fruit crumbles of every sort – simple, honest dishes and things I love to this day. But for me, Mum's baked apples were best of all: honey-sweet and bursting with nuts and dried fruit. Invariably I would scald my tongue by eating them before they'd cooled down, but it didn't matter. They were so good.

Honey & Pecan Baked Apples

SERVES 6

60 g pitted dates, coarsely chopped
60 g raisins
60 g roasted pecans, coarsely chopped
¼ cup (90 g) clear honey
¼ cup (60 ml) double thick cream
¾ teaspoon ground cinnamon
1 teaspoon finely grated lemon zest
1 teaspoon vanilla extract
6 pink lady, fuji or royal gala apples
2 cups (500 ml) good-quality clear apple juice
1½ tablespoons clear honey, extra
thick cream or Greek-style yoghurt, to serve

What is it about the aroma of apples baking that is so comforting? It immediately takes me back to my school days, and arriving home after the long journey on the school bus to be greeted at the front door by the glorious fragrance of apples and cinnamon as Mum baked an apple crumble or pie (or simple baked apples like these) for dessert on a wintry evening.

I must admit that I always rather hope that no-one will come back for seconds of these, as they re-heat beautifully in the microwave and are such a treat for breakfast with a spoonful of Greek-style yoghurt.

- Preheat your oven to 180°C.
- In a small bowl, stir together the dates, raisins, pecans, honey, cream, cinnamon, lemon zest and vanilla. Set the bowl aside.
- Baked apples rarely have lids, and you can just lop the tops off (doing this always makes me feel like the Queen in *Alice in Wonderland*, shouting, 'Off with their heads!'), however I love the rather whimsical look lids give them. If you want to make little lids, cut the top off each apple far enough down to include the stalk when you lift the 'lid' off. Trim the finest sliver off the base of the apples if necessary too, so they sit up straight without wobbling about.

- Now, core the apples. You can use an apple corer or one of those little gadgets that is used to make melon or potato balls. (I must admit mine has been languishing in my kitchen drawer for at least 25 years and is mainly used for coring – I don't think it has caught sight of a melon in years!) Core each apple, widening the hole out quite a bit towards the top so it will hold plenty of the filling. Make the finest, most shallow slit around the middle of the apples with a sharp knife to help stop the apple bursting as it bakes (not all apples do this, but some are more prone to it than others so it's a good idea to be on the safe side).
- Stand the apples in a small gratin or shallow baking dish that fits them fairly snugly. Divide the filling evenly among them, pressing it into the hollow and mounding it up generously on top. Sit the lids on the apples then trickle the apple juice around them.
- Put the dish in the oven and bake the apples for about 50 minutes or until they're fairly tender (I like them to still have a bit of 'body'), basting them once or twice with the juices. This is only a rough guide to the timing, as it may vary considerably depending on the variety and size of the apples you use, and the thickness of the dish they are baked in. To check if they're ready, pierce one with a fine skewer – it should go in fairly easily. If at any time the tops start to look a bit burnt, sit a sheet of foil loosely over them. ›

- When the apples are ready, remove them from the oven. Use a slotted spoon to transfer them to a plate then set them aside in a warm spot. Strain the liquid left in the dish into a medium saucepan and add the extra honey. Stir until the honey has dissolved, then bring the liquid to the boil over high heat. Continue to boil it until it's somewhat reduced and syrupy – this may take 15 minutes or so, depending on the size of your pan.
- To serve the apples, sit one on each plate and trickle some of the reduced juice over the top. They are lovely with a little thick cream or yoghurt.

17th April

Oh no, the wind is howling around the house and the rain is back with a vengeance, beating almost horizontally onto the windows and causing the downpipes to spout water as they try to cope with the deluge. Well, it will certainly fill the water tank again – and put paid to any gardening this weekend. Still, there is something very cosy and comforting about cooking when it's wild and woolly outside, and it's just the sort of weather that says 'soup' to me. So soup it will be.

I don't know if you do this, but I tend to have a run on particular dishes, where I cook them a lot and then for some reason don't make them for ages. It's not that I've stopped enjoying them, it's just that something else has come up to take their place for a time. However at some stage they inevitably come back around again and I enjoy them all the more – it's rather like finding a long-lost friend. This earthy lentil soup is just such a thing, and I'm so glad that it's back on the menu again.

Middle Eastern Double Lentil Soup

SERVES 6–8

I almost feel as though this heady, spicy soup is some sort of magic elixir – it is the dish I turn to whenever I'm feeling a bit below par or need comforting. With each spoonful I can feel it weaving its spell; warming me up and sending all sorts of goodies scurrying through my body to fight off bugs and build up my immune system. I'll often add a handful of baby spinach leaves to the pan just before I take it off the heat for a little bit of 'green' and always have chunks of bread close by for dunking. The soups keep well for at least 5 days in a tightly sealed container in the fridge and only improves over time.

250 g split red (orange) lentils
250 g puy-style lentils, or similar, plus 1 tablespoon extra
2 tablespoons extra virgin olive oil
4 onions, finely chopped
6 cloves garlic, finely chopped
1½ teaspoons sea salt flakes
2 small red chillies, finely chopped
2½ tablespoons finely chopped ginger
3 teaspoons ground cumin
1½ teaspoons curry powder
1 teaspoon ground coriander
¼ teaspoon ground cinnamon
2 teaspoons sweet Hungarian paprika
1 teaspoon smoked paprika
2.25 litres water or homemade chicken stock (see page 210)
juice of 2–3 limes (or substitute lemon juice), to taste
sea salt flakes, extra

- Thoroughly wash and drain both lots of lentils separately. To do this, I usually put them in a big fine sieve and swish them around in lots of cold water, changing the water regularly. Initially the water will be cloudy, particularly with the orange lentils, but after a few goes it will clear. While they're in the sieve, stir the lentils around to check for any little bits of gravel or dirt as they're notoriously gritty.
- Divide the oil evenly between two medium-sized saucepans then warm them over medium heat. Divide the onion, garlic and salt evenly between the pans and cook for 10 minutes, stirring them from time to time. Now divide the chilli, ginger, cumin, curry powder, coriander, cinnamon, sweet Hungarian paprika and smoked paprika between the pans. Cook, stirring constantly, for 3 minutes or so to bring out the fragrance of the spices.
- Now tip all the red lentils into one pan and all the puy-style lentils into the other. Mix them in well and cook, stirring occasionally, for another few minutes. Divide the water or stock evenly between the pans. Increase the heat to high and bring it to the boil. Once it's bubbling merrily, reduce the heat to low and simmer the soups gently, partially covered, for about 25 minutes until the lentils are very soft (the puy-style lentils may take longer to soften).
- While the soups are cooking, bring a small saucepan of water to the boil and cook the extra spoonful of washed puy-style lentils for 15–20 minutes until the lentils are tender to the bite but retain their shape. Drain them and set them aside.
- When both soups are ready, cool them slightly then purée them (ideally, use a stick blender for this so you can do it all in the pans). Add the lime or lemon juice and extra salt to taste – it's worth fiddling with this a bit to get the balance just right.
- To serve, pour each batch of soup into a large jug. Now pour from both jugs simultaneously into each bowl – I know this sounds a bit fiddly but it's easy to do. Try to pour each on opposite sides of the bowl so they show a clear line of separation where they meet. Sprinkle the cooked lentils over the top.

PUY LENTILS . . .

These lovely grey–green lentils are a French variety now being grown in Australia (here they are labelled as 'puy-style' lentils). They have a terrific earthy flavour and tend to keep their shape more than other lentils – not that that is important in this case!

20th April

We have a huge cupboard in the garage where I store all the really 'serious' cookware that's just too cumbersome to put elsewhere. Last night, when I was out there rummaging for some platters to serve dinner on, the loveliest thing happened. As I pulled out a pile of platters a dear little green frog popped up from underneath one – goodness knows how he had managed to find his way there, but he looked perfectly at home. I'm pleased to say he is even more so now, as we've put him in the front garden by the pond where a number of frogs live, so hopefully our nightly chorus will have a new voice added to it.

I am sitting here writing this wearing my gardening clothes in the rather forlorn hope that the weather will improve. I managed to get half an hour in earlier, but the heavens have opened again and I suspect we're in for a very wet Sunday afternoon. The upside is that it's good cooking weather so I shall console myself by baking a cake for afternoon tea, and I know exactly what cake it will be: a buttery lemon and almond cake soaked in a tangy lemon syrup.

Almond & Lemon Syrup Cake

SERVES 10–12

1¼ cups (185 g) plain flour
1½ teaspoons baking powder
¼ teaspoon salt
1 cup (220 g) caster sugar
200 g marzipan, cut into smallish chunks
5 large (70 g) eggs
280 g unsalted butter, at room temperature
finely grated zest of 3 large lemons
¾ teaspoon almond essence
1½ teaspoons vanilla extract
flaked almonds, for topping, optional
icing sugar, for dusting, optional
thick cream or lemon-scented cream (see page 188), to serve

continued next page

For those of you who don't like marzipan, please don't be put off by its inclusion in this recipe – it really provides more of a background note and gives a lovely, delicate almond flavour to this quick and simple cake.

All modesty aside, this has all the hallmarks of the perfect cake: it's quickly whizzed up in a food processor; it keeps well for up to 5 days (if anything the flavour improves after a day or two); it's moist and has a plush, velvety crumb; it freezes like a dream; and it's versatile – effortlessly making the transition from a pristine, 'proper' afternoon tea-type cake to a beautiful and luscious dessert cake. I love it simply with a spoonful of cream, and if that cream is lemon-scented so much the better.

- Preheat your oven to 170°C. Butter a 23 cm springform tin, line the base with buttered baking paper, then dust the tin with flour. Set it aside.
- To make the cake, put the flour, baking powder and salt into the bowl of a food processor fitted with the steel blade. Whiz them together for about 20 seconds, so they're thoroughly mixed, then tip them into a bowl. Now add the caster sugar and marzipan chunks to the processor, and whiz them together until the two are thoroughly pulverised. (Sometimes the marzipan sticks to the blade, so you may have to stop the machine a few times and carefully dislodge any bits that do.) Add the eggs to the processor bowl and whiz them into the marzipan sugar for 1 minute. Now scatter the butter chunks on top and whiz them in too for 40 seconds or so until the mixture becomes thick and creamy. Don't be alarmed if it looks quite liquid-y or even slightly curdled at this stage – that's just as it should be. Add the lemon zest, almond essence and vanilla extract and whiz briefly. Now tip in the reserved flour ›

LEMON SYRUP

⅔ cup (150 g) caster sugar
zest of 2 lemons, cut into 1 cm wide strips
½ cup (125 ml) lemon juice, strained
1 cup (250 ml) water

BY THE WAY . . .

If you want to gild the lily, serve the cake with a smattering of berries in summer, or tender vanilla-scented poached rhubarb in winter.

mixture, and pulse it in with quick on-off bursts of the processor, until the mixture is just combined – don't overdo it or the cake may end up being a tad tough.

- Scrape the batter into the prepared tin, and gently smooth it out. At this stage, I quite often sprinkle a thick layer of flaked almonds over the top. Bake the cake for 55–60 minutes until it feels softly springy when gently pressed in the middle, or when a fine skewer inserted into the centre comes out clean. Remove the cake to a rack and let it settle for 10 minutes. Release the sides of the tin, and gently invert the cake onto the rack. Sit another rack on top, and turn the cake again so it's right-side up. Leave it to cool completely.
- While the cake is cooling, make the syrup. To do this, put all the syrup ingredients into a medium-sized saucepan over high heat. Stir them until the sugar dissolves, then stop stirring and bring the syrup to the boil. Let it bubble fairly rapidly for 10–12 minutes, or until the mixture looks thicker and more 'syrupy', then turn off the heat and set it aside to cool.
- To serve, transfer the cake to a platter or cake stand and dust it with icing sugar if you like. Serves slices with a dollop of lemon-scented cream and some lemon syrup, making sure you get a few curls of zest on each plate too. (Alternatively, you can pour syrup over each slice, in which case don't dust the cake with the icing sugar.) Serve any leftover syrup separately.

Lemon-Scented Cream

1 cup (250 ml) thickened cream
2 tablespoons icing sugar or icing sugar mixture
3 teaspoons very finely grated or chopped lemon zest

I use this lemon-scented cream with lots of desserts and cakes. It's ever so easy to make and adds another dimension to whatever it's being served with – be it cake or something as simple as a bowl of lightly sugared strawberries or peaches. It's lovely made with lime, orange or tangelo zest too.

- Put the cream, icing sugar and zest in a small saucepan over low heat. Bring the mixture very slowly to just below boiling – there should be tiny bubbles forming around the edge of the pan. Turn off the heat, cover the pan and leave the cream to cool.
- Once it reaches room temperature, pour the cream into a container, cover it tightly and put it in the fridge for a few hours or overnight. When you're ready to use the cream, strain it through a fine sieve into a chilled bowl and whip it to soft peaks. (If you find the cream has thickened considerably overnight, you may need to use the back of a spoon to help push it through the sieve.) Pile it into a serving bowl and it's ready to go.

21st April

When I went for a walk this morning there was a huge bank of cloud over the escarpment – it looked just like a taller range of mountains rearing up behind the cliffs, and I wondered if it might be raining up the valley. There's a quite a breeze here, which is lovely as it has blown any cloud away and feels as though it will dry things out a bit. Such a treat after the sogginess of the last few months.

I seem to be finding green tree frogs everywhere at the moment. There were two more in the garage again this morning – one nestling very happily in a cup, and the other under the garage door. I have set them both back with the others in the garden and hope they will be fine. Goodness me, at this rate we shall have a veritable orchestra of them down by the pond!

Having said that, we do have to keep a very sharp eye on them, as cane toads have well and truly taken up residence in this region. I hate killing anything, and we do it in the most humane way possible, but they cause such destruction of the other wildlife that there is no alternative. Sometimes I feel we are fighting a losing battle: I have seen whole hillsides come alive with tiny cane toads after a few days of good solid rain – so much so that the land literally seems to heave with them.

On a brighter note, we have just come back from a long walk through the fields that belong to the farm at the end of the road, and from the dam in the middle came the heartening chorus of a family of frogs (quite different from the song of cane toads). We often stride out on these beautiful autumn afternoons as it's one of the best times of year here – there's a real nip in the air and the hills seem so blue and close in the clear, cool light. Before we head off, if I'm organised (which I'm certainly not always, but fortunately am today) I leave a casserole bubbling away in the oven. There's nothing quite like returning home with glowing cheeks and a hearty appetite to the wonderful savoury aroma of red wine, onions and herbs wafting through the house. The lovely thing is that there is little else to do once we're back except boil some potatoes to mash (soft polenta is good too, but it just doesn't wash with my mob – they're potato lovers from way back) and steam some beans or make a green salad to go with it.

An Autumn Casserole of Lamb Forequarter Chops with Red Wine & Thyme

SERVES 4

1½ tablespoons red wine vinegar
750 ml fruity red wine (shiraz or merlot work well)
2 bay leaves
5 large cloves garlic, very finely sliced
10 thyme sprigs (not lemon thyme)
8 lamb forequarter chops
⅓ cup (80 ml) olive oil, or more as needed
about ⅔ cup (100 g) plain flour
6 large brown onions, finely sliced
1–2 teaspoons sea salt flakes, or more to taste
freshly ground black pepper
fresh bay leaves or thyme sprigs, to garnish

As you may have noticed by now I'm a bit of a lamb-chop girl. It doesn't really matter what sort, I love them all – loin for grilling, neck chops for a good Irish stew and large forequarter chops for dishes like this, where long, gentle cooking brings out their succulent best. It's a super casserole with simple flavours and not too many of them – just my cup of tea. On more than one occasion (like today) I haven't had time to marinate the chops overnight and have simply begun the recipe from frying them, using the red wine marinade only at the point it is poured over them before they go into the oven. I must say it works very well, so don't let the marinating time stop you from trying this.

If you don't have a flameproof casserole to cook this in, just sauté the chops and onion mixture in a large frying pan, then transfer them and the marinade to a casserole dish to go into the oven.

- In a container that will fit the chops comfortably, mix together the vinegar, red wine, bay leaves, half the sliced garlic and 5 thyme sprigs. Add the chops, making sure they are submerged in the wine, then cover them tightly and refrigerate the container overnight.
- The next day, remove the chops from the marinade (but hang on to it as you will need it later) and pat them dry with paper towels.
- Gently warm half the oil in a flameproof cast-iron casserole dish (I use a medium-sized, deep Le Creuset casserole for this) over low-ish heat. Shake two or three chops at a time in a bag with the flour so they're well coated in it. Add however many chops will fit comfortably in a single layer in the pan and fry them for 2–3 minutes each side or until they're speckled brown. Remove them to a plate and continue flouring and cooking the remaining chops in the same way. You will find as you do this that some of the flour will come off the meat into the pan – it tends to burn easily so you will have to adjust the heat as you go to stop this happening. (If the flour has blackened, use some tongs to hold a wad of paper towel and swish it around the pan to wipe away the worst of it – if you do this, you may well have to add a bit more oil to continue cooking the chops.)
- When all the chops are browned, add 2 more tablespoons of oil to the dish and warm it over low heat. Add the onion and remaining garlic and cook, stirring them occasionally, for 12–15 minutes until they're pale golden.
- Meanwhile preheat your oven to 175°C and strip the leaves from the remaining thyme sprigs.

- When the onions are done, scoop most of them out, leaving just a thin layer over the base of the dish. Now add a layer of chops, more onion and more chops, and finally a layer of onion, seasoning the layers with salt and pepper and sprinkling them with the thyme leaves as you go. Increase the heat and pour the reserved marinade over the top. Once the liquid is gently bubbling, turn off the heat, press a sheet of baking paper onto the surface, then cover with a lid and transfer the dish to the oven.
- Cook the lamb for 2 hours. Lift the dish out of the oven and leave it to settle for 10 minutes or so. After this time, remove the lid and paper and blot up any excess oil floating on the surface with paper towels. You can transfer everything to a warm serving dish, or clean up the sides of the casserole dish and serve it in this. Garnish it with a few fresh bay leaves or thyme sprigs.

22nd April

I've read that at dusk magpies will often sit on a branch and warble their way through the sounds they have heard that day, apparently even down to things like mimicking a barking dog. I'm often reminded of that when I have nights that I think of as my 'magpie memory' nights. I suspect we all have them. For no reason at all I will wake in the middle of the night and lie there, sifting and sorting my way through the events of the day – good, bad and indifferent. It's not exactly something I welcome as I would much rather be asleep, but these things happen and there is not much to be done for it.

Last night, to break the loop, I ended up re-working our plans for the veggie garden and got so carried away that I couldn't wait for morning, so I could get out and see if what I was thinking would actually be feasible . . . and to make a much-needed cup of tea – there is nothing quite like it to restore body and soul, is there?

23rd April

A glorious day has dawned – cool, bright and crystal clear. What is it about the air some days that makes everything seem so sharp and defined, as though it has been etched against the sky? The breeze is stiff again and a flock of ibis are wheeling over the valley, riding the thermals higher and higher. They look so graceful with their wings spread wide to catch the currents.

We called out to see some dear friends who live along the valley and when we arrived were greeted by the sight of the exquisite passionfruit flowers in the photo. The vine was draped all over the shed and I have taken some cuttings to see if I can get it to grow here.

When I was potting them later I heard a familiar chattering by one of the bird baths, and when I looked was delighted to see a baby white-eared monarch swaggering up and down along the rim, bossily waving his tail about and chattering at the other birds to stay away while he bathed in peace. They're quite rare and very endearing little bundles of fluff. I do hope he stays for a bit, as he looks far too young to be out in the world on his own.

24th April

Gosh, market day comes around quickly, and our weekly visit is one of the things I so love about living here. There are always new things, and today's surprise was that we now have not one, but two local cheese-makers. Between them they make a wide range of cheeses and we've stocked up on a wonderfully pungent washed-rind cheese, a small disc of 'white' cheese with a lovely mushroomy aroma and camembert-like crust, a streaky blue, and a jar of labneh balls bathed in olive oil. All in all, a real bonanza!

Risoni with Saffron & Lemon

SERVES 6–8

salt, for cooking
2 generous pinches of saffron threads
30 g unsalted butter
1 heaped tablespoon very, very finely chopped onion
1 small clove garlic, peeled and squashed
160 ml cream
4 fresh bay leaves
500 g risoni
sea salt flakes and freshly ground black pepper
finely grated zest of 1 medium-sized lemon
2 tablespoons lemon juice, or more to taste
fresh bay leaves, to garnish, optional

RISONI OR RISOTTO?

I like serving this with osso buco (see my version on page 206), as it's a bit of a surprise take on its classic accompaniment of risotto alla Milanese or saffron risotto. Using risoni (rice-shaped pasta) makes it look similar, but there is that delicious surprise when you take your first bite and realise it's not rice. The trick is not to overcook the risoni initially, otherwise it will be a bit gluggy (don't worry if it is, it still tastes great!).

This is a lovely dish – simple to make but very effective and just a bit different. I got the idea for it from Geraldene Holt's terrific *Complete Book of Herbs*. I've tweaked it somewhat, but credit is due to her for the original.

- Preheat your oven to 150°C.
- Bring a large saucepan of water to the boil for cooking the risoni. Salt it well once it is boiling.
- Meanwhile, sit the saffron threads in a small ovenproof dish, and warm them gently in the oven for 3 minutes or so. Crush them a little, then tip them into a small heatproof bowl or jug, and stir in 2 tablespoons very hot water. Set aside to infuse, stirring the mixture occasionally. (If you do this even further ahead of time, the saffron flavour will be stronger.)
- Melt the butter in very large, heavy-based frying pan over medium–low heat. (If you don't have a big frying pan, it's best to make this recipe in two smaller ones, dividing the ingredients equally between each pan. Alternatively, if you only need enough risoni for four people as a side dish, halve the quantities and make it in one pan.)
- Add the onion and garlic to the frying pan and cook them, stirring regularly, for 4 minutes or so until they're tender and translucent. Now add the saffron mixture, cream and bay leaves. Cook them gently for 3 minutes, stirring often.
- In the meantime, add the risoni to the boiling water. Give it a good stir, and return the water to the boil. Cook the risoni for about 4 minutes, or until it is half-cooked (fish a few grains out and bite them to be sure). Drain it in a fine sieve or colander, reserving about 2½ cups of the cooking water (you probably won't need all this water, but I prefer to have a bit extra rather than find I don't have enough when I need it later on).
- Tip the drained risoni into the frying pan with the onion mixture. Cook it, stirring regularly, for another 4–5 minutes (depending on the heat it might take a bit longer still). Dribble in some of the risoni cooking water from time to time as the mixture absorbs it and starts to look a bit dry when you scrape your spoon across the base of the pan (it really is just like cooking a classic risotto).
- Try a little to check whether the risoni is ready – it should be tender but still have a bit of body to it. Add salt, pepper, lemon zest and juice. Taste a spoonful and add more lemon juice or salt if necessary. Tip the risoni into a warm bowl, grind on a bit more pepper and garnish with bay leaves (or even a few fine strands of lemon zest).

27th April

I've been chortling with laughter. It all started when I heard a commotion by one of the bird baths earlier and went around to check what was happening. Two rainbow lorikeets had discovered it and the other birds were trying, without success, to shoo them off. I don't think I've ever seen two birds look quite so sodden and bedraggled. They soaked themselves for so long that when they finally wanted to fly away, they could hardly get off the ground because their feathers were heavy with water.

While I was there I picked some bay leaves – gosh, I love their spicy fragrance. This lot are destined for another batch of risoni that I'm going to serve with slow-cooked veal shin in red wine (see page 206).

28th April

There was great excitement this morning. Clive came into the office to check on something and as I looked up to talk to him a movement outside the window caught my eye. Lo and behold, a rather large yellow-faced whip snake was poised on a pile of mulch we haven't got around to spreading in the garden bed. He lay there basking in the sun for ages, and then in an impossibly sinuous movement, glided off through the garden. Fascinating as it is to see one, I'm rather hoping it was a temporary visit! I am just so glad I didn't spot it when I was gardening yesterday just near where it lay.

I must admit that, despite numerous encounters during our seven years here, I still find the snakes a challenge. I've certainly got more used to them, but there is something almost primal about my reaction to seeing one.

29th April

Gosh it's beautiful today, if somewhat nippy. The air was incredibly crisp and clear earlier when I was out walking. I hate to say it, but it was just before dawn – I'm a real morning person and my friends and family groan in disbelief that I'm up and about at this hour. I can't help it. I love the stillness and peace – there's hardly a sound until the birds set up their dawn chorus.

My timing was perfect today as I arrived at the crest of the hill into town just as the sun's rays were creeping over the horizon. I watched the fingers of sunlight move up the valley until everything was bathed in the incredible clarity of that golden early-morning light. It was one of those truly blessed moments of grace and complete contentment. By the time I got home a brisk wind had sprung up and my fingers had started to tingle with the cold. I know lots of people loathe wind but I love this weather. It's so invigorating, and it just says 'comfort food' to me so I shall cook up a batch of soup for lunch. I can think of nothing nicer.

Watercress, Leek & Potato Soup

SERVES 4–6

As you read through this book you may notice that watercress turns up time and again. I love its lively peppery flavour, which really shines through in this elegant pale green soup. When we had it for lunch I served it with some leftover sweet potato, cheese and thyme soda bread (see page 277) on which we squashed ripe avocado. The flavours and textures all worked so well together and the colours looked beautiful. Just one thing: as is the case with so many recipes, you need to taste the soup once it's made and adjust the flavours to suit you. It's particularly important here as the flavour of the cress can vary considerably – sometimes it tastes quite intense and earthy, at other times (especially if it's hydroponically grown), it's mild and I often find I need to add a little more at the end.

75 g unsalted butter
3 medium-sized leeks, trimmed, halved and well washed
400 g potatoes, peeled, quartered and cut into 5 mm chunks
about 700 g watercress (3–4 big bunches)
1.25 litres homemade chicken stock (see page 210)
3 teaspoons sea salt flakes, or more to taste
2 tablespoons lemon juice, or more to taste
⅓–½ cup (80–125 ml) cream, plus extra to serve
small watercress sprigs, extra, to serve
fine lemon wedges, to serve
freshly ground black pepper
soft goat's cheese, to serve, optional

- Melt the butter in a nice big saucepan over low heat. When it is bubbling gently add the leek and potato and cook them, stirring occasionally, for 10 minutes.
- Meanwhile, thoroughly wash the watercress and trim away the roots. Reserve about a third of the cress and add the remainder to the saucepan. Swish it around to coat it in the buttery leek mixture – it will wilt as you do. Now pour in the chicken stock and add the salt. Increase the heat and bring the mixture to the boil.
- Once it's boiling, reduce the heat so the soup bubbles gently but steadily. Cook it for about 25 minutes or until the potato chunks are tender. To check, squash one or two pieces against the side of the pan – they should feel soft and disintegrate easily (although if the potatoes are waxy you may find they are a bit more resistant). When they are tender, remove the pan from the heat.
- Now purée the soup. (Ideally, do this with a stick blender – it's so much easier and less messy to purée soup in the pan than going through all the business of ladling it into a blender and puréeing it in batches.) When it's smooth (it will have lots of tiny flecks of watercress), pour in the lemon juice and cream, then add the reserved raw watercress. Give it another burst with the blender to purée the cress. The colour will become noticeably greener and fresher.
- Finally, taste the soup and adjust the flavours to suit you. I often add a bit more salt or lemon juice, and occasionally if the cress is mild, another handful or two of raw cress and purée it again.
- Reheat the soup briefly if necessary, then ladle it into warm bowls. Serve with a trickle of cream and top with a sprig or two of watercress, a lemon wedge, a touch of black pepper and a little goat's cheese, if liked.

A BIT OF CRUNCH . . .

I must admit I rather like chopping up a few raw watercress stalks and sprinkling them in the bottom of my soup bowl before ladling in the hot soup. The heat of the soup wilts them slightly but they retain a rather nice crunch, which is a lovely contrast to the smooth soup.

MAY

1st May

What a breathtakingly beautiful morning. Earlier on, the market was humming – everybody was out and about enjoying the sunshine and stocking up for the week ahead. You could almost smell the change of seasons in the air as the stalls were awash with all sorts of late-autumn treats: vivid green peas and creamy heads of cauliflower nestled alongside fat bunches of flat-leaf parsley and small, but very sweet, mandarins.

As soon as I see produce like this I find my mind is off and running, trying to decide what to do with it all. I think it's just the way cooks' minds work, don't you? I love the way we're immediately sifting and sorting combinations of ingredients to put together. Almost without realising it, in our heads we're balancing sweet, sour, salty and sharp tastes with crunchy, soft, chewy, crisp textures – it's a wonderful process, and is one of the things I love most about cooking. I'm sure it's why it takes me an inordinately long time to go around the market, as I keep heading off on tangents when something catches my eye, and then I see something else to go with it, and so it goes on . . .

I've already decided on what to do with the cauliflowers. I've been toying with the idea of making a lemony cauliflower salad for ages, combining the curd-like heads with chunks of soft goat's cheese and sharp little ligurian olives, so now is my chance to do so (see page 203). And inevitably another treat will be cauliflower cheese for Sunday night's dinner – simple, satisfying and just the thing after a hard day's work in the garden. I probably shouldn't admit to this, but it's usually eaten on trays on our laps while we watch whatever period drama happens to be unfolding on the ABC. I'm sure it wouldn't taste quite the same if we were to eat it at the table!

Cauliflower Cheese

SERVES 2 HUNGRY GARDENERS OR 4 AS A SIDE DISH

It seems a bit funny to be giving you a recipe for cauliflower cheese, as you probably have your own. But having mentioned it, I feel I should put it in here. It's one of our favourite stand-bys in winter – if peas are in season we have it with a bowlful of them and some big flat mushrooms that have been drizzled with olive oil and roasted in a hot oven until their juices are bubbling. Not exactly a gourmet dinner, but very comforting and delicious. By the way, a little flat sauce whisk is ideal for making roux-based sauces like this, as it gets right into the corners of the pan and helps prevent the sauce from catching and burning.

60 g unsalted butter
⅓ cup (50 g) plain flour
2 cups (500 ml) cold milk
180 g good tasty cheese, grated
30 g freshly grated parmesan (or grana), plus a little extra to serve, optional
sea salt flakes and freshly ground white pepper
squeeze of lemon juice
1 medium-sized cauliflower, cut into large florets

- Melt the butter in a medium-sized saucepan over low–medium heat. When it has melted and is gently bubbling, tip in the flour. Cook the roux (as this mixture of butter and flour is called), stirring pretty much constantly, for about 5 minutes. This is where that sauce whisk comes in handy, as it allows you to completely cover the bottom of the pan and get right into the corners where the roux can stick and burn.
- Add the milk all at once, and allow the mixture to come to the boil. Whisk the sauce regularly during this time to prevent it scorching or becoming lumpy. Don't worry if a few lumps appear initially – they should whisk out once the sauce has boiled.
- Once it starts to bubble, reduce the heat so there is a slow but steady plop, plop, plop of bubbles. Cook, stirring regularly, for 10–15 minutes until the sauce is thick and smooth. Taste a little to check that it doesn't taste floury – if it does, cook it a bit longer. When it's done, it should have a gentle, milky flavour.
- Turn off the heat and add the two cheeses, whisking them in until the sauce is smooth. Taste it again and add salt and pepper if it needs it, plus a good squeeze of lemon juice to 'brighten' the flavour. If you're not using the sauce straight away, press a sheet of baking paper onto the surface to stop it forming a skin, then cover the pan with a lid. Give it a good stir before you use it.
- Meanwhile, cook the cauliflower. I usually steam the florets until they are just tender, but still have a bit of bite to them. If you prefer boiling them, by all means do so.
- Truth be told, if it's just us, when the cauliflower is ready I drain it, scoop the florets onto our plates and spoon an unseemly amount of sauce over the top, finishing off with a good grinding of black pepper. However, if you want to be a little more refined about things, you can scoop the florets into a lightly buttered ovenproof dish, pour the sauce over the top, and sprinkle on the extra parmesan. It can then go under a hot grill to brown the top, or you can pop it into a preheated 190°C oven for 15 minutes or so, until a golden crust forms.

Cauliflower, Feta & Preserved Lemon Salad

SERVES 6–8

I'm pleased to say this salad worked a treat. The colours are so soft and subtle and the tangy preserved lemons and bite of the cheese are a lovely foil to the crisp florets. Ligurian olives are the ones to use here – small and black, they have a lovely buttery olive flavour and tiny stones. The salad would also be divine served as antipasto, with a few curls of prosciutto on the side. (By the by, if you would rather not use anchovies, try this with the lemon-pressed oil dressing on page 300.)

- Before you start the dressing, put a large saucepan of water on to boil for cooking the cauliflower (or you can cook it in a steamer, if you prefer).
- The easiest way to make the dressing is to put all the ingredients in a blender and whiz them all together until the dressing is smooth. Taste it, and adjust the flavours to suit you – if you are one of my mob who loves anchovies, you may well add another anchovy or six! You can also make the dressing by putting the anchovies and preserved lemon in a bowl and squashing them with the back of a spoon to make a paste; once that's done, whisk in the remaining ingredients. Pour the dressing into a large bowl and set it aside.
- Give the cauliflower a good wash, as little snails and slugs love to nestle inside it. Break, or cut, it into small florets. Once the water in the saucepan is boiling, salt it well then tip in the florets. Cook until the cauliflower is just tender, but still has a bit of bite – this should take about 8 minutes or so, depending on the size of the florets. It's best to slightly undercook them, as they will continue to cook a little in the dressing as they cool down.
- As soon as they are ready, drain the florets in a colander. Give them a really good shake to remove any extra water so it doesn't dilute the dressing – if they still seem a bit wet, tumble them into a thick clean tea towel and wrap them in that for a minute or so to absorb the excess moisture. Tip the cauliflower into the bowl with the dressing and gently mix the two together. Leave to cool, turning the florets about in the dressing every now and then.
- Just before serving, mix in most of the olives, preserved lemon rind, feta and rocket, reserving a little of each for garnishing. Pile the salad up into a bowl and sprinkle the reserved bits and pieces over the top. Finish off with a good grinding of black pepper.

just over 1 kg cauliflower (you need about 1 kg trimmed florets)
16–20 ligurian olives
2–3 tablespoons very finely sliced preserved lemon rind
180 g good-quality feta (goat's feta marinated in olive oil is particularly good)
2 big handfuls of small rocket leaves
freshly ground black pepper

DRESSING

1–2 anchovy fillets, or more to taste
1–2 teaspoons finely chopped preserved lemon rind
½ cup (125 ml) lemon-pressed extra virgin olive oil
2 tablespoons extra virgin olive oil
sea salt flakes, to taste
¼ teaspoon sugar
1–2 tablespoons lemon juice

2nd May

If you read my last book, *Mix & Bake*, you will know that I have rather a fetish for tea cosies, and it certainly hasn't abated in the intervening years. In fact if anything it has been allowed to flourish, blessed as we are to live in an area where selling all sorts of knitted paraphernalia is one of the principal ways of fund-raising – which is why I'm now the proud owner of three more cosies to add to my ever-expanding collection.

It all started off innocently enough this morning when I popped into town to pick up some bits and pieces for dinner, but I came back with rather more than I'd bargained for. The ladies from the local St Vinnies had set up a street stall and I happened by just as they were unpacking the most wonderful hand-knitted tea cosies. Before you could say 'Jack Robinson' I'd bought three – as you do! The one that has really taken my fancy reminds me of a hat that I remember seeing the Queen Mother wearing. It has a band of gorgeous crocheted flowers around the crown and is so quirky and divine that I've been walking around with it on my head, wondering if I could perhaps turn it into a beanie for winter! Thank heavens no-one can see me.

I also managed to find room in my basket for three pretty crocheted coat hangers, two jars of rosella jam, some mustard pickles and half a dozen scones to go with the jam. All in all, it was a very successful trip!

(When we were shooting, Rodney happened upon my tea cosy cache and insisted on taking a pic of them. I didn't dare confess I had even more tucked away . . .)

3rd May

The most extraordinary sight greeted me this morning when I went outside. For days we've watched a golden orb weaver spider spinning a web from one of the lemon trees to the jasmine that climbs up the wall. It's an incredible feat, especially when you catch sight of it at just the right angle and can see the intricately woven strands glistening in the sunlight. I've narrowly missed it a few times when I've been head down on a mission, but as it turns out, one of our resident male red-brow finches wasn't quite so lucky.

He must have flown into the web only minutes before I arrived, for I rounded the corner to be greeted by the sight of him firmly enmeshed in it and becoming more so as he struggled to escape. The web was so strong that he couldn't break free, so he was just hanging there in mid-air.

I managed to disentangle him as best I could, being mindful that it's not a good idea to handle wild birds as it stresses them terribly, but there really wasn't much choice as he was firmly trapped. I set him down on the grass and was relieved to see him flap away under a bush and start grooming his feathers. I don't know quite how he got the sticky strands off, but when I checked a short time later he had gone, thank goodness.

4th May

A small green tree frog has become my writing companion these last two weeks. As I sit here tap-tap-tapping away, he has made his home at the top corner of my window, and peers in at me as I work. Each day I expect him to have moved on, but so far he seems very happy, and it's a real delight to come into the office and see him, for writing is such a solitary occupation and that little bit of companionship is very welcome. He gets to hear all I write, as I tend to sit and read it out aloud . . . goodness only knows what he makes of it!

Oh, but it's chilly tonight. I've just gone around drawing the blinds and as I looked up the valley, I could see Mount Wollumbin (Warning) silhouetted against a cold red sky – it's beautiful, but has that really icy look to it. It's just the sort of night for something warm and comforting, and fortunately I cooked just such a dish on the weekend when I had a bit more time. That all sounds terribly Martha Stewart-ish, doesn't it? But I should add my life is rarely this organised. I just try to do a bit of extra cooking when I can, as it's such a relief to have something delicious on hand during the week when things are hectic. My mum would be proud of me!

So tonight we're having my version of osso buco. I'd been meaning to make it for a while, and a visit to the butcher decided me as when I arrived he had just finished cutting some beautiful veal shins into thick, meaty rounds. This recipe is by no means a classic version: I don't use the traditional sprinkle of gremolata just before it's served (although you can, if you like); I cook the veal in red wine not white; and I use tomatoes in it too – which is like heresy to some cooks! But when all is said and done it tastes rather wonderful, which is the most important thing. If you would like an authentic touch you could always serve it with its classic partner, risotto alla Milanese – a glorious golden risotto infused with saffron; although I must admit I tend to take the easier option and serve it with light and fluffy polenta (see page 290) or risoni with saffron and lemon (see page 194).

Slow-Cooked Veal Shin in Red Wine with Herbs (a sort of Osso Buco)

SERVES 4–6

- ⅓ cup (80 ml) extra virgin olive oil, or more as needed
- 3 large brown onions, finely diced
- 4 large cloves garlic, finely chopped
- 3–4 carrots, finely diced
- 2 tablespoons sun-dried tomato pesto
- ⅓–½ cup (50–75 g) plain flour, for dusting
- 6–8 meaty pieces of veal shin (approx 1.5 kg), cut about 3 cm thick
- 1 × 400 g can diced tomatoes
- 2 cups (500 ml) fruity red wine (I tend to use a shiraz)
- ¼ cup (60 ml) water
- 2 teaspoons sea salt flakes
- freshly ground black pepper
- 1 tablespoon thyme leaves
- 1 tablespoon finely chopped rosemary
- 2 bay leaves
- fresh bay leaves or sprigs, to garnish (or a sprinkle of chopped parsley)

The ideal pan to cook this in is one of those lovely wide, relatively shallow, enamelled cast-iron pans-cum-casseroles that can go from cooktop to oven with ease. They weigh a tonne and are rather expensive, although in the scheme of things they are a good investment as they last a lifetime. That said, all is not lost if you don't have one – I don't either, but it doesn't stop me making this dish. I start off in a large frying pan, then transfer everything to an ovenproof casserole to finish cooking.

Many butchers label thickly cut veal shin as 'osso buco'; if possible, ask them to cut it from the hind legs, as it is usually meatier and more tender. Just one more thing, when you eat this, make sure you scoop the delicious marrow out of the bones – it's the best part.

- Preheat your oven to 165°C.
- Warm half the olive oil in a large heavy-based frying pan (or a large enamelled cast-iron pan) over low–medium heat. Once it's warm, add the onion, garlic and carrot and cook, stirring regularly, for 10 minutes or so until they have softened somewhat and the onion is golden. Spoon in the tomato pesto and cook it, stirring constantly, for another minute or two. Scrape the mixture into a bowl and set it aside.
- Wipe out the pan with some paper towels and return it to medium heat. Add the remaining oil.
- Meanwhile, tip the flour into a sturdy plastic bag. Put two or three pieces of veal in the bag and shake them about to coat them in the flour. Shake off the excess flour and sit the pieces, slightly apart, in the pan – they should sizzle gently and steadily. Repeat with the remaining veal. You may well have to cook it in batches (adding a bit more oil, if necessary) as you don't want to overcrowd the pan or the veal won't brown. Cook the pieces for about 5 minutes until they are well browned, then repeat on the other side. As they are ready, transfer them to a plate.
- Wipe out any excess oil from the pan and return it to medium heat. Tip the onion mixture back into the pan. Now add the canned tomatoes, red wine, water, salt, pepper, thyme, rosemary and bay leaves. Increase the heat and bring the mixture to the boil, stirring vigorously to scrape up any of the lovely caramelised bits that have stuck to the bottom of the pan (they add so much flavour to the final dish). ›

- If you're using an ovenproof pan, you can now just tuck the veal pieces into the pan in a single layer, pushing the vegetables aside a bit to fit them in. If not, carefully transfer the veal pieces and wine mixture to a large casserole dish – ideally one that will fit the meat in a single layer. (If your casserole dish is too small to fit the veal in one layer, it's best to divide everything evenly between two smaller dishes.) Now press a sheet of baking paper on top of the mixture, scrunching it slightly so it fits snugly, and cover tightly with a lid or a double thickness of foil.

- Place in the oven and cook for 2–2½ hours or until the veal is very tender (the meat should be starting to pull away from the bone when it's ready). It's a good idea to check the veal from time to time as it cooks – if it looks too dry, sprinkle in a little more wine or water.

- Carefully remove the dish from the oven and leave it to settle for 5–10 minutes, then check to see if you need to sop up any excess oil from the surface with paper towels. I often serve this straight from the pan at the table, having cleaned up the sides if they look a bit manky, and added a sprig or two of fresh bay leaves. I usually carefully turn the veal pieces over (just be careful if you do this as they are so tender that they're rather fragile and can fall apart), for they tend to look a bit dry, and scoop a spoonful or two of the thick carroty 'sauce' over the top which gives them a lovely gloss. It also looks rather rustic and lovely served on individual dinner plates, or in wide, shallow bowls, beside a little risoni or polenta.

6th May

I often see a family of wood ducks on my walk, and today they were busily foraging by the side of the road. The parents kept a close eye on me as I approached to see if I represented any danger, but as they're accustomed to me now they let me pass by without further ado. And believe me, they can make quite an ado at times, especially when the ducklings are young and on their first outings into the big, wide world. The parents show incredible courage and will fend off even the biggest creatures to make sure they don't get anywhere near their young. They start off by hissing and taking little runs towards whatever disturbs them, and if it continues to do so they will launch into a full-blown attack while herding the ducklings out of danger – it seems that parents are the same whatever species they belong to.

I must admit that often my heart is in my mouth when I see them, as they insist on taking quite leisurely strolls across the road, stopping slap-bang in the middle to check that all's clear. Fortunately, the locals are aware of this propensity and keep an eye out for them; I've even seen traffic, including enormous B-double trucks, banked up on the Pacific Highway to allow a pair of ducks to shepherd their seven ducklings across four lanes of traffic – it doesn't bear thinking about, does it? I do wish they would find a safer route.

7th May

Tonight's sunset is exquisite – the skyline looks like the backdrop for some old-time western movie set. The Nightcap Ranges are black silhouettes against a pale orange glow that gradually dissolves into the indigo of the night sky, with the finest sliver of a new moon floating above. I'm reluctant to go inside but know I need to get weaving if we're to eat tonight.

I'm in the mood for something warming, and I started making some parsnip soup earlier which I'm about to finish off. I must say, I do like a parsnip or two – the early-season ones are sweet and tender and can be turned into a remarkably delicious soup.

Parsnip Soup with Roasted Pecans & Persian Feta

SERVES 8

60 g unsalted butter
2 large leeks, well washed and finely sliced
1.25 kg parsnips (about 8 or 9), peeled and cut into 1.5 cm chunks
2 potatoes, peeled and cut into 1.5 cm chunks
2.25 litres homemade chicken stock (see below)
2–3 teaspoons sea salt flakes, or more to taste
⅔ cup (170 ml) cream
handful of finely sliced roasted pecans, optional
handful of finely sliced kalamata olives, optional

TO SERVE

80 g roasted pecans, thinly sliced crossways
a smidgen of extra virgin olive oil
120 g Persian feta (soft goat's cheese is excellent too)
4–5 kalamata olives, very finely sliced, optional
freshly ground black pepper

OUT OF STOCK?

When I first made this soup I found I didn't have quite enough homemade stock, so I used about 2 cups (500 ml) of water to make up the difference, and it was fine (just thought I'd mention that, in case the same thing happens to you).

I love this silky, satisfying soup, with its subtle ivory, gold and tan tones – they remind me of autumn leaves. And autumn is the time to make this, when the first parsnips are dug from the garden and new-season pecans are dropping from the trees. Before serving, I sometimes stir in a good handful of finely sliced kalamata olives and toasted pecans, and sprinkle a few olive slivers over the top.

- Melt the butter in a very large saucepan over low heat. Add the leek and cook, stirring regularly, for about 8 minutes until it has softened and collapsed a bit. Now tip the parsnip and potato into the pan and swish it around in the buttery leek mixture. Cook the vegetables gently so they don't colour, stirring now and then, for 10 minutes.
- Add the chicken stock and salt to the pan. Increase the heat to high and bring the stock to the boil. As soon as it's boiling reduce the heat to low, cover the pan with a lid, and simmer the mixture (it should bubble gently) for about 40 minutes, or until the parsnip and potato are very tender. I usually squish a few pieces of parsnip against the side of the pan with a wooden spoon to check if they are tender enough – when they are, turn off the heat.
- Blend the soup until it is very smooth. (Ideally do this in the pan with a stick blender, which is a lot less messy than puréeing batches of soup in a regular blender.) Stir in the cream, then taste the soup and add more salt if necessary. Mix in the pecans and olives if you are using them, then warm the soup gently, but don't let it boil.
- To serve, mix the sliced pecans with the olive oil (this gives them a lovely gloss). Ladle the soup into bowls and scatter little pieces of feta into the middle of each bowl. Sprinkle the pecan and olive slivers over the feta, then finish off with a grinding of black pepper and a few tiny drops of olive oil.

SIMPLE CHICKEN STOCK

I don't go to much fuss when I make chicken stock as I like a pure unadulterated chicken flavour. Basically all you need to do is get some chicken carcasses from the butcher (many give them away or sell them cheaply) and put them into a very big saucepan. Add about 1 litre of cold water per carcass, making sure they're completely covered in water – sit a plate on top if necessary to keep them below the surface. Bring the water to the boil, then reduce the heat until the occasional lazy bubble floats to the surface, and cook the stock for a couple of hours, skimming off any froth or scum that comes to the surface. When it's ready, strain the stock into containers, leave it to cool, then cover it tightly and keep it in the fridge if you are using it within 2 days. Otherwise it's best to freeze it – it'll keep well for a couple of months.

9th May

It's a glorious evening. A gentle golden light is casting a soft glow over everything, including the grevilleas outside my window, which are almost luminous with it. And for once all is quiet – the constant chatter of parrots and honeyeaters calling to each other is fading away, leaving only the occasional enquiring trill to see if anybody is about.

It's also time for me to start battening down the hatches, as I can feel the temperature dropping rapidly. No doubt I shall warm up soon enough as I'm about to throw myself into a marathon cooking session. We have visitors arriving for the weekend and I want to get a few things under way so I'm not cooking non-stop while they're here.

One of the dishes I'm making is a lemon-scented flan (which is the Spanish equivalent of a crème caramel). It's such a simple dessert to make, yet there is something extraordinarily special and luxurious about the pristine shimmer of the caramel with the golden, eggy custard beneath. Whenever I make it I wonder why I don't do so more often – I don't know about you, but I find it so easy to forget just how beautiful these familiar dishes can be.

Lemon-Scented Flan

SERVES 8

180 g caster sugar
½ cup (125 ml) water
400 ml milk
550 ml cream
finely grated zest of 2 lemons
1 tablespoon lime or lemon marmalade
4 eggs
5 egg yolks
120 g caster sugar, extra
1½ teaspoons vanilla extract
2 teaspoons lemon juice, strained
1 teaspoon finely grated lemon zest, extra

The only thing that's a bit nerve-racking about making this (at least, it is for me) is turning it out. I hold my breath when I do so, as it often forms a little air lock and the flan refuses to shift from the tin. I've found the best way to tackle this is to do some very gentle probing down the sides of the tin with a fine metal spatula to help loosen the flan and allow some air to seep in and break the vacuum.

Just one thing to keep in mind: be a little bold when you're caramelising the sugar. Allow it to become just that tad darker than you are comfortable with, for it is the ever-so-slightly bitter edge this imparts that gives the flan its character.

- Preheat your oven to 150°C. Line the base of a roasting tin with a folded tea towel (this helps to diffuse the heat when you bake the flan). Sit a 20 cm round cake tin on the tea towel.
- To make the caramel, put the sugar and water in a heavy-based saucepan over high heat. Stir until the sugar dissolves, then stop stirring and bring the mixture to the boil. Allow it to boil, undisturbed, washing down the sides occasionally with a brush dipped in water to remove any sugar crystals that may form. (If you are wondering why you do this, it's because if these crystals stay on the sides they can cause the caramel to candy.) Once the syrup turns a light amber colour, watch it like a hawk – you want it to become a deep rich brown, but not so dark that it burns. ›

A NOTE ON TINS . . .

Make sure you use a regular cake tin for this, rather than non-stick or springform. The caramel will not cling to a non-stick tin, and a springform tin will leak, or water will leak in.

- Once it's ready, pour the caramel into the cake tin. Leave it a few minutes then, using oven gloves to protect your hands, tilt and rotate the tin to coat the base and sides in caramel. Keep swirling the caramel around the sides until it starts to thicken and set. Put the cake tin back in the roasting tin.
- For the custard, put the milk, cream, lemon zest and marmalade in the saucepan you used to make the caramel (don't rinse it out first) and warm it over low heat. Give the mixture a good stir, then heat it until it's very hot but not boiling – as it heats, any caramel that has stuck to the pan dissolves into the milk and this in turn will deepen the flavour of the custard. When it's ready, turn off the heat, cover the pan and leave the milk mixture to infuse for at least 30 minutes.
- In a large-ish bowl, whisk together the whole eggs, egg yolks and extra caster sugar. Slowly pour in the infused milk mixture, stirring constantly but trying not to whisk in too much air. Mix in the vanilla and lemon juice. Strain this mixture through a fine sieve into a jug, then stir in the extra teaspoon of lemon zest. Slowly pour the custard into the caramel-lined cake tin, then use a spoon to skim away any air bubbles that form on the surface.
- Fill the roasting tin with enough hot tap water to come halfway up the side of the cake tin. Put the lot in the oven and cook the flan for about 1 hour, or until the edges are set and the centre wobbles very slightly when you gently jiggle the tin.
- Remove the roasting tin from the oven, then carefully lift out the cake tin and transfer it to a rack. Leave the flan to cool completely in the tin. When it's cool, cover the tin and refrigerate the flan overnight (better still, leave it for 2–3 days as the longer it sits the more the caramel coating dissolves, forming a lovely syrup around the flan when it's turned out).
- Time to un-mould the flan. If the custard part of it is attached to the sides of the tin, carefully run the tip of a knife around the top edge of the flan to loosen it. Now comes the turning-out part I mentioned in my intro . . . take a deep breath and sit a serving dish on top of the cake tin (make sure it has a lip to catch the caramel). Now grasp the edges of the cake tin and the serving dish and quickly flip the whole thing over. All being well, the flan will gently plop onto the dish; if it doesn't, carefully re-invert it, loosen it a little more and try again. Leave it for 10 seconds or so then gently lift off the cake tin. Bravo! There you have it – one beautiful, shiny lemon flan.

Lemon, Leek, Pea & Prosciutto Risotto

MAKES 4 SMALL SERVES

It's funny how your confidence grows as a cook; I always used to find the thought of cooking risotto daunting, as there seemed to be so many rules to follow to make it properly. However, I reached the point where I had to overcome the fear (how could a girl who cooked in an Italian restaurant for years admit to being intimidated by the thought of making risotto?), and the only way to do that was to cook it and keep on cooking it until I was comfortable with the process. Like so many things we avoid, it turned out that it wasn't nearly as difficult as I imagined. Quite the opposite in fact, and I now look on it as a relatively quick and easy dinner at the end of a busy day.

I should preface this recipe by saying that I'm more than happy to take short-cuts when I'm cooking if the results are just as good as going the long way around. However, in the case of risotto, I make an exception. I know it seems easier to use stock made from stock cubes or out of a can or tetra-pack, but a truly good risotto is totally dependent on starting with a well-flavoured, delicious stock (which generally means you have to make it yourself) and good-quality rice. In this case I use chicken stock, which really is a cinch to make and takes only a minute or two of actual work to put together. I tend to make rather a lot and freeze it in 1.5 litre amounts, so I can pull out exactly the quantity I need to make a batch of risotto.

Any leftover risotto makes wonderful arancini – plump little balls of rice and cheese, fried until they're crisp and golden. In fact, I think they are almost better than the risotto itself, so I usually try to make sure we have enough risotto left to make a plateful of these the next day. They're perfect with a simple tomato salad and a bowl of mixed salad greens.

70 g unsalted butter
2 large leeks, well washed and finely sliced
1 large clove garlic, finely chopped
about 1.5 litres homemade chicken stock (see page 210)
200 g arborio or vialone nano rice (see page 4)
2 teaspoons extra virgin olive oil
70 g prosciutto, finely sliced
180 g peas (frozen are fine)
2 tablespoons finely chopped flat-leaf parsley
finely grated zest of 1 lemon
1–2 tablespoons lemon juice, to taste
1–2 tablespoons cream (or a tad more butter)
50 g freshly grated parmesan, plus extra to serve
sea salt flakes
a little sliced taleggio, fontina or fresh goat's cheese, optional
tiny parsley leaves, to garnish

- Melt the butter in a large, preferably deep-sided frying pan over medium heat. Add the leek and garlic and cook, stirring regularly, for 8–10 minutes, or until they are soft and wilted.
- In the meantime, heat the chicken stock in a separate saucepan until it's very hot, but not quite boiling. Reduce the heat so it barely bubbles.
- When the leek mixture is ready, tip the rice into the pan and cook it for a couple of minutes, stirring constantly, so it's slightly toasted and coated in the buttery leek and garlic. Add a ladleful of the hot stock, just so it covers the rice (it will most likely hiss and steam) and cook, stirring regularly, until the rice has absorbed the stock. Add another ladle of stock, and again let it bubble and be completely absorbed by the rice, stirring regularly (the bubbling should be relatively gentle and even over the surface of the rice). I know many recipes say to stir risotto constantly, but it's not entirely necessary – a good stir every 20–30 seconds is fine. Continue to ›

RISOTTO PANS

There are some rather gorgeous pans that are specifically designed for making risotto – I've had my eye on a beautiful copper one for years (which costs the earth, of course!). However, until that day comes, I use a very large, deep-sided, heavy-based frying pan which works beautifully. The heavy base distributes the heat evenly, and the deeper sides allow me to stir away to my heart's content without spilling risotto all over the stovetop.

add the stock, one ladleful at a time, until the rice is done to your liking – the grains should still be slightly firm and the whole mixture should be a bit sloppy and creamy. Just be aware that depending on the rice you use, you may not need all the stock: what you are after is rice that mounds slightly on the plate when you serve it, but slowly collapses on itself. All up, it takes about 18–20 minutes to get to this stage.

- While the rice is cooking, warm the olive oil in a frying pan over medium heat. Add the prosciutto and cook for a minute or so until it is translucent. Add the peas (straight from the freezer is fine) and toss them about until they are heated through and tender – this only takes a few minutes. Remove the pan from the heat and keep warm.
- When the rice is ready, turn off the heat and stir in the parsley, lemon zest, juice, cream, parmesan and salt to taste. Now mix in most of the pea mixture – if the risotto firms up a bit too much with these additions, just add about half a ladleful of stock to loosen it. (Occasionally I mix in slices of taleggio, fontina or little nuggets of fresh goat's cheese at the very end, just before serving the risotto.) Serve in warm pasta bowls, scatter the remaining pea mixture on top and garnish with tiny parsley leaves. Serve with extra parmesan, if liked.

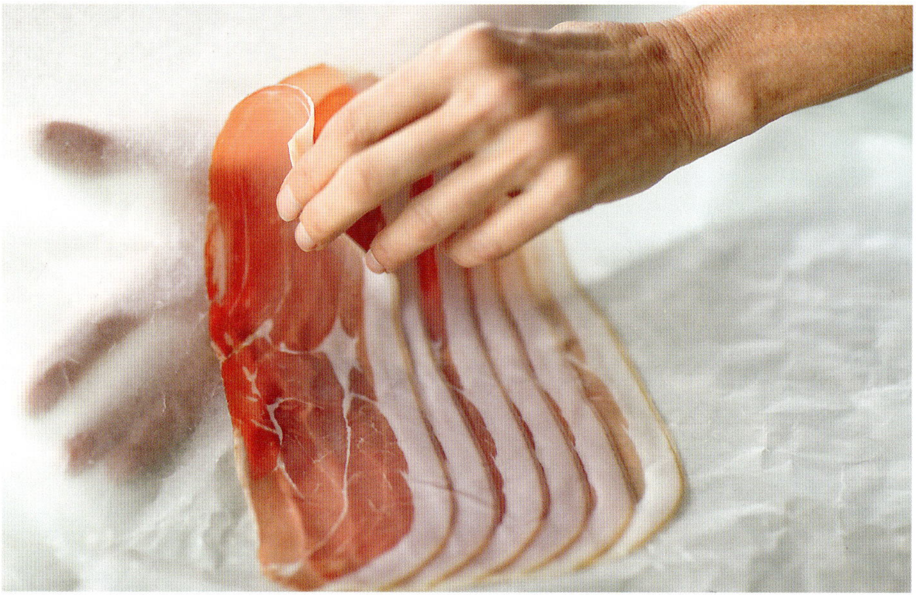

12th May

Well, it's a day of threes again. We were standing outside earlier when three sulphur-crested cockatoos screeched their way across the sky then dropped down low over our house and literally skimmed the tops of our heads – we could actually feel the wind on our faces from the flapping of their wings.

At the same time, three blue-faced honeyeaters were busy foraging in the banksias. They absolutely love them and are guaranteed to be around at this time of year, when the nectar is flowing.

But the third visitor is somewhat of a surprise: I've spent the better part of the morning chasing a very elusive grey and white rabbit around the garden! He's obviously someone's escaped pet and he's having a ball nibbling the sweetest shoots from our newly planted snow peas. He lets us get close enough to feed him with rocket leaves, but as soon as we try to pick him up he's off, with both of us in hot pursuit. It's quite mad and feels like something out of *Alice in Wonderland*!

I'm relieved to say that I eventually tracked down the rabbit's young owner, and between the two of us and a rather large bunch of salad greens, we managed to lure him back into his hutch. I'm delighted to report that both rabbit and owner are doing well.

14th May

During these colder months my marmalade pan is rarely off the stove. Even our smallest citrus trees are laden, and between our own fruit and that of our friends, who generously leave full boxes and baskets on our doorstep, we have a never-ending stream of oranges, lemons, limes, tangelos, grapefruit and mandarins. It's rather wonderful, but at times a little daunting as I feel almost obliged, in that way only cooks can, to preserve this bounty while it lasts. Last year was such a bumper season that at one stage I even contemplated setting up a stall on the roadside as we couldn't possibly eat the amount of oranges we had, and nor could I keep up with the marmalade-making!

That said, I do so enjoy the whole preserving business. I can almost feel marmalade-makers of the past leaning over my shoulder, watching as I rhythmically slice the fruit and tumble the pips out into a square of muslin, just as they did. I so clearly remember watching my mum do the self-same thing, and asking her why she was tying the pips up and leaving them to soak overnight with the fruit. Her explanation that this helps extract the pectin from them, which is what makes the marmalade set, made the whole process seem magical to me then and, I would have to say, it still does today. How extraordinary to take something as simple as fruit, sugar and water and transform them, by some wonderful alchemy, into a jar of potted sunshine.

Orange, Mandarin & Lemon Marmalade

MAKES 5–6 MEDIUM JARS

This recipe may seem a little long-winded, but that is mainly because I want to explain the process of marmalade-making in some detail, rather than because there is anything tricky about it. In fact, once you get the hang of it, you'll find you really don't need the recipe and can make it off the top of your head. See page 165 for guidance on how to sterilise your jars before you begin.

Ideally, as all the old jam-making manuals say, you should use freshly picked, early-season fruit for marmalade as it contains more pectin, but I realise that is not always possible. However, if you can get your hands on citrus from your local farmers' or growers' market, the finished marmalade will certainly benefit.

clean piece of muslin, for the pips
3 large oranges (not navels)
4 mandarins (or tangelos)
2 large lemons
about 2.25 litres cold water (or better still, use equal quantities of freshly squeezed orange or mandarin juice and water)
about 2 kg granulated sugar

- Line a small bowl with a double thickness of muslin.
- Give the fruit a really good scrub before you start. Quarter the oranges and slice them as finely as you can. As you come to the pips, scrape them away and put them into the muslin-lined bowl. Put the orange slices into a very large ceramic or stainless steel bowl. Repeat this with the mandarins and lemons.
- Pour the cool water over the sliced fruit. As I mentioned above, if you are fortunate enough to have heaps of oranges and mandarins, squeeze some and use the resulting juice to replace part of the water that you need – it makes for a much more intensely flavoured marmalade. If you do this, add any pips to the others in the bowl as it's a case of 'the more the merrier' to help set the marmalade.
- Bundle up the pips in the muslin to form a little swag, then tie it tightly with a double thickness of cooking twine to prevent the pips escaping. Dunk it into the bowl of fruit and water, making sure it sits under the surface. Now cover the bowl tightly with plastic film and leave it overnight in a cool spot.
- The next day, pour the fruit and liquid (including the bag of pips) into a very large saucepan – if you are lucky enough to have one, a preserving pan is ideal (see note overleaf). Bring the mixture to the boil over high heat, then reduce the temperature to very low and simmer, uncovered, for 2–2½ hours until the skins are tender.
- After this time, remove the pan from the heat. Now the next bit is a little messy, but essential. First, remove the bag of pips to a small bowl. Press down on the bag with a spoon to extract as much of the liquid as possible, and return this to the pan (you may well notice that the last of this liquid is quite 'gelled'-looking from the pectin in the pips and pith). Now you need to measure the amount of liquid and fruit you have. To do this, have a large heatproof measuring jug at hand and ladle the liquid and fruit from the pan into this. Once it is full, empty it into a large bowl and continue to measure the rest. You should have somewhere around 2.25 litres, but don't worry if it is more or less – it will all work out! ›

- Return the fruit and liquid to the pan, and for every cup (250 ml) of this mixture add 200 g of sugar. For example, if you have 2.25 litres of liquid and fruit you will need 1.8 kg of sugar; 2.5 litres and you will need 2 kg, and so on.

- Put the pan over high heat. Stir the mixture until the sugar has dissolved, then stop stirring and bring the mixture to the boil. You now need to boil it rapidly until it is at setting point. I'm afraid it's hard to be accurate about how long this will take as it depends on a number of factors, such as the pan you use and the amount of pectin in the fruit. It could take anywhere between 25 and 40 minutes.

- As the marmalade gets closer to its setting point, it will start to bubble up in the pan (which is why you need a big pan to start with). It does this alarmingly quickly so it's important to stay close by and adjust the heat to stop it bubbling over. I tend to hover about at this stage, adjusting the heat up or down to keep it at a fairly even, steady boil.

- It's around about now that you need to start checking the marmalade to see if it's set. There are a few ways to do this, but the two I like best, and use in combination, are the classic 'spoon' and 'saucer' tests.

- For the spoon test, all you do is dip a large wooden spoon into the boiling marmalade then lift it up high above the pan and let the marmalade on it drip back in. What you're hoping to see is those last few drops looking quite thick and syrupy, and ideally running together and joining up then falling as more of a 'sheet' than individual drops (however, long fine tails on them will do nicely!).

- For the saucer test, sit two or three saucers in your freezer while the marmalade is cooking. When you think the marmalade is nearly ready, spoon a little of it onto one of the ice-cold saucers and return it to the freezer for 2 minutes, then push your finger through it. If it feels set and the surface wrinkles up a little, it's ready. You may find this doesn't happen first time around; if this is the case just continue boiling the marmalade and check it again after another minute or two. Keep testing it until it's right.

- As soon as it's ready, take the pan off the heat and let the marmalade settle for at least 10–15 minutes. Skim any frothy scum off the top then give it a good stir so the fruit is suspended in it (initially the fruit floats to the top, but as the marmalade cools and thickens, stirring will distribute it evenly through the marmalade). Ladle it into hot, sterilised glass jars. Cover them loosely with a sheet of baking paper to protect them, and leave them to cool completely (this may take 6 hours or more). Remove the paper and seal the jars tightly. Label and date them, then store them in a cool, dry, dark place for up to 8 months.

15th May

Like many people who love to cook, I get a lot of pleasure out of growing some of the herbs that I use. And the nice thing is that it doesn't take much space to grow them. For many years we lived in an old attic apartment, so the only herbs we had lived in tiny pots on a window ledge, yet it was amazing just how many of them thrived; there were always a few sprigs of thyme or oregano to plop in a casserole, or delicate Greek basil leaves to scatter over a salad. Eventually I graduated to a couple of large window boxes on our bedroom windowsill, which were stuffed so full that the perfume wafting in at night made us feel as though we were sleeping in a scented garden. And with our move here, at last I have the delight of a small but 'proper' herb garden. The trouble is that now I can let loose a bit, I do, and tend to get carried away and plant masses of everything. To say we have a glut of herbs at times is somewhat of an understatement! Which is how this recipe came about. With flat-leaf parsley to burn, I remembered reading about a recipe of Peter Gordon's (of Sugar Club fame) for a parsley pesto and thinking how delicious it sounded. I began experimenting to come up with something similar, and this pesto is the result. I love it with the sweet potato, but give it a try with other veggies too – it's remarkably good on all sorts of things.

Roast Sweet Potato with Smoked Paprika, Parsley & Macadamia Pesto

SERVES 8–10

10–12 medium-sized sweet potatoes, peeled
olive oil, for coating
tiny parsley leaves, to garnish

SMOKED PAPRIKA, PARSLEY AND MACADAMIA PESTO

150 g macadamias, roasted
2 cloves garlic, coarsely chopped
½ cup (15 g) coarsely chopped flat-leaf parsley
1 tablespoon smoked paprika
100 g feta, crumbled
150 ml extra virgin olive oil
200 ml olive oil
1–1½ tablespoons lemon juice
sea salt flakes, optional

It fascinates me how in rural areas such as this, we can buy some rather exotic things that would have been unheard of even a short time ago. Recently I was wondering where I was going to find smoked paprika as my stocks were running low, when of all things I walked into a deli in Murwillumbah to find myself spoilt for choice, with not one but three varieties of smoked paprika available. The times are definitely a-changing! There was sweet, hot (which is quite tangy and piquant) and bitter-sweet (probably the most aromatic). I opted for the bitter-sweet, but use what you have to hand – all three would work beautifully in the pesto. By the way, this recipe makes rather a lot, but the quantities can easily be halved.

- Preheat your oven to 220°C. Line two large baking trays first with foil, then with a sheet of baking paper (if you have a very large oven tray the sweet potato may all fit on the one – just make sure it isn't too crowded or it won't colour properly). Set the trays aside.
- Cut the sweet potatoes into largish pieces (I usually get four to six chunks from each one) and spread them in a single layer on the prepared trays. Drizzle a little olive oil over them, then use your hands to mix everything together so the chunks ›

are lightly coated with oil. Put the trays in the oven and roast the sweet potato, turning it carefully once or twice, for 45–50 minutes or until it has lovely dark caramelised edges.

- In the meantime, put the parsley leaves for garnishing in a small bowl and cover them with iced water. Cover the bowl and store it in the fridge until you are ready to serve. This chilly spell will crisp and curl the parsley so it looks really fresh and pretty.
- While the sweet potato is roasting, make the pesto. Put the macadamias, garlic, parsley and smoked paprika in a food processor fitted with a chopping blade and whiz them together to make a coarse paste. Now add the feta and extra virgin olive oil and whiz the mixture again for about 15 seconds. Pour in the olive oil and lemon juice and purée everything for 20 seconds or so, stopping and scraping down the sides once or twice as you go.
- Taste the pesto and, if necessary, add salt and more lemon juice. Scrape the pesto into an airtight container or jar, seal it tightly and store it in the fridge. It keeps well for about 10 days (surprisingly, it freezes rather well too, and can be kept for 2 months or so).
- When the sweet potato is ready, spoon some pesto over it (you won't need it all, but I always make the extra to have on hand for other things) and return the tray to the oven for a minute or so to warm the pesto. Remove the tray and very gently stir the mixture so the sweet potato is coated in pesto. Pile it all into a bowl and decorate it with the parsley leaves. Serve warm or at room temperature.

17th May

The garden is full of birds. We were both stopped in our tracks this morning by the sheer number and variety of them. As we watched, a brown honeyeater and a rainbow lorikeet were jockeying for position in the bird bath, while a tiny scarlet honeyeater darted in and out between splashes; two baby blue fairy wrens settled briefly on top of the lavender, looking somewhat bemused at all the activity around them; a friar bird dangled upside-down in the grevilleas making its peculiar 'dedadelada dedadelada' call; and our usual band of red-brow and double-barred finches were fossicking for seed on the terrace. These lovely creatures give us so much pleasure and we go about our day with huge smiles on our faces. I suspect the current burst of activity is because our crimson callistemons are just starting to flower and the nectar is drawing everyone from near and far.

I remember reading in Simon Barnes' wonderful book, *How to be a Bad Birdwatcher*, about the joy to be had in recognising bird calls without being able to see the actual birds, and I now know exactly what he means. As I sat in my office (which is on the other side of the house to all the activity) I could hear but not see two birds calling this morning and I recognised the song of the blue-faced honeyeaters. It was really lovely to know they were there even though I couldn't see them.

19th May

Mount Wollumbin marks the tide of our days. Sometimes in the early morning it's so wreathed in cloud it's invisible, then unexpectedly, as though a veil has been lifted, the peak appears and floats like an island in a sea of white. Later in the day, it's as clear as a bell, so much so that we can see the trees marching up its flanks and the sheer cliff faces near the summit. By late afternoon it's bathed in a golden glow as the sun sets behind it – the gold gradually turning into spectacular crimson and violet streaks shooting up into a sky that progressively grow softer and more delicate as the light fades. And at the very end of the day, especially when the moon is full, we sit outside in the dark and watch the stars appear above it until it's bathed in their cool light.

20th May

Tomorrow we're doing a big morning-tea fundraiser for the Cancer Council, and I'm delighted to say that I've just put my eighth batch of scone dough mixture in the fridge, ready to bake in the morning. The kitchen and I are both coated in a film of flour; in fact, as I write this, I can see a fine dusting settling onto my keyboard. Everyone else's keyboard disasters seem to involve spilled coffee – in my case it's gummed up with flour!

21st May

Phew! We've just arrived back from the morning tea and it was a great success – such a special thing to be part of. There is a tangible sense of community in all the villages here, and Federal (where the morning tea was held) is no exception. There always seems to be a willing band of volunteers ready to bake cakes, man the tea- and coffee-making facilities and wash up a never-ending stream of cups and saucers.

The tea was held in the lovely old village hall in Federal and, as the weather was fine, we had tables outside on the lawn too. We started bright and early so we could put the finishing touches to the hall and make it look warm and welcoming – and even at that early hour many people arrived unsolicited with flowers for the tables, donations and freshly baked cakes to add to the already impressive array. In one corner there was a special table where those who wished could have their tea leaves read (we're fortunate to have an extraordinarily skilled tea-leaf reader in our midst), and I began baking just before the first arrivals. From that point on, we couldn't keep up with the demand and, despite all the gorgeous cakes, I think I must have baked about 160 scones in just a few hours. It seems there is nothing like a freshly baked scone to go with a cup of tea.

Fluffy Buttermilk Scones

MAKES 18–20

- 2 cups (300 g) self-raising flour
- 2 cups (320 g) wholemeal self-raising flour
- ¼ cup (55 g) caster sugar
- 1 teaspoon salt
- 160 g cold unsalted butter, cut into small chunks
- 200 g sultanas, currants or chopped dates, optional
- 2 cups (500 ml) buttermilk
- flour, for dusting
- milk, for glazing, optional

I published this recipe in my last book, *Mix & Bake*, however as it is the one I use all the time, and as I've had such a wonderful response to the scones every time I make them, I thought it was timely for me to repeat it here. Mind you, I've made them so many times that I could almost do them with my eyes closed now – especially after today's effort! They really do live up to their name and they have a lovely 'wheaty' flavour from the wholemeal flour. My favourite way to eat them is to use lots of big chunks of dates in the dough, and serve them warm with butter and a really good pot of tea. It's a hard-to-beat combination, although a little jam and cream doesn't go amiss either.

- Preheat your oven to 200°C. Dust a sturdy baking sheet with flour and set it aside. (If you don't have a heavy baking sheet, you can use a lightweight one but line it with a double thickness of baking paper so the bottoms of the scones don't burn.)
- Put the flours, sugar and salt into a large bowl. Whisk them together with a balloon whisk for a minute so they're thoroughly combined and aerated. Scatter the little chunks of butter over the top, and use your fingers to rub the butter into the flour mixture until it resembles coarse breadcrumbs. (If you like, you can make this step faster by using a food processor – I certainly do; then just tip the resulting mixture into a big bowl.)
- Add the dried fruit (if using) and toss it about so it's well coated. Now, make a well in the centre of this mixture. Pour in the buttermilk and stir it in very lightly until the mixture starts to come together into a somewhat sticky dough. Turn this mixture out onto a floured board and knead it gently until it's just combined. Pat it out into a 4–5 cm thick round. Dip a scone-cutter or small tumbler into some flour to stop the dough sticking to it, then cut out the scones, dunking the cutter back into the flour between each one. Gently knead together any scraps and cut them again.
- Sit the scones closely together on the prepared baking sheet and either brush the tops with a little milk or dust them very lightly with flour. Put the tray in the oven and bake the scones for about 20 minutes, until they're golden. When they're ready, remove them from the oven and immediately wrap them in a clean tea towel. Leave them for 5 minutes, then serve them with butter or lashings of jam and cream.

22nd May

I had to laugh when Rodney arrived back today for another week of shooting this book. His car was the most extraordinary sight, packed to the gunwales with pans and dishes, old boards, shutters, tins of olive oil, rice and olives for me, props, photographic gear . . . and perched on top (along with his fishing rod, which is a faithful travelling companion) a wonderful pale green laminex-topped table that we have both fallen in love with. It looks as though he stopped at every op shop between Sydney and here!

The house is already turned upside-down as we get ready for another bout of photography. Our house isn't very large, and for the week or so Rodney visits, it literally becomes a photographic studio in which we all just happen to sleep and eat! Fortunately, we're old friends and manage to survive the close quarters. Dinner is more often than not eaten on our laps, as the dining table is covered in dishes and bowls. Not only the dining table, I might add: every spare horizontal surface is laden with 'stuff' that we might happen to need – tea towels, wooden spoons, pots, pans, glasses . . . It's all very mad, but rather wonderful too.

I've prepped all day today for we begin shooting in earnest tomorrow. No matter how many years I've been doing this, I never lose that nervous feeling in my stomach and the fear that it may not all come together. Rodney and I have discussed this and he feels much the same way, which makes me feel a lot better and not quite so silly.

One of the dishes I've been preparing is olive-oil poached salmon and as I have a bit more salmon than I need, we shall have that for dinner tonight.

Salmon Poached in Olive Oil

SERVES 4

1½–2 lemons, very, very thinly sliced
4 salmon fillets (about 180–200 g each), skin on
sea salt flakes
2½ tablespoons of the smallest capers you can find (see page 3)
¼ cup (15 g) chopped flat-leaf parsley
about 2 cups (500 ml) extra virgin olive oil
salsa romesco (see page 236), to serve

This is such an easy way to cook fish, and remarkably good. Although you might imagine that the salmon would taste rather oily, it's surprisingly light and wonderfully moist from its gentle poaching in the oil. The same poaching softens the sharpness of the lemon slices and infuses the salmon with a lovely lemony note. (Although I use salmon in the recipe, I have also poached thick fillets of snapper the same way and they were delicious.)

I tend to serve this with olive-oil mashed potatoes (see page 451) and a simple salad. In this case it's paper-thin slices of fennel and sprigs of peppery watercress dressed with a smidgen of lemon-pressed oil dressing (see page 300) – a made-in-heaven combination with the salmon. And if you can't be bothered to make the salsa romesco to accompany the salmon, then don't; it's a lovely dish with or without it (although I must admit, I do love the vibrancy it adds to the flavours). If you are going to make the salsa, do so before you start cooking the fish.

- Preheat your oven to 125°C.
- Spread half the lemon slices evenly over the base of a ceramic or glass ovenproof dish that will hold the salmon fillets snugly in a single layer. Set the dish aside.

- Pat the salmon fillets dry with paper towels then rub each one with a little salt. Sit them, skin-side down, in the dish with the lemon and sprinkle half the capers over the top. Now overlap the remaining lemon slices down the length of each fillet. Scatter the parsley and remaining capers over the top. Pour in enough oil to entirely cover the fillets (don't worry if the tops of the fillets just break the surface of the oil – they will be fine).
- Sit the dish in the oven and cook the salmon for 30–35 minutes. At this point, you will notice some small milky droplets clinging to the fillets. Remove the dish from the oven and leave it to settle in a warm spot for 10 minutes. Then, using a fish slice, carefully remove one fillet at a time from the oil, trying not to dislodge its cargo of lemon slices (if you like, you can gently pull the skin away from the fish, although it's a bit difficult to do this without disturbing the lemon topping). If you find the milky residue on the sides of the fillets a bit unappealing, carefully scrape it away.
- Sit a fillet on each warm dinner plate, and spoon a little of the oil from the dish, along with a few capers and extra lemon slices, over the top. Serve the salsa romesco separately.

NOT SO FISHY, AFTER ALL . . .
Surprisingly, the leftover oil is not particularly fishy, and can be strained through a fine sieve and stored in the fridge for a week or so, to poach another batch of fish.

Salsa Romesco

MAKES ABOUT 1½ CUPS (375 ML)

400 g ripe tomatoes (about 5 medium-sized tomatoes), cored and cut in half
½ cup (125 ml) extra virgin olive oil
sea salt flakes
caster sugar, for sprinkling
2 very large red capsicums (peppers)
2 large cloves garlic, peeled
1 small red chilli, finely chopped
½ teaspoon smoked paprika
60 g blanched almonds, lightly roasted
splash of white wine vinegar, optional

I love this vivid orange, robustly flavoured salsa and dollop it onto all sorts of dishes – steamed or roasted veggies, sandwiches, soups and salads. It works a treat with no end of things.

- Preheat your oven to 150°C.
- Place the tomatoes, cut-side up, in a roasting tin. Drizzle them with a little of the olive oil and sprinkle each half with a tiny pinch each of salt and sugar. Slip the tin into the oven and roast the tomatoes for an hour or so, until they're soft and wrinkled. Set them aside to cool a little in the tin.
- Meanwhile, line a grill tray with foil. Slice the capsicums down their natural contour lines into large pieces, then remove the cores, seeds and white ribs. Sit them, shiny-side up, on the prepared grill tray, then place them under a hot grill until the skins blister and blacken.
- When they're ready, take them out and cover them with a thick tea towel. Leave them to sweat for a few minutes then, as soon as they're cool enough to handle, peel away and discard the skins. Set the capsicums aside.
- In a small saucepan, gently warm the garlic cloves in the remaining olive oil until they're pale golden. Meanwhile, put the chilli and smoked paprika into a heatproof jug (or bowl). When the garlic and olive oil mixture is ready, pour it into the jug and stir everything together.
- Now put the tomatoes and any of their cooking juices into a blender. Add the peeled capsicums (saving a sliver or two for garnishing if you like), garlic oil mixture, almonds and salt to taste. Whiz everything together, stopping and scraping down the sides occasionally, until the mixture is as smooth as possible (it will be a little grainy looking due to the almonds).
- Now, taste the salsa, and add more salt or a splash of vinegar if necessary (I sometimes do and sometimes don't, depending on the sweetness of the capsicums). Scrape the mixture into a container, cover it tightly and store it in the fridge for up to 5 days.
- To serve the salsa, scoop it into a bowl and garnish it with a sliver of reserved capsicum, if you like.

24th May

Because I knew I would be cooking most of today, I crept out of bed early so I could have an hour or two in the garden before I started. It was glorious – cold (so I had Clive's huge old woollen jumper pulled over everything else), but beautiful. My breath was frosty in the crisp air, and the little birds darted back and forth, urging me to put their seed out. I love the way they do this and am always delighted that they have learned to trust us and realise we're not a threat.

29th May

For the past week Rodney has been playing cat and mouse with the scarlet honeyeaters that arrive as soon as the callistemons and grevilleas burst into flower. Each time he raises his camera to photograph them they stop just long enough for him to get them into focus, but in that split second before the shutter clicks they seem to know and dash off to the next bloom. We've been laughing about it, and decided that there is a lesson in there somewhere – certainly one of patience, if nothing else.

Of course now he has packed up his camera and is getting ready to leave, they're putting on a real show – darting through the branches to feed, perching in full view for seconds at a time, and pirouetting like models so we see them from every angle. It's almost as if they're poking fun at us. It remains to be seen if, by the end of this book, we have a photo of one for you to see . . . (If you can't wait to find out, turn to page 332.)

JUNE

1st June

Phew, well that was the week that was . . . how can it have zoomed by so quickly? It seems as though one minute the house was bursting with props and photographic gear and people, and the next it's just Clive and me again – the only indication of what's passed being a fridge bulging with food. However, despite the bounty, I'm longing for something plain tonight and can think of nothing nicer than mashed potato with some minted peas and roasted mushrooms.

2nd June

Winter has arrived with a vengeance. There was torrential rain last night, the force so intense that it felt like a giant hand was hurling it at the house; at one stage the wind was so strong I thought the roof was going to take off. However, this morning the rain has abated somewhat to a steady downpour. The poor little birds are looking woefully bedraggled as they sit on the windowsill, trying to get out of the worst of it. Gus, who is the only dog I know who hates getting his paws wet, has just banged on the front door to be let in and given me a real 'you've got to be kidding' look when I told him to come around the back, through the waterlogged garden, for his morning treat!

It may sound a little peculiar in this damp and chilly weather but I'm actually making ice-cream today (any ice-cream aficionado will well understand that the weather has no bearing at all on such things). I always think of this particular ice-cream as a winter one, if there is such a thing, because the flavours are so warm and spicy – pumpkin, cinnamon, nutmeg, ginger and maple syrup, topped off with crunchy fingers of pepita brittle.

Pumpkin & Maple Ice-Cream

SERVES 6

840 ml thickened cream
2 teaspoons ground cinnamon
1 teaspoon ground nutmeg
1 teaspoon ground ginger
8 egg yolks
160 ml pure maple syrup
2 cups (800 g) cooked mashed butternut pumpkin (see note overleaf)
2 teaspoons vanilla extract
pepita brittle, to serve (see page 243)

You may wonder why I'm so specific about using butternut pumpkin for this ice-cream. Basically it's because it tends to be more intensely flavoured than other varieties, and generally the flesh is somewhat drier too after baking – just what you want for this, as watery pumpkin can make the ice-cream a bit icy and hard.

- Pour the cream into a large, heavy-based saucepan and sit it over low heat. Add the cinnamon, nutmeg and ginger and slowly heat the cream until it is hot, but not boiling (allowing it to boil will give the cream a 'scalded' taste).
- Meanwhile, put the egg yolks and maple syrup into a large bowl and whisk them together until they're well combined. When the cream is hot, slowly add it to the egg yolk mixture in a thin stream, whisking all the while. Once it's thoroughly combined, pour this mixture back into the saucepan. ›

COOKED PUMPKIN . . .

To cook the pumpkin for the ice-cream base, line a baking tray with baking paper and preheat your oven to 180°C. Split the pumpkin in half lengthways, scoop out the seeds and place each half (or one half only if the pumpkin is very large) on the baking tray, cut-side down. Pop the tray in the oven and bake the pumpkin until it's very soft when pierced in the thickest part with a fine skewer. It usually takes about an hour or so, however the time can vary a bit, depending on the size of the pumpkin. When it's done, remove it from the oven and let it cool, then peel away the skin and scoop the pulp into a container. It keeps well in the fridge for about 5 days. You'll probably end up with more than you need, but you can turn any leftovers into a delicious side dish – just mash it and heat it with a good dob of butter, then season to taste with salt, pepper and nutmeg.

- Return the pan to the stovetop over moderately low heat and cook the custard (for that's what it is), stirring constantly, until it has slightly thickened. Try to stir in a 'figure of eight' movement so you completely cover the bottom of the pan as you go. I use a combination of a flat-based sauce whisk and wooden spoon for this – I find the sauce whisk gets into the corners of the pan, but the spoon is best towards the end of the cooking time as the mixture thickens (ideally use a flat-based wooden spoon too – they're really terrific for this sort of thing).
- The most important thing to remember is that you don't want the custard to boil, or it will curdle. Just take your time and watch it like a hawk once it starts to thicken. It's ready when it seems thicker and leaves a trail when you run your finger through the mixture on the spoon. It won't be super-thick though, so don't expect it to have the consistency of a white sauce. I wish I could explain this better, but I'm afraid it's one of those things in cooking where practice makes perfect – the more often you do it, the more confident you become. Once you get the hang of it you can speed things up by increasing the heat a bit, however I wouldn't do this until you feel good and ready!
- As soon as the custard is ready, remove it from the heat. Pour it into a bowl and whisk in the cooked pumpkin. Leave the mixture to cool. Stir in the vanilla, then cover the bowl and pop it in the fridge. (By all means make the custard a day ahead – the flavour only improves on sitting.)
- If you're lucky enough to have an ice-cream churn you can churn the custard in this. If you don't have one, you will need to be just a little more patient. For the non-churn method, pour the mixture into a large stainless steel bowl and freeze until the ice-cream is frozen 5 cm in from the edges of the bowl – the time will vary, depending on your freezer, but it will probably take a few hours. Remove the bowl from the freezer and give the ice-cream a really good whisk with a balloon whisk or hand-held electric beater (you could also scrape it into a food processor and process it until it's smooth, but it makes for a bit more washing up!). Put the bowl back in the freezer, freeze the ice-cream as before, and repeat the whisking. (If you're wondering why you are doing all this, I promise you it's worth it, as it helps break up the ice crystals in the ice-cream into smaller ones so the texture becomes smoother and creamier each time you do it.)
- Now pack the ice-cream into a container, cover it tightly and freeze it overnight or until it's firm. Check it a while before you want to eat it: if it seems hard, pop it in the fridge for 40 minutes or so before serving, so it's soft enough to scoop easily.
- To serve, use an ice-cream scoop or large serving spoon dipped in hot water to scoop the ice-cream into chilled bowls or glasses and finish off with a shard of pepita brittle.

Pepita Brittle

Before we start, I should mention that you really need a sugar thermometer to make this brittle. The process is a bit fiddly, to be honest, as the pepita caramel is poured out onto baking paper, covered with another sheet of paper and rolled out thinly with a rolling pin before being left to set. It's one of those jobs that needs to be done rapidly, so if you feel at all anxious about it, it may be better to start off using the method for the pecan praline on page 356 (substituting pepitas for the pecans), then when you get your confidence up have a go at this.

1 cup (220 g) caster sugar
½ cup (125 ml) water
tiny pinch of salt
125 g raw green pepitas

- Sticky-tape a large sheet of baking paper to a heatproof work surface (a large wooden board works well), to stop it moving about.
- Put the sugar, water and salt into a medium saucepan and clip a sugar thermometer to the side of the pan. Place the pan over high heat. Stir constantly until the sugar dissolves, then stop stirring and bring the mixture to the boil. As it boils, wash down the sides from time to time with a pastry brush dipped in water to dissolve any sugar crystals that may form. The mixture will slowly change from being quite liquid to more of a thick syrup with lots of lazy bubbles all over the surface. When the sugar thermometer shows it is at the soft ball stage (this is marked on the thermometer), remove the pan from the heat. Stir in the pepitas with a wooden spoon and keep on stirring the mixture until the sugar in the syrup crystallises and it becomes stiff and creamy white – this may take a few minutes.
- Return the pan to the heat, and cook the mixture, stirring as best you can, until the sugar melts completely. Don't worry if this takes a while – initially the sugar will become even stiffer and drier before melting again. Continue to cook the mixture until the pepitas smell and look toasted and the mixture is a deep caramel colour. This should only take a few minutes.
- As soon as it's ready, take the pan off the heat and carefully pour the mixture onto the prepared baking paper. As quickly as possible, sit another sheet of baking paper on top and use a rolling pin to press down heavily on the brittle and roll it out as thinly as you can (this is hard work and needs quite a bit of heft). It firms up rapidly, so you need to be fast too! Remove the top sheet of baking paper and leave the brittle to cool and set. When it's ready, peel it off the paper then break it into large shards.
- To store the brittle, layer the shards in an airtight container between sheets of baking paper or freezer wrap to stop them sticking together, then freeze. When you need some brittle, take out as much as you want and return the rest to the freezer, where it will keep for up to 4 months.

BRITTLE VS PRALINE

You may well be wondering what the difference is between this brittle and regular praline when the ingredients are pretty much identical – and what makes it worth the extra effort. In some ways they are similar, but whereas regular praline is always sparkly and clear (apart from the nuts!), stirring and rolling the mixture as you do for the brittle results in a glossy, opaque sheet. Known as nougatine in pastry work, these rolled sheets can be cut with an oiled knife and formed into shapes or even little bite-size 'tart' shells.

3rd June

What a blow: I've just had to cancel a cooking class I was meant to teach tomorrow. It's rare for me to do such a thing and I feel awful about it, however in my over-enthusiastic onslaught on the pruning at the weekend I managed to slip on a rock and fall heavily. (What is it that gets into a gardener with a pair of secateurs in their hands? I suddenly have a terrible urge to prune everything in sight.) The fall happened so quickly that I have no real idea how I ended up flat on my face. Thank goodness I didn't knock any teeth out, but I did manage to jar my shoulder and hip quite badly.

I keep telling myself that this enforced rest will be very good for body and soul as I normally tend to whiz around doing things at full bore and will now have to lessen the pace – not a bad thing, by any means. It has also meant I have a heap of food intended for the class and only two of us to eat it. So I have taken the opportunity to do a bit of experimenting, particularly with sweet potato as I seem to have a small mountain of them!

Sweet Potato & Bacon Frittata

SERVES 4–6

800 g sweet potato, peeled and cut into 1 cm chunks
2 tablespoons olive oil
sea salt flakes
splash of balsamic vinegar
6 large rashers of bacon, rind removed
1 onion, halved and thinly sliced
2 tablespoons thyme leaves
a generous handful of chopped flat-leaf parsley
8 eggs
freshly ground black pepper and nutmeg, to taste
⅓ cup (25 g) freshly grated parmesan
100 g feta
tiny thyme sprigs, to garnish

Try to use the best eggs you can find for this, for they make all the difference to the flavour. The 'girls' up the valley laid the eggs for the frittata in this photo and as you can see, the lovely, outdoor, scratching-about life they lead shows in its extraordinary golden hue. Sometimes the cakes I make with their eggs are so brilliantly coloured that everyone thinks I've added a pinch of saffron to the mixture!

- Preheat your oven to 220°C and line a large baking tray with baking paper.
- Spread the sweet potato chunks in a single layer on the prepared tray. Drizzle 1 tablespoon of the olive oil over the top, sprinkle on a little salt then toss everything together so the chunks are lightly coated in oil.
- Pop the tray into the oven and roast the sweet potato for 15–20 minutes or so, until it's tender when pierced with a fine skewer. Remove the tray from the oven, sprinkle a little balsamic vinegar onto the sweet potato and gently stir it in, then set aside.
- Cut the bacon into thin matchsticks. Put these into a large, non-stick frying pan (mine is about 30 cm in diameter) and turn the heat to medium. Fry the bacon, stirring regularly, until it is just cooked and the fat has that lovely translucent look to it, then remove the pan from the heat. Tip the bacon matchsticks out onto crumpled paper towels to drain.

- Return the pan to the stovetop and reduce the heat a little. Pour in the remaining oil, add the onion slices and cook them, stirring now and then, for 6–8 minutes until they're pale golden. Now add the bacon, sweet potato, thyme and parsley to the onion. Thoroughly mix them in and warm them through.
- Meanwhile, crack the eggs into a bowl and add pepper, nutmeg and a little salt to taste. Whisk everything together until the eggs are just combined, then stir in the parmesan.
- Increase the heat under the frying pan to medium. Pour the beaten eggs evenly over the sweet potato mixture and cook for a few minutes, stirring frequently with a fork. Now reduce the heat to low and continue to cook, still stirring regularly, for a few more minutes until the egg forms small curds and is starting to look more set. At this stage, crumble the feta over the top, half mix it in, then stop stirring and leave the frittata to cook until it's nearly set (the top will still be a bit wet). This usually takes another 4–5 minutes, depending on the pan. ›

- One of the secrets to making a good frittata is not to overcook it, or it will become tough: the egg should be just set and tender. Frittatas are also quite easy to burn and as the flame on my cooker is a bit uneven, I rotate the pan a quarter turn every so often in the hope the heat will be more evenly distributed and the egg won't catch on the bottom.
- When the egg is nearly set, remove the pan from the heat and put it under a hot grill for a minute or so, just to firm the top of the frittata. Leave it to settle in the pan for a couple of minutes before serving.
- I usually slice and serve the frittata straight from the pan, but if you like, you can carefully loosen it and slide it out onto a serving plate. Finish it off with a good grinding of black pepper and a smattering of tiny thyme sprigs over the top. Left-overs are delish too (although quite rare in our house) – when we do have them, they often find their way into a sandwich, with a good dollop of mayonnaise and some rocket leaves.

6th June

My dad loved a bargain and, much to my mother's dismay, he would buy everything in bulk. We could barely open cupboards at times, they were so stuffed with cartons of Sao biscuits (his favourite), tissue boxes, 5-kilo tins of olives, or whatever else he thought was a particularly good buy.

The up-side to this was that he bought fruit the same way, and would arrive home with wooden crates of grapes; three or four watermelons; trays of mangoes, persimmons and squashy custard apples, and all sorts of other things. I'm sure it drove Mum to distraction at times, but we kids thought it was wonderful.

I rather suspect I've inherited his tendencies as I often arrive home with all manner of 'finds' stuffed in the back of the car. This morning I have a huge basketful of lemons that I picked up from a road-side stall and a very large tub of gorgeous bright-green Sicilian olives – they're quite hard to come by here and I couldn't resist when I saw they were so well-priced. Poor Clive, he despairs of me at times when the car pulls up in the driveway, laden with my latest buys. However, to prove my purchases are sound I've launched myself into cooking up a veritable storm of lemony dishes. These next two are favourites of his so hopefully all will be forgiven . . . and then I can tell him about the four bags of chook manure I also managed to fit in the car and dragged into the shed when he wasn't looking!

A Fine Winter Dish of Chicken, Slow-Cooked Onions & Lemons

SERVES 4–8, DEPENDING ON HOW HUNGRY EVERYONE IS

This comforting dish is a mainstay for me when I want something delicious to eat that doesn't require much work. If I'm making it for dinner, I tend to cook it in stages – caramelising the onions and garlic a few hours ahead of time, and spreading them into the roasting tin; then browning the chicken pieces just before I'm ready to put the whole lot in the oven. By the way, the preserved lemon isn't essential in this dish, however if you do have some on hand, give it a try as it adds a tremendous depth of flavour to the chicken.

- ⅓ cup (80 ml) extra virgin olive oil
- 4 large brown onions, halved and thinly sliced
- 4 large cloves garlic, finely sliced
- sea salt flakes and freshly ground black pepper
- 1 generous tablespoon thyme leaves
- 8 very small thyme sprigs
- 8 chicken chops (partly boned leg and thigh portions)
- flour, for dredging
- 1½ cups (375 ml) chicken stock (see page 210)
- 1½–2 tablespoons finely chopped preserved lemon rind, optional
- 3 large lemons, scrubbed and dried
- 24 green olives (bright-green Sicilian olives are particularly good)

- Warm half the oil in a large frying pan over low heat. Add the onion and garlic and cook, stirring regularly, for 20–25 minutes or until they're soft and pale golden. Season with salt and pepper, then stir in the thyme leaves. Spread this onion mixture evenly over the base of a roasting tin that will fit the chicken pieces snugly in a single layer. Sprinkle the thyme sprigs over the top and set the tin aside (you can do this step up to 6 hours ahead of time and keep the tin in a cool place). Wipe out the frying pan and set it aside too.
- Preheat your oven to 180°C. Heat the remaining oil in the frying pan over medium heat. Coat the chicken chops in flour, shaking off any excess, then add them to the pan and cook them for 3–4 minutes each side until they are a rich golden brown all over. Try not to crowd the pan or the chicken pieces will sweat rather than brown – cook them in batches if they look a bit too snug, adding a little more oil if necessary. As the chicken chops are ready, sit them on top of the onion mixture.
- When all the chicken pieces have been browned, use paper towels to blot up any excess oil in the pan, then pour in the stock. Bring it to just below the boil, stirring regularly to scrape up any of the caramelised bits that have stuck to the pan. Add the preserved lemon rind (if using).
- Meanwhile, cut 16 thin slices of lemon. Remove the seeds, and overlap two slices on each piece of chicken. Squeeze the juice from the remaining lemons into the frying pan, then pour this lemony stock into the tin around the chicken.
- Put the tin in the oven, and cook the chicken for 45–50 minutes until it is browned. Scatter the olives around the chicken for the last 15 minutes of cooking time.
- Remove the tin from the oven and let the chicken settle for 5 minutes. Then carefully transfer the chicken, onion and cooking juices to a warm deep serving platter. It's delicious with wilted spinach and soft polenta or olive oil mashed potatoes (see page 451) to soak up the cooking juices (a simple green salad is pretty good too).

Homemade Limoncello

MAKES ABOUT 1.5 LITRES

8 large plump lemons, scrubbed (the fresher the better)
1 litre vodka
500 g caster sugar
2 cups (500 ml) filtered water or still mineral water
juice of ½ lemon

I first tasted homemade limoncello about 10 years ago and was immediately bowled over by its wonderful, mellow lemon flavour. You can of course buy it from good bottle shops, but making it is easy as long as you can bear to wait to let it mature. You can double the recipe as it keeps indefinitely and is wonderful to use in all sorts of lemon desserts. I often add a splash to the syrup for a lemon cake (try it with the almond and lemon cake with lemon syrup on page 186); drizzle it over lemon ice-cream or gelato; make it into a long drink by adding loads of ice and sparkling mineral water; and use it to subtly flavour cream to go with lemon or berry desserts. Or you can just do as the Neapolitans do and drink it icy-cold as a digestif.

- Using a veggie peeler, carefully peel away the zest from each lemon, making sure you trim off any white pith from the strips of zest (as this can make the limoncello bitter).
- Put the zest into a 2-litre sterilised jar (see note on page 165) and cover it with half the vodka. Seal the jar tightly and leave in a cool, dark place for 40 days (or up to 3 months if you want a more intense flavour and colour), after which time the vodka will have started to take on the flavour and rich yellow colour of the zest. At this point, put the sugar and water into a saucepan over high heat and stir until the sugar has dissolved, then stop stirring and bring it to the boil. As soon as the mixture boils, turn down the heat and let it simmer for 5 minutes. Turn off the heat and let it cool completely.
- Add the cool sugar syrup, lemon juice and remaining vodka to the jar of zest-infused vodka. Mix well, then cover tightly and leave for another 40 days in a cool, dark place. After this time, strain the limoncello into a sterilised bottle and store in the freezer until ready to use.

9th June

I'm sitting here, snug and warm in my office as the rain tumbles down again. The frogs have already welcomed it with a cacophony of croaking and no doubt there is much to-ing and fro-ing going on in the undergrowth. Just as long as they're careful going about their business, for despite it being winter, I saw two snakes earlier in the week (actually, I suspect it was the same snake that I disturbed twice).

It made me realise how far I've come since we first arrived, for not all that long ago you wouldn't have seen my feet for dust if I stumbled across a snake. Now, although I find it startling, I'm not averse to seeing them and marvel at the way they move. In this case it was a yellow-faced whip snake, which is quite a sight – its slender body ranging from olive green to a rusty orange flush towards its head, with remarkable black and white yin/yang commas around its eyes.

When I first disturbed it, I was picking some herbs to flavour a roast chicken. More often than not, this is what we have when I run out of ideas for dinner, as there really is nothing like a beautifully roasted, crisply golden chicken. It's one of the easiest things to cook as it only takes about 10 minutes to prepare the chicken and then it happily minds its own business while it roasts and fills the house with its mouth-watering aroma. I'm always surprised when guests rave about how fabulous it is, and suspect it has more to do with the chickens we use rather than the cook, for we're fortunate to be able to buy really top-quality organic chooks that are full of flavour.

Roast Chicken with Oodles of Herbs

SERVES 4

140 g unsalted butter, softened
sea salt flakes, to taste
a bundle of fresh herbs (tarragon, thyme, rosemary and sage all work really well) – you want to end up with 2–3 tablespoons chopped herbs, with some left over to scatter on top
1.8–2 kg organic (or free-range) chicken
1 lemon, halved

I must admit this is a very general recipe, as I tend to just wander out to the herb garden and pick whatever happens to be flourishing at the time. Mostly I use thyme and rosemary, and always but *always* tarragon when it's in season. Although tarragon is one of those love-it-or-leave-it herbs, it has a wonderful, powerful anise flavour that I think goes particularly well with chicken.

In the warmer months, I serve this with a simple salad (some sliced tomatoes drizzled with good olive oil and scattered with a bit more tarragon) along with a bowlful of tiny mint-flavoured new potatoes. Or, if the weather is cooler, I'll sit some parsnips, pumpkin, potatoes and onions around the chook as it cooks and we'll have a 'proper' roast with all the trimmings.

- Preheat your oven to 230°C.
- Put the butter and salt into a bowl. Use a wooden spoon to thoroughly beat them together and lighten the butter a little. Add 2–3 tablespoons chopped herbs to the butter and thoroughly mix everything together.
- Pat the chicken dry, then carefully slide your fingers between the skin and the flesh at the neck end. Gently loosen the skin all over the breast, thighs and drumsticks. ›

Take your time and try to avoid piercing the skin if you can. (Having said that, I should admit that I do this occasionally, particularly if I am rushing, and it is no big deal if you do – just close it over as best you can. You can even use a bit of the loose neck skin to patch it if necessary.)

- Now scoop up some of the herb butter with your fingers (you may like to wear prep gloves to do this) and spread it onto the flesh under the skin you have loosened. It's a bit awkward to do, but you soon get the hang of it. Do this all over the chook, reserving any leftover butter. When that is done, sit the chicken in a roasting tin that fits it comfortably.
- I rarely truss a chicken – I find it enough to loosely tie the drumsticks together at their base with a bit of kitchen twine and tuck the wingtips under the neck. Once you've done this, spread any remaining butter over the outside of the chicken, then pick off leaves or tiny sprigs from the leftover herbs and scatter these all over the top. Squeeze on the juice from the lemon then tuck the lemon halves and any leftover herbs into the cavity.
- Place the tin in the oven and roast the chicken for 20 minutes, then reduce the heat to 205°C and continue to cook it for another 50 minutes. If I remember, I baste it every now and then, but many's the time I have just left it be and still ended up with a very delicious chicken.
- When it's ready – and it will look and smell divine at this stage – remove the chicken from the oven. Leave it to settle in a warm spot for at least 15 minutes before carving it. While it's settling, I usually tip the herby, lemony juices left in the roasting pan into a jug and let them sit for a bit, then spoon the fat off the top. Serve the juices with the chicken. (You can also make gravy if you like, using these juices to make up some of the liquid, however, I rather like just spooning on the flavourful juice.)
- I'm not the world's best carver, by any means, so I tend to carve the chicken in the kitchen where no-one can see my efforts! However, if you happen to have a good carver on hand, it does look very beautiful served whole on a big platter with fresh herb sprigs tucked around it.

10th June

After all my talk about the elusive scarlet honeyeaters, we've had a closer encounter with one than we would wish. Earlier this morning a tiny male, probably dazzled by the light, flew into one of the windows and knocked itself out. We covered it with our bird rescue box, and much as we've longed to see one of these beautiful little birds up close and capture it on camera, we would have given anything for it to fly off and continue to lead us a merry dance. There is nothing quite as vulnerable as a wounded bird – it's heartbreaking. Hopefully it will rally round.

Late morning . . . and we have a happy ending! Just 10 minutes ago I went to check on the patient and he was rather groggily coming to his feet, fortunately with no wing damage. When I lifted the box he took off into the tree, and we've all breathed a big sigh of relief.

Sadly, the outcome isn't always so happy, and our garden is testament to the fact that not all the birds survive such an impact. We've buried more than I can bear to remember, but I like to think the plants near the burial sites thrive, attracting and feeding many of their companions so in some form or other their deaths are not in vain.

12th June

Today is a diamond day with a capital D. We've just had a long walk on the beach and it was *beautiful*. The sunlight shimmered and bounced off the water, the light so bright and sharp that it almost hurt. The sea here, which is often quite wild, was benign and so clear that we could see tiny fish swirling around our feet as we waded through the shallows. And we weren't the only ones who could see them – the crested terns with their endearing Nigel Kennedy haircuts wheeled overhead, then plummeted like darts into the surf to scoop them up.

We had hoped to see some whales, as they pass quite close to the shore at this time of year, but today there wasn't a whale in sight. Luckily, this absence was more than made up for by the antics of a family of dolphins. These beautiful creatures were having a ball, soaring down the waves just below the surface of the water, then swinging off them before they broke and going back to catch another one – just like any good surfer would!

We have come back home hungry and, as I was recently given an armful of parsnips, I have decided to make a gratin with them.

Parsnip, Parmesan & Nutmeg Gratin

SERVES 4–6

700 g medium-sized parsnips
30 g unsalted butter
100 g freshly grated parmesan
sea salt flakes, to taste
freshly grated nutmeg, for sprinkling
300 ml cream (or a mixture of cream and good stock or milk)
100 ml milk, or thereabouts
⅓ cup (25 g) fresh breadcrumbs

I don't use much cream in my cooking, however I have made an exception for this, and it's worth it – the gratin is indecently rich and buttery and perfectly scrumptious. Not the sort of thing to eat too often but a treat in small quantities. Paired with a sharp salad of watercress and mustard leaves to cut through the richness, it makes a wonderfully satisfying meal. It's also terrific with the herb-roasted chicken on page 252.

- Preheat your oven to 190°C.
- Peel the parsnips and cut them in half crossways, so you end up with a thick fat piece and skinnier tail end. Cut all the pieces lengthways into 3–4 mm slices (if you have a mandolin, it's perfect for this).
- Use roughly half the butter to grease a medium-sized gratin dish (mine is oval, about 26 cm long and 6 cm deep). Layer the parsnips in the gratin dish, sprinkling a little parmesan, salt and nutmeg between each layer. I usually put the slices from the skinny ends in the bottom of the dish, keeping the better-looking larger slices for the top layers. Don't overdo the seasonings – it only needs the lightest sprinkling of salt and smidgen of nutmeg. Finish with an overlapping layer of parsnips (peel and slice another one if you're a bit short), and sprinkle the remaining parmesan over the top.
- Whisk the cream and milk together then drizzle it over the parsnips. Sprinkle the breadcrumbs evenly over the top and dot with the remaining butter.
- Now pop the dish in the oven for 50–60 minutes, until the parsnips are tender and the top is speckled brown. Check it every so often and tent some foil loosely over the top if it is looking a bit too dark. The house will be filled with a wonderful cheesy fragrance as it bakes.
- When the gratin is ready, carefully lift it out of the oven. It's not the most beautiful dish in the world, but it has a really rustic look that I love. If the sides of the dish are a bit too speckled and sploshed, use some wet paper towels to wipe off the worst, then serve it straight away.

19th June

Three black cockatoos (why do they always seem to fly in threes?) flew low over my head today, battling a gusty wind. I don't know what it is with these birds, but there is something strangely mournful, yet magical about them. They're regarded by many Indigenous communities as harbingers of rain, in which case it looks like we may be in for a downpour.

And they're not wrong – just an hour ago I heard the first telltale pitter-patter on the roof. There is something peculiarly comforting about the sound of rain on a tin roof. I've heard many people speak of this, but it is only now that we have one of our own that I fully understand what they mean.

However, that's not what I was going to write about at all. I wanted to give you the recipe for a rather special fennel dish we had with dinner last night. It was one of those lovely meals where everything came together without too much ado, which was slightly unexpected and hugely gratifying.

We had butterflied leg of lamb, encrusted with spices and fresh coriander, which we barbecued until it was charred outside and rosy-pink within (see page 446). Alongside was this dish of sweet and sour 'wilted' fennel and red capsicum (the edges of the capsicum and fennel just a bit burnt to bring out their sweetness), as well as some roasted sweet potato dressed with parsley and smoked paprika pesto (see page 226) – a jar of which I unearthed in the back of the fridge. I hate to think what else may be lurking there . . . Add to this a bowl of rocket leaves tossed in lemon juice and olive oil, and it really was a feast.

Caramelised Fennel & Red Capsicum with Pine Nuts and Sultanas

SERVES 4

2 medium–large red capsicums (peppers), cut into 1.5 cm chunks
1 large bulb fennel, cut into 1.5 cm chunks
1 large red onion, cut into 1.5 cm chunks
¼ cup (40 g) sultanas, ideally naturally dried (see note below)
¼ cup (40 g) roasted pine nuts
about 1½ tablespoons shredded mint
mint leaves, to garnish, optional

DRESSING

⅓ cup (80 ml) extra virgin olive oil
¾–1 teaspoon sea salt flakes
½ teaspoon freshly ground black pepper
1 small clove garlic, squashed and halved
1½–2 tablespoons balsamic vinegar, or more to taste
2–3 level teaspoons caster sugar

FINISHING TOUCHES . . .

If you can find dark, naturally dried sultanas, do use them as their colour and texture are perfect in this. I quite often put a few handfuls of small rocket leaves in the bottom of the serving bowl before adding the fennel mixture – they go really well with the other flavours.

This is a very useful dish to have up your sleeve as it is best eaten barely warm or at room temperature (so no last-minute cooking – I do love that). It goes well with just about anything that has been simply barbecued. Fish, chicken, pork or beef would all work a treat, as would bundles of goat's cheese wrapped in vine leaves and quickly grilled until the cheese is molten.

- To make the dressing, put all the ingredients into a bowl and whisk them together until the sugar dissolves, then set it aside. (You can shake these together in a jar if you prefer, but I sometimes find the sugar doesn't completely dissolve when I do this.)
- Place a large frying pan over high heat and pour in about 2 tablespoons oil from the top of the dressing (it will have separated as it sits). When the oil is hot, add the chopped capsicum, fennel and onion to the pan and sauté for about 10 minutes, or until they have softened but still have a little bit of crispness about them and some of the edges are turning golden. You may find you need to spoon in a bit more of the oil as you go. Add the sultanas after 5 minutes.
- Pour the remaining dressing into the pan, along with the pine nuts. Give everything a really good stir then remove the pan from the heat. Taste the mixture and adjust the salt, vinegar and sugar balance, then scoop into a bowl and leave to cool. Just before serving, stir in the shredded mint and garnish with mint leaves, if liked.

21st June

I always think of my mum on the solstice as it's her birthday tomorrow and I have a clear recollection of her telling me about the shortest day of the year when I was little. It all seemed quite mysterious to me then (and I still find this time quite magical), so somehow it seems fitting that we're off to a solstice party under the stars tonight. It's being held in a paddock on a friend's property and is what we call a BBB night – beer, bangers and bonfire. I so love get-togethers like this – they remind me of my childhood and staying up for cracker night. The kids all have a ball tearing around in the dark, half the time trying to frighten each other to death, and the other half downing awe-inspiring quantities of sausage sarnies with oodles of tomato sauce. There is inevitably a bit of dancing (many of us are old hippies at heart!), guitar strumming and a lot of laughter.

As well as taking a mountain of sausages I've also made a big batch of spicy pumpkin and coconut soup. The nights are really icy now and we shall need something to keep us warm – apart from our beanies and about ten layers of jumpers of course.

So . . . the clock is about to strike midnight and we've just arrived home, managing to disturb a bandicoot who was having a field day digging up the garden. What a night! The air is so keen it almost hurts to breathe, and the Milky Way is extraordinary – how can there be so many stars in the sky? I find it impossible to grasp the scale of it, especially on nights like this when we're out in the open. I am dumbstruck by the sheer grandeur of it all.

Spicy Pumpkin, Ginger & Coconut Soup

SERVES 8

- 2 tablespoons extra virgin olive oil
- 2 onions, sliced
- 4 large cloves garlic, finely chopped
- 2½ tablespoons finely chopped ginger
- 2 small red chillies, finely chopped
- 3 heaped teaspoons ground cumin
- 2 heaped teaspoons ground coriander
- ½ teaspoon ground cinnamon
- 1 heaped tablespoon curry paste (I use Patak's Tikka Masala paste)
- 2 tablespoons sun-dried tomato pesto or regular tomato paste (purée)
- 2.5 kg butternut or Kent pumpkin, peeled and cut into 3 cm chunks
- 1 × 400 g can diced tomatoes
- 1 tablespoon sugar
- 2–3 teaspoons sea salt flakes, or to taste
- freshly ground black pepper
- 1.75 litres water
- 270 ml light coconut cream
- juice of ½–1 lemon, to taste
- coriander leaves (or herb flowers), to serve, optional

This recipe makes rather a lot of soup, however it freezes wonderfully well and I love knowing that I have it on hand for those days when I forget to think about what we're going to have for dinner – which happens more frequently than I care to admit! The soup goes particularly well with pide bread, which is gorgeous as is, but sometimes I like to add a bit more flavour by brushing it with olive oil, scattering extra nigella seeds over the top (there can never be too many, as far as I'm concerned) and heating it up in a warm oven – it's terrific.

By the way, if you're wondering what the flowers are on the soup – both my tarragon and Thai basil were flowering when we took the photograph and I couldn't resist scattering a few blossoms over the top to finish it off.

- Warm the olive oil in a very large saucepan over medium heat. Add the onion and cook, stirring often, for 10 minutes. Now add the garlic, ginger and chilli and cook, stirring occasionally, for 2 minutes. Scoop in the spices, curry paste and tomato pesto or paste and cook, stirring constantly, for another minute or so to release their fragrance. I love doing this as the warm aroma of the spices smells brilliant.
- Tumble in the pumpkin and give it a good swizzle around so it is coated in the spicy mixture (you will need a bit of elbow grease to do this as there is rather a lot of pumpkin). Finally, add the tomatoes, sugar, salt, pepper and water. Increase the heat to high and bring the soup to the boil, then reduce the heat to low so it bubbles gently. Partly cover the pan and cook the soup for 35–40 minutes, or until the pumpkin is very tender.
- Remove the pan from the heat and allow the soup to cool slightly, then purée it in batches in a blender, or with a stick blender in the pan. Gently reheat it, then stir in most of the coconut cream, keeping a little bit back for serving. Taste the soup and add more salt or lemon juice if necessary.
- To serve the soup, ladle it into warm bowls. Dribble a little of the reserved coconut cream over the top, along with a good grinding of black pepper and a few coriander leaves (or herb flowers).

THE PERILS OF PUMPKIN

Oh, BTW, having spent two days with rather exotic orange-tinted palms after my last go at peeling and chopping vast quantities of pumpkin, I am now sworn to wear prep gloves when I tackle the job. No matter how hard I scrubbed I couldn't wash the stain off – I can only think it must make the most fantastic dye!

22nd June

Mum's birthday. If possible, I shall spend some time pottering in the garden this afternoon, as she loved hers and it was a great source of peace for her, as it is for me. (I had to smile as I wrote the word 'potter' as it's far too gentile a word for my efforts – slash and burn is more like it!)

Our wild menagerie appears to be growing: along with our resident echidna, whip snakes, frogs, blue-tongue lizards, all the birds (at last count 45 different species that visit regularly) and a rather large python that slips across the lawn on warm evenings hunting for its dinner, we've now acquired some newcomers.

The first time I saw one I nearly died, thinking it was a rat, but on closer inspection I could see that it was more mouse-like, with somewhat pretty, crinkly ears. I realised this was a creature I'd heard about since we moved here, but never seen – a dear little nocturnal native marsupial called an antechinus. They tend to live in the rainforest, well away from humans, but there is a patch of rainforest just down the road, and I suspect they have come from there. If they plan to stay in our garden, I just hope that they watch out for our python friend once he comes out of hibernation – he is a big fella (at least 2 metres long) and I imagine they would be the perfect snack for a hungry snake!

It only seems right to cook Mum's smoked fish pie for dinner tonight. It brings back so many happy memories – not only of her, but of all the family sitting around the dining table, chatting and laughing. Isn't it wonderful the way food can do that?

Cooee's Famous Smoked Fish & Mash Pie

SERVES 6

600 ml milk
1 kg smoked haddock or cod, cut into a few large pieces
4 hard-boiled eggs, peeled and coarsely chopped
1 tablespoon finely chopped flat-leaf parsley
160 g good tasty cheese or gruyère, grated
40 g unsalted butter
2 tablespoons plain flour
sea salt flakes, ground white pepper and nutmeg
1½ tablespoons capers
big squeeze of lemon juice
1½ tablespoons grated parmesan
snipped chives, to serve, optional
lemon wedges, to serve

continued next page

About this time of year when the cold weather well and truly bites, I invariably find myself buying the ingredients for this heart-warming pie. My mum, Cooee, regularly made it in winter and, for me, it immediately conjures up such a clear image of her. She always let us mash the potatoes and, best of all, pile them up like Mount Vesuvius on top of the pie. (I suspect she always cooked far more potato than she needed, as nearly as much went into our mouths as went onto the pie!) The aroma as it baked was tantalising and we would all line up, waiting for it to come out of the oven, burning our tongues on the first few spoonfuls we were so eager to eat it. If I remember rightly she served it with minted peas, or occasionally a salad, and it goes wonderfully well with both; but perhaps my favourite accompaniment is a big mound of sautéed spinach leaves – their earthy, mineral sharpness beautifully offsets the mellow flavour of the pie.

- First you need to make up a batch of mashed potato. To do this, boil the potatoes in plenty of salted water until they're tender. Drain them, then return them to the heat briefly to dry them off. Now thoroughly mash them with a potato masher. Add the butter and most of the warm milk, then mash a bit more, pouring in a splash more milk if necessary, so you end up with a pretty thick mash. Add salt to taste, then set aside in a warm spot.

- Preheat your oven to 200°C.
- To cook the smoked fish, pour the milk into a large frying pan over low heat and bring it to a simmer. Add the fish, then cover the pan and gently poach the fish until it flakes easily with a fork – this could take anywhere between 5 and 10 minutes, depending on the thickness of your fish. (By the way, if your pan is small you may have to cook the fish in batches.) Use a slotted spoon or egg slice to scoop the fish pieces onto a plate – reserve the milk in the pan.
- I tend to wear prep gloves for this next bit, as it's a little messy. You need to peel away the skin from the haddock, remove any bones, then flake it into chunky pieces. Put these into a bowl, and gently mix in the eggs, parsley and grated cheese. Set the bowl aside in a cool spot.
- The last step before you put the pie together is to make a white sauce from the reserved poaching milk. To do this, melt the butter in a smallish saucepan over medium heat. As soon as it stops bubbling, add the flour and cook, stirring constantly, for 3 minutes or so. Slowly dribble in the reserved poaching milk, stirring all the while, and bring the mixture just to the boil. At this stage the sauce will have thickened somewhat – I like it to be reasonably thin, so I'll quite often add a splash of regular milk if it seems a bit too thick. Let the sauce bubble gently for 5 minutes or so, then spoon out a little to taste – I always do this to check the flour has been cooked long enough to lose its raw taste. When it's ready, take the pan off the heat and sprinkle in salt, pepper and nutmeg to taste. Now, pour this over the fish mixture, add the capers and lemon juice and gently fold everything together.
- Lightly butter a reasonably large ovenproof dish (or if you want to make it a bit more special, use individual dishes) and scoop in the fish mixture. Stir the parsley into the mash, if using, then pile the mash up over the pie and score with a fork – this isn't vital, but it's something Mum always did, so I can't not do it! Sprinkle the parmesan on top, then bake the pie for 25–30 minutes (check after 20 minutes if you're making individual pies), or until the mash is flecked with gold.
- When it's ready, remove it from the oven, snip some chives over the top if you like, and serve it straight away with lemon wedges and a bowl of sautéed English spinach or lightly cooked peas or green beans.

MASHED POTATO

1.3 kg potatoes, peeled and quartered, if large
50 g butter
350–400 ml very warm milk
sea salt
small handful of chopped flat-leaf parsley, optional

25th June

My fingers are freezing and it's no wonder as the temperature dived last night and we've woken to a crystal-clear frosty morning. Our house sits at the top of a hill so the frost never climbs this high, but down in the fields it's a different story.

Rugged up from head to toe, we went down to look – and what a sight it was. The fields stretched away, looking like some extraordinary jewel box where every plant glittered as though encrusted with diamonds, and they crunched beneath our boots as we walked.

Beautiful as it is for us, I know for many of the local orchardists it spells heartache. They will have been up all night, setting heaters in amongst their trees in a desperate effort to ward off the deadly crystals, for many of the stone-fruit trees are flowering now and a dose of frost at the wrong time is fatal to the coming year's crop.

It's just too cold to be outside, so I've been sorting out my kitchen cupboards (an extremely overdue task). It has taken me an inordinately long time, but I'm now feeling very virtuous – for the first time in ages, I can actually open drawers and see the bottoms of them. I also found some buried treasures, including a lovely old cast-iron skillet I was given many years ago – it's such a lovely pan, softly burnished with age and use. It has built up a non-stick patina over time and everything I cook in it slides out easily. I know these pans require a bit more maintenance than Teflon-coated ones, but there is something supremely satisfying about cooking in them, and for cakes such as this one, they're perfect.

Upside-Down Apple & Polenta Skillet Cake

SERVES 8

This rustic, not-too-sweet cake needs to be eaten while it's still warm, however it's very easy to make and a real favourite of mine. The polenta gives it a beautiful golden colour and adds an intriguing grittiness to the texture. I often think this would make a terrific addition to a brunch – a meal that always seems so civilised to me, although one that we rarely have.

If you don't have a cast-iron skillet, don't despair – I have also made this in a good, heavy-based non-stick frying pan. I wrapped the handle (which wasn't oven-proof) in four thick layers of foil to protect it from the heat, and it worked beautifully.

SWEET APPLES . . .

I mentioned using sweet apples in this recipe, and what I mean by that are apples that have a high sugar content, as they tend to hold their shape well as they cook. Pink lady, fuji, golden delicious and royal gala all fit the bill.

60 g unsalted butter
1 tablespoon pure maple syrup
5 medium-sized sweet apples (see note above), peeled, quartered and cored
pure maple syrup, to serve
yoghurt or cream, to serve
continued next page

- Preheat your oven to 220°C.
- Melt the butter in a well-seasoned 22–24 cm cast-iron skillet over medium–high heat (most cast-iron pans have ovenproof handles, but if your pan doesn't, wrap the handle tightly in three or four thicknesses of foil to protect it). The handle of the pan gets very hot, so you will need to use an oven mitt or extra-thick tea towels to manoeuvre the pan. ›

POLENTA TOPPING

⅔ cup (125 g) fine yellow polenta
½ cup (75 g) plain flour
2 tablespoons caster sugar
1½ teaspoons baking powder
¼ teaspoon salt
1 egg, lightly beaten
⅔ cup (160 g) sour cream
¼ cup (60 ml) milk
1 teaspoon vanilla extract
60 g unsalted butter, melted

- Pour the maple syrup into the pan and swirl it about to mix it with the butter. When the mixture is quite hot, remove the pan from the heat. Now fill the pan with the quartered apples. I've found the best way to tackle this is to first sit the apples on their sides around the edge of the pan, wedging them in as tightly as possible (it's a little awkward as they tend to move about a bit, but try using a spoon to help prop them up as you go). Now, tightly fill the centre of the pan with more apples, cutting them to fit if necessary. It may seem like an awful lot of apple but they shrink substantially as they cook, so you need to fit in as many as possible.
- Return the pan to the heat and cook the apples for 10–12 minutes until they are deep golden and caramelised, but not collapsing, turning them carefully halfway through cooking. You will find the apples will slip and slide a bit as you do this, but when they are ready just push them back together as best you can.
- Meanwhile, for the polenta topping, pour the polenta into a medium-sized bowl, then add the flour, sugar, baking powder and salt. Use a balloon whisk to whisk everything together for 1 minute. In another bowl, thoroughly whisk together the egg, sour cream, milk, vanilla and melted butter until they are well combined. Make a well in the centre of the polenta mixture and pour in the wet ingredients. Stir everything together until they are well mixed.
- When the apples are ready, scrape the polenta mixture over the top of them, spreading it out as evenly as you can – it can be a little awkward, so just do the best you can.
- Pop the skillet into the middle of the oven. Sit a sheet of foil underneath it to catch any drips as the caramel may bubble up. Bake the cake for 15–18 minutes, until it's a deep golden and a fine skewer inserted in the centre comes out clean.
- When it's ready, carefully (the handle will be red-hot) remove the skillet from the oven to a heatproof surface. Gently loosen the cake around the edges of the pan, then leave it to settle for a minute or two. Sit a serving platter on top and very carefully invert the cake onto the platter (watch your hands when you do this as the pan will still be very hot). Remove the skillet – don't worry if some chunks of apple have stuck to it, just gently loosen them and sit them back on top of the cake.
- Serve the cake while it's warm and tender, with maple syrup and yoghurt or cream.

26th June

As June ends, great swathes of pink and mauve-tipped flowering molasses grass patchwork the countryside – it's spectacular and incredibly fragrant. As you can imagine from the name, it really does smell malty, just like warmed molasses. It's the scent of home for me, and I feel a great sense of belonging and contentment when I first sniff it after being away for a time.

28th June

Still no whales, but on our whale-watching walk this afternoon we could see two really large birds fishing just off the break-wall. As we got closer we could see they were gannets, and their aerobatics display was breathtaking as they swooped and dived to feed on the shoals of tiny fish that were teeming around the rivermouth. We'd never seen shoaling like this before. There must have been hundreds of thousands of tiny silver and brown fish, swerving and veering as one in a desperate effort to survive not only the attack of the gannets, but also schools of bigger fish – bream and mullet – leaping out of the water in their eagerness to catch them. Within minutes, these big fish caught the attention of a family of dolphins, who picked them off for supper with incredible ease and grace. Seeing the stark reality of the food chain laid out before us like this was a real eye-opener. And I guess in a way we completed the cycle, for we stopped at the Fishing Co-op on the way home for fish and chips, which we ate with our legs dangling over the edge of the wharf.

29th June

I've just been rather guiltily weeding the garden. A dear friend of mine calls weeds 'little misplaced plants' and ever since I heard him say this I've had to steel myself to pull them out, as I feel rather mean. However, I ameliorate my guilt somewhat by reminding myself that I do dig them back into the garden or make weed 'tea' from them so the soil and other plants get the benefit . . . and perhaps this is just what they are there for.

Despite the 'little misplaced plants', I was delighted to see the celery is thriving, as is some rather handsome ruby chard. I have picked a big bunch of each to use for dinner tonight, along with some dill that I discovered when I finally squelched my way around to the herb garden after an absence of a few days. To my delight I saw the feathery fronds peeping out from behind a bay tree that I've been meaning to prune for ages – fortunately, despite my neglect, the dill has flourished. It's a herb I love: there's nothing quite like its refreshing aniseed flavour, and as it can be a little tricky to grow here (bolting to seed quickly), this is a real treat.

I shall use it to make pesto with some macadamias – it will go perfectly with the celery in a winter salad that I have been constructing in my mind for ages (see page 270). And I think I shall put the chard into a savoury tart with a rich cheese filling and crunchy almond top (see page 368).

I can't begin to explain just how satisfying I find growing even the few herbs and vegetables we do. For me, it somehow completes the circle of cooking and eating in a very special way, and I suspect our veggie garden is only going to expand as time goes by.

A Winter Salad of Fennel, Smoked Salmon & Avocado with Dill & Macadamia Pesto

SERVES 4

- 2–3 large celery stalks, trimmed
- 1 smallish bulb fennel
- 3 teaspoons finely chopped dill (or fennel fronds), optional
- 2–3 tablespoons lemon-pressed oil dressing (see page 300), or your favourite vinaigrette
- 1 just-ripe avocado, thinly sliced
- 140 g smoked salmon, torn into bite-sized pieces
- tiny dill leaves, to garnish

DILL AND MACADAMIA PESTO

- 4–5 large spring onions (or enough to make 1 cup, chopped)
- ½ cup (15 g) chopped flat-leaf parsley
- ½ cup (30 g) chopped dill
- ½–1 tablespoon white wine vinegar
- 120 g macadamias, lightly roasted
- ¾ cup (180 ml) extra virgin olive oil
- sea salt flakes and coarsely ground black pepper

GREEN STUFF . . .

To prevent the acid in the vinegar from dulling the lovely green colour of the pesto if you're making it ahead of time, leave out the vinegar, then add it just before you use the pesto.

This lovely salad is beautifully balanced, if I do say so myself. The lush richness of the salmon and avocado are offset by the clean, fresh flavour of dill and the crunch of the fennel and celery. All cool whites, greens and pinks, the salad makes a terrific starter for a special winter dinner as it looks fabulous and is dead easy to make.

You will find that this recipe makes more of the dill and macadamia pesto than you need for the salad, however it's so versatile and keeps so well that I'm always happy to have the extra on hand. If you're wondering what to do with it, I find it's terrific tossed with green beans or peas as a vegetable dish; spooned onto roasted tomatoes, which you can then sprinkle with feta and warm through; or mixed with marinated goat's cheese and used to top bruschetta, along with smoked salmon or salmon roe (this is particularly good!).

- First, make the pesto. To do this, roughly chop the pale green and white parts of the spring onions, then measure them out to make sure you have 1 cup. Now put the chopped spring onion, parsley, dill, vinegar, macadamias and a third of the oil into a blender or food processor and whiz them all together. With the motor running, slowly drizzle in more oil until the mixture is smooth and thick. Taste the pesto and add salt and pepper – you may find it needs a little more vinegar too, if you would like it to be a bit sharper. Scrape the mixture into a container, seal it tightly and place it in the fridge. (The pesto keeps well for at least 2 weeks as long as there is a thin film of oil floating on the surface to seal it.)
- To make the salad, slice the celery stalks very finely on the diagonal, then tip them into a bowl. Now halve the fennel, make a V-shaped cut to remove the core in each half and slice it lengthways as finely as possible. Add it to the bowl of celery, along with the chopped dill or fennel fronds (if using). Pour in the dressing and mix everything together.
- Now line up four dinner plates along your bench. Dollop two dessertspoonfuls of pesto into the middle of each plate, flattening it out a little with the back of the spoon as you go. Sit a little pile of the fennel and celery salad on the pesto, then top this with a couple of slices of avocado and some loosely rolled-up pieces of smoked salmon (if you like you can dot a little bit more pesto in amongst everything too). Add another layer of salad, avocado and smoked salmon, finishing off with a few slivers of fennel from the salad. Sprinkle each salad with tiny dill leaves and serve immediately.

JULY

1st July

My neighbour has just given me the most beautiful basket of big, fat field mushrooms – what a treat! I have decided that fate sometimes takes a hand in these things, for in a serendipitous turn of events, a mushroom strudel recipe that I misplaced ages ago has finally floated to the top of a pile of papers on my desk. Strudel for dinner is clearly meant to be!

Coiled Mushroom, Hazelnut & Dill Strudel

SERVES 4–6

Rather than being rolled into a log, this strudel is made into slender ropes that are coiled and joined together to make a rather spectacular dish, as you can see. However, it is a little fiddly to do, so if it all seems a bit daunting, just make it into a regular strudel shape instead – it will taste just as good. Using a variety of mushrooms will give more complexity to the flavour and texture; however, this version with the field mushrooms also tastes wonderful.

12 sheets filo pastry, plus a few extra in case of tearing
150 g unsalted butter, melted and cooled
poppy, sesame or nigella seeds, for sprinkling
dill sprigs, to garnish

MUSHROOM FILLING

⅓ cup (80 ml) olive oil
60 g unsalted butter
1 clove garlic, finely chopped
2 large onions, finely chopped
1 kg mushrooms, fairly thickly sliced
½ cup (120 g) sour cream
2 teaspoons Dijon or honey mustard
lemon juice, to taste
sea salt flakes and freshly ground black pepper, to taste
¼ cup (15 g) firmly packed finely chopped dill
60 g roasted hazelnuts, coarsely chopped

- Start by making the filling. I know it's a bit more work, but unless you have an enormous frying pan, I'm afraid you'll have to cook the mushrooms in two pans – it's nigh on impossible to fit them all into one pan, and even if you manage to do so they will tend to stew rather than fry. So first off, divide the oil and butter evenly between two large frying pans. Warm them over medium heat, then put half the garlic and onion into each pan and cook, stirring occasionally, for about 8 minutes until they have softened. Now increase the heat and divide the mushrooms evenly between the pans. Cook them for about 15 minutes, tossing regularly, until the juices have evaporated and the mushrooms are starting to sizzle. It's really important to ensure the liquid has boiled off the mushrooms – if not, the filling will be too wet, and the excess liquid may seep into the pastry, making it soggy (the bottom is always a bit soggy, but ideally the rest should be crisp).
- When the mushrooms are ready, turn off the heat. Combine them all in one pan, then mix in the sour cream, mustard, lemon juice and salt and pepper. Leave the filling to cool, then stir in the dill and hazelnuts. (You can make the filling the day before you want to use it and store it in the fridge, but if you do this, don't add the dill and hazelnuts until the last minute so the dill flavour is fresh and the nuts keep their crunch.) Whatever you do, make sure the mushroom mixture is cool before you start making the pastry coils, otherwise you'll have the devil of a job handling them as the warmth of the filling will soften the filo too much and melt the butter. ›

BY THE WAY . . .

I should also say I have made many variations of this, adding cubes of tangy goat's cheese, slivers of reconstituted dried porcini mushrooms or different herbs, and all have worked very well. I rather suspect you could add whatever takes your fancy.

- Lightly butter a 26 cm springform cake tin and line the base with baking paper.
- Unroll the filo sheets onto the bench and cover them with a slightly damp tea towel to stop them drying out. Lay three sheets of filo directly on top of each other, buttering each sheet lightly as you go. Spoon about a quarter of the filling in a rough log shape down one long side of the filo, making sure it's about 3 cm in from the edge. (I find a small palette knife comes in very handy at this point, to neaten up the mixture and shape it more easily.) Now roll up the filling in the filo to form a narrow rope, making sure the pastry at the far end is well buttered so it seals properly. Now lightly butter the rope, then cut it in half. If you are anything like me, by this stage your hands and the bench will be very buttery and messy, but do persevere as it does get easier as you go. By the way, you could use olive oil instead of butter, but I find the oil doesn't give the pastry quite the same lovely crispness and flavour as butter does. Then again, I would say that, as I'm a bit of a butter girl! Whatever you decide, it's important that the coil is well lubricated as it will help make it supple enough to bend.
- Now, coil one half of the rope into a tight snail shape. This is easier said than done as the first coil is the trickiest one to do. Don't worry if it splits – mine often does, but it is easily patched later. Now sit this in the centre of the tin. Attach the other half of the rope to this by pushing the ends together so it looks like one continuous coil (you may have to smooth the join together with your fingers). Make three more ropes from the remaining filo and filling, however don't cut these ones in half. As each one is ready, just add it to the coil. By the end, the coil should fill the pan (you may have to squash it in a bit to make it fit).
- When it's finished, brush a little more butter over the top and patch any joins or tears that need it with a small piece of filo. Sprinkle the seeds over the top, then put the tin in the fridge for 30 minutes or so to firm up the pastry.
- In the meantime, preheat your oven to 190°C. Sit the tin on a baking sheet to catch any drips of butter, and bake the strudel for 35–40 minutes or until it is golden.
- When it's ready, transfer it to a cooling rack and leave it to settle for 10 minutes or so. If the top isn't as brown as you would like, you can slip the tin under an overhead grill (on medium heat) for a few minutes to colour it a bit more – watch it like a hawk if you do this, as it catches quickly.
- Slip off the outer ring of the tin, and slide the strudel onto a serving plate. I find a couple of large egg slices help with this, as does using a bit of leverage from the baking paper underneath. Garnish with dill sprigs.
- To serve, slice the strudel into wedges – a wide-bladed server comes in handy here to lift each slice off the plate intact, but if the coils pull apart a bit just push them back together again. No-one will ever know, I promise.

5th July

My love of nasturtiums started with my mum, for she always had them in the garden and when we were little we would help her pick big bunches of them. The leaves and flowers would go into salads, as would the funny knobbly seeds, but only after she had pickled them in vinegar first so they were quite sharp and tangy – a flavour somewhat reminiscent of capers. Whenever we helped her with this, we would have nasturtium sandwiches for lunch – made with thick slices of fresh brown bread spread with butter or mayonnaise, a layer of the spicy green leaves and scattering of their vivid orange, crimson and yellow petals. As a four year old, it seemed awfully exotic to be eating flowers!

So when I was making the bread recipe below and saw that my nasturtiums were flowering, it seemed only right to make a batch of these magical sandwiches. They were just as I remember and brought back really happy memories.

Sweet Potato, Cheese & Thyme Soda Bread

MAKES 1 LARGE LOAF

Although this easy soda bread is wonderful for making nasturtium sandwiches, its gorgeous sunny colour and warm nutmeg and thyme fragrance also make it a natural with winter soups.

- 2 medium-sized sweet potatoes (ideally the orange-fleshed ones)
- 2 cups (300 g) plain flour, plus extra for dusting
- 1 cup (150 g) self-raising flour
- 1 teaspoon bicarbonate of soda
- 2 teaspoons sea salt flakes
- ½ teaspoon caster sugar
- 1 teaspoon freshly grated nutmeg
- 1½ tablespoons thyme leaves
- 70 g grated parmesan
- 70 g grated tasty cheese
- 300 ml buttermilk
- 1 egg, lightly beaten
- 60 g unsalted butter, melted and cooled
- tiny thyme sprigs, to garnish
- marinated feta or goat's cheese and unsprayed nasturtium leaves and flowers, to make sandwiches, optional

- Preheat your oven to 180°C and line a baking tray with baking paper. Prick each sweet potato five or six times with a fine skewer then sit them on the baking tray. Pop them in the oven and bake them for 50–60 minutes until they're tender. To check, run a fine skewer into the centre of each one – it should slide through easily. When they're ready, remove them from the oven and let them cool down.
- Once the sweet potatoes are cool enough to handle, peel away the skin and mash the flesh in a bowl. Measure out 1 cup (230 g) of the mashed sweet potato and set it aside. (You may have a bit leftover; if you do, try squashing it onto a sharp cheddar cheese sandwich, along with a thick smear of chilli jam or chutney – a great combination.) By the way, the sweet potatoes can be cooked a few days ahead if you like, and stored in the fridge.
- When you're ready to bake the bread, preheat the oven to 180°C. Line a baking sheet with baking paper and lightly dust it with flour.
- Sift the flours, bicarbonate of soda, salt and sugar into a bowl. Mix in the nutmeg and thyme leaves – I tend to use a balloon whisk for this as it's really effective at distributing them evenly. Now thoroughly mix in the parmesan and tasty cheese.
- In another bowl, whisk together the buttermilk, egg and melted butter until well combined. Whisk in the mashed sweet potato – you will find the mixture will be ›

a little bit lumpy, but that's absolutely fine. Now, make a well in the middle of the flour mixture and pour in the buttermilk mixture. Use a wooden spoon to mix the two together. After a certain point I find the dough becomes a bit thick and awkward to mix with the spoon so I usually finish it off with my hands. When it has come together, tip it out onto the baking sheet. Pat it into a flat-ish round or rectangluar shape, about 4 cm thick. Sieve a fine layer of flour over the top and use a blunt knife to score the round fairly deeply into eight wedges, or the rectangle into eight chunks. Scatter some thyme sprigs over the top.

- Put the bread in the oven and bake it for about 45 minutes, or until a skewer inserted in the centre comes out clean. When it's ready, remove it from the oven and let it cool on a rack until barely warm – I know this is hard as it smells so good, but the flavour really comes out when it has cooled a bit. Like all soda breads, this is best eaten the same day it is made, however I have often frozen leftover bread for up to a fortnight and with a bit of gentle warming, it's been just fine.
- If you want to make nasturtium sandwiches, either break the bread into wedges or cut it into thickish slices. Squash some chunks of marinated feta or goat's cheese onto each slice (I add a good grinding of black pepper too) and top the cheese with washed and dried nasturtium leaves and petals . . . If the weather is fine, there is no better place to eat this than a warm, sunny corner of the garden.

9th July

Have you ever seen snowpeas growing? They're lovely! The tendrils remind me of toddlers' fingers as they reach out to cling to the nearest support, and the delicate pink and purple flowers only last a day or so before the familiar curved green pods start to form. Once they take off you can't stop them – mine are well and truly above my head now and growing taller by the day, and they're covered with peas. We can hardly keep up with the pace and I am flinging them willy-nilly into just about everything we eat while they're so young and sweet. The lot I have just picked are destined for this simple pea salad.

Sugar Snap, Snowpea & Green Pea Salad with Goat's Cheese

SERVES 1 RATHER HUNGRY PERSON

It's funny that I turned out to be a recipe writer, for my natural inclination when I cook is to just put things together and eat them without thinking too much about the details. But of course that's not the way to work out a recipe. A while back, in one of my rare fits of organisation, I drew up a format sheet to use when I cook – needless to say that lasted all of two days before I was back to my usual habit of scrawling on bits of paper and then spending ages trying to decipher what on earth I'd written! It's not a very scientific approach, I know, but all I can say is that it works for me.

This particular recipe is a good example. I have made the salad several times over the past few weeks, but it was only when a friend happened by at lunchtime and asked for the recipe that I realised I had no real clue as to quantities. However, you will be pleased to hear I've actually taken notes this time around and this is the result – all I ask is that you don't feel beholden to use exactly the same amounts of everything as it's really just a guide.

As far as the dressing goes, I generally use a spoonful or two of whatever I happen to have made up, but if you're looking for a recipe try the lemon-pressed oil dressing on page 300.

150 g peas in their pods
100 g sugar snap peas
100 g snowpeas (mange-tout)
sea salt flakes and freshly ground black pepper
4–6 cherry tomatoes, halved or quartered
2 tablespoons salad dressing, or more or less to taste
as many small basil leaves as you would like
50–60 g goat's cheese or feta marinated in olive oil

- Bring a large saucepan of water to the boil.
- Meanwhile, shell the peas and trim the tops of the sugar snaps and snowpeas, stringing them as you go.
- Once the water is boiling, salt it lightly. Add all three lots of peas, and cook them for 2–3 minutes until they are bright green and tender, but still a little crisp. ›

- Tip them into a colander as soon as they are ready and run them under cool water to stop them cooking. Finally, dunk them in a bowl of ice and water to set the colour – I don't always do this last part if the salad is just for me, but if I want them to be bright-green and gorgeous for someone else, I do. Now, wrap the peas in a clean tea towel to dry them off a bit.
- Tip the peas into a bowl and add the tomatoes. Drizzle some dressing over the top and gently mix it in. Pile the salad into a serving bowl, dotting it here and there with basil leaves and pieces of goat's cheese or feta. Grind some black pepper over the top.
- While I am putting the salad together I usually warm up a bit of Turkish bread in the oven, as it's perfect for sopping up the juices in the bottom of the bowl – the best part of any salad, as far as I'm concerned.

11th July

How can it be that in the dead of winter so much is blooming? Our garden is far more vibrant now than it is in mid-summer, which surprises me as I've always thought the opposite would be true. In summer it's a sea of green and purple foliage with just the odd flower blooming here and there, but right now it's an absolute riot of colour – reds, yellow, pinks, oranges, blues and maroons (some of which shouldn't go together, but it all just seems to work). My primary school sewing teacher used to insist that 'blue and green should never be seen unless they're in the washing machine'. I heartily disagreed then, and I do even more so now as I look around me. (The ending to that particular story is that she obviously felt my scorn for I was thrown out of the sewing class at the tender age of 10 and told never to darken her door again! I must admit it was a huge relief . . .)

In amongst this explosion of colour I can hear a young male blue fairy wren trilling his little heart out. His brilliant blue feathers were only just starting to colour a few weeks ago, but now they are positively iridescent. The Buddha's head is a favourite perch and he is fluffing about on it now, showing off to his two female companions – the start of his harem, no doubt.

12th July

A friend has dropped in a big bunch of cavolo nero, which I love. Do you know it? The name translates from the Italian as 'black cabbage', although its leaves are more a lovely dark green with just a tinge of blue. They're narrow and crinkly, and when you wash them they almost seem to be waterproof, as the drops slip off them, leaving silvery trails. We'll have it for dinner tonight with some grilled polenta. Perfect.

Sautéed Cavolo Nero with Crisp Polenta

SERVES 2

½ batch light and fluffy polenta (see page 290)
sea salt flakes and freshly ground black pepper
1 bunch (approx 600 g) cavolo nero, thoroughly washed
¼ cup (60 ml) extra virgin olive oil, plus extra for brushing and drizzling
1 large clove garlic, finely chopped
1 small red chilli, finely chopped
lemon juice, to taste
marinated goat's cheese or Persian feta, optional
lemon wedges, to serve

If you like the earthy flavours of silverbeet and kale, then cavolo nero is for you. It's generally more 'chewy' and slightly sweeter than the other two, leaning more in flavour towards the cabbage family. Cooked this way it's delicious – there is a good hit of heat from the chilli, and a touch of garlic to enhance its robust flavour. We make a meal of it with the polenta, but it's great as a side dish too. Or up the ante a bit with the amount of oil, garlic and chilli, add grated parmesan (and even some crumbled Italian sausage, if you like) and toss it with pasta – orecchiette is ideal because the little dimples catch the strands of cabbage beautifully.

Oh, I meant to say, because the polenta takes a while to cook, I often make it a day or two ahead, so it's ready to go when I want to quickly throw the meal together.

- Make up the polenta. When it's ready, scrape it into a shallow rectangular container or baking tray lined with baking paper. Smooth it out as best you can with a wet palette knife and leave it to set. Cover it tightly and store it in the fridge. (You probably won't need quite all of it for two of you, but I find that leftovers never seem to go amiss – there is always something in the fridge that is better for being served with a wedge of grilled polenta!)
- Bring a large saucepan of water to the boil and salt it well. Meanwhile, slice the cavolo nero leaves crossways into 2–3 cm pieces. Scoop them into the boiling water and cook for at least 5 minutes or until they're quite tender. Depending on the size and age of the leaves, this may take a little while – they should be a bit chewy, but not overly so. (If you prefer, you could steam the cavalo nero until tender.) Drain the leaves well in a colander, pressing down on them to extract as much liquid as possible. Use a fork to fluff them up a bit.
- Now return the saucepan to the stovetop over low heat. Pour in the oil. Once it's warm, add the garlic and chilli and cook them gently for a couple of minutes, stirring them regularly. You don't want the garlic to brown or it will taste bitter. Stir in the cavolo nero, then cover the pan and increase the heat to medium. Leave it to cook for 10 minutes or so, stirring occasionally. The only way to tell if it is ready is to try a forkful – it should be delicious and not at all 'raw' tasting. When it's done, season with salt and pepper, and stir in some lemon juice, to taste.

- While the cavolo nero is cooking, slice the polenta into triangles or sticks. Heat a non-stick chargrill pan or frying pan over medium–high heat. Brush the polenta generously with oil and add it to the pan. Leave it to cook until it forms a golden crust, then turn it over and repeat on the other side. Remove it to a plate and keep it warm.
- To serve, sit two or three slices of polenta on each plate, top them generously with the cavolo nero mixture, then crumble on some goat's cheese or feta (if using). Now give it a good grinding of black pepper and drizzle a little more extra virgin olive oil over the top, if liked. Serve with lemon wedges.

14th July

We've had steady soaking rain for a few days now, but not enough to stop me walking this morning. It was lovely – not a soul about, and the first wattle flowers were glowing softly in the dawn light. I couldn't resist nipping off a sprig which is now sitting in a vase on my desk, looking as if a little ray of sunshine has crept into the room. It smells wonderful too, with a crisp fragrance that always reminds me of sun-dried washing.

On the weekend I had a planting marathon as part of my ongoing experiment to find out what grows best where, so we can finally site the veggie garden. In amongst the grevilleas I planted some rather exotic-sounding crimson carrot seedlings, half a dozen delicate elk-horn lettuce, six bushes of Italian flat beans and four stands of mustard greens. I now have to keep my fingers crossed for the next few weeks and see how they go.

One thing I *don't* need to worry about is the silverbeet. I have an absolute glut of it at the moment and I'm about to make a silverbeet and chickpea 'pie' to use some up.

Silverbeet & Chickpea Bake

SERVES 4

2 very large (or 4 small) leeks
⅓ cup (80 ml) extra virgin olive oil, or more to taste
1 large clove garlic, finely chopped
650 g silverbeet (Swiss chard), ruby chard or English spinach
400 g can chickpeas, rinsed and drained
good grating of fresh nutmeg
sea salt flakes and freshly ground black pepper, to taste
3 eggs
¾ cup (60 g) freshly grated parmesan, plus a little extra for sprinkling

There is something about this simple, earthy dish that's very satisfying and wholesome. Tomatoes seem to have a real affinity with it so I tend to serve it with a tomato salad or something along the lines of a ratatouille. Occasionally, I'll stir a can of tuna into the mixture before baking it, which is rather good too and makes it just that bit more substantial.

- Preheat your oven to 180°C. Lightly grease a medium-sized gratin dish or shallow earthenware dish.
- Trim the dark green tops off the leeks. Now cut the leeks in half lengthways and wash them really well to remove any grit (leeks have a habit of trapping little bits of soil between the leaves so give them a thorough going over). Slice them finely and set them aside.
- Heat the oil in a large frying pan over medium–low heat. Add the leek and garlic and cook, stirring regularly, for 10 minutes or so, until they have softened and become somewhat translucent.
- In the meantime, thoroughly wash the silverbeet, ruby chard or spinach. Leave the water on the leaves and chop them crossways into 2 cm wide strips. Put these strips into a large saucepan and sit it over high heat. Cover the pan tightly and cook the leaves, stirring from time to time, until they have wilted and collapsed. This should only take about 2–3 minutes – keep an eye on them so they don't scorch. As soon as they're ready, take them off the heat. Tip the leaves into a colander and drain them well, pressing down on them to extract as much moisture as possible.
- Once the leek mixture is ready, add the drained leaves to the pan and cook for 5 minutes, stirring regularly to break up any clumps. If it seems a bit dry, add a little more olive oil.
- Remove the pan from the heat, and mix in the chickpeas, nutmeg, salt and pepper. Set the pan aside.
- In a large bowl, lightly beat the eggs then stir in the parmesan. Scrape in the leaf mixture and thoroughly mix everything together – more often than not I squish it together with my hands. Transfer the mixture to the prepared dish and spread it out evenly, then sprinkle the extra parmesan over the top.
- Bake the gratin for 35–40 minutes, or until the top seems firm and is flecked with gold. Leave it to cool a bit, then serve it warm or at room temperature.

16th July

Many of our friends are amazed at how cold it gets overnight here in winter, despite being in the sub-tropics – it's certainly something I never expected when we arrived. I'm not quite sure why this is, but I suspect that with none of the tall buildings and generated energy that a city has to trap in heat, the air here cools to a much lower temperature and the warmth of the day dissipates more rapidly. In fact, the fields below our house are white and crunchy with frost at least half a dozen times in winter.

But oh, these spectacular winter sunsets . . . The sky this evening is blue as blue, apart from an extraordinary bruise of a cloud edged with gold from the sun's last rays. Tonight I can't stop for long to enjoy it, though, as I'm on a mission – I'm off to France to teach in a few months' time (it sounds a bit like taking coals to Newcastle, doesn't it?). I must admit to feeling a mixture of excitement and apprehension at the prospect, but right now I can't afford either, as I have to get the recipes I shall be teaching together and send them off – all 28 of them. So I suspect we shall be having some rather eclectic meals over the next few weeks. Some recipes are done and dusted, like the lamb shank and polenta ones on the following pages, but at least another half dozen need to be tested and written.

17th July

One of the recipes for my teaching stint in France that is well under way (literally – I can hear the churn whirring in the background as I write this) is one for honey and pecan ice-cream (see overleaf). This batch should be extra good as it's made with Frank the pecan man's fabulous pecans and our local white mahogany honey, which has a beautifully rounded flavour and gorgeous, clear amber colour.

Speaking of honey, Colin (the man who delivers our gas bottles) is a bee-keeper. On a recent visit he stopped at one of the grevilleas that was alive with bees and pulled off some of the flowering brushes to show me how, when the bees are collecting nectar, nothing will disturb them. It was remarkable – they barely seemed to realise they had moved. He then gently shook them away and slapped the flower into the palm of his hand. I was fascinated to see the amount of sticky-sweet nectar that gathered there – no wonder the bees and honeyeaters love grevilleas.

Honey & Pecan Ice-Cream

SERVES 6–8

80 g caster sugar
100 g coarsely chopped pecans
200 g honey
600 ml pure cream
4 eggs
1½ teaspoons vanilla extract
450 ml thickened cream, lightly whipped
pecan praline (see page 356), to serve, optional

This ice-cream really does taste divine and has the most glorious melt-in-the-mouth texture, however whenever I've taught it to a class I've noticed a few people turn a whiter shade of pale when I mention we have to make a custard first, and even paler still when they realise it's not done in a double boiler but straight in the pan! This is really not hard to do, but I know it can seem a bit scary first time around. The most important thing is to stay focused and be a bit brave, as the custard needs to be cooked until it's quite thick. Probably the best way to approach this is to cook the custard over low heat the first time you make it, then as you gain in confidence you can increase the heat – soon you'll be whipping it up in no time.

- Put the sugar into a medium-sized heavy-based saucepan or copper pan over low heat and allow the sugar to melt. You will find that initially the sugar melts in patches, but don't stir it as this can cause the sugar to 'candy' – just move the pan about over the heat, and use a wooden spoon to push and poke about, rather than stir it. When the sugar has melted and is just starting to turn golden, tip in the pecans. Stir the mixture gently, but constantly, until the nuts smell 'toasty' and the sugar has caramelised and become a lovely deep golden brown.
- Immediately scoop in the honey (this helps stop the sugar caramelising any more). Give the mixture a stir and, once the honey has melted, pour in the pure cream. Increase the heat to medium and bring the mixture to just below the boil.
- Meanwhile, lightly whisk the eggs, then tip them into a jug. Now, pour the beaten egg into the hot honey cream in a slow, steady stream, whisking all the while. Continue to cook the honey mixture, stirring it constantly (I use a combination of a flat-based sauce whisk initially and then revert to a flat-based wooden spoon as the mixture thickens) until it forms a thick custard. The most important thing to remember here is not to allow the custard to come to the boil or it will curdle.
- As soon as the custard is ready, remove the pan from the heat and sit it in a large dish or sink of iced water. Continue to stir it until the custard is cool (you may need to change the water if it gets too warm). Once the custard has cooled, stir in the vanilla. Pour the custard into a container or bowl, cover it tightly and chill it. (You can make the custard the day before you need it if you like – in fact the flavour only improves if you do.)
- Fold the cold custard and whipped cream together. If you have an ice-cream churn, simply churn the mixture in batches in it. If not, you will have a bit more work to do, I'm afraid. For the non-churn method, pour the mixture into a large stainless steel bowl and freeze until the ice-cream is frozen 5 cm in from the edges of the bowl – the time will vary, depending on your freezer, but it will probably take a ›

BY THE WAY . . .

The flavour of any homemade ice-cream is always best after it has sat in the freezer for a day or two so it has a chance to 'ripen' and allow the flavour to fully develop.

few hours. Remove the bowl from the freezer and give the ice-cream a really good whisk with a balloon whisk or hand-held electric beater (you could also scrape it into a food processor and process it until it's smooth, but it makes for a bit more washing up!). Repeat this freezing and beating twice more. (If you are wondering why you are doing all this, I promise you it's worth it, as it helps break up the ice crystals in the ice-cream into smaller ones so the texture becomes smoother and creamier each time you do it.)

- Finally, pack the ice-cream into a container, cover it tightly and freeze it until it's firm – at least overnight (see note, left).
- When you're ready to serve the ice-cream, scoop it into chilled bowls or glasses and sprinkle crushed pecan brittle over the top. If you want to highlight the pecan flavour even more, try serving it with pecan butter-crunch biscuits (see page 363).

THE SILENCE OF THE SPOON!

What I'm going to say next might sound a bit odd and I don't quite know how to explain it, but here goes. Over the years, whenever I've made custard I've noticed a phenomenon which I think of as the 'silence of the spoon'. This occurs when the custard is nearly cooked and beginning to thicken: if you listen you will notice that instead of slopping wetly against the sides of the pan and making little splashing sounds as you stir it, the custard goes quiet. This is a really good indicator that it has thickened and is just about ready.

18th July

It's becoming colder by the day, yet when I was out this morning the sweet fragrance of jasmine filled the air in one of the most densely wooded parts of the track. It was like a small miracle. I couldn't spot it at first, but then saw a cluster of the delicate pink and white blossoms dangling from a branch above my head – obviously an escapee from somebody's garden. I can't bring myself to pull it out, but it's a bit rampant so I shall bring some secateurs with me on my next walk and cut it back a little so it doesn't smother any of the trees, which it could well do if left unchecked.

Oh gosh, as I read over those last words I realise that I'm becoming more and more like my mother! As I child I used to die of embarrassment when she pinched off plant sprigs that happened to be bobbing over a fence or creeping beneath one . . .and now here I find myself armed with secateurs about to do much more!

19th July

It's our local market today and I have triumphantly returned with a clutch of seedlings to plant out: Rouge de Marmande tomatoes, Chandler strawberries, and the big prize – a White Shahtoot mulberry tree. The latter is something I've coveted for a long time. They are a lovely weeping tree, with long pale greeny-white mulberries that are sweet as sweet. I remember first reading about them many years ago in British travel writer Eric Newby's book, *A Short Walk in the Hindu Kush*, however it's only since we moved here that I've actually seen them and eaten the mulberries he described in such mouth-watering detail. And now I have one of my own to plant. Whoopee!

I also succumbed to half a dozen fat bulbs of fennel (they were far too pristine and beautiful to walk past), two big bags of strawberries and a startlingly crimson bunch of rhubarb.

As I write this, the rhubarb is already poaching – in a snap-lock bag. I know that sounds a bit bizarre but it's a terrific way to cook it, as it helps keep its shape and somehow intensifies the colour like no other method I know. I'm going to mix it with the strawberries and we'll have it for dessert. I'm hoping it will be just the right finish for what has become a very colourful dinner from the garden: sweet potato and bacon frittata (see page 244), served with crunchy rosemary potatoes (see page 145) and fennel, watercress and pear salad (see page 300), then the rhubarb and strawberries with a little cream and wedge or two of shortbread (see page 86).

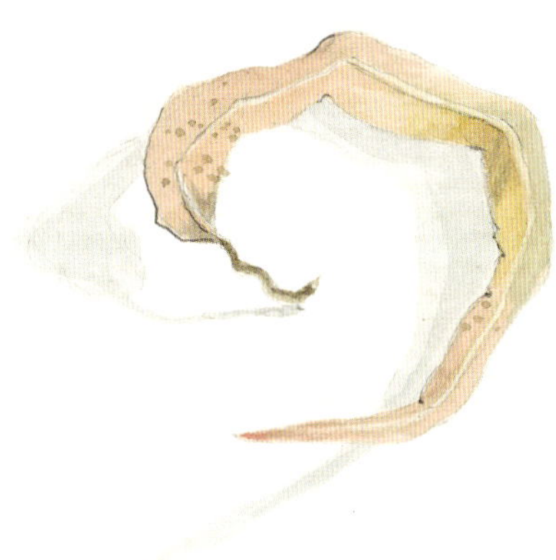

19

Poached Rhubarb with Strawberries

SERVES 4

about 500 g rhubarb, thoroughly washed
1¼ cups (275 g) caster sugar, or more to taste
1½ teaspoons vanilla extract
¼ cup (60 ml) clear apple juice or water
1 punnet (250 g) medium-sized strawberries
cream, to serve

BY THE WAY . . .

This simple dessert goes well with many things – a spoonful of rich cream, good vanilla ice-cream, homemade custard or, for something a little more exotic, try it with lightly sweetened mascarpone scented with a few drops of rosewater. A crisp sweet wafer or wedge of shortbread wouldn't go astray either.

As I said, this method of cooking rhubarb may seem rather unusual but the results are fantastic. The bag, rhubarb and all, is lowered into a large saucepan of simmering water and cooked gently for about 20 minutes. The resulting rhubarb is the most gorgeous rosy pink and is tender, but holds its shape beautifully, which is one of the most difficult things to get rhubarb to do, as it goes from being separate pieces to a mush in the blink of an eye.

- Slice the rhubarb on the diagonal into 4–5 cm chunks, then place in a bowl and sprinkle the caster sugar, vanilla extract and apple juice or water over the top. Mix everything together, cover the bowl, and leave to sit for an hour or so, gently stirring from time to time to help dissolve the sugar.
- Just before you want to cook the rhubarb, bring a large saucepan of water to the boil over high heat.
- Give the rhubarb mixture another stir – the sugar should be partly dissolved and somewhat slushy (the more dissolved it is, the better). Scoop it into a large snap-lock bag, squeeze out most of the air, then seal the bag tightly.
- Now, fold a tea towel and lower it into the pan of boiling water so it covers the base and comes up the sides a bit. (Don't worry that it waves around in the water – as soon as you add the rhubarb it will settle.) Lower the bag of rhubarb into the water, making sure it rests on the tea towel and doesn't touch the base of the pan, for if it does, the plastic will most probably melt (I learnt this the hard way!).
- Partly cover the pan, and adjust the heat so the water bubbles very, very gently. Cook the rhubarb for about 20–25 minutes, or until it is tender. To check, use tongs to carefully lift the bag partly out of the water and gently squeeze a couple of pieces of rhubarb through the bag – if they are still a bit firm, give them another couple of minutes then check again.
- When the rhubarb is ready, hold a bowl beside the pan and use tongs to carefully lift the bag out of the water into the bowl (the plastic is quite soft at this stage so do this quickly otherwise the weight of the rhubarb mixture might tear it). Leave it to cool. Once it's cool, open the bag and carefully pour or spoon the rhubarb into a container, seal it tightly and store it in the fridge. You may find that some of the sugar hasn't quite dissolved, but it will do so as the rhubarb sits.
- When you are ready to serve, hull the strawberries and halve them or slice them lengthways. Gently mix them into the rhubarb. Transfer the lot to a serving bowl and serve with cream.

Fennel, Watercress & Pear Salad with Lemon-Pressed Olive Oil

SERVES 6

2 large (or 5 baby) bulbs fennel, halved and cored
1 very large bunch watercress, washed and broken into sprigs
1 large just-ripe pear, finely sliced
150 g roasted pecans, coarsely chopped
150 g marinated goat's cheese, crumbled into small chunks
freshly ground black pepper

DRESSING

¾ cup (180 ml) lemon-pressed extra virgin olive oil
sea salt flakes, to taste
⅓ teaspoon sugar
1½–2 tablespoons lemon juice
small dash of balsamic vinegar

We eat this salad again and again during winter, usually for lunch with chunks of good bread to wipe the plate clean. I do all sorts of variations on the theme – sometimes substituting rocket for watercress, witlof for fennel or adding silky slivers of avocado. The simple dressing is a great favourite of mine and terrific in many other salads too – it's perfect whenever you want a bright lemony flavour. Just one thing to keep in mind: lemon-pressed oils vary considerably from brand to brand, so remember to taste the dressing and adjust the balance of flavours once you have made it.

- To make the dressing, whisk everything together until the salt and sugar have dissolved. Taste it and adjust the flavours to suit you, then store it in the fridge until you need it.
- Slice the fennel very, very finely (if you are fortunate enough to have a mandolin, it is ideal for this). Put the slices into a large bowl as you go, and toss them with a little dressing to stop them discolouring. Add the watercress, pear slices, half the pecans and half the goat's cheese to the bowl. Pour in the remaining dressing (or as much as you would like) and use your hands to gently mix everything together. Pile the salad into a serving bowl (or you can pile it up onto individual plates to serve as a starter) and scatter with the remaining pecans and goat's cheese. Grind a little black pepper over the lot and serve.

21st July

It's the coldest day of the year so far. The temperature went down to 3°C overnight and the thermometer is hovering around 12°C at the moment. We were so swathed in beanies, scarves, gloves and various layers of clothing for our morning walk that we looked like two toy roly-poly men. Knock us down and I'm sure we would have bounced back up again!

But despite this cold snap, the mulberry trees are covered in a fuzz of pale green leaves and tiny clusters of mulberries; the lilly pillys are adorned with their hectic pink new shoots; and, as we passed the peach orchard, the first faint blush of misty blossom hovered over the branches.

But that is not the only indicator that the seasonal wheel is turning. There is a flurry of activity amongst our bird population too. Although it seems far too cold to us, it would appear that this is the time for a lot of billing, cooing and courting. Most of the male birds are strutting their stuff in their resplendent winter finery, while the females pretend not to be too interested (sounds horribly familiar, doesn't it?). Some lucky protagonists are already nesting, and we see them fly past, trailing long streamers of palm frond to reinforce their new homes. At this rate our bird population could well double over the coming months!

22nd July

We have some new additions to the neighbourhood – the sweetest little lambs. They must have been born about a week ago and they still look terribly uncertain about the world around them. However, they are very dear and rush up to the fence whenever we walk by. This morning there was one little chap who was so new he could barely stand on his very wobbly legs.

When we got back from our walk I cleaned some fennel I bought in the market. Gosh, it's beautiful. I've munched my way through half a bulb already and must stop or there won't be enough to cook. I do so love the way its flavour and texture changes, depending on how it's prepared. When it's raw, the aniseed flavour is quite intense and it has a wonderful crunch when you bite into it; once cooked, the flavour mellows and becomes softer and more rounded, and it's so meltingly tender you can cut it with a fork.

I'm rather fond of this particular way of cooking it. It's very simple, yet it tastes far more complex than you might expect. Do let it cook until it is quite caramelised in patches – it may even look a bit burnt but will taste wonderful.

Caramelised Fennel with Carrots

SERVES 4

I am the first to admit that this is not the most beautiful-looking dish, but the flavour is superb. When I serve it, I usually turn the slices of fennel over so the side that was on the bottom of the pan is facing up, as it tends to be more glazed and glossy than the other side. I also cook the slices in two frying pans as even my biggest one can't quite take all the fennel in one layer, which is what it needs to develop a rich, brown colour.

- 3 large bulbs fennel
- ½ lemon
- 60 g unsalted butter
- ⅓ cup (80 ml) extra virgin olive oil
- 2 onions, finely chopped
- 2 carrots, finely diced (about 5 mm chunks)
- 1 cup (250 ml) good chicken stock
- 2 bay leaves
- sea salt flakes, to taste
- lemon juice, to taste

- To trim the fennel, cut off any green leafy fronds pretty much level with the top of the bulbs. (At one time, all fennel sold had these graceful fronds, but these days it is rare – more's the pity, as they make a gorgeous garnish and are also wonderful to add flavour to barbecued fish.) Now trim the base flat, and check the outside layer of fennel – if it is really coarse or badly bruised, peel this outer layer away. Cut each bulb, from top to bottom, into 8 mm thick slices. Generally the core is removed from fennel, but in this case leave it intact as it holds the slices together. Rub each slice with the cut side of the lemon to help stop them discolouring, then set aside.
- Divide the butter and oil evenly between two large frying pans over medium heat. When the butter has melted and the mixture is hot, divide the onion and carrot evenly between the pans and cook, stirring regularly, for about 8 minutes or until the onion is golden. ›

- Tuck the fennel slices into the pans so they sit in a single layer. The easiest way to do this is to push some of the carrot and onion out of the way and nestle in a slice of fennel, then scoop the veggies as best you can over the top. Cook the fennel slices for about 8 minutes on each side, or until they are partly golden. Divide the chicken stock evenly between the pans and add a bay leaf to each too.
- Now cover the pans – if you don't have lids, sit a baking tray on top of each one, but be careful to use oven gloves or a thick tea towel when you move them as they get very hot. Cook the fennel for another 20 minutes or so, carefully turning it once halfway through the cooking, until it is meltingly tender and deep golden brown on the bottom, with a few dark caramelised patches. If the slices don't look brown enough when you turn them over, increase the heat slightly.
- Use a wide-bladed spatula or egg slice to transfer the fennel to a serving dish. Spoon the carrots and onions over and around the fennel. There shouldn't be much in the way of liquid left in the pan – if there is more than about ⅓ cup (80 ml), increase the heat to boil off the excess. Sprinkle in some salt and add a good squeeze of lemon juice. Taste it, and when it's as you like it, pour it over the fennel slices.
- You can pretty much eat this at any temperature: hot, cool or barely warm (my favourite as I think it does the flavours the most justice). It keeps well for days.

27th July

The Byron Bay Writers' Festival is always held at the very end of July or early August. It's something we never miss because it's the most wonderful, stimulating event. And this year was no exception, despite the freezing cold and wet – so many fascinating people with so much to say. Among the highlights was Miriam Margolyes reading some of her favourite pieces. She read with such warmth and skill, it was magical stuff and she had everyone in the palm of her hand.

Today, of course, it's back to earth with a bump, although the festival has been a real shot in the arm and it has prompted me to attack my writing with renewed vigour, which is wonderful. So if you notice any changes from here on in, you know why!

28th July

I've had a bowl of pears ripening on the kitchen bench these past few days as I've been meaning to make a pear and almond cake. They look so lovely that I've been reluctant to use them, however I've noticed those tiny little fruit flies starting to hover about and if I don't do something with them soon the flies will have a field day. I shall slice a couple of pears into a fennel and pear salad (see page 300) to eat with dinner tonight, as we have become somewhat addicted to it, and the rest will go into the cake.

It's a lovely cake too. I've always loved the flavour of pears and almonds together – for me, it's just one of those perfect combinations where the whole is greater than the sum of its parts. It's actually a bit of a running joke in the family that I can rarely walk past a patisserie which has any sort of pear and almond tart, cake or muffin in the window, without ducking in to buy one.

Fragrant Pear & Almond Cake

SERVES 8–10

180 g almond meal
80 g self-raising flour
¼ teaspoon salt
4 free-range eggs
250 g caster sugar, plus extra for sprinkling
1½ teaspoons vanilla extract
¼ teaspoon almond essence
200 g unsalted butter, melted and cooled
icing sugar, for dusting
cream, to serve

MUSCAT-POACHED PEARS

2 fairly large just-ripe pears
1 cup (250 ml) muscat
a squeeze of lemon juice

This cake is very simple to make, and is really moist and buttery. Just the sort of thing that is perfect served plain for tea, or can be turned into a rather lovely dessert if it's dusted with icing sugar and served with cream. The muscat really enhances the flavour of the pears (a luscious dessert wine would be rather fabulous too), but if you would rather not use alcohol, you can cook them in pear nectar instead.

- To make the muscat-poached pears, peel, quarter and core the pears. Sit them in a small frying pan or saucepan so they fit fairly snugly in a single layer, then pour in the muscat and lemon juice. Turn the heat to medium–high and warm the muscat until it comes to the boil – as soon as it does, turn the heat down so it bubbles gently. Cover the pan and poach the pears for about 10 minutes or until they're just tender, carefully turning them once while they cook.
- When the pears are ready, gently transfer them to a bowl with a slotted spoon. Now, increase the heat under the pan and boil down the remaining cooking liquid until only ½ cup (125 ml) or so remains. Pour this over the pears and leave them to cool (you can do this a day ahead and leave them in the fridge overnight).
- Preheat your oven to 180°C. Butter a shallow 24 cm cake tin and line the base and sides with buttered baking paper. Dust the tin lightly with flour and set it aside.
- Put the almond meal, flour and salt into a large bowl and whisk them together with a balloon whisk for 40 seconds, or until they are well mixed.
- In a separate bowl, whisk together the eggs, sugar, vanilla extract and almond essence until they're thoroughly combined, then mix in the cooled butter until it disappears. Now, scrape this buttery mixture into the almond meal mixture and stir them together. Spread the resulting batter evenly into the prepared tin.
- Take the pear quarters out of their liquid and pat them dry. Now, halve each quarter lengthways and lay them decoratively over the top of the batter (there is no need to press them in as they will sink a bit as the cake bakes). Sprinkle a tiny bit of caster sugar over each slice of pear.
- Bake the cake for about 45–50 minutes, or until the top springs back slowly when gently pressed and a fine skewer inserted in the centre comes out clean. You may find that after 40 minutes or so the top is looking quite brown enough – if this is the case, just sit a sheet of foil loosely on top of the cake to stop it getting any darker.
- Transfer the cake to a rack and leave it to cool in the tin until it's barely warm. Carefully invert the cake onto the rack, remove the tin and paper, then invert it again onto a plate so it's pear-side up. Dust lightly with icing sugar and serve with cream.

30th July

What a sight – the oriole is back! I looked up from my toast and tea this morning to see him delicately sipping water from the bird bath. It's the second time he has appeared and he is oh-so-beautiful. He's a big bird, about the size of a friar bird, with a deep-green back, striated black and white breast, and brick-red bill and legs. The first time we saw him, over a week ago, we thought he must be passing through, however here he is again so perhaps he has decided to make this his patch for a bit – I do hope so.

I'm making a warm egg and bacon salad for lunch and I feel a bit like the Cat in the Hat from the Dr Seuss books as so many of the egg shells are the most delicate shade of green . . . anyone for green eggs and ham?

Frisée, Poached Egg & Bacon Salad with Croutons (aka Green Eggs and Ham)

SERVES 4

I do love this classic salad, and often end up making a version of it for dinner when I'm on my own as it's an ideal meal for one. Basically I just use any salad greens I happen to have on hand – they all seem to work a treat; however, I must admit that I'm particularly proud of the beautiful lacy elk-horn lettuce that I used in the salad the day we took this photo, as it was one of my gardening experiments that worked! If you manage to find some, do give it a go as it has a robust, slightly 'hot' flavour that can stand up to the warm dressing.

1 medium-sized head of fine frisée *or* 1 large bunch of elk-horn lettuce, well washed
4 slices good dense bread, crusts removed
olive oil, for pan-frying
splash of white vinegar
4 very fresh free-range eggs
250 g slab or thickly cut bacon, cut into 5 mm wide pieces
freshly ground black pepper

DRESSING

100 ml extra virgin olive oil
2 tablespoons white wine vinegar
sea salt flakes, to taste

- Pick over the frisée, discarding any coarse leaves; break the rest into bite-sized tendrils. Put these into a roomy bowl, then cover and chill.
- Make the dressing by whisking all the ingredients together in a bowl. Set it aside.
- To make the croutons, cut the bread into small chunks (about 1 cm square). Heat a thin layer of olive oil in a large frying pan over medium heat. When the oil is hot, add the bread chunks and fry them, turning regularly, until they're golden brown all over. Scoop them onto paper towels to drain, then wipe out any excess oil from the pan (you'll be using it again soon to cook the bacon). If you are anything like me you will need to put the croutons as far away from yourself as possible if you want any left by the time you are ready to eat the salad!
- To poach the eggs, fill a frying pan with cold water to the depth of about 3 cm. Bring the water to a simmer and add a splash of vinegar. Break an egg into a cup and slide the egg into the water, as close to the surface as possible to help stop the yolk breaking. Quickly repeat this with the remaining eggs. Poach the eggs ›

for about 4 minutes, or until they are done to your liking. (I like mine with a runny yolk so it mingles with the dressing once you cut it – it's one of the best parts of the salad.) When the eggs are ready, carefully lift them out of the water with an egg slice and trim off any raggedy bits of white with a sharp knife. Slip the cooked eggs into a shallow dish (a gratin dish is ideal) of tepid water until you need them. (If you get your timing right with cooking the bacon and tossing the salad, there is no need to hold the eggs in the tepid water – just lift them out of the pan onto the salad.)

- While the eggs are cooking, return the wiped-out frying pan to the heat. Once it's fairly hot, add the bacon pieces. Fry them until they're crisp and golden, then scoop them out of the pan onto a plate. Leave any bacon fat in the pan. Pour in the dressing and swirl it around – it will hiss and spit a bit. Remove the pan from the heat, carefully taste the dressing and add a bit more vinegar and salt if needed.
- Tip the dressing over the frisée and toss them well together. Divide the frisée evenly among four plates then scatter some croutons and bacon strips over the top. Sit a poached egg in the middle of each salad. Scatter more croutons and bacon around the egg and grind on some black pepper. Serve immediately.

AUGUST

1st August

We have just received the news that a dear friend's mother, whom I have known since childhood, has died. Although not unexpected, we are both deeply saddened, as it just doesn't seem possible that someone so vital and seemingly invincible is no longer here.

There is something about times like this that sends me scuttling into the kitchen to stir, knead, slice and chop my way through the day, cooking dish after dish in some strange hope that the steady, soothing rhythm of all this activity will assuage the grief and create some sort of order out of the chaos. I know I'm not alone in doing this. It's as though we somehow work out our sadness amidst the pots and pans and welcome domesticity of our daily life.

I have pretty much cooked myself to a standstill and around me are jars of biscuits, cakes cooling on their racks, two batches of preserved lemons and the comfort of a homely casserole gently bubbling away in the oven. One of the cakes I baked is the marzipan and pear cake on page 320, which we shall eat for dessert with a little cream. It tastes wonderful in that lovely old-fashioned way that some cakes and puddings do – and I suspect it will be just what our battered spirits need.

Beef with Red Wine, Prunes & Pecans

SERVES 4–6

⅓–½ cup (80–125 ml) olive oil
3 large onions, thinly sliced
2 large cloves garlic, finely chopped
about ⅓ cup (50 g) plain flour
1.5 kg blade steak, trimmed and cut into 4–5 cm chunks
1½ cups (375 ml) red wine
300 ml chicken or veal stock
1½ tablespoons thyme leaves
2 teaspoons brown sugar
2 heaped teaspoons Dijon mustard
1 teaspoon sea salt flakes, or more to taste
freshly ground black pepper
18 plump prunes
18 roasted pecans
thyme sprigs, to garnish

I remember my mum making something very similar to this classic beef stew when we were kids. We had quite a long trip home from school so were always ravenous by the time we got there – it was heavenly to be greeted with such a wonderful aroma wafting through the house. Invariably she would serve it with a big dollop of mashed potato, which was perfect to soak up the juices. I still serve it like this, but I imagine it would also be terrific with light and fluffy polenta (see page 290). Just one thing about casseroles in general: more often than not it's best to cut the meat into bigger chunks than you might think, as they shrink quite a lot as they cook.

- Preheat your oven to 160°C.
- I use a lovely big enamelled cast-iron casserole for this, but if you don't have a flameproof casserole, use a large frying pan for the stovetop cooking, then transfer everything to a casserole dish before it goes in the oven. Heat 1 tablespoon of oil in the casserole (or frying pan) over medium heat, add the onion and garlic and cook them, stirring regularly, for 10 minutes or until they have softened and coloured just a little. When they're ready, scoop them out into a large bowl and return the casserole to the heat. Add another tablespoon of oil to warm up.

- Meanwhile, tip the flour into a plastic bag. Add enough of the steak chunks to fill the casserole in a single layer and jiggle the bag to coat the chunks in flour. Tip them into a strainer to shake off the excess flour before adding them to the casserole. Brown them all over, turning them as they need it – you want them to be a good rich brown. As they're ready, remove them from the pan and add them to the onion mixture. Continue flouring and cooking the meat like this, adding more oil to the pan as necessary. When all the meat is cooked, stir the meat and onion together until thoroughly mixed.

- Add the red wine, stock, thyme leaves, sugar, mustard, salt and pepper to the casserole dish (or frying pan). Bring the mixture to the boil, stirring really well to scrape up all the lovely sticky brown bits from the base of the pan. Return the meat and onion mixture to the casserole (watch out as it will splash up when you do this) and mix them in well. Now cover the dish tightly and transfer it to the oven.
- Cook the casserole for 1½ hours. After this time, remove the lid and stir in the prunes and most of the pecans (reserve a few for garnishing). Return the dish, without the lid, to the oven and cook the casserole for another 30–40 minutes or until the juices have thickened to a sauce consistency, giving it a good stir halfway through the cooking time. This time may vary quite a bit, depending on the size of your casserole dish – the liquid in a large one tends to reduce more quickly than it does in a smaller dish.
- When it's ready, remove the casserole from the oven and leave it to sit for a few minutes. If it needs it, blot up any surface fat with some paper towels. Taste the sauce, and add a little more salt if necessary.
- I like to take this out to the table in the casserole, but as the sides of the dish can get a bit messy, I usually clean them up a bit first with damp paper towels. To finish, tuck the reserved pecans here and there over the top of the dish and scatter with a few thyme sprigs.

Upside-Down Marzipan & Pear Cake

SERVES 10–12

1¼ cups (185 g) plain flour
1½ teaspoons baking powder
¼ teaspoon salt
1 cup (220 g) caster sugar
200 g marzipan, chopped into small chunks
5 × 70 g eggs, lightly beaten
280 g unsalted butter, at room temperature, cut into chunks
1 teaspoon vanilla extract
1 teaspoon finely grated lemon zest
golden syrup, for glazing, optional

PEAR TOPPING

5–6 medium-sized just-ripe pears (you need about 900 g)
90 g unsalted butter
⅓ cup (75 g) caster sugar
pinch of salt

There are a few steps to making this lovely golden cake, however it's not difficult to do – it's one of those cakes to make when you have settled in for a baking day. A slice is lovely with a cup of tea, but is definitely special enough for dessert too.

- Butter and flour the sides of a 24–26 cm round cake tin and line the base with buttered baking paper. (I used a fluted tin for this which looks rather lovely.)
- For the topping, peel, quarter and core the pears. Melt half the butter in a large frying pan over medium heat. Sit the pear quarters in the pan and cook, turning them now and then, for 6–8 minutes until they are partly tender and a mottled golden brown.
- When they're ready, remove the pears from the pan and arrange them decoratively over the base of the cake tin, rounded-side down. Return the frying pan to the stovetop over high heat. Add the caster sugar and 2 tablespoons water and stir to dissolve the sugar, then stop stirring and let the mixture come to the boil. Cook it for about 5 minutes until it becomes a deep golden caramel colour, then swirl in the remaining butter and a pinch of salt. Stir it briefly to melt the butter and form a thick, dark caramel sauce. Immediately drizzle this sauce (there won't be much) over the pears, then set the cake tin aside. Preheat your oven to 180°C.
- Put the flour, baking powder and salt into a food processor fitted with the steel blade. Whiz them together for about 20 seconds, so they're thoroughly mixed, then tip them into a bowl. Now add the caster sugar and marzipan chunks to the processor, and whiz them together until the two are thoroughly pulverised. Add the eggs to the processor bowl, and whiz them into the marzipan sugar for 1 minute. Now scatter the butter chunks on top and whiz them in too for about 40 seconds, so the mixture becomes thick and creamy. Don't worry if it looks quite liquid at this stage – that's just as it should be. Add the vanilla extract and lemon zest, and whiz briefly. Now tip in the reserved flour mixture, and pulse it in with quick on-off bursts of the processor until the mixture is just combined.
- Scrape this batter evenly over the pears in the tin (the caramel sauce may seep up the sides a bit). Pop the tin in the oven and bake the cake for about 1 hour, or until the top, which will be quite dark, springs back when lightly pressed and a skewer inserted in the middle of the cake comes out clean.
- Remove the cake to a cooling rack, and leave it to settle in the tin for 5 minutes. Sit a flat serving plate on top and carefully invert the cake onto this. Gently remove the tin. Leave the cake to cool and serve it warm or at room temperature. If the pears lose a bit of their gloss as they sit, brush a little golden syrup over them just before serving the cake.

3rd August

Great stands of bamboo are an iconic feature of the landscape here, although somehow incongruous as they spring up willy-nilly in farm paddocks and by the roadside, their enormous yellow canes (as thick as my arm) rattling like sabres in the wind. Close up, the colours are quite extraordinary, as you can see. I wish we had enough space to plant a grove of them here, but I suspect Clive is very grateful that we don't, as he gets rather alarmed by my gardening endeavours at times!

5th August

There is a manic wind whipping through the treetops today. It's the sort of wind that's somewhat unsettling and leaves me feeling a bit scratchy. I have just been in town and people have their heads down, clutching coats around them as they battle their way up the main street. I must admit I didn't loiter either – a quick stop at the butcher to pick up a ham hock and I'm already back home, dicing onions and potatoes to make some pea and ham soup. Today is definitely a soup sort of day, and I have a hankering for this comforting old favourite. Mind you, this hasn't always been the case – as a child I couldn't bear the stuff. I well remember stubbornly sitting at the dining table long after the lights were turned out with a now-cold and congealed bowl of it in front of me, which I refused to finish. I honestly can't remember the outcome, but I suspect I surreptitiously scraped it into the dustbin and Mum and Dad turned a blind eye! And now all these years later I love the stuff and we often have it for lunch on a cold day – with all the trimmings of course, for it just wouldn't be the same without the crunchy little nuggets of fried bread my mum called sippets scattered over the top.

Split Pea & Ham Soup with Sippets

SERVES 6

It never ceases to delight me the way just a few simple ingredients can be transformed into such a soothing and delicious meal with so little work. 'Meal' is the operative word here, for it really sticks to your ribs and I can't imagine following it with a main course!

- Split peas always need a good wash and soak before you use them, so the night before you want to make the soup, tip the peas into a large bowl and fill it with cold water. Swish the peas around with your hand – the water will become quite milky – then drain them. Do this another three or four times at least, until the water becomes relatively clear. Once that happens, cover the peas again with cold water and leave them to soak overnight in a cool spot. (A cool spot is important, because they can ferment if they are too warm. This is something I learnt early in the piece, when we had an unseasonably warm autumn night – when I checked on the peas in the morning they had fermented and were merrily bubbling away!) ›

500 g green split peas
1 large meaty ham hock (ask your butcher to saw it into 3 or 4 pieces as they'll be easier to fit in the pan)
1 bay leaf
2 large onions, chopped
3 large potatoes, peeled and cut into chunks
2.5 litres water
sea salt flakes and freshly ground black pepper
flat-leaf parsley, to garnish
sippets (see note overleaf), to serve

SIPPETS . . .

These tiny little cubes of fried bread are awfully addictive and I invariably make heaps more than we need as at least half of them mysteriously disappear off the draining paper as soon as they are cool enough to eat! To make them, remove the crusts from slices of white or wholemeal bread, and cut the bread into small chunks (about 1.5 cm). Pour olive oil into a large frying pan to a depth of 4 mm and heat over medium heat. When the oil is hot, toss in the bread cubes and cook, turning them regularly, until they're golden all over – this doesn't take long and you will need to keep an eye on them as they burn quite rapidly. As soon as they are ready, scoop them out onto paper towels to drain. Pile them into a bowl and serve them with the soup. (My mum used to fry the bread chunks in bacon fat, which would probably not be considered quite the done thing these days, but gosh they were delicious!)

- The next day, rinse the peas well then drain them. Tip them into a very large saucepan or stockpot, and add the ham hock pieces, bay leaf, onion, potato and water. Bring the soup to the boil over high heat, then reduce the heat and let it simmer, partially covered, for 1¼–1½ hours until the peas and potatoes are mushy and disintegrating. Every so often while the soup is cooking, skim off any froth that floats on the surface. To check it's ready, squash some pieces of potato against the side of the pan – they should disintegrate easily.
- When the soup is ready, remove the chunks of ham hock and reserve them. Discard the bay leaf. Purée the pea mixture to form a thick soup (ideally with a stick blender so it can all be done in the pan), then add salt and pepper to taste.
- As soon as the ham hock pieces are cool enough to handle, strip the meat from them, discarding any skin and fat. Chop the meat into little chunks and return it to the soup, reserving a handful for garnishing. If the soup has cooled down a bit too much, warm it gently. Ladle into bowls and sprinkle each serve with some of the reserved ham and parsley leaves. Serve a bowlful of sippets separately.
- P.S. As the soup sits it thickens even more, so if you make it ahead of time, you will have to thin it with more water when you reheat it.

8th August

Oh, but Jack Frost has been hard at work overnight. The cold glitter of frost is painted in great swathes over the fields and the new lambs are huddled together in the nursery paddock, trying to keep warm. They are funny little things – although slightly different in age, they have formed a gang of three and do everything together. One of their main games (and, I suspect, something that is a part of sheep culture) is to head-butt each other constantly. As they do this, they push up and down the paddock and from a distance they look like some sort of bizarre new animal – a reverse of Dr Doolittle's famous pushmi-pullyu!

We have been up in the hinterland today and it's gorgeous. The macadamia plantations, which roll their way over the hills as far as the eye can see, are flowering, the trees spangled with long creamy catkins. But it's the fragrance that's extraordinary: as soon as we stepped out of the car we were enveloped in their intoxicating scent. It was positively heady as we walked through the orchard – the densely planted trees a sight to see as the sun sent its beams streaming under their skirts.

13th August

The brilliant blue skies of the last few days have gone and today it looks as though a flock of sheep are stretched across the sky – each small cloud a fluffy powder puff. It's not quite as cold, thank goodness, and on my rounds of the garden earlier I was chuffed to find that my basil still has some sturdy leaves hanging on. It amazes me how it survives through winter – most of the plants die back, but inevitably one or two in the most sheltered spots soldier on, providing us with a welcome taste of summer, despite the cold. I shall use what I've picked in a tart for dinner, along with a good pinch of saffron threads to add their sunny colour and distinctive fragrance to the mix.

With the tart in the oven, I am about to launch myself into cleaning up a bunch of beautiful leeks that I bought at the market. Cooked with tomatoes, olives and lemon, they should go well with the tart, along with a bowl of whatever salad greens I can find.

Saffron, Basil & Ricotta Tart

SERVES 6

This tart goes back a long way to the time I worked at Taylors restaurant in Sydney's Surry Hills. The restaurant was ahead of its time and I learnt so much from its two extraordinarily talented owners, Anne Taylor and Ian McCulloch. Ian and I were both mad about pastry and any dishes to do with it, so we often made a selection of savoury tarts for the antipasti plates. This particular one is quite unusual as the saffron gives the filling a gorgeous sunshine-yellow colour, which is flecked with the vivid green of the basil. Because of its simplicity, the ingredients need to be the best you can find: buy the ricotta from a deli where they sell it fresh out of the hoop colanders, and if fresh basil is out of season, use good-quality basil pesto instead.

- 100 ml dry white wine
- about ¾ teaspoon loosely packed saffron threads
- 1 pre-baked pastry shell in a 25–26 cm tart tin (see page 371)
- 3 × 70 g eggs
- 700 g fresh ricotta
- 100 g freshly grated parmesan
- ¼ cup (15 g) firmly packed basil leaves *or* 2–3 heaped tablespoons basil pesto, or more to taste
- sea salt flakes and freshly ground black pepper, to taste
- 100 g unsalted butter, melted and cooled
- small basil leaves, to garnish

- Before you do anything else, gently warm the wine (I do this in the microwave in a heatproof jug) and add the saffron threads to it. Mix well, then leave to steep for 30 minutes.
- In the meantime, preheat your oven to 180°C. Sit the tart tin with the pastry shell on a baking tray.
- Pour the saffron mixture into a food processor. Add the eggs, ricotta, parmesan, basil (or pesto), salt and pepper and whiz everything together. With the motor running, pour in the melted butter. Mix it in, stopping and scraping down the sides once or twice as you go, until the mixture is thick and smooth. (I use a large food processor for this, which will mix it all in one hit, however if you don't have a large one, it may be best to do it in batches.)
- Scrape the ricotta mixture into the tart shell and shake it gently to even out the top. Pop the tray with the tart into the oven and bake it for 30 minutes or so, until it is puffed and a speckled dark-golden brown on top, and feels set when you gently press your fingers on the surface and jiggle it.
- Remove the tart tin to a rack and leave it to settle for 5 minutes or so before sliding it onto a serving platter. Garnish with a sprinkling of small basil leaves. Although it looks rather resplendently puffed when it comes out of the oven, I'm afraid it sinks as it cools, but the flavour is simply wonderful.

Leeks with Tomatoes, Olives & Lemon

SERVES 4–6

6 medium-sized leeks
about 100 ml extra virgin olive oil
2 medium-sized just-ripe tomatoes
12 small black olives (niçoise or ligurian are good)
zest of ⅓ small lemon, very thinly sliced
1 tablespoon lemon juice, or more to taste
sea salt flakes, to taste
crusty bread, to serve

I have always adored leeks, finding their flavour so much mellower and more rounded than their robust onion cousins – a characteristic that is brought out in this dish by gently cooking them in olive oil. The recipe is inspired by that remarkable cook Elizabeth David, who wrote with such eloquence about simple dishes like this.

- Trim the dark green tops from the leeks, then slice off the roots so that you leave just enough of the root end to hold the leeks together. Now cut each one in half lengthways. Give them a really thorough wash in cold running water as leeks are notoriously gritty and harbour soil in the most unlikely places. Pat them dry.
- Warm the oil in a large frying pan over low heat. Sit the leek halves in the pan, side-by-side. When the oil starts to bubble gently, turn the leeks over and cook them for a minute or so, then cover the pan and cook the leeks for another 10 minutes, turning them carefully once or twice. You may need to adjust the heat as they cook so the oil keeps up a gentle bubble. They're ready when they are well tinged with gold and the root end is tender when pierced with a fine skewer.
- While the leeks are cooking, bring a small saucepan of water to the boil. Cut a shallow cross in the tip of each tomato and when the water is boiling, drop them into it. Leave them for a minute, then scoop them out and dunk them briefly into cool water – basically what you are doing here is loosening the skin without cooking the flesh of the tomatoes. Carefully peel away the skin, then halve the tomatoes and scoop out the seeds. Cut the flesh into small chunks and set aside.
- When the leeks are ready, carefully lift them out of the pan and sit them on a shallow serving plate. Add the tomato dice to the oil left in the frying pan and quickly warm it through. Swirl in the olives, lemon zest, lemon juice and salt, then remove the pan from the heat. This lovely lemony mixture now gets tipped over the leeks, but taste it first in case the flavours need a bit of adjusting – it often needs a tad more lemon or salt. Spoon it over the leeks and serve them barely warm or at room temperature with lots of good bread to soak up the scrumptious juices.

14th August

Drum roll . . . At last, ladies and gentlemen, I am delighted to present the famous (or should I say, infamous) and much-sought-after scarlet honeyeater. Taa-daa!

After all this time we were beginning to think we would never get a photo of one, but just now Rodney and I walked outside with the camera to take some shots of the garden and who should be waiting for us in the grevilleas but the elusive scarlet honeyeater – more like Pimpernel, if you ask me . . . We are all so excited that Clive is going out to buy a lottery ticket to celebrate!

And it seems we're on a roll, for there were also some gorgeous scaly-breasted lorikeets in residence. They look impossibly gaudy yet the brilliant emerald greens, golds and reds of their feathers form the most perfect camouflage when they are in the right habitat. Their underwings are bright red too and look spectacular when they fly overhead.

16th August

I sometimes wonder if we aren't situated on some kind of bird super-highway, for as we sat having breakfast this morning the birds were literally fanging by the window. Each time I looked up from a sip of tea, birds of one feather or another were zipping purposefully back and forth. As they found their destination, they would veer off into a tree or bush while the others continued their journey – it was fascinating, and I wish I knew more about them.

Speaking of breakfast, I'm afraid we both made little pigs of ourselves, as yesterday I was fiddling about with a recipe for a quick fruit and nut bread and decided to try the leftovers for our morning toast. Well, I can say with some certainty that the recipe is a success! But so more-ish that we both kept cutting off 'just another small slice' and now all I want to do is have a little siesta to let it all settle. Not quite the idea, but the bread is delicious.

Roasted Pecan, Pumpernickel & Date Soda Bread

MAKES 1 MEDIUM LOAF

At the moment, I'm baking at least two or three loaves of this quick and easy-to-make bread a week. It is richly flavoured and densely textured, chock-full of dried fruit and roasted pecans. The nearest thing I can equate it to is a sourdough loaf – but, I should add, without all the work. What's nice is that you can mix and match the nuts and dried fruits to your heart's content – sometimes I add sunflower seeds or pepitas, at other times hazelnuts or cashews, and I'm forever changing the dried fruit according to what I happen to have on hand.

¼ cup (40 g) fine polenta (preferably organic stone-ground), plus extra for dusting
¾ cup (120 g) stone-ground wholemeal flour, plus extra for dusting
½ cup (75 g) unbleached plain flour
½ cup (60 g) rye flour
1½ teaspoons baking powder
½ teaspoon bicarbonate of soda
1 teaspoon salt
1 teaspoon caraway seeds
125 g pitted prunes, halved
125 g pitted dates, halved
200 g roasted pecans, very coarsely chopped
1⅓ cups (330 ml) buttermilk
1 tablespoon honey
1 tablespoon blackstrap molasses

- Preheat the oven to 200°C. Line a baking sheet with baking paper, then dust the paper with a little polenta.
- Tip the polenta, flours, baking powder, bicarbonate of soda, salt and caraway seeds into a large bowl. Whisk them together for a minute or so with a balloon whisk. Add the prunes, dates and 180 g of the pecans (reserve the rest for later) then toss them about so they are well coated in the flour.
- In a separate bowl, mix together the buttermilk, honey and molasses (if you gently warm the honey and molasses first they'll mix into the buttermilk more easily).
- Next dust your work bench with flour. Make a well in the middle of the flour mixture in the bowl, pour in the buttermilk mixture and mix them together – I start off with a wooden spoon and then resort to using my hands once it gets too awkward. Bring the dough together as best you can (it will be quite soft and sticky) then tip it onto the floured bench. With floured hands, knead the dough very gently for a few moments so it just comes together – sprinkle a little extra flour (no more than 2 tablespoons) on it if it sticks to your fingers. Shape it into a 'football', then sit it on the prepared baking sheet. With a serrated knife make 4 or 5 very shallow slashes diagonally across the loaf (if they're too deep the loaf opens out a bit too much during cooking, making it drier than it should be). Press the reserved pecans into the loaf, then sieve a fine dusting of flour over the top.
- Bake the loaf for about 35–40 minutes, or until the bottom sounds hollow when you tap it with your knuckles. Transfer the loaf to a wire rack and leave it to cool for about an hour before slicing. (This is easier said than done, as it smells wonderful – but it will slice more readily when it is cooler, and the flavour will be even better.) Unlike many quick soda breads, leftovers keep remarkably well for up to 4 days in a sealed container and, as you will have gathered from my comments on the previous page, it makes the most terrific toast.

BLACKSTRAP MOLASSES

This nearly black, treacly syrup isn't used so much nowadays, but when we were children, Mum used to give us a spoonful as a tonic every now and then as it is high in minerals, especially iron, calcium, manganese, copper and potassium; interestingly, if your iron levels are low, you may find you actually crave it once you taste it. It has a robust bitter-sweet flavour that I find quite addictive, and it's available from health-food stores.

18th August

I ache this morning. Having spent most of the last week indoors, glued to my computer (by the end of which my poor old keyboard was just about smoking), by the weekend I was desperate to get outside, so I volunteered to be Clive's off-sider in the garden. He had hired a chainsaw and skip to do some major pruning, and we both launched ourselves into it with great gusto, fuelled by numerous cups of tea, sandwiches and the odd biscuit or three. It was hard work, but thoroughly satisfying and relatively mindless too – just the tonic I needed after a week of staring at a computer screen. Something that made me chuckle though was that within minutes of Clive starting up the chainsaw, he had a captive audience of four little boys, who appeared from nowhere on their bikes and stood watching with eyes as big as saucers. What is it about boys and noisy machinery? The louder it got, the more they loved it!

Needless to say, we were both so tired last night after two days of pruning, sawing and carting endless barrow-loads to the skip that we could barely put one foot in front of the other. I'm afraid dinner was nothing to write home about: after a long soak in an Epsom salts bath, the best we could manage was peanut butter on toast and a cup of tea. Then we fell into bed and I don't think either of us moved all night.

20th August

Oh gosh, Squeaky Door is at it again today. He is a sweet little rosella, who is not very old and can't bear to let his mum out of his sight. As soon as she disappears from view he starts up his plaintive cries (which are much like the sound of a squeaking door hinge, hence the moniker). I suspect she is trying to encourage him to fend for himself but he's clearly none too happy about it.

I have been bitten by the baking bug today and have decided to make a linzertorte. This classic Austrian cake-cum-tart is traditionally made with almond or hazelnut meal but my version is decidedly Aussie, using local pecans and jam made from Davidson plums, which thrive in the nearby rainforest.

Spicy Pecan & Davidson Plum Jam Linzertorte

SERVES 8–10

125 g pecans
250 g plain flour
½ teaspoon salt
1 teaspoon ground cinnamon
¼ teaspoon ground cloves
¼ teaspoon freshly ground nutmeg
250 g unsalted butter, at cool room temperature
1⅓ cups (300 g) caster sugar
2 heaped teaspoons finely grated lemon zest
2 eggs
1 teaspoon vanilla extract
½ cup (160 g) good-quality raspberry jam
½ cup (160 g) Davidson plum or regular plum jam
icing sugar, for dusting
thick cream, to serve

I have always loved the complex flavour and nose-tingling aroma of linzertorte – the rich fragrance of cinnamon, nutmeg and cloves invariably reminds me of Christmas. And it is at Christmas that I most often make it, as the plums are ripe for picking then, so I usually christen my first batch of jam in one of these impressive tortes. Of course, you don't need to use Davidson plum jam to make this (regular plum jam is perfectly fine), but if you can lay your hands on a jar do give it a go – its distinctive tang is the perfect foil to the buttery spiciness of the torte.

Although the torte may look as though it's a bit tricky to make, it's not. The pecan base is simply pressed into the tin, so there is no rolling involved, and you can squeeze the mixture for the lattice top out of a thick plastic bag – no piping skills required!

- Put the pecans into the bowl of a food processor and pulse them a few times so they're coarsely chopped. Add the flour, salt, cinnamon, cloves and nutmeg, and keep on processing until the nuts are very finely chopped (just don't get too carried away or the mixture will start to clump together as the oil comes out of the pecans). Tip the mixture into a bowl and set it aside.

- Now put the butter and caster sugar into the processor and whiz them for a minute or so until they're light and creamy-looking. Give the bowl a good scrape, then add the lemon zest and whiz it in briefly. With the motor running, add one egg at a time, making sure the first one is well absorbed before adding the second. Trickle in the vanilla extract and whiz briefly just to mix it in. Scrape around the sides of the bowl to make sure everything is well mixed together. Tip the pecan mixture into the food processor and whiz for 10 seconds or so until thoroughly combined.

- Scrape two-thirds of the dough into one bowl, and the remainder into another. Cover them both with plastic film, then put the larger portion in the fridge and chill it for 1–1½ hours until it has firmed up. Store the smaller portion in a cool spot (preferably not the fridge – you are going to pipe with it, so the dough needs to be quite soft).

- Remove the chilled dough from the fridge, then press it as evenly as you can all over the base of a 24–25 cm loose-based tart tin or springform cake tin. (I have made it successfully in both, however if you are using a loose-based tin, sit it on a baking tray so it's easier to manoeuvre.) The dough is quite soft, so you will find if you sit your hand in the middle of the tin and turn the tin slowly you can easily even it out. Push gently around the edges of the dough to form a very slight rim up the side of the tin – no more than 5–6 mm high. After all this handling, the dough will be quite soft again so it's a good idea to chill it for 30 minutes or so to firm it up. While it's chilling, mix together the raspberry and Davidson plum jams.

- When the dough base has firmed up, spoon the jam onto it and spread it out evenly, without going quite to the edge of the tin. Now, scoop the smaller portion of dough into a large piping bag fitted with a 6 mm plain tube. If you don't possess such a thing (which I know many people don't), use a large, strong snap-lock bag. Just force the dough towards one corner and twist the rest of the bag so the mixture forms a little pouch. Carefully snip the corner off the bag (be careful not to make the hole too big) and you're ready to go. ›

A COUPLE OF HELPFUL TIPS . . .

If you are a bit of a dab hand with cake decorating, please don't make the same mistake I did first time around with this and use a star-tip for the piping – the larger bits of chopped nut clogged up the tip, causing me to make a right mess of things.

The pecan dough can be made a day ahead. Chill both portions, but remove the one for piping from the fridge well ahead of time so it can soften.

- Make a lattice top by piping five or six parallel strips of dough evenly across the jam-coated base, then pipe another five or six strips of dough across these to form a lattice. If necessary, press the edges of the strips gently to the dough rim to seal. Use the remaining dough in the bag to pipe a border around the rim, over the sealed edges, then chill the linzertorte for 30 minutes or so. (By the way, don't worry if your piping is a little wiggly and wonky – mine always is too, but by the time the torte is baked and dusted with icing sugar, it will still look beautiful. Anyway, I always console myself with the thought that this handmade look adds character to the cake!)
- Preheat your oven to 160°C. Slide the torte into the oven and bake it for 1¼ hours or until the lattice top is golden and the jam is slightly bubbly (don't be surprised that the dough spreads as it bakes – it's meant to!). When it's ready, transfer it to a rack and leave it to cool in the tin.
- When the linzertorte is barely warm, carefully loosen around the edges of the tin with a fine palette knife (if necessary), then remove the sides of the tin and leave the torte on the base to cool completely. Once it is completely cool, use a large spatula to help slide it off the base onto a serving plate. Dust the edges with a little icing sugar and serve it with cream (it's rich, so you only need smallish slices). Leftovers keep well for up to 5 days at room temperature and 10 days or more in the fridge.

21st August
The best thing has happened – I have seen two kingfishers in one day! I can't believe it. These improbably beautiful birds are such a rare sight that to see one is special enough, but two is extraordinary. And not only did I see two; they were different species. The first was the smaller azure kingfisher, while the one we have just seen on the fence is its larger cousin, the sacred kingfisher. They really are the most magical birds and the flash of blue as they take off is mesmerising.

The second best thing to happen is that Rodney arrived earlier clutching a freshly caught snapper (he certainly has a way with a fishing rod!) and we're about to cook it for dinner. I tend to cook fish simply, however some years ago I tried the Lebanese dish Samke Harrah and since then have always had a bit of a 'thing' for it. It's a sumptuous dish, with a wonderful range of contrasting textures and flavours – unctuous tahini sauce, smoky barbecued fish and crisp, roasted nuts. When we eat it I always feel we should really be in a far more exotic setting to do it justice: if I close my eyes I can just see myself reclining on piles of silk cushions, the fragrance of a rose garden wafting in through the windows, the gentle tinkle of a fountain in the distance and low mosaic-topped tables covered with platters and bowls of exquisite little morsels to eat. Did I mention that I have an extremely vivid imagination?

Samke Harrah

SERVES 6

The spicy tahini sauce in this dish is particularly delicious, and really lovely with other things too. If there is a bit leftover I will often stir it through a bowl of jasmine rice or toss it with some peas or green beans. However, just be aware that it does tend to thicken as it sits so you may have to thin it quite a bit with extra water, depending on how far ahead you make it. If you do this, the balance of flavours may be affected, so it's a good idea to taste the sauce just before you serve it and add a little more salt or lemon juice if necessary. By the way, traditionally this is made with a large whole baked fish, which looks really spectacular.

- **¼ cup (30 g) pecans, cut into fine slivers**
- **¼ cup (40 g) pine nuts**
- **¼ cup (35 g) slivered almonds**
- **olive oil, for roasting and brushing**
- **6 × 180 g snapper fillets (gold-band snapper is particularly good for this), skin on, well dried**
- **sea salt flakes and freshly ground black pepper**
- **1–1½ cups (30–45 g) coriander leaves**
- **lemon or lime wedges, to serve**

continued next page

- Preheat your oven to 180°C. Toss the pecans, pine nuts and slivered almonds in just enough olive oil to lightly coat them. Spread them on a baking tray and roast them for 5 minutes or so until they are golden and smell toasty, stirring them now and then so they cook evenly. Set them aside to cool.
- To make the tahini sauce, heat the olive oil in a large frying pan over low–medium heat, add the onion, garlic and chilli and cook them, stirring regularly, for about 12–15 minutes until they're tender and pale golden. Add the ground coriander, cumin, both types of paprika and the chopped coriander and cook, stirring regularly, for another 2 minutes to release the flavour of the spices. Turn off the heat but leave the mixture in the pan on the stovetop as you will use it again shortly. ›

TAHINI SAUCE

2 tablespoons extra virgin olive oil
1 large brown onion, finely chopped
4 large cloves garlic, finely chopped
1 small red chilli, finely chopped
1½ teaspoons freshly ground coriander seeds
¾ teaspoon freshly ground cumin seeds
1 teaspoon sweet Hungarian paprika
½ teaspoon smoked paprika
⅓ cup (20 g) chopped coriander
1 cup (250 ml) tahini
300 ml water
80–100 ml lemon juice, to taste
1½–2 teaspoons sea salt flakes, or more to taste

- Scoop the tahini into a bowl. Gradually pour in the water, whisking all the while with a balloon whisk, until the mixture looks smooth and creamy. Now add the lemon juice and salt – it should have the consistency of a thin-ish pancake batter. Set it aside.
- Preheat your barbecue plate or chargrill pan to hot.
- Meanwhile, reheat the onion mixture in the frying pan. When it's warm, pour in the tahini mixture, stirring all the while, then reduce the heat to very low and cook the sauce gently for 6 minutes, stirring regularly. The sauce becomes thicker as it heats – if it seems too thick, add more water (it may absorb up to a cup more) and/or lemon juice. When it's ready, turn off the heat and keep it warm.
- Cut a few very fine slashes in the skin of the snapper fillets. Brush each fillet well with olive oil then sprinkle with salt and pepper. Put the fillets on the barbecue or chargrill pan, skin-side down, and cook them for 2–3 minutes. Carefully turn them over and cook them for a further minute or two, or until the flesh is just opaque.
- When they're ready, transfer the fillets to a long oval or rectangular platter. Spoon some tahini sauce over the top of each one and sprinkle them with the roasted nuts and coriander leaves. Serve with lemon or lime wedges, and the remaining sauce in a separate jug (any leftovers will keep in the fridge for up to a week).

22nd August

There are potatoes galore at the moment: the market is awash with kipflers, king edwards, nicolas and dutch creams, and we've been happily eating them every which-way. Best of all have been the tiny, freshly dug new potatoes, which taste like essence of potato and have skins so papery and fine that I can rub them off with my fingers. I nearly always cook these as simply as possible – boiling them briskly until they're tender, then tossing them with a little butter, shredded mint leaves and sea salt . . . there's nothing nicer. But sometimes, for a change of pace, I cook them like this.

New Potatoes with Olive Oil & Garlic

SERVES 4

It's hard to believe just how scrumptious these potatoes are – they look somewhat wrinkled and plain, but have the most wonderful creamy texture and subtle garlic flavour. I cook them in a big, solid frying pan with a thick glass lid that is just the right size to fit the potatoes in a single layer. If you don't have such a thing, divide them between a couple of frying pans – the most important criterion is that they have tight-fitting lids.

1 kg small new potatoes
¼ cup (60 ml) extra virgin olive oil, or a little more to taste
2 cloves garlic, crushed
needles from two large rosemary sprigs, plus an extra sprig to garnish, optional
sea salt flakes and freshly ground black pepper

- Give the potatoes a good scrub, but don't peel them.
- Sit them in a single layer in a large, heavy-based frying pan that has a tight-fitting lid (or use two pans). Now pour in enough cold water to fill the pan to a depth of 4 mm. Cover the pan tightly, sit it over high heat and bring the water to the boil. As soon as it boils, reduce the heat to low and simmer the potatoes until all the water has evaporated or been absorbed. Immediately remove the pan from the heat, take off the lid and wipe off any condensation that has formed on the underside of it.
- Pour in the oil and give the pan a good shake so the potatoes are well coated in the oil. Cover the pan and return it to the stovetop over low–medium heat. Cook the potatoes for about 25 minutes, shaking the pan regularly so they move about a bit. Now and then wipe the steam from the underside of the lid. They're ready when they are speckled with gold and feel soft if you poke a fine skewer into one. They don't colour evenly so tend to be a mottled golden brown, however if they look a bit too pale, increase the heat a little and cook them a bit longer. At the end of the cooking time, add the garlic, rosemary and salt and pepper to taste. Swirl the pan so they are mixed in and cook everything for another minute. Tip the potatoes into a warm bowl, sit a rosemary sprig on top if you like and serve them immediately.

24th August

We have been visiting some friends and on our way back home have just seen the most extraordinary thing: a Mexican stand-off between a sheep and two plovers protecting their nest. The sheep was nose to beak with the furiously squawking male plover, while the female bravely remained settled on her eggs. The sheep wasn't being at all aggressive – if anything I think it was curious, as it very gently nosed the birds and didn't try to disturb the female. How I wish I knew what was going on!

Our friends sent us home laden with oranges from their trees, including a dozen blood oranges which are *such* a treat. I've kept a few for breakfast (they make the most glorious crimson juice) and I've just sliced the rest to go into this exquisite dessert.

Caramelised Blood Oranges & Navel Oranges

SERVES 4–6

3–4 large navel oranges
3 cups (660 g) caster sugar
about 3 cups (750 ml) water
6 blood oranges
cream, or vanilla or orange ice-cream, to serve

I've always wished I was one of those terribly organised cooks who has lots of interesting things squirrelled away in the fridge and freezer so they can whip up a fabulous meal in no time. Despite my good intentions this is rarely the case, for like everyone else I know, what with work, family, friends, gardens and other commitments, there is precious little time left for anything else.

That said, one thing I nearly always make sure I have on hand is a stock of the gorgeous toffee syrup that coats the oranges in this recipe. It's such a useful thing, for as long as you can lay your hands on some oranges you can put together a really simple but lovely dessert in no time flat. There is far more syrup here than you need for the number of oranges, but as it's little more work to make a larger quantity, I always do and just pour the leftover syrup into a jar and store it in the fridge where it happily keeps for a year or more.

- Remove the coloured zest only from the navel oranges – this is a bit fiddly but you want to avoid the white pith underneath as it's quite bitter. Slice the zest as thinly as you can into fine shreds.
- Now you need to blanch the shreds to soften them and remove any residual bitterness. To do this, bring a small saucepan of water to the boil; once it's bubbling rapidly add the zest and boil for a minute, then tip into a strainer. Repeat this blanching again, then leave the shreds in the strainer to cool.
- For the syrup, put the caster sugar and 2 cups (500 ml) of water into a large saucepan over high heat. Stir constantly until the sugar has dissolved, then stop stirring and bring the mixture to the boil. Leave it to boil until it is a lovely deep golden colour, washing down the sides occasionally with a brush dipped in water to ›

BY THE WAY . . .

If you don't want to peel the oranges at the last minute, you can do them a few hours ahead of time, then store them (unsliced) in a tightly sealed container in the fridge. Slice them just before you need them.

remove any sugar crystals. As always with caramel, there's just that right moment to halt its cooking, when it's neither so pale that it will taste wishy-washy, nor so dark that it becomes bitter and burnt. I know it's tempting to err on the side of caution and take the pan off the heat when the syrup is quite pale, but try to be a bit brave and not whisk it off too quickly – it will taste so much more delicious with a little more colour.

- When it's ready, take the syrup off the heat and carefully pour in just under a cup (250 ml) of water. Be sure to protect your hands and arms when you do this because the syrup will spit and bubble up like anything and can cause bad burns.
- Now, return the pan to the heat, add the blanched orange zest and swirl the pan to mix it in. Sometimes the syrup hardens into toffee when the extra water and zest are added – if it does this, just stir it gently until it dissolves again. Take the pan off the heat and leave the syrup to cool completely. (If it seems a bit thick once it cools just add a little more water and warm it gently.)
- To store it, pour the syrup into a jar and keep it in the fridge. Return it to cool room temperature before using it as it thickens up a bit in the cold.
- When you're ready to serve the oranges, peel them all – including the ones you used for the zest – with a very sharp knife (a blunt knife just tears the oranges), making sure you remove all the white pith. When they are peeled, slice them into rounds. Carefully remove as many seeds as you can from the blood orange slices. Now layer both lots of slices in a serving bowl, overlapping the two different types of oranges – I love the stunning contrast between the deep red veining of the blood oranges and the vivid orange of the navels. Spoon a generous amount of syrup and zest over the orange slices and serve them with cream or ice-cream.

25th August

I woke really early this morning, long before sunrise, and just lay there in that lovely day-dreamy state between sleep and wakefulness. As I did I became aware of the slowly building dawn chorus of birds, sounding just like an orchestra tuning its instruments before a performance. The very first calls were those of the brown honeyeaters – these somewhat nondescript little birds have the sweetest song and they were trilling up and down the scales long before there was even a faint glow in the east. Their song was soon joined by the enquiring chirps of the finches calling gently to each other, the strident territorial cries of the magpies, and the exquisite chimes of the butcherbirds as they sang their hearts out, welcoming the new day.

27th August

As I mentioned earlier, I'm off to teach in France in October. The region where the classes are held is famous for its prunes, so I've been trying out no end of recipes to see what might work well. I've finally settled on a chocolate, prune and pecan cake (although walnuts also grow in the same area so I suspect we shall use these instead of the pecans). I hesitated about including it here because it is so extraordinarily rich that at times I wonder if it isn't a bit too much. 'Impossible!' replied two chocoholic friends, between mouthfuls, when I asked them the self-same question. To prove the point they both went back for seconds – one even contemplated thirds, but finally decided that discretion was the better part of valour!

Flourless Chocolate, Pecan & Prune Truffle Cake

SERVES 16–20 (YOU ONLY NEED A SMALL SLICE)

- **250 g pitted prunes, quartered**
- **220 ml prune juice**
- **1½ tablespoons armagnac or cognac (or use extra prune juice, if you prefer)**
- **Dutch-processed cocoa powder, for dusting**
- **250 g unsalted butter**
- **250 g good-quality dark chocolate, chopped**
- **¾ cup (75 g) Dutch-processed cocoa powder, extra**
- **125 g roasted pecans, chopped into small pieces**
- **8 eggs, at room temperature**
- **2 egg yolks**
- **400 g caster sugar**
- **pinch of salt**
- **2 teaspoons vanilla extract**
- **½ quantity ganache (see page 354)**
- **pecan praline (see page 356), optional**
- **thick cream, to serve**

This beautiful cake is best made at least a day or two ahead of time, as the flavour only benefits from sitting (I've even eaten a slice after three weeks and it was still terrific). The texture is that of a mousse, with the prunes adding a sensuous lushness and the pecans contributing not so much their flavour but rather a welcome crunch. Interestingly, like many very rich cakes, it does actually benefit from a small scoop of cream to cut the intensity of each mouthful. And I imagine (not that I've tried it) that instead of the icing, the cake could look lovely with a drift of softly whipped cream and some splinters of roasted pecans on top – or even just a dusting of icing sugar. But for my money, I do love the look of the rubble of coarsely chopped praline.

- Put the prunes into a small bowl and pour in the prune juice and armagnac or cognac, if using. Stir them together, then set the bowl aside.
- Tightly wrap a 23–25 cm springform cake tin with foil – as the cake is baked in a water bath, this will help stop any water seeping into the batter. I find a sheet of foil from a roll of extra-wide foil is best for this. Butter the tin and line the base with buttered baking paper. Dust the tin with cocoa powder, tap out the excess, and sit it in a large roasting tin. Preheat your oven to 170°C.
- Melt the butter in a large saucepan over low heat. Add the chopped chocolate and whisk it in with a balloon whisk until the mixture is smooth. Take the pan off the heat, tip in the extra cocoa powder and whisk until it's thoroughly incorporated. Now stir in the pecans and prunes with their juice, then set the mixture aside to cool to lukewarm.
- Tip the eggs, egg yolks, sugar and salt into the bowl of an electric mixer and beat on medium speed for a minute or so, until the mixture starts to look a bit foamy (unlike many cake recipes of this type, you don't need to beat them until they are fluffy). Pour in the chocolate mixture and vanilla and whisk again until the batter is well combined (don't be alarmed that it looks quite wet and sloppy – it's meant to be like that). Pour the batter into the prepared cake tin.
- Now, pour enough very hot tap water into the roasting tin so it comes halfway up the side of the cake tin. Carefully lift the lot into the oven and bake the cake for 1¼–1½ hours, or until the surface appears to be dry and crusty (with, quite possibly, a crack or two) and the cake feels set if you lightly rest the palm of your hand on top and gently wobble it. ›

A CLEAN CUT

The easiest way to slice soft cakes like this is to use a hot dry knife. It helps to have a tall jug of very hot water nearby so you can dip the knife blade into the water in-between cutting slices. Wipe it dry and make the next cut and so on; the slices will look really neat and sharply defined.

- When the cake is ready, carefully remove it from the oven. Lift the cake tin out of its water bath, peel away the foil (be careful as a little water sometimes gets trapped in the foil) and sit it on a rack so the cake can cool completely in the tin. Cover the tin and refrigerate it overnight.
- The next day, loosen around the sides of the cake with a fine palette knife. Gently release the sides of the tin and lift the ring away. Carefully invert the cake onto a flat plate and remove the base and baking paper, then sit a cooling rack on top of the cake and invert it again onto this. I have a cardboard cake round that I use for mousse cakes like this as they can be very soft and awkward to handle – I sit it on the cake before turning it over onto the rack so it forms a base for the cake, which makes it so much easier to manoeuvre. (I made my round by cutting it from a strong piece of cardboard and covering it with foil.)
- Pour the barely warm ganache evenly over the cake so it trickles down the sides. I don't cover the sides completely as I like the look of the rivulets of chocolate running down them. Leave the ganache to set, then carefully transfer the cake to a serving plate or cake stand. Scatter coarsely crushed praline around the edge of the cake, if you are using it, then serve with a bowl of thick cream. Store any leftover cake in the fridge.

Ganache (Shiny Chocolate Icing)

MAKES ABOUT 1¾ CUPS – ENOUGH TO ICE 2 MEDIUM-SIZED CAKES

250 g good-quality dark chocolate, broken into small chunks
125 g unsalted butter
50 ml water

Ganache is lovely stuff and terribly easy to make. There are lots of different versions of it (many use cream rather than butter), but whatever recipe you use, you end up with a silky, chocolate glaze that forms a glossy icing when it's poured over a cake.

- Put the chocolate, butter and water into a medium-sized, heavy-based saucepan over low heat. Let the chocolate and butter melt, stirring the mixture frequently, until the ganache is smooth. (I use a small, flat sauce whisk for this, as it gets right into the corners of the pan where the chocolate tends to clump a bit.) The most important thing to keep in mind when you're making ganache is that it mustn't get too hot and boil – if it does, it becomes oily and grainy and there's not much chance of salvaging it, I'm afraid. Once it's silky smooth, take it off the heat and let it cool until it's barely warm and of a thick pouring consistency. Pour as much as you need over the cake.
- Scrape any leftover ganache into an airtight container, seal it tightly and store it in the fridge. When you're ready to use it, gently warm it over very low heat, then let it cool to the right consistency.

A FEW EXTRA NOTES ON GANACHE . . .

I always make a full quantity of ganache even if I don't need it all, as it keeps well in a tightly sealed container in the fridge for at least 3 months. It's wonderful to have on hand when you want to dress up a cake in a hurry – all you need do is swoosh some ganache over it and it immediately looks chic and special.

Just a word of advice about setting: ganache sets beautifully most of the time, however, like all chocolate, it's a bit temperamental in hot, humid weather. This is the norm where I live, so I've come up with a few strategies to deal with it.

If it just won't set and is still sticky I put the ganache-coated cake, uncovered, in the fridge for a short time, so the quick burst of chilled air sets it. (It can also dull the sheen if it's in too long so you need to keep an eye on it.)

I also find I have to store such cakes in the fridge, otherwise the ganache is just too soft and awkward to handle and ends up with my finger prints all over it when I try to move it about. To store it like this, just put the cake, uncovered, in the fridge until the ganache has set, then cover it in plastic wrap. But before serving it, remove the wrap and return the cake to cool room temperature so the ganache regains its sheen.

Pecan Praline

1 cup (220 g) caster sugar
½ cup (125 ml) water
100 g pecans, sliced crossways

BY THE WAY . . .
I'll sometimes stir a spoonful or two of crushed praline into whipped cream and serve it with lightly sugared strawberries; other times I'll go the whole hog and use beautiful long shards of it to decorate a special cake.

This will make more praline than you need for the cake, however it keeps indefinitely in the freezer and you can use it to dress up all sorts of other cakes and desserts (see, for example, the recipe for honey and pecan ice-cream on page 292). You can make this with other nuts too – almonds and hazelnuts are particularly delicious.

- Line a large shallow baking tray with baking paper and sit it on a board or thick tea towel.
- Put the sugar and water into a small saucepan over high heat. Stir it constantly until the sugar dissolves, then stop stirring and bring the mixture to the boil. As it boils, wash down the sides from time to time with a pastry brush dipped in water to dissolve any sugar crystals. The mixture will slowly change from being quite liquid to a thicker syrup, with lots of lazy bubbles all over the surface.
- From here on in you need to watch it like a hawk as it changes colour quite rapidly. As soon as it turns a light amber colour, add the chopped pecans and swirl the pan to mix them in (be careful as it may froth a bit at first). Continue to cook the syrup until it's a deep golden brown, then immediately take it off the heat and carefully pour the mixture onto the prepared baking tray. Hold the tray with a thick cloth to protect your hands and tilt it gently to spread the mixture as evenly as you can. (Be careful doing this as both the syrup and the baking tray are very hot.) Leave the praline to cool and set, then break it into large shards.
- To store the praline, layer the shards in an airtight container between sheets of baking paper or freezer wrap to stop them sticking together. Freeze for up to 12 months, taking out as much as you want and returning the rest to the freezer.

29th August
I've just had the nicest surprise: I was out picking some snowpeas for lunch and heard a rustle near my feet. As I looked down I saw the distinctive stubby tail of a blue-tongue lizard disappearing under a pile of timber. I sat quietly nearby for a bit and lo and behold, out it came again to bask in the sun – so beautiful.

By the way, the remarkable relationship between the plovers and the sheep continues . . . A lamb has now entered into the fray, and it too carefully avoids the nest but comes right up to the birds. Knowing nothing about sheep behaviour, I decided to do some investigating and now have a new-found appreciation of these dear woolly creatures. It would seem that they are quite intelligent and capable of emotionally responding to things, so I'm starting to wonder if this particular sheep is acting as some sort of guardian angel to the two birds and their nestlings, for you couldn't find a more exposed place for a nest than slap-bang in the middle of the paddock.

SEPTEMBER

1st September

Whew! It's the first day of spring but it feels more like the beginning of summer – there's a hot, wild wind blowing and, after months of dryness, the humidity has suddenly arrived. No doubt we shall still get some cool weather, but it seems that Mother Nature is more than ready to shed her winter clothes.

We've just been up the valley to visit friends near Wilson's Creek (which you can't really even call a hamlet – it's more an idea than a place, the focal point being a quirky cafe where all roads meet). Before we set out I baked a batch of biscuits to take with us for afternoon tea. I'd been meaning to try a pecan biscuit recipe (see page 363) for ages, and this was the ideal opportunity to do so. I must say I was chuffed with the results – the biscuits were scrumptious and were wolfed down in no time. I'm just pleased that I have a few more rolls of the biscuit dough in the freezer, for I can see they're going to become a great favourite.

On our way home there was a bushfire close to town, which is a real worry this early in the season. Fortunately it was under control, but there were four fire crews in attendance, and it doesn't augur well for summer. The snakes have obviously felt the new-found warmth too, for as we pulled into the driveway a whip snake took off at a great pace into the bushes. It's the third we've seen in as many days.

I've come back bearing, amongst other things, a huge bunch of coriander that is covered in flowers – they're so delicate and beautiful that I often put them in a vase, where they last for ages. However, today I've nipped off a few, as I already had some chicken marinating for dinner and couldn't resist using the flowers to garnish it.

Coconut Chicken with Spicy Cucumber Ribbons

SERVES 4 HEARTY EATERS OR 6 LIGHTER ONES

- 2 × 270 ml cans coconut cream
- ¼ cup (75 g) your favourite curry paste (I use Patak's Tikka Masala paste)
- ¼ cup (45 g) finely chopped ginger
- inner hearts of 3 stalks lemongrass, finely chopped
- ⅓ cup (20 g) finely chopped coriander
- 8 chicken chops (partly boned leg and thigh portions) or skin-on chicken thighs
- a few lacy coriander leaves, to garnish
- steamed jasmine rice, to serve

continued next page

This scrumptious chicken dish is perfect for times like today when we've been out and about for most of the day and the thought of cooking something from scratch is less than inspiring. The marinade only takes a few minutes to make and basically you just plonk the chicken into it the night before you need it, make sure it's well coated (and covered, or everything in your fridge will smell rather exotic!) then leave it until you're ready to cook it.

I nearly always serve this with jasmine rice and something cucumber-y, as their cool freshness is a lovely balance for the spicy chicken. The cucumber ribbons look really pretty and I love to make them when time is on my side. When it isn't, I'm just as likely to seed and slice the cucumbers then mix them with a little plain yoghurt, fresh mint and salt, and serve this instead.

- In a large bowl, thoroughly mix the coconut cream, curry paste, ginger, lemongrass and coriander.
- Line a lidded container large enough to hold the chicken with a large, sturdy plastic bag. Sit the chicken pieces in the bag and scoop in the marinade. Tie a knot ›

SPICY CUCUMBER RIBBONS

800 g Lebanese or other small cucumbers, washed and dried
2 tablespoons light olive oil
2 tablespoons very finely shredded ginger
1 large clove garlic, finely chopped
1 tablespoon rice (or white wine) vinegar
1 teaspoon caster sugar
2 small red chillies, finely chopped
3 teaspoons sesame oil
up to 1 tablespoon lime juice
sea salt flakes, to taste

in the top of the bag, then squish it about in your hands so that the chicken is thoroughly coated in the marinade. (Make sure you use a good strong bag for this or, as I've found to my cost, the bag could tear as you squish the chicken, making rather a horrible mess!) Put the bag back into the container and cover it tightly with a lid. Now just pop the lot into the fridge for at least 3–4 hours or, better still, overnight. If you remember, give the chicken pieces another squish from time to time.

- When you are ready to cook the chicken, preheat your oven to 190°C. Line a shallow baking tray with baking paper and sit the chicken pieces on it, skin-side up. Squeeze any leftover marinade in the bag over the chicken. Slip the tray into the oven and cook the chicken for about 40 minutes, until it is deep golden brown on top.
- While the chicken is cooking, make the cucumber ribbons. To do this, run a vegetable peeler repeatedly down the length of a cucumber to form long narrow ribbons, stopping when you get to the seeds. Rotate the cucumber and do the same again. Repeat with the remaining cucumbers, then put the ribbons into a large bowl, cover them with plastic film and chill them. (I discard the seedy cores and the first ribbons on each side as they are all skin and a bit chewy.)
- When the chicken is nearly done, combine the olive oil, ginger, garlic, vinegar, caster sugar, chilli and sesame oil in a small saucepan. Sit the pan over medium heat and bring the mixture to the boil. As soon as it boils, remove it from the heat and stir in a little of the lime juice. Taste it and add salt and more lime juice, if necessary. Pour this over the cucumber ribbons and thoroughly mix it in.
- When the chicken is ready, sit one or two pieces on each plate and place a tangle of cucumber ribbons alongside. Finish off with a sprinkling of coriander leaves and, if by any chance you have them, coriander flowers. This is delicious with a bowl of jasmine rice.

Pecan Butter-Crunch Biscuits

MAKES ABOUT 40

These simple biscuits are lovely and buttery, with a melt-in-the-mouth texture which is most satisfyingly balanced by the crunch of the pecans. I also love the fact that the rolls of biscuit dough freeze well, so when I get a craving for something sweet, I can slice and bake a batch in no time. I rather like serving biscuits with ice-cream and these would go beautifully with the pumpkin and maple ice-cream on page 240, or the honey and pecan one on page 292.

2 cups (300 g) plain flour
½ teaspoon baking powder
¼ teaspoon salt
250 g unsalted butter, at room temperature
⅓ cup (75 g) caster sugar
⅓ cup (75 g) brown sugar
2 egg yolks, lightly beaten
1½ teaspoons vanilla extract
80 g roasted pecans, chopped
pecan halves, for topping, optional

- Put the flour, baking powder and salt into the bowl of a food processor. Whiz them together for 15 seconds so they're well mixed, then tip them out into a bowl.
- Now add the butter, caster sugar and brown sugar to the processor bowl. Whiz them together for about 40 seconds until they're creamy, stopping the machine once or twice to scrape down the sides. Meanwhile, mix the egg yolks and vanilla together in a small jug. With the motor running, drizzle the egg yolk mixture in through the feed tube and whiz until well combined with the butter and sugar. Tip the flour mixture back in and pulse it into the butter mixture with quick on/off turns (too much mixing once the flour is added can cause the biscuits to toughen when they bake). Add the chopped pecans and very briefly pulse them in – this only needs a couple of quick bursts or the nuts will become too finely chopped.
- Scrape the dough, which will be quite soft, into a bowl, then cover and put it in the fridge for about 30 minutes to firm up a bit.
- Scrape the dough out onto a board and divide it in half. Lay a large sheet of foil on the bench and cover it with a sheet of baking paper. Gently roll one portion of dough into a log about 5 cm in diameter. Sit the log on one edge of the baking paper and roll it up in the paper. Next, roll it so it's wrapped in the foil, then twist the ends of the foil tightly in opposite directions so you end up with something that looks like a long bonbon. Do the same again with the remaining dough. At this stage you can freeze the logs until you need them (they keep well for about 5 weeks; just defrost them in the fridge overnight before slicing them). If you're baking the biscuits the same day, chill the logs for 2–3 hours in the fridge until they're firm enough to slice.
- Preheat your oven to 150°C and line one or two baking trays with baking paper. Unwrap the log (or logs) and slice into 6–7 mm thick rounds. Sit the rounds on the trays, about 2 cm apart, and press a pecan half into the middle of each one, if using. ›

- Bake the biscuits, in batches if necessary, for 25 minutes or until they're light golden brown and feel crisp to touch. (I often take a peek at the bottom of one too, to check it's cooked.) If your oven cooks a bit unevenly, turn the trays around halfway through the baking time and swap the shelves they are on.
- When the biscuits are ready, remove them from the oven and leave to cool on the trays for 5 minutes. Then gently transfer them to a wire rack and leave to cool completely. Store the biscuits in an airtight container, where they will keep well for 5–6 days. Or you can freeze them for up to 3 weeks – when you want them, just defrost at room temperature for about 20 minutes.

3rd September

I have always wanted to grow broad beans, but so far I've had little success. I suspect it's just a bit too warm where we are, but our friends who live just a little further and higher up the valley have no such problem, and last time we visited I was absolutely green with envy at the massed plantings of broad beans in their veggie garden. They grow them not only for the delicious beans, but also to help the soil (being legumes, their roots have amazing nitrogen-fixing properties) and, once the beans are picked, they use the plants as green mulch. They look glorious – the tall green spikes festooned with their distinctive black and white flowers, and here and there a velvety pod or two. As we roamed about we picked the pods and ate the vivid green beans straight from their spongy nests – they tasted wonderful, delicate and resoundingly 'green', with none of the mouth-furring properties that more mature beans can have. When I taste them like this, I understand why in Italy they serve these first tiny beans fresh, with just a drizzle of olive oil and some parmesan cheese or wisps of prosciutto.

4th September

Well, I've finally discovered who has been eating my strawberries! For the last week or so, every time I've made a mental note that the strawberries were nearly ripe and only needed another day or so before picking, they would be gone before I got to them – very neatly removed from their stalks. This morning I happened to be outside sweeping, and saw a magpie casually strolling over to my strawberry patch. He paused momentarily when he saw me, then looked me dead in the eye, bent down and meticulously plucked a strawberry off its stem before – again, very deliberately – flying off with it. I was left standing there, shaking my head half-admiringly and half in frustration at his audacity! Still, there are enough for us both and I have managed to pick a small basketful, which I'm going to marinate in red wine syrup. They make a lovely dessert that only needs a splodge of cream or yoghurt to finish it off.

Strawberries in Red Wine Syrup with Rosewater Cream

SERVES 6–8

¾ cup (165 g) caster sugar
1½ cups (375 ml) pinot noir (one with a fruity, berry flavour is ideal)
⅓ cup (110 g) strawberry jam
3 cm piece of cinnamon stick
zest of 1 lemon, cut into 1 cm wide strips
1 vanilla bean, split
about 650 g strawberries

ROSEWATER CREAM

1 cup (250 ml) double thick cream
1 tablespoon icing sugar, sifted
1 teaspoon rosewater, or more to taste
1 teaspoon vanilla extract

BY THE WAY . . .

You can double or triple the recipe very successfully, just cook the syrup longer so it looks 'syrupy'. As a guide, if you triple the recipe the syrup will take about 35 minutes to cook.

There are many ways to serve this dessert. For the photo I scooped the rosewater cream into tiny tumblers and spooned the strawberries and their syrup over the top, which all looks rather sharp and sleek. However, they're also lovely just piled in a bowl with the lemon zest and vanilla bean tucked in amongst them, and the rose-scented cream served alongside. The serves are quite small, but you don't need a lot as it's quite intensely flavoured.

- Put the sugar, wine, jam, cinnamon stick, lemon zest strips and vanilla bean into a medium-sized saucepan over medium–high heat. Stir the mixture until the sugar dissolves, then stop stirring and bring it to the boil. Adjust the heat so the mixture bubbles gently and steadily (but not at a rolling boil) and leave it for 12–14 minutes, or until it has reduced somewhat and become quite syrupy.
- Remove the pan from the heat. Discard the cinnamon stick and leave the syrup to cool. Once it has cooled down, strain it through a fine sieve into a bowl to remove any seeds from the jam. Return the vanilla bean and lemon strips to the syrup, cover the bowl with plastic film and chill the syrup until you need it (you can keep it in a tightly sealed container in the fridge for at least a couple of weeks).
- About half an hour before you're ready to serve the strawberries, hull them and cut them in half lengthways (if they are really large, I slice them). Put the strawberries into a bowl and pour the syrup over the top. Gently mix and leave in a cool spot.
- For the rosewater cream, combine all the ingredients in a chilled bowl and whip until soft peaks form.
- To serve the berries in little glasses, scoop some of the cream into each glass, then spoon some of the berries and their syrup over this, sitting a few more berries jauntily on top. Otherwise, serve them in one big bowl with the cream to the side.

THE SCENT OF A ROSE . . .

The rose-scented cream is lovely with the berries, but be careful not to go overboard with the rosewater – or it could be rather like eating a spoonful of rose-scented body lotion! Start off by adding a bit less than you need, taste the cream, then add a tiny bit more, taste it again, and keep on going like this until it's how you like it.

I sometimes use sour cream instead of regular cream for desserts like this, as I rather like the slight tang it gives, especially when matched with something quite sweet or rich.

11th September

The markets are full of rainbow and ruby chard at the moment. It looks so vibrant and cheery with its hot pink and bright yellow stalks and deep green leaves, and it tastes terrific – softer and a bit more subtle than its better-known cousin, silverbeet. My favourite way to cook it is to wash it well, then briefly cook the leaves in a covered saucepan in only the water that clings to them. When they are wilted and tender, I drain them, chop them coarsely, then toss them in a pan with a good slosh of extra virgin olive oil, lemon juice and salt (a bit of chilli and garlic wouldn't go astray either). It's soooo delicious.

As rainbow chard is only in season for a relatively short time, I try to use it as much as possible when I can, and the tart recipe that follows turns up again and again on our table at this time of year. The cheese and eggs soften the earthiness of the chard, giving a lovely balance to the flavour, while the almond topping adds a satisfying crunch.

Rainbow Chard, Cheese & Almond Tart

SERVES 4 GOOD EATERS (WITH A BIT LEFT OVER!)

- 1 blind-baked simple shortcrust pastry shell (see page 371) in a 26–28 cm loose-bottomed tart tin
- 30 g unsalted butter
- pale green parts of 5 spring onions, finely sliced
- about 500 g rainbow chard or silverbeet (Swiss chard)
- 4 eggs
- 1¼ cups (310 ml) milk
- ½ cup (125 ml) cream
- sea salt flakes and freshly ground black pepper
- ¼ teaspoon grated nutmeg
- 60 g grated mozzarella
- 200 g grated good-quality tasty cheese
- handful of flaked almonds

Last time I felt like making this I had neither chard nor spring onions, however after rummaging through our spare fridge (which, I'm somewhat embarrassed to say, can become a museum for any excess or leftover bits and pieces that I've forgotten about) I did manage to unearth a bunch of English spinach and one rather old leek that had found its way to the very back. As it turns out they made a terrific pairing, so if chard is hard to find you can always give this a whirl with spinach and leeks.

- Preheat your oven to 180°C. Sit the tart tin with the pastry shell on a baking tray.
- Melt the butter in a very large frying pan over medium–low heat. Add the spring onion and cook, stirring regularly, for 4–5 minutes until it has softened.
- In the meantime, thoroughly wash the chard or silverbeet, then shake off the excess water and slice it finely, stalks and all. There is rather a lot of chard, so I find it easiest to do half a dozen leaves at a time, rolling them up in a bundle then cutting across the bundle to shred them. When it's all shredded, add the chard to the frying pan (there's a mountain of the stuff so your pan needs to be large, or else it's best done in two pans or in batches). Cook the chard over medium heat, stirring it occasionally, for 8–10 minutes or until it has collapsed and wilted but the leaves and stalks are still deeply coloured. If, at this stage, there is a little liquid left in the bottom of the pan, briefly increase the heat to evaporate it. Turn off the heat and set the pan aside for the chard to cool completely (it can be cooked the day before and refrigerated until you need it). To hasten the cooling, transfer the chard to a shallow bowl and stir it regularly to allow any steam to escape.

- In a bowl, whisk the eggs to break them up, then whisk in the milk, cream and a little salt, pepper and nutmeg to taste. (It's a good idea to taste the cheese you are going to use in the tart before salting the egg mixture – if the cheese is salty, you probably won't need to add any extra salt.)
- When the chard is cool, mix in just over half of the combined cheeses, then spoon this mixture evenly into the tart shell. Sprinkle the remaining cheese over this, then scatter the flaked almonds evenly over the top. Give the egg mixture another quick whisk in case it's settled a bit, then drizzle it into the tart shell. (Depending on the size of the tart tin you are using, you may not need the last 2–3 tablespoons – be careful that it does not overflow.)
- Slide the tart, on its baking tray, into the oven and bake it for about 45 minutes, or until it's deep golden on top and lightly set. To check, insert the tip of a fine knife into the centre of the tart and gently press the sides of the cut apart. The filling should be softly set with no liquid running into the cut. Remove the tart from the oven and leave it to cool and settle for at least 10 minutes before serving. Then just slip off the outer ring of the tin, and gently slide the tart off its base onto a flat serving plate.

BY THE WAY . . .

This tart goes particularly well with other robustly flavoured vegetables, such as roast beetroot, slow-cooked tomatoes or garlicky grilled field mushrooms. I made it again last night to double-check the recipe, and we had it with a fennel, butter lettuce (the first from the garden, says she proudly!) and avocado salad, and a big bowl of herb-roasted potatoes. It was lovely.

Simple Shortcrust Pastry Tart Shell

MAKES ONE 26–28 CM TART SHELL

This recipe may seem a bit long-winded, but please don't be put off by that – I just wanted to explain it as best I could. It makes lovely pastry that is short and buttery, without being too difficult to handle. In fact it's quite forgiving and can withstand a fair bit of push and pull without disintegrating. However, I should warn you that things can get a bit tricky in summer, as the pastry can soften rapidly in the heat and therefore become harder to handle. As it can get terribly steamy here, I try to get around this by rolling the pastry in the cool of the morning before it heats up too much.

1½ cups (225 g) plain flour
¼ teaspoon salt
125 g cold unsalted butter, cut into small chunks
¼ cup (60 ml) iced water
1 egg yolk mixed with 2 teaspoons water

- Whiz the flour and salt together in a food processor. Add the butter and whiz again until the mixture resembles medium-fine breadcrumbs. With the motor running, pour in the iced water and process only until the pastry forms a ball around the blade. (The time for this varies a bit depending on the weather – when it's warm it comes together faster.)
- Take the pastry out and shape it into a ball. Now, flatten it into a disc and wrap it tightly in plastic film. Chill the disc for about 40 minutes or until the pastry is firm, but supple enough to roll (the timing of this depends on how cold your fridge is). By the way, you can make the pastry a day or two ahead of when you want to use it and store it in the fridge, but you will need to bring it back to cool room temperature so it's pliable enough to roll.
- On a lightly floured board, roll out the pastry into a large round to fit a 26–28 cm loose-based tart tin. Roll the pastry around your rolling pin to transfer it to the tin. Carefully drape it over the tin – watch that you don't press it down onto the sharp edges which may cut through it.
- Use your knuckles to gently press the pastry into the tin, leaving an overhang all around; trim a little pastry from the overhang and keep it in the fridge in case you need to patch any cracks later on. Sit the tin on a baking tray – this makes it much easier to manoeuvre both now and later when the tart is baking – and chill it for 40 minutes or so, until the pastry is firm (pop it in the freezer if you're running short of time).
- Preheat your oven to 200°C.
- Completely cover the pastry with a large sheet of foil, pressing it gently down into the corners. Spread pie weights, uncooked rice or dried beans all over the base to a depth of about 1 cm to weigh it down.
- Slide the baking tray into the oven and bake the tart shell for 20 minutes, or until it's nearly set. Remove it from the oven and run a rolling pin over the foil on the top edge to cut off the pastry overhang. Return the tin to the oven, with the foil ›

and weights still intact, and bake the pastry for a further 8–10 minutes, or until it is lightly coloured and feels firm and dry. Take it out again and carefully remove the foil and weights. Don't worry if there are any fine cracks in the pastry shell – just patch them with the reserved pastry.

- Brush the egg wash over the pastry, making sure it is well coated, then return the tart shell to the oven for a few minutes so the egg wash sets to a shiny glaze (this helps to seal the pastry and stop the bottom getting soggy once it's filled). When it's set, remove the tart shell from the oven and leave it to cool in the tin on a rack. It is then ready to be filled.

12th September

Our drunken parrot tree is well and truly living up to its name! Its slender grey branches are adorned with shiny seed pods and, at this time of year, tufts of soft new leaves and leathery red buds. It is these buds that are attracting more than their fair share of attention from the local lorikeets, as they are just starting to blossom and the birds are wild about the nectar, which literally drips from the flowers when they're fully open. And it's from this abundance of nectar that the tree gets its rather extraordinary name – for if the nectar sits for a bit and warms up, it starts to ferment and becomes quite alcoholic, which in due course has a rather intoxicating effect on the birds! Occasionally we see one or two birds staggering around the base of the tree, and more than a few loop-the-loop on the branches!

13th September

I've already mentioned the jasmine which grows over the track where I walk – well today I discovered that it's not just jasmine that thrives there. I veered off the path down the slope to where a tiny creek flows, and much to my delight saw that a veritable orchard in the wild has sprung up. All garden escapees, I'm afraid, but it is rather wonderful too: there are at least three cherry tomato plants, a young pawpaw, a thorny old bush lemon, two Davidson plums and a mulberry sapling. There are birds galore feeding on them, so although they shouldn't be there, they're providing a welcome source of food.

Having come this far in the book, you've probably noticed that I'm rather keen on spices and tend to use them liberally when I cook – I love the warmth and vibrancy they add to food. So it's inevitable that whenever I'm wondering how to liven something up I'll often make up some kind of spice rub or paste to give it a boost. The paste on the facing page is a version of chermoula. There are so many recipes for this floating around – just about every cook I know has their own take on it. I tend to be pretty relaxed about it, making all sorts of versions according to what it's going with (and, truth be known, what I happen to have on hand).

Salmon, Spinach & Chermoula Rolls

SERVES 4

More often than not I'm perfectly happy with a simple piece of grilled salmon accompanied by nothing more than a squeeze of lemon juice. But sometimes I get a craving for something a bit more complex and interesting, and when I do it's hard for me to go past this tart, spicy Moroccan marinade that adds so much verve to whatever it's used with.

This particular dish came about through one of those happy coincidences when I happened to have rather a lot of leftover chermoula in the fridge and was wondering how to dress up some salmon fillets for dinner. Well, one thing led to another and these lovely rolls are the result. They look and taste wonderful, and are fantastic for a dinner party, as they can be made well ahead and simply popped in the oven to cook when you need them.

- For the chermoula, put all the ingredients into a bowl and thoroughly mix them together. Set the bowl aside in a cool spot while you prepare the salmon.
- Trim the fillets up a bit, removing the thinner 'tail' if necessary, so they are roughly log-shaped (hang on to the trimmings as you can make extra rolls from these). Pop all the fish onto a plate and into the fridge.
- Now lay a sheet of foil large enough to comfortably enclose one fillet on your work surface, then put a slightly smaller sheet of baking paper over this. Overlap two to three large leaves of English spinach, shiny-side down, in the middle of the baking paper. Now, thoroughly coat one piece of salmon in the chermoula and sit it in the middle of the leaves. Using the paper to help you, wrap the leaves completely around the fish (use some extra leaves if the salmon isn't covered) then wrap the paper around it too, to form a log. Roll this up snugly in the foil. Secure the ends of the foil by twisting them tightly in opposite directions so the whole package resembles a neat bonbon. Pop it in the fridge and repeat the rolling and wrapping with the remaining fillets. (At this stage, I mix the trimmings with some of the remaining chermoula then bundle them together into one or two rolls as well – they don't slice quite as neatly as the rolls made with the whole fillets, but I usually chill them once they're cooked and have them cold the next day, by which time they cut beautifully.) Chill all the rolls for a couple of hours.
- Preheat your oven to 200°C.
- Sit the salmon bonbons on a baking sheet, then put them in the oven and bake for 15 minutes – if the fillets are very thick, allow an extra couple of minutes. Remove them from the oven and leave the rolls in their wrappings for at least 20 minutes to settle and firm up a bit – the foil will keep them warm. (You can also chill them and serve them cool if it's a really hot day.) ›

4 small fillets of Atlantic salmon (or ocean trout), skin off
12–16 large English spinach leaves, washed and stalks removed
lemon wedges, to serve

CHERMOULA

2 teaspoons freshly ground black pepper
2 teaspoons freshly ground cumin seeds
2 teaspoons freshly ground coriander seeds
1 teaspoon smoked paprika
2 teaspoons sweet Hungarian paprika
½ teaspoon cayenne pepper
6 large cloves garlic, finely chopped
¼ cup (60 ml) lemon or lime juice
1 small red chilli, seeded and chopped
½ cup (25 g) finely chopped coriander
¼ cup (60 ml) extra virgin olive oil

continued next page

TOMATO SALAD

4–5 large ripe tomatoes, seeded and sliced
½ small red onion, very finely sliced
¼ cup (60 ml) extra virgin olive oil
½ teaspoon freshly ground cumin seeds
good pinch of smoked paprika (you could use sumac instead)
1 tablespoon lemon juice, or more to taste
sea salt flakes, to taste
handful of small black olives
tiny coriander leaves, to garnish

- While the rolls are settling, put the tomato, onion, olive oil, cumin, paprika, lemon juice and salt into a bowl and gently stir them together.
- To serve the salmon, put a good spoonful of salad onto each plate, then scatter some olives and tiny coriander leaves on top. Unwrap the logs. Using a sharp knife (preferably not a serrated one as it tends to tear the flesh), slice the salmon into thick rounds. Overlap these on the plate beside the salad and serve with lemon wedges.

14th September

The spring blueberries have finally arrived in the market and we've made little pigs of ourselves these past few days, eating them every which-way – straight out of the bucket (yes, we buy them by the bucket!); with yoghurt for breakfast; or baked into a particularly good lemon and blueberry cake. But best of all, yesterday afternoon when we were ravenous after a few hours of mulching, I made a batch of pikelets and sprinkled a handful of blueberries into the batter. What a hit! A neighbour who was working out in his garden came over too, and between the three of us we proceeded to reduce what I thought was a rather large pile of pikelets to virtually nothing in an embarrassingly short time! The blueberries became lovely and jammy as they cooked so we didn't need extra jam, and with just a smidgen of butter they were wonderful (a bit of cream would have been rather good too). When I cook things like this, I am forever reminded of just how delicious simple dishes are.

Blueberry Pikelets

MAKES 20–24

This is a recipe that I cut my 'cooking' teeth on, for on a wet, wintry weekend my mum would often suggest making a batch of pikelets as a treat for afternoon tea. It was a wonderful way to keep us kids occupied, and the recipe was perfect as it's so easy and the results so immediate. We would make big batches of them, happily devouring them and licking our sticky, jammy fingers as we went. All three of us have gone on to really enjoy cooking – two to make a career out of it – and I suspect it comes down to times like these when we cooked together. (If you're making them with your own kids, for safety's sake, you need to be in the background when it comes to the cooking stage, but otherwise let them go for it!)

1 cup (150 g) self-raising flour
½ teaspoon bicarbonate of soda
¼ teaspoon salt
2 tablespoons caster sugar
1 free-range egg
1 cup (250 ml) buttermilk
20 g unsalted butter, melted and cooled a little, plus extra for cooking
1½ teaspoons vanilla extract
⅔ cup (150 g) blueberries, fresh or frozen
butter, or jam and thick cream, to serve

- Tip the flour, bicarbonate of soda, salt and sugar into a medium-sized bowl and whisk them together with a balloon whisk for 40 seconds, so they're well mixed. In a separate bowl, whisk together the egg, buttermilk, melted butter and vanilla until they're combined. Make a well in the flour mixture and pour this buttermilk mixture into it. Whisk them together to form a smooth-ish batter. Leave it to sit for a few minutes, then just before cooking the pikelets, stir in the blueberries.

- Heat a large non-stick frying pan over low heat. (If you don't have a non-stick pan, use a regular one but make sure you keep it well buttered because the berries can sometimes 'catch' a bit and stick to the base of the pan.) Melt a small nugget of butter in the pan then use a thick wad of paper towel to swizzle the butter all over the base, wiping out any excess, as you only need a thin film.

- Drop dessertspoonfuls of batter into the pan, leaving a gap between each one as the pikelets spread a bit. They won't all be perfectly round, but for me that's part ›

REHEATING

Surprisingly, these do reheat rather well. Last time I made them, miracle of miracles, there were a few left over, which I put in the fridge. The next day, I warmed them briefly in the microwave and they were still really light and fresh-tasting.

of their charm – if you like, you can use the back of the spoon to swirl the batter a little to make them more regular. Cook the pikelets gently for about 3 minutes until small bubbles appear all over the surface. Then take a peek underneath, and if they're a light-ish tan colour, use a palette knife or egg slice to turn them over. Cook them for another 2 minutes or so on this side until they are done. (This turning-over bit may feel a little awkward as the tops are still uncooked, but you will soon get the hang of it.) By the way, you may well have to adjust the heat as you go – it's only really once you've cooked the first batch that you can figure out just the right temperature.

- When they're done, lift the pikelets out and sit them on a plate. Cover them loosely with foil to keep them warm while you cook the rest. (If necessary, swish a bit more butter around the pan as you go.)
- While they're cooking, we usually get the kettle on and make a pot of tea so we can sit down and enjoy them while they're still warm. There's nothing nicer. (By the way, you don't have to add blueberries to the recipe – Mum rarely did. More often than not we made plain ones, which we spread with blackberry jam and cream. They were sooo delicious.)

16th September

Clive is away for the rest of the week and I find I cook quite differently when it's just me. I make up all sorts of dishes from whatever bits and pieces happen to be in the fridge. Tonight I'm cooking up a panful of spring vegetables – or perhaps I should practise my French for the trip next month and call it a mélange or meli-melo of vegetables or even verdure de printemps! It sounds somewhat grander, doesn't it?

A Panful of Spring Vegetables

SERVES 4 AS A SIDE DISH, OR 1–2 PEOPLE AS A MEAL

500 g prepared mixed spring vegetables, such as peas, asparagus, zucchini (courgettes), sugar snap peas, broad beans
2 tablespoons extra virgin olive oil or good butter, or more to taste
sea salt flakes and freshly ground black pepper
lemon wedges, to serve
goat's curd, marinated goat's cheese or fresh ricotta, optional

It may sound a bit silly, but I found writing this recipe quite a challenge as it's another one of those dishes that I rarely actually measure out. I usually just prepare whatever veggies I have to hand in whatever quantities I think we can eat, cook them briefly then toss them about in as much butter or olive oil as I think they need! So you certainly can't go wrong using this as a guide and adjusting the amounts to suit you. I'll often make a meal of them, dotting a bit of lemony goat's curd or delicate fresh ricotta here and there when I tip them out onto my plate, and finishing off with a generous grinding of black pepper and squeeze of lemon juice – it's so very delicious.

When it comes to the vegetables themselves, I use whatever is best and freshest in the market: tiny zucchini, finger-length broad beans, sweet little sugar snap peas, green peas, and if I'm really lucky, delicate spears of asparagus. The weight given is just a guide, and when I say 'prepared' I mean the weight once the vegetables have been shelled, trimmed and sliced.

- The first thing to do is to prepare all your veggies: shell the peas, slice the asparagus and zucchini, string the sugar snaps and pod the broad beans. On that particular note, I rarely double-peel broad beans as I rather like the chewy skins – but I will if they're very large with tough skins, or if I want everything to look green as green.
- Bring a steamer or large saucepan of water to the boil and salt it lightly. Cook one group of vegetables at a time until they're just tender and still bright green. Immediately they're ready, scoop them out of the pan and dunk them into a bowl of ice and water. Repeat this with the remaining vegetables. When they're all done and cooled, drain them and wrap them in thick tea towels to dry them off.
- Now heat the olive oil or butter in a large frying pan over medium heat. Once it's hot, add all the vegetables and toss to coat them in the oil or butter. Cook for a few minutes, stirring regularly, until they are warmed through, then sprinkle with a little sea salt. When they're ready, slide them into a warm serving bowl. Grind some black pepper over the top and serve with lemon wedges. If you want to make this into more of a meal, dollop some goat's curd, cheese or ricotta onto your plate, pile the veggies on top, then scatter a bit more cheese over everything.

18th September

As luck would have it, Rodney was out in the garden taking some pictures this morning when he saw what we call our 'birds in the bush' phenomenon. We have a blue potato bush growing just near the bird bath – Clive gave it one of his famous (or should I say infamous!) haircuts last winter, and the poor thing still hasn't recovered. Our finch families have adopted the bush as their home with great gusto. They absolutely love it, as they can scuttle in and out of the maze of branches with ease, but none of their larger predators (magpies and butcher birds) can do the same. And it is from this safe haven that they merrily flit to the bird bath for their morning drink and swim before ducking back into the bush to dry off. They look so comical as they drink, dipping down to the water then throwing back their heads to swallow. Afterwards, the whole bush vibrates and hums with the whirring of their wings as they dry themselves off. Rodney managed to capture some of the crew as they were preening and warming themselves in the early-morning light.

20th September

As you can see from the last entry, Rodney is back and we're hard at work again. It has been fascinating photographing this book throughout the year, as it has made me more conscious than ever of the subtle changes in the countryside, the garden and the food I cook as each season progresses. Right now the mustard greens are glorious. I rarely cook them, preferring to tear up the hot, spicy leaves and use them in a salad. You know, I'm really surprised that they aren't as readily available as rocket, for they're very easy to grow and just as delicious – I'm sure there would be a huge market for them if they were better known.

The hippeastrums are out as well, looking wonderfully gaudy, and after its winter dormancy the herb garden is starting to perk up again too. Everything is brighter, fresher and greener. The garlic is in bud and looks exquisite, and I've just picked a big bunch of parsley, rosemary and thyme to flavour a breadcrumb coating for some racks of lamb.

Herb-Crusted Racks of Lamb

SERVES 4

This is a classic dish and well worth perfecting as it's just so easy to make, and the results are spectacular. The herb mixture coats the racks thickly, becoming lovely and crunchy as it cooks, and the racks themselves look really impressive with their crisp green-and-gold coating.

I know that if you haven't cooked rack of lamb before the idea might seem a bit intimidating, but if you just think of it as a whole lot of lamb cutlets joined together it becomes much less worrisome! I cook this dish when I want to make something special but know I'm not going to have much time. More often than not I serve it with roast onions with goat's cheese and thyme (see page 181) and either something steamed and green, like spinach, or a simple watercress and fennel salad (see page 300). By the way, if you're not a fan of garlic, by all means leave it out – the meat is still perfectly delicious and a bit more delicate if the crust is simply flavoured with herbs.

2 racks of lamb (ideally each comprising 8 or 9 cutlets)
¼ cup (70 g) Dijon mustard (or a mixture of Dijon and honey-flavoured mustard)
rosemary or thyme sprigs, to garnish

HERB COATING

120 g coarse-ish fresh white breadcrumbs (made from a fairly dense loaf like stale sourdough or ciabatta)
generous handful of finely chopped flat-leaf parsley
2 tablespoons finely chopped thyme
2 tablespoons finely chopped rosemary
1–2 large cloves garlic, finely chopped (or to taste)
sea salt flakes, to taste
about ¼ cup (60 ml) extra virgin olive oil

- Preheat your oven to 220°C. Line a baking tray with baking paper.
- Sit the racks, fat-side up, on the prepared tray. Pop them in the oven to roast for 12 minutes. When they're done, take them out and leave them to cool a little while you make the herb coating.
- To do this, just put the breadcrumbs, chopped herbs, garlic and salt into a bowl and stir them together. Now drizzle in the olive oil and mix well.
- Spread a layer of mustard over the fat side, base and cut sides of the lamb racks (there's no need to spread it over the rib bones or undersides of the racks). Use your fingers to press a thick layer of the herb coating all over the mustard. Don't worry if a few little bits of coating drop off onto the tray – I just leave them there, pushing them up against the racks, so that as the lamb cooks the crumbs soak up some of the juices and become lovely and crunchy. (I must admit, these succulent little morsels often don't make it to the table, as I end up eating them while the racks are settling after cooking.)
- When the racks are coated with the herb mixture, return them to the oven and cook them for 20–25 minutes for pink lamb; unfortunately, you have to wing it a little with the cooking time, as it depends on the size of the racks. The ones we buy here are fairly substantial whereas when we lived in the city, I used to get much smaller ones that took less time to cook. The way I check is to prod the thickest part of the meat carefully (so I don't dislodge the crust) when I think it's ready – it should feel a little springy, but not bouncy, if that makes sense. ›

HOT STUFF . . .

I often vary the mustards that I use to coat the lamb, or mix two together to create a more subtly flavoured crust. I'm particularly fond of using a mixture of Dijon and the slightly hot Honeycup mustard – the Honeycup adds a little sweetness that balances out the more tartly flavoured Dijon.

- Remove the tray from the oven, cover the racks loosely with foil and leave them in a warm spot to settle for at least 10 minutes.
- To serve the lamb, slice down between the cutlets – you can carve them into single cutlets if you like; I usually carve them into racks of three, as they look a bit more impressive like this. Sit the lamb on individual plates and garnish with herb sprigs.

A GOOD REST

When a piece of meat cooks, the juices are forced to the outside of it; so if you slice it as soon as it comes out of the oven, these juices run out and the meat becomes dry and chewy. However, if you let it settle for a bit, the juices are redistributed through the meat and it stays beautifully succulent.

22nd September

Phew, what a week! Apart from photographing with Rodney, I've also been involved with our big film-night fund-raising dinner. The dinner was instituted a few years ago and has gone from strength to strength – in fact it has become so popular that it books out early and we reluctantly have to turn people away. It's always a fantastic night and this year was no exception, thanks to the hard work and planning of a small but dedicated band of volunteers.

A group of us are kept busy in the kitchen and, although we don't get to see the film, it's a small loss as we have just as much fun as those attending the dinner. It all gets a bit mad during service but in a very happy, chaotic sort of a way. Once dinner has been served, the film starts and everyone goes inside, and this is the signal for us cooks and waiters to down tools and eat our dinner. This year it was such a balmy evening that we set up a table outside and as we sat, chatting under the stars, I felt so fortunate to be a part of such a special night.

This year's film was *Mostly Martha,* and as we loosely (at times very loosely!) base the food around the theme of the film, Italian was on the menu. The tables were set up with bowls of olive and sun-dried tomato tapenade (see page 388) waiting to be spread on crusty loaves of bread. For the main course, there was a choice of chicken thighs roasted until crisp with a jumble of lemons, herbs, potatoes and golden shallots, or thick wedges of eggplant, mozzarella and parmesan torta (see page 142) with a scoop of luscious peperonata (see page 144) and soft parmesan polenta (see page 290). Bowls of green beans tossed with tomatoes, basil and tiny pearl bocconcini (yes, the colours of the Italian flag) were passed down the long tables, and everyone tucked in. It was a rollicking, joyful night.

I can't finish the menu there without mentioning the desserts, as we always try to make them very special. There was a gorgeous flourless orange and pine nut cake served with sticky caramelised oranges and cream, and a Torta di Verona, which is a glorious tiramisu-like confection of mascarpone custard laced with marsala and amaretto-soaked panettone, topped with blueberries and sugared almonds.

FEDERAL
SCHOOL OF ARTS
1895

Olive & Sun-Dried Tomato Tapenade

MAKES ABOUT 1½ CUPS (360 G)

- 360 g good-quality kalamata olives, pitted
- 120 g semi-dried tomatoes, finely chopped
- 2 cloves garlic, finely chopped
- 2 tablespoons salted capers, thoroughly rinsed, then soaked in cold water for 15 minutes and drained
- freshly ground black pepper
- 1 tablespoon lemon juice, or more to taste
- 3 teaspoons finely chopped thyme
- 4 anchovy fillets, optional
- 100 ml extra virgin olive oil
- thyme sprigs, to garnish
- crackers or pide toasts (see note below), to serve

This can be made well ahead of time, and is an incredibly useful thing to have on hand: serve it simply as a dip, use it to add a bit of oomph to a tomato pasta sauce or soup, or swirl a spoonful into lightly cooked green beans with a dash of extra virgin olive oil and serve with some soft goat's cheese or feta sprinkled on top. You can also make tapenade mayonnaise or butter from it just by mixing it with either one: the butter is super on grilled salmon or tuna, and the mayo is terrific in all kinds of sandwiches.

As you will see, I've made the anchovy fillets optional. They are a traditional ingredient in tapenade, but with quite a few vegetarians to feed at our film night dinner, we made the tapenade both ways and they were equally delicious – all we did for the vegetarian one was slightly increase the quantity of capers to maintain the salty balance.

- Put the olives, sun-dried tomatoes, garlic, capers, pepper, lemon juice, thyme and anchovies (if using) into a food processor and pulse until they're mixed, stopping and scraping down the sides occasionally. With the processor going, drizzle in the oil until everything comes together and forms a thick, chunky paste. At this stage it's a good idea to taste the tapenade and adjust the flavours – I find it sometimes needs a little more lemon juice or thyme. When it's right, scrape it into an airtight container. Trickle a thin layer of oil over the top of the mixture, then seal the container tightly and store it in the fridge. It keeps well for at least 3 weeks.

- When you're ready to use it, spoon the tapenade into a bowl and garnish with a few thyme sprigs. Serve it with crackers or pide toasts. If I'm offering it as a nibble with drinks I sometimes make little crostini, spreading the tapenade onto slices of baguette that have been brushed with olive oil and crisped in the oven. Finish them off with a dollop of goat's curd and a few tiny thyme sprigs.

PITTING OLIVES

The easiest way to pit olives is to squash a few at a time by pressing down on them firmly with the flat side of the blade of a chef's knife. This loosens the pits and they should pull away easily from the flesh.

PIDE TOASTS . . .

If I have leftover pide bread I often dry it to make these little toasts. Simply slice the bread thinly (a thickness of 5 mm or so), lay the slices on a baking tray and dry them out in a low oven until they are crisp and very lightly coloured. Transfer them to a rack and leave them until they're cool. Store them in an airtight jar and serve with dips.

23rd September

Oh, I do so love spring! Walking through town early this morning was like strolling through a perfumed garden – with so much in bloom, the air was positively intoxicating. Because I'm so familiar with what grows where, I could almost close my eyes and find my way home purely by scent. Heavenly! But as soon as I rounded the corner for home my reverie was broken, for that blasted magpie was back and as bold as brass, snipping off yet another strawberry for his dinner. I shall have to net the plants at this rate!

Speaking of beautiful perfumes, one of the first things I planted as soon as we arrived here was a rose geranium. It is a plant that holds such happy memories for me: its musky scent reminds me of my mum's garden, as she always had scented geraniums growing. I remember her having lemon, peppermint and cinnamon varieties – but the rose geranium, with its fragile mauve flowers, was most definitely her favourite.

Rose Geranium Leaf Cake

SERVES 12–16

12–16 medium-sized unsprayed rose geranium leaves
250 g unsalted butter
3 cups (450 g) plain flour
½ teaspoon bicarbonate of soda
½ teaspoon salt
3 eggs, at room temperature
2 cups (440 g) caster sugar
1 cup (250 ml) buttermilk
1½ teaspoons vanilla extract
1 teaspoon rosewater
icing sugar, for dusting
rose geranium or other herb flowers, for garnishing
softly whipped cream, to serve

I realise that this cake isn't going to be possible for everyone to make, but if you have a rose geranium in your garden, or can convince someone who has one to give you some leaves (and I feel sure that most gardeners will – they're a generous-hearted lot), then you're on your way. The cake is delicate and the elusive rose fragrance is quite subtle, but I love it and make it regularly in spring as it seems so appropriate for this time of year. It keeps surprisingly well too, and the flavour seems to grow stronger over time.

I use a large food processor which will fit this quantity of ingredients fairly easily, but if you only have a small one, you will probably have to combine the butter, egg and sugar mixture with the dry ingredients in a separate bowl.

- The day before you're going to make the cake, rinse and thoroughly dry four of the rose geranium leaves. Wrap these firmly around the block of butter. Wrap the butter tightly in greaseproof paper then plastic film and store it in the fridge overnight. Return it to room temperature before making the cake.
- Preheat your oven to 160°C. Lightly butter and flour a 26–28 cm fluted bundt tin. Rinse and dry the remaining rose geranium leaves then press them, face-down, decoratively into the cake tin as best you can – they won't stick all that well, but the weight of the batter will flatten them out once it's poured in. Set the tin aside.
- Whiz the flour, bicarbonate of soda and salt in a food processor so they're well mixed, then tip them into a bowl. Put the eggs and sugar into the processor and whiz them for 1 minute. Cut the butter, still wrapped in its leaves, into chunks and add these to the eggs and sugar. Whiz everything again for a minute, stopping ›

Café

and scraping down the sides occasionally. Now add the buttermilk, vanilla and rosewater and process everything for 10 seconds. Finally, tip in the flour mixture and blend it in with on/off pulses until it's just combined – it's a good idea to stop and scrape down the sides once or twice as you do this to ensure the flour is thoroughly incorporated. What you end up with is a lovely thick, creamy-coloured batter speckled with the green of the rose geranium leaves.

- Spoon the batter into the prepared tin, doing your best to keep the leaves in place (this gets easier the more batter you add). Smooth the surface, then pop the cake in the oven. Bake it for about 70 minutes, or until a fine skewer inserted in the middle comes out clean. Leave it to cool in the tin for 12 minutes, then carefully invert the cake onto the rack, remove the tin, and leave it to cool completely – I love the look of it at this stage with its rather wonderful leafy pattern.
- To serve, carefully slide the cake onto a large serving plate and dust with icing sugar (do this lightly, so you don't disguise the outline of the leaves), then decorate with rose geranium flowers. Serve with cream. As this is such a big cake, you may well have leftovers – these can be wrapped tightly and frozen for up to 3 weeks, or kept in an airtight container in a cool spot for 5 days or so.

27th September

When Clive and I moved here we didn't imagine that along with our new life we would also be adding another hat to the somewhat motley assortment we already share between us: auctioneer, valuer, cook, food writer, author . . . and now, tourist guides extraordinaire! For, in our naivety, we hadn't realised that living in such a popular holiday area tends to make one's home a sought-after destination too. In fact, so numerous were our visitors during our first year here that at one stage a rather pragmatic friend suggested it might be easier if we just hung out a B & B shingle and be done with it!

We have become authorities on scenic drives, back roads, picnic spots, walking tracks, guesthouses, where the best surf break is, and a host of other miscellanea that are all-important to our numerous holidaying friends and family. And, as most of them love their food with a passion, where to find and eat great food is nearly always at the top of the agenda (of course, it's somewhat flattering when they say they would prefer to eat here with us than go out – but also daunting!). Lovely as all this is, it's not something we bargained for when we bought our house, which really needs to be twice as big!

This influx has also encouraged me to put together a repertoire of very quick, very easy recipes (perhaps my next book should be *50 Recipes You Can Make in Under 20 Minutes*!) so that I can spend time with our visitors and not in the kitchen. The gelato overleaf is one I pull out again and again as it's so simple and everyone seems to love it. Sometimes I just serve it as is with a wafer biscuit on the side (not homemade, I have to confess); other times I'll serve it with sliced strawberries, peaches, honeydew melon or whatever else happens to be in season.

Tingly Lemon Gelato

SERVES 8

very finely grated zest of 3–4 lemons
2 cups (500 ml) lemon juice, strained
1½–2 cups (330–440 g) caster sugar
½ cup (125 ml) cold water
1 cup (250 ml) thickened cream

This tingly, tart–sweet gelato is wonderfully refreshing, especially after a substantial main course. It's really quite sharp, which I like, but if you prefer a softer, more rounded flavour then try to track down some Meyer lemons. Funnily enough, although these thin-skinned lemons are difficult to find in some areas, they thrive here and are probably the sturdiest in our humid climate. Their flavour is less sharp, fuller and slightly sweeter than their more common cousins, Eureka and Lisbon lemons, and for this reason they're particularly good in desserts and cakes. (To my mind a classic lemon tart or Sussex pond pudding are at their best when made with these fat, golden lemons.) You will notice that you can vary the quantity of sugar – if you go for the slightly sweeter version, just be mindful that the gelato will be a bit softer in texture.

Unfortunately, I have to tell you that the gelato really does have a finer texture if it's churned in an ice-cream maker; however, with patience and a bit of elbow grease, you can make a more than respectable version without a machine.

- Put the lemon zest, lemon juice, caster sugar and water into a large bowl and whisk them together until the sugar has dissolved. Add the cream and whisk it in just until it's well combined – don't worry if it looks slightly curdled initially, it will smooth out as you whisk.
- If you have an ice-cream maker, pour this mixture into it, and churn until it is frozen (I find I have to do this in two batches in my machine). To freeze the gelato without an ice-cream maker, pour the mixture into a large stainless steel bowl and freeze it for 4–5 hours, or until it's frozen 5 cm in from the edge (the time will vary, depending on your freezer). Remove the bowl from the freezer and give the gelato a really good whisk with a balloon whisk or hand-held electric beater to break up the ice crystals and smooth it out. Put the bowl back in the freezer, freeze it again as before and repeat the whisking. (For an even smoother texture, repeat this step a few more times.)
- Scrape the gelato into a cold container, cover it tightly and put it in the freezer for at least 6 hours or, better still, overnight to allow it to 'ripen'. Ripening is a funny expression for it, but that's exactly what it does, for the flavour improves over a few days.
- The gelato keeps well for up to a fortnight. There are lots of ways to serve it: I often just scoop it into waffled sugar cones, or small chilled bowls or glasses. If by any chance you have made an almond and lemon cake (see page 186) and have any of the zest and syrup leftover, it's lovely spooned on top; or, for a more sophisticated dessert, drizzle a little limoncello (see page 250) over each serving.

OCTOBER

2nd October

We have a plethora of bananas at the moment as some friends have given us the most beautiful bunch they have just harvested. The cut end is still sticky and sappy so we've swaddled it in newspaper until it dries out. Seeing them reminds me of where we grew up near Pittwater, for we had a thicket of banana trees in our back garden (as did all our neighbours – they were de rigueur along with passionfruit and choko vines). They were a perfect bolt-hole when we played hide-and-seek as we could wriggle into the middle of the dense clump so no-one could find us. I remember looking up in fascination at the clusters of bananas forming – and I wasn't the only one. I think the possums and bush rats had an eye for the main chance too, as some of the bananas would mysteriously disappear just when they were beginning to change colour.

We would all watch eagerly for the first big bunches to develop to the point where Dad would cut them down and hang them in a cool spot under the house to ripen. In nature's own amazing way they tended to mature a few at a time rather than all at once, so we had a constant supply. But when it was really humid they would all ripen at the same time and my poor mum would suddenly find herself cooking up a storm of banana cakes, tea loaves, puddings and anything else she could think of. She would also freeze as many as possible to use when supplies were a little less prolific. The thing I loved most was her wonderfully sticky banana cake. Sadly she never wrote the recipe down, but after much experimenting (a good way of using up our own abundance of bananas!), this version of her cake has become a firm family favourite.

Upside-Down Sticky Banana Cake

SERVES 6–8

This cake really needs to be eaten the day it's made to look its most beautiful, glossy best. Not, I hasten to add, that I've ever found that to be a problem – the hardest thing is trying to keep everyone away long enough for it to cool down a little! However, in the interests of seeing whether it would keep, I managed to snaffle a slice when I made the one in the photo and refrigerated it overnight (with a big note on it threatening dire things to anyone who even *thought* about eating it!). The next day I gently warmed it and then of course had to eat it – in the interests of research, you understand – and it was terrific! The bananas weren't quite as glossy as when it was freshly turned out, but the taste and texture were perfect.

180 g self-raising flour
¼ teaspoon salt
½ teaspoon ground cinnamon
¼ teaspoon freshly ground nutmeg
1 medium-sized very ripe banana
2 tablespoons sour cream
2 eggs
180 g caster sugar
90 g cultured unsalted butter, in small chunks, at room temperature
1 teaspoon vanilla extract
golden syrup and thick cream or vanilla ice-cream, to serve

CARAMEL TOPPING

60 g unsalted butter
¾ cup (165 g) brown sugar
large pinch of salt
4–5 large just-ripe bananas

- Preheat your oven to 180°C. Butter a 24–25 cm round cake tin and set it aside.
- For the caramel topping, melt the butter in a heavy-based saucepan over medium heat. Add the brown sugar and salt and cook the mixture, stirring occasionally, for a few minutes until it's glossy. Don't be alarmed if the sugar doesn't dissolve completely – it tends to form a slush. Just be a little careful as you cook this: don't let it cook for too long or get too hot, or else the butter will separate out. This is not a major tragedy as you can still use the mixture – it's just a bit more awkward to do so as the sugar hardens.
- When the caramel is ready, pour it into the prepared tin and tilt it to coat the bottom evenly. (If the topping has separated a bit and the sugar has hardened, just press it in as best you can – it will melt again as the cake bakes.) Now, peel and slice the bananas fairly thickly (about 6–7 mm), then sit the slices in overlapping circles over the base of the tin so they completely cover the caramel. Set the tin aside while you make the cake batter.
- Put the flour, salt, cinnamon and nutmeg into a food processor and whiz them together for 10 seconds. Tip them into a bowl. In another bowl, mash the banana then stir in the sour cream. Set both bowls aside.
- Put the eggs and sugar into the processor, then whiz them together for 1 minute, occasionally stopping and scraping down the sides with a rubber spatula. Add the butter and vanilla, and whiz again for 40 seconds or so. Now, scrape the mashed banana and sour cream mixture into this and whiz them together for 10 seconds or until they're just combined. The batter may well look a little curdled at this stage, but don't worry – it will be fine. Add the flour mixture to the food processor and pulse them together until they're just combined.
- Dollop spoonfuls of the cake batter into the tin over the bananas and spread it out evenly. Do this fairly carefully so you don't disturb the bananas underneath. ›

A NOTE ON BANANAS . . .
It's important that the bananas for the caramel topping aren't too ripe, otherwise they collapse and become mushy as they bake. The cake will still taste great – it just won't look as pretty. This works in reverse for the banana that's part of the cake batter: it's best if it's really ripe because it's sweeter and mixes in more evenly.

- Bake for 45–50 minutes until the cake is golden and springy when you give it a gentle prod in the centre. Remove it from the oven and leave it to settle in the tin for 3 minutes. Then carefully loosen it around the sides (watch out for your fingers as the tin will be very hot). Sit a serving plate on top of the tin and, holding the tin with a tea towel to protect your hands, flip the cake and plate over. Sit the plate on the bench and leave the tin on top for 20 seconds: this creates a little bit of steam which helps the cake come out of the tin easily. Gently remove the tin. Don't worry if some banana slices stick to the bottom of it – just scrape them off and press them back onto the cake. Occasionally, I've found the caramel has hardened a little and some bits have stuck to the base of the tin – if this happens to you, very gently and briefly warm the base of the tin on the stovetop to dissolve the hardened caramel then drizzle it over the cake. Let the cake cool.
- Just before serving, brush a little golden syrup over the top. This cake is lovely served warm or at room temperature with cream or ice-cream.

3rd October

As kids, one of our favourite dinners was lamb rissoles with mashed potatoes and a big splodge of tomato sauce on the side. I was thinking about this recently as I was driving about the countryside, as you do – food is never far from my thoughts. (Clive always teases me about this, saying he wishes he could make my toes curl as much as good food does!) Anyhow, I was playing around with ideas for making a somewhat Asian version of rissoles and potatoes and came home all fired up to experiment, the result being the two recipes that follow: one an old favourite, the other a newcomer. They can each happily stand alone, however I can thoroughly recommend trying them together – there wasn't a skerrick left on anyone's plate when we ate them, which is a sight that always gladdens a cook's heart.

Thai-Style Chicken 'Rissoles' with Chilli Dipping Sauce

MAKES 10–12 (ENOUGH TO SERVE 4)

I love the way water chestnuts add such a delectable crunch to anything they go in. I tend to fling them willy-nilly into any sort of grain salad that I make (rice and barley are particularly good) and they're terrific in these rissoles too, adding a really interesting texture. Although we generally eat these as a main course, I sometimes make wee rissoles and serve them with drinks, and they are invariably vacuumed up. You can use a good bottled chilli sauce to dribble over the rissoles, but I prefer to make this sharp–sweet vinegar-based one as it's a bit less cloying than straight chilli sauce.

1 stalk lemongrass
1 clove garlic, finely chopped
2 teaspoons finely chopped ginger
2 tablespoons chopped spring onion (white part only)
1 small red chilli, finely chopped
2 tablespoons chopped coriander or basil
2 tablespoons finely shredded mint
1 teaspoon Thai red or green curry paste
2 tablespoons coconut cream
1 teaspoon fish sauce
sea salt flakes and freshly ground black pepper, to taste
1 small or ½ large red capsicum (pepper), very thinly sliced into strips about 3 cm long
⅓ cup (65 g) finely chopped water chestnuts
500 g minced chicken
20–24 coriander or mint leaves

continued next page

- As you probably know, lemongrass is pretty tough, so you need to do rather a lot of trimming. Firstly, cut off the top of the stalk so you're left with about 7 cm of the base. Peel away the coarse outer layers of the base until you reach the more tender heart area, and chop this very, very finely. (I rarely throw out my lemongrass tops; they usually end up in either a curry or my teapot – see page 414 for a simple lemongrass and mint tea.)
- Scrape the chopped lemongrass into a large bowl. Add the garlic, ginger, spring onion, chilli, coriander or basil, mint, curry paste, coconut cream, fish sauce, salt and a good grinding of black pepper. Stir everything together so it's thoroughly mixed. Now add the capsicum strips, water chestnuts and finally the chicken and mix together until well combined. Hands are definitely best for this, as they mix so much more evenly and gently than a spoon, although I must admit I usually slip on a pair of prep gloves first as it's pretty gloopy. Once the mixture is well combined, cover the bowl and pop it in the fridge for half an hour or so. ›

light olive oil, for pan-frying
large herb leaves (such as basil), to serve, optional
lime wedges, to serve

CHILLI DIPPING SAUCE

½ cup (125 ml) rice vinegar or mild white wine vinegar
½ cup (110 g) caster sugar
1 teaspoon salt
1 tablespoon very finely shredded ginger
1 small red chilli, seeded and finely chopped
½ kaffir lime leaf, very finely shredded

- While the mixture is chilling, make the dipping sauce. Put all the ingredients into a bowl and whisk until the sugar has completely dissolved. Pour into a jar, seal tightly and chill the sauce until you need it.
- To shape the rissoles, remove the chicken mixture from the fridge and form it into 10–12 patties with clean hands. The strips of capsicum may stick out a bit – if so, just press them back onto the surface. Press a coriander or mint leaf onto each side of the rissoles then sit them in a single layer on a plate lined with baking paper. If you're in a hurry you can cook them straight away, but they're easier to handle if they're covered and chilled briefly so they firm up a bit.
- To cook the rissoles, pour a thin layer of oil into a large frying pan and heat it over low–medium heat. Once it's hot, add the rissoles (in batches if necessary) and cook them for about 7 minutes all up, turning them once halfway through the cooking time. As they're ready, lift them out of the pan and sit them on paper towels to drain.
- To serve, put a couple of large basil leaves on each of four dinner plates and sit the rissoles on top. Garnish with lime wedges and serve the sauce separately.

Stir-Fried Sichuan Pepper Potatoes

SERVES 4

Gosh, I must have first cooked these delicious little matchsticks over 25 years ago. They're extraordinarily good and although it's somewhat tedious slicing all the potatoes (and it is, there is no denying it) the resulting dish is well worth it. I could quite happily make a meal from a bowlful of these and nothing else, however more conventionally they're great with any simply grilled or barbecued meat, fish or chicken, or of course Thai-style rissoles (see page 401).

4–5 large old potatoes
½ cup (125 ml) light olive oil
2 teaspoons whole Sichuan peppercorns (see note below)
2 small cloves garlic, peeled and lightly crushed
2½ tablespoons white wine vinegar, or to taste
2 tablespoons dry sherry or vermouth
1–2 small red chillies, very finely chopped
2 teaspoons sesame oil
4 spring onions, very finely sliced on the diagonal
sea salt flakes
½ teaspoon crushed Sichuan peppercorns, extra, for sprinkling

- Peel the potatoes, then slice them into 6 mm × 3 mm matchsticks, dropping them into a bowl of cold water as you go.
- When they're done, pour the oil into a wok or large, heavy-based frying pan. Add the whole peppercorns and garlic cloves to the pan and heat them slowly and gently in the oil until the garlic is pale golden – don't let the garlic become too dark or it will impart a bitter flavour to the oil. Take the pan off the heat and carefully strain the oil into a heatproof jug, discarding the peppercorns and garlic.
- Drain the potatoes, tip them out onto a couple of thick clean tea towels (or do as I do and use an old bath towel for this – it soaks up the moisture beautifully) and pat them as dry as possible.
- Use a thick wad of paper towels to wipe out the wok or frying pan to remove any fragments of peppercorn, then return it to the stovetop over high heat. Pour in the strained oil and when it's hot, tip in the potatoes (watch out as they will splash and spit a bit), tossing them about constantly so they're well coated in the fragrant oil. Continue to cook them, tossing all the while, for 2 minutes. Add 2 tablespoons vinegar to the pan and partly cover it. Cook the potatoes for another 5 minutes or so until they're nearly tender, stirring them regularly. Now sprinkle in the sherry or vermouth, chilli, sesame oil and half the spring onion and stir-fry the potatoes for another minute. They should be done by now – fish one out, blow on it to cool it down, then take a bite and see. When the potatoes are tender, sprinkle in the remaining vinegar and salt to taste, then stir-fry for another 30 seconds or so until the liquid evaporates.
- Immediately slide the potatoes into a warm serving bowl and sprinkle them with the crushed peppercorns and remaining spring onion. Serve straight away.

SICHUAN PEPPERCORNS . . .

Sichuan peppercorns have a wonderfully exotic peppery flavour. When a recipe calls for them to be crushed, first toast them lightly in a hot, dry frying pan over medium heat until they start to pop. As soon as they do, take the pan off the heat and tip the peppercorns into a mortar. Grind them finely, then sieve out the woody casings and stalks before using them.

5th October

The water dragons are out and about again, and I do so love them. As we crossed the creek on our walk this morning a family of four were cooling themselves in the water – the parents all but submerged with just their eyes peeping above the surface, while the babies scrambled over the rocks, plopping into the water whenever something startled them. They're the most extraordinary, almost prehistoric-looking creatures and truly wonderful to see.

I rather wish we could have joined them in the creek as the weather is hotting up, with waves of steamy heat rising from the road. I can see it's time to get the barbecue into good working order again – it tends to take a bit of a bashing from now on in as I find myself increasingly reluctant to cook inside. In fact, I'm just making the marinade now for some lamb steaks we shall use to christen it tonight.

Barbecued Lamb Steaks with Cucumber, Currant & Yoghurt Relish

SERVES 4

4 lamb leg steaks (cut about 3 cm thick), fat scored
extra virgin olive oil, to serve
tiny mint leaves, to serve

MARINADE

2 teaspoons freshly ground cumin seeds
3 teaspoons sweet Hungarian paprika (I sometimes add a smidgen of smoked paprika too)
1½ teaspoons freshly ground black pepper
1½ teaspoons freshly ground coriander seeds
½ teaspoon ground turmeric
4 large cloves garlic, finely chopped
¼ cup (60 ml) extra virgin olive oil
¼ cup (60 ml) lemon juice
⅓ cup (20 g) finely chopped mint or coriander

CUCUMBER, CURRANT AND YOGHURT RELISH

2 Lebanese or other small cucumbers
2 cups (560 g) thick Greek-style plain yogurt
1 small clove garlic, finely chopped
1 teaspoon sea salt flakes
½ cup (25 g) finely chopped mint
1 tablespoon lemon juice
¼ cup (40 g) currants

It's only since we moved here that I've discovered lamb leg steaks and just how fantastic they are for barbecuing. We have a super butcher who sells organic lamb – he cuts the steaks quite thickly, leaving a good rim of fat to keep them moist and give them plenty of flavour (I do love a bit of fat on my meat). The cucumber relish is virtually a staple for us in summer as it works beautifully with just about anything that goes on the barbecue – salmon, chicken, pork and even veggies (especially eggplant and zucchini). It's a little different from standard mint and yoghurt, as the cucumber is seeded and grated and the currants add an unusual fruity sweetness.

- To make the marinade, mix all the ingredients together to form a paste. Set it aside while you prepare the steaks.
- The first time I made this I discovered that the steaks tend to fall apart as they cook, so now I thread a couple of thick toothpicks through the meat of each one to hold them together. Once they're 'toothpicked', sit each steak on a sheet of plastic film and smear the marinade thoroughly over both sides. Wrap the steaks up tightly in the plastic film and refrigerate them in a sealed container (or else your fridge will smell *very* garlicky) for at least 3 hours or, for a stronger flavour, overnight.
- About 2 hours before you're going to cook the lamb, make the cucumber relish. To do this, halve the cucumbers lengthways and scoop out the seeds with a teaspoon. Now grate the halves on the coarsest side of a box grater. Bundle the grated cucumber into the corner of a clean tea towel, then squeeze it over the sink to remove as much liquid as possible. Once this is done, shake the cucumber shreds into a large bowl. Mix in the remaining ingredients, then taste the relish and adjust the amount of lemon juice and salt, if necessary. Cover the bowl and chill.
- Half an hour before you're ready to cook the lamb, remove it from the fridge. Preheat your barbecue so it's on a good, steady medium heat. Put the steaks on the barbecue and cook them for about 4 minutes each side for pink lamb. (If your barbecue has a lid, close it for cooking.)
- While the lamb is cooking, scrape the relish into a small serving bowl. Drizzle a thread of olive oil over the top and garnish it with tiny mint leaves. Serve the lamb with the relish.

Oz.10
Gr.300

6th October

Everything looked green as green as I was driving through the hinterland this morning. The grass is so thick and lush after three weeks of rain followed by bursts of sunshine that I'm tempted to stop the car and stretch out in it. Sadly, I'm too aware that passers-by (or curious cows) may wonder at the mad woman lying in the field! However, I did stop to pick some delicate native violets, which will look divine on the citrus creams I've made for dessert.

Little Lemon & Lime Creams

SERVES 6

2 cups (500 ml) thickened cream
½ cup (80 g) icing sugar, to taste
1 generous tablespoon finely grated lime zest (from about 3 limes)
1 generous tablespoon finely grated lemon zest (from about 2 large lemons)
¼ cup lime juice, strained
1 tablespoon lemon juice, strained
4 drops vanilla extract
unsprayed violets, to garnish, optional

I can't begin to tell you how often I make these dear little creams, nor how much everyone seems to love them. They're the quickest and easiest dessert I know. The actual preparation is a breeze and only takes about 10 minutes, but you do need to allow time for setting. I try to make them the day before I need them, though you can get away with less setting time – as little as 4 hours, if push comes to shove . . . which it quite often does at our house!

As you can see, the violets look beautiful on the creams, however you could also use raspberries, sliced strawberries, strips of candied lemon zest – pretty much anything that goes with their tangy flavour.

- Put the cream, icing sugar and grated lime and lemon zests into a medium-sized saucepan over very low heat. If you have a heat diffuser, use it – you want the cream to warm through at a snail's pace to extract as much flavour from the zests as possible. Stir the mixture only until the sugar dissolves, then leave the cream to come slowly to just below the boil – keep an eye on it so it doesn't actually boil, though, as this will alter the flavour. When it reaches this stage (it will have steam coming from it and very small bubbles around the side of the pan), turn off the heat.
- Cover the pan and leave the cream to cool until it is barely warm. At this point, stir in the lime and lemon juices and the vanilla. Strain the mixture through a very fine sieve into a large jug, pressing down on the zest with the back of a spoon to extract as much cream as possible.
- Sit six ½ cup (125 ml) ceramic dessert pots (I usually use small Chinese tea cups) on a plate and divide the cream mixture evenly among them. Gently tap each one a couple of times on the counter to disperse any air bubbles, then sit them back on the plate. Cover them with plastic film and put them in the fridge to chill and set.
- To serve the creams, set each one on a small plate and scatter a few violets on top, if using. If you want to dress them up a bit more, serve them with thin, crisp biscuits or fine fingers of shortbread (see page 86).

8th October

I woke at first light after a raging storm in the wee small hours of the morning. It was silent and uncannily serene after the crashing and banging that kept us awake half the night. When I was walking into town for the newspapers, I could feel my steps slow as everything had a dreamy quality about it that enveloped me too. The trees were shrouded in a soft, damp haze and the avenue of silky oaks by the creek glowed gently as the sun's rays pierced the mist – it looked just like a stage-set from *Swan Lake*. Further on, the scarlet flame tree and purple jacaranda that stand side-by-side were almost luminous, and I wondered if town planners of the past had an eye for all this when they planted out the streets, or if it was just a wonderful piece of serendipity.

Speaking of serendipity, I was *very* serendipitously given a huge bag of pecans by two of the local farmers. They have a beautiful plantation out near Eltham where they grow not only pecans but coffee too, and sell both in a lovely old cottage-cum-tea-room in the middle of the orchard. It's my treat to stop there whenever I drive over to Lismore – there's nothing quite like sitting out on the wide veranda, sipping coffee grown just down the road and eating a pie made from pecans grown only metres away.

My All-Time Favourite Pecan & Maple Pie

SERVES 8–10

1 blind-baked simple shortcrust pastry shell (see page 371) in a 25–26 cm loose-bottomed tin
about 1½ cups (180 g) pecan halves, for topping
icing sugar, for dusting, optional
cream or ice-cream, to serve

PECAN AND MAPLE FILLING

1½ cups (180 g) pecans
125 g brown sugar
1 cup (250 ml) pure maple syrup
2 teaspoons vanilla extract
80 g butter, melted and cooled
⅓ cup (80 ml) cream (or for a lighter option, buttermilk)
4 eggs

I've always had such a soft spot for pecan pie – there is something about the combination of short, crisp pastry, sticky caramel filling and roasted pecans that is alarmingly addictive. I tend to try it wherever I go, and am constantly tinkering about with recipes for it. This one is the latest in a long line of experiments – and I would have to say it has become my favourite. Unlike most, the filling is made from ground pecans, which give it a surprising lightness, but it still gets a delectable crunch from the pecan halves studded over the top.

- Preheat your oven to 180°C. Sit the tin with the cooked pastry shell on a baking tray.
- For the filling, put the pecans and brown sugar into the bowl of a food processor. Whiz them together for 20 seconds or so to chop the pecans. Pour in the remaining ingredients and whiz everything together to thoroughly combine them – the mixture will be quite wet and the pecans finely chopped.
- Pour the pecan mixture into the pastry shell, remembering to leave space for the remaining pecans – depending on the depth of your tin, you may have to hold back just a little filling or it could overflow with the weight of the nuts on top. Arrange the remaining pecan halves decoratively over the top of the filling. (I try to manoeuvre them so that when the pie is baked I can cut down between the rows for each slice. It's no big deal if you don't do this – just bear in mind that if the pie is warm or at room temperature when you slice it, the pecan halves tend to tear and pull the filling as you cut into them.)
- Put the pie, on its tray, into the oven and bake for 45–50 minutes until the filling is set. It will be puffed up and glorious when it's ready, but don't be alarmed when it sinks as it cools. Transfer the pie to a wire rack and leave it to cool completely; the filling will be softly set at room temperature, although it firms up if you chill the pie.
- To serve, slip off the outer ring of the tin and slide the pie onto a serving plate. If you like, dust it very lightly with icing sugar, then slice with a sharp knife and serve with cream or ice-cream.
- Leftover pie (if there is such a thing!) keeps very well in the fridge for up to a week, although the pastry does soften over time. It also freezes well for a month or so.

THE REAL DEAL . . .

You'll notice I specify pure maple syrup in the ingredients lists. I urge you not to succumb to the lure of cheap maple-flavoured syrup – it is nothing like the real thing and is terribly disappointing. Your pie will suffer for it, I'm afraid. Pure maple syrup is readily available in supermarkets.

10th October

As I sit here writing, I'm inhaling the intoxicating fragrance of a cup of fresh mint and lemongrass tea. This glorious brew is a clear, pale straw colour with just a few curls of mint leaves floating in it. I find it refreshing and soothing at the same time, and love that I can just go and pick the makings from the garden. I imagine it would make a wonderful sorbet or granita too.

When I'm cooking with lemongrass, the leaves (that are usually trimmed off in most recipes) rarely make it into my compost heap. Invariably I knot them and plop them into a curry, or they go towards making a pot of this fragrant tea. It's wonderfully refreshing and makes a terrific digestif after a meal – it's also easy as pie to make. I always brew it in a lovely old Chinese teapot as I greatly enjoy the sense of ritual it brings, and its delicacy somehow seems fitting for the brew. To make it, all you need do is pick a few large sprigs of mint and put them in a china teapot, along with a coarsely chopped stalk or two of lemongrass (or just use the leaves). Pour boiling water over the lot and leave it to infuse for 5 minutes or so. Occasionally, I'll add a slice of fresh ginger – this is especially good if you've eaten too much or are feeling a bit queasy after a rich meal. Once the tea has brewed, pour it into small tea bowls or cups and sweeten it with a smidgen of honey.

Mint and lemongrass aren't the only things running riot in the herb garden. I have parsley to burn again and have picked masses of it, which I'll use to make some salsa verde and a rather sprightly parsley salad that will be just the thing with the snapper fillets I've bought for dinner.

Fish Fillets with Salsa Verde & Lemon & Parsley Salad

SERVES 4

You may have noticed that rather a lot of dishes in this book use parsley . . . I love its fresh, vibrant flavour and feel it has been somewhat overlooked of late as we've focused our attention on other herbs. Unfortunately, there was a whole era when a sprig or handful of chopped parsley was the only garnish any dish ever had, and I think eventually everyone became utterly sick of it and made a point of using anything else they could lay their hands on.

However, like all things, it can be fantastic when used in the right way, and I for one would love to see it make a comeback. But I should add a proviso here: when I speak of parsley, I mean flat-leaf parsley (which is also called Italian or Continental parsley). It has a softer, rounder flavour and far nicer texture than its somewhat scratchier cousin, curly parsley. And if any dish were to highlight parsley's good points and versatility, then this is it. In the salsa verde, its robust green flavour is tamed to a more subtle note, and this is repeated in a more potent way in the lemon-scented parsley salad that tops the fish. It's a beautiful dish, too: all clean greens, gold and white, with the contrasting glossy black of the olives. The secret to making it look as lovely as possible is to seek out the smallest, most tender parsley leaves for the salad – it's a bit time-consuming but looks so much nicer.

- To make the salsa verde, put all the ingredients except for the oil, lemon juice and salt into a blender or food processor. Turn the machine on and drizzle in the oil until a thick purée forms. I find I usually have to stop the machine and scrape down the sides a few times when I do this. Now whiz in the lemon juice and salt to taste. Scrape the salsa verde into a container, seal tightly and store in the fridge if you're not using it immediately.
- For the salad, mix the parsley leaves, olives and capers in a bowl. Cover the bowl and pop it in the fridge. To make the dressing, put the olive oil, anchovies, lemon juice and preserved lemon rind into a blender and purée it well. It's a good idea to taste it and adjust the flavours to suit you – it may well need more salt or lemon juice, depending on just how salty and sharp the anchovies and preserved lemon are. Pour the dressing into a jar, seal tightly and store in the fridge.
- To cook the fish, heat a little olive oil in a heavy-based frying pan over high heat (or preheat the barbecue and brush the fillets with a little oil). Season the fillets with salt and cook them for 2–3 minutes until they're pale golden on one side – the actual cooking time will depend on the thickness of the fillets. Turn them over and cook for another 2–3 minutes, or until they are tender but just cooked through. ›

olive oil, for pan-frying
sea salt flakes
4 × 200 g white fish fillets (blue eye, mahi-mahi, bream and snapper are all good options)
lemon wedges, to serve

SALSA VERDE

1 cup (about 40 g) tightly packed coarsely chopped flat-leaf parsley
1 tablespoon fresh breadcrumbs
½ hard-boiled egg, coarsely chopped
1 tablespoon capers, rinsed and drained
1 small clove garlic, chopped
3 anchovy fillets
2 teaspoons finely chopped preserved lemon rind, optional
1 tablespoon grated parmesan
½ cup (125 ml) extra virgin olive oil
1 tablespoon lemon juice, or more to taste
sea salt flakes

continued next page

LEMON AND PARSLEY SALAD

50 g small flat-leaf parsley leaves
24 small black olives (tiny ligurian ones are terrific)
1½ tablespoons capers, rinsed and drained
⅓ cup (80 ml) extra virgin olive oil, or to taste
6 anchovy fillets
3 teaspoons lemon juice, or to taste
1 tablespoon chopped preserved lemon rind

The only way I find I can really check is to prod a piece gently: it should 'give' a little, without being soft and mushy, or firm and bouncy. It takes a bit of practice to get used to just the right feel, but you will find the more you do it, the more familiar you become with it.

- While the fish is cooking, toss the salad with some of the anchovy dressing, keeping the rest for later.
- When the fillets are ready, give the salsa verde a good stir then dollop a couple of spoonfuls into the centre of each plate. Sit a piece of fish on this. Scoop some parsley salad on top of the fish and drizzle with the reserved dressing. Serve with lemon wedges and any leftover salsa verde.

SALSA VERDE . . .

Salsa verde keeps well in the fridge for about 5 days and, surprisingly, it retains its vivid green colour too. It's lovely with any seafood, but it's also really good stirred through steamed vegetables (particularly beans), dolloped onto a barbecued steak, or trickled over thinly sliced poached chicken for a light summer meal.

11th October

If I had the time to potter at my leisure when I cook, I think I would have the most fabulously stocked pantry and fridge ever. It would be full of all those little things that are so incredibly useful to have on standby – homemade tapenade, preserved lemons (at least I can boast a stock of those after a marathon bottling session in winter, when the trees were laden with fruit), spicy-hot harissa, marmalade, jars of caramelised orange syrup, ganache (perfect for dressing up a cake in no time flat) and always, but always a supply of praline in the freezer. I invariably make more of this than I need so I can squirrel the rest away and bring it out when I'm caught short trying to dress up a dessert. I really can't think of many things that don't benefit from its toasty, nutty, crunchy presence: chocolate cake, ice-cream and all sorts of sweet mousses and simple compotes of fruit.

Drunken Strawberries with Praline Cream

SERVES 4

- 2 punnets (about 500 g) medium-sized strawberries, hulled and halved lengthways
- 1–2 tablespoons caster sugar or pure icing sugar
- 2 tablespoons strawberry liqueur
- coarsely broken praline, or praline shards, to garnish

PRALINE CREAM

- 1 cup (250 ml) double thick cream or sour cream
- 1 tablespoon icing sugar, sifted
- 1 teaspoon vanilla extract
- ⅓ cup (55 g) finely crushed almond, hazelnut or pecan praline (see page 356)

WILD STRAWBERRIES

These occasionally make an appearance in good fruit shops, but because they bruise easily not all that many grocers tend to stock them. Fortunately, they're not hard to grow (we had a couple of pots on our windowsill when we lived in the city and it's amazing just how many berries we picked). White or deep crimson in colour, they are positively ambrosial – even a few mixed into a fruit salad or berry compote will add the most exquisite flavour.

This is a very simple dessert – perfect if you have unexpected visitors as it takes so little time to prepare (less if you already have some praline tucked away in your freezer). Even if you do have to make the praline from scratch, the whole thing comes together with little to-do. If you don't have strawberry liqueur, Grand Marnier, Cointreau and kirsch all work well in its place.

- Put the halved strawberries into a large bowl and sprinkle the sugar and liqueur over the top. Stir very gently so the berries don't bruise, then cover and leave in a cool spot, stirring from time to time. I try not to refrigerate the strawberries unless it's very hot, as the cold tends to dull their flavour. (You can prepare them up to an hour or two ahead of using them – any longer and they get a bit mushy.)

- Meanwhile, make the praline cream. To do this, put the cream, icing sugar and vanilla into a chilled bowl. Use a balloon whisk to softly whip the cream – be careful not to overdo this or the cream may become a bit too stiff and grainy. Lightly fold in the praline.

- To serve the berries, scoop them, along with their juices, into dessert bowls or glasses. Spoon some of the praline cream over the top and garnish them with either very coarsely broken praline or long, slim shards of it.

STRAWBERRY LIQUEUR . . .

The best strawberry liqueur I've tried is a French variety sold as Crème a la Fraises des Bois. It's made from tiny wild strawberries and has a remarkably intense fragrance – almost heady if you take a good long sniff (it's hard not to once you've uncorked it!). As you've probably guessed, it's not cheap but a little goes a long way and it's rather fabulous for adding a real verve to things – a splash in a glass of sparkling white wine or fizzy mineral water makes a lovely rosy-pink aperitif; try it drizzled over a scoop or two of vanilla ice-cream with a few berries scattered on top; or stir it into mascarpone and serve it with a mixture of berries, or sliced strawberries and pineapple.

13th October

I don't know what it is about markets, but in a rather endearing way no one seems to know anybody's surname, so they refer to each other by profession, much as people did in mediaeval times. It's always Frank the pecan man, Heather and Hugh the tomato growers, Liz and Bob the flower people and, inevitably, Belinda the cook!

Today the stalls were full of the most gorgeous red capsicums – big, even ones with tight, shiny skins and bright green stalks. I bought heaps, not only for cooking but to pile in bowls around the kitchen as I love their vibrant colour and voluptuous curves. Nature is so remarkable, isn't it? I also bought some tomatoes and a jar of marinated feta from our local cheesemaker – it's delicious, and the creamy chunks look divine in their olive oil bath. I shall have to think about what I am going to do with them.

It's now nearly bedtime, but while I can still remember I wanted to write down what I ended up concocting from my market purchases. Basically, I made a simple capsicum gratin, topped with goat's cheese, thick slices of tomatoes and a layer of crunchy olive-oil-crisped breadcrumbs. I must say it went down a treat.

Red Capsicum, Tomato & Goat's Cheese Gratin

SERVES 4 AS A MAIN OR 6 AS A STARTER

- 4 large red capsicums (peppers)
- ⅓ cup (80 ml) extra virgin olive oil
- 2 large brown onions, halved and thinly sliced
- 2 cloves garlic, halved and sliced paper-thin
- about 700 g medium-sized ripe tomatoes (about 6)
- 2 tablespoons capers (the tiny salt-packed ones look best), rinsed and drained
- 2 tablespoons thyme leaves
- 2 heaped tablespoons finely chopped flat-leaf parsley
- sea salt flakes and freshly ground black pepper
- about 200 g marinated (or fresh) goat's cheese
- 70 g coarse-ish fresh breadcrumbs, made from a good country-style or sourdough loaf
- thyme or parsley sprigs, to serve, optional

I have now formalised this recipe somewhat so that I can include it here. We made a meal of it with chunks of good bread (vital for sopping up the lovely oily juices) and a handful of salad greens tossed in vinaigrette. However, since then we have eaten it as part of a 'leftovers' dinner (fondly known around here as 'what on earth is that lurking in the back of the fridge?') alongside a slice of the rainbow chard, cheese and almond tart (see page 368), which I had frozen weeks ago and almost forgotten about. It would also be excellent with barbecued lamb steaks, chops or a simple herb-roasted chicken.

- Slice the capsicums into large pieces along their natural contour lines and remove the seeds and white ribs. Put them, skin-side up, on a grill tray and run them under a hot grill until the skins blister and blacken. Remove and cover them with a clean tea towel to sweat and loosen the skins. Peel them as soon as they're cool enough to handle, then slice them into 1.5 cm wide strips. Set them aside.
- Meanwhile, heat half the oil in a medium-sized frying pan over low heat. When it's warm, add the onion and garlic and cook them so they sizzle softly, stirring them regularly, until they're a pale golden brown – this will take about 20–25 minutes. When they're ready, turn off the heat and set them aside.
- Cut the tomatoes into thick slices (about 8 mm) and put them aside too.
- Preheat your oven to 180°C. Lightly oil a medium-sized gratin dish – the one I use is 30 cm × 18 cm, and is 4.5 cm deep.
- To put the gratin together, mix half the capsicum strips, most of the capers and 1 tablespoon each of the thyme and parsley into the onion mixture. Season with salt and pepper. Spread this mixture over the base of the gratin dish, then crumble the goat's cheese evenly on top. Overlap the tomato slices attractively on the cheese, slipping a strip of the remaining capsicum between each slice (if the strips are a bit big, cut them in half).
- Now, thoroughly mix the breadcrumbs with the remaining herbs and capers and 1 tablespoon of the remaining olive oil. Scatter this mixture evenly over the tomato slices then dribble what's left of the oil on top.
- Bake the gratin for 35 minutes, or until the top is golden and you can hear it gently bubbling. Remove and leave to cool a little before serving (it tastes best when it's warm rather than hot). If the rim of the gratin dish looks a bit splattered, just wipe it with damp paper towel to clean it up. Scatter with a few herb sprigs, if liked.

15th October

When it comes to travelling I'm a bit of a funny 'coot', as my dad would have said. Being born on the cusp of Leo and Cancer, I find the Leo part of me is excited and ready to be out and about in the world, while the Cancer crab is retreating further and further into its shell the closer we get to leaving (tomorrow, in fact!). I can see that I'm going to have to be reluctantly prised out of my safe haven. This is not at all helped by the fact that October is a glorious time of year here and I'm sad to be leaving, as the garden grows more beautiful each day.

The jasmine by our bedroom is a cascade of starry flowers and we sleep a soothing, scented sleep as gusts of perfume waft in through the doors at night. The gardenias are covered in buds, and will be a mass of flowers in a few weeks – hopefully some will last the distance until we return. And sadly for the cook in me, my rouge de Marmande tomatoes are heavy with green fruit, which will no doubt ripen while we're away. I'm tying the stems to thicker, more substantial stakes today, which will hopefully stop them collapsing under the weight of what looks to be a bumper crop. I suspect the birds will get the most benefit from them, however I have told our neighbours to come and help themselves, as they are truly special tomatoes with the most wonderful 'old-fashioned' tomato flavour. They look rather whimsical too, with their funny ridged, squashy shape covered in mottled green and red skin. They're certainly the antithesis of their even, perfect supermarket cousins – but all the better for it, I would have to say!

We've spent the weekend mulching to try to get the garden in order before we leave; otherwise, a few weeks away at this time of year when everything has a major growth spurt could see us needing a machete to slash our way through to the front door when we get home!

Fortunately, friends have offered to cook dinner for us tonight as the cupboard is very nearly bare. I'm just scratching around now, using up the last bits and pieces in a cake to take for dessert.

Toska Torte with Homemade Caramel Sauce

SERVES 8–10

1½ cups (225 g) plain flour
1½ teaspoons baking powder
pinch of salt
180 g unsalted butter, melted and cooled
2 tablespoons milk
1½ teaspoons vanilla extract
3 × 60 g eggs, at room temperature
1 cup (220 g) caster sugar
thick cream and homemade caramel sauce (see facing page), to serve, optional

TOPPING

80 g unsalted butter
½ cup (110 g) caster sugar
½ cup (125 ml) cream
heaped ½ cup (80 g) flaked almonds, lightly roasted

My mum, Cooee, was a really good cook and she especially loved to bake. In my mind, I can see her so clearly in the kitchen of our family home, swathed in an apron and enveloped in a cloud of flour as she rolled pastry or whipped up a cake for us to try.

The cake tin was rarely empty and she would always make a cake on Friday to have as a treat over the weekend. Her cakes were mainly plain and tasted wonderful – orange butter loaf and apple and cinnamon tea cake were great favourites. However, as we got older she started to go to cooking classes (there were very few people giving them at that time), and our diets expanded greatly as she took us on a whirlwind gastronomic world tour. We tried things we'd never tasted before: dolmades, hummus, homemade pâté, sticky cinnamon-scented baklava and rich European-style cakes, including this scrumptious Toska Torte. Basically it's a buttery, somewhat firmly textured sponge with a wonderfully chewy toffee and almond glaze. I remember many times that it was pressed into service as a birthday cake. Mum would split it in half and spread a generous layer of lightly whipped vanilla cream in the middle before sitting the top back on, adding a swag of candles and serving it with lashings of homemade caramel sauce. It was the best!

- Preheat your oven to 175°C. Butter and flour a 24–25 cm non-stick springform cake tin and set it aside.
- Either sift the flour, baking powder and salt together into a bowl, or tip them all into the bowl and use a balloon whisk to mix them all together for 1 minute. Set the mixture aside.
- In a jug or bowl, mix together the melted butter, milk and vanilla.
- With an electric mixer or hand-held electric beater, beat the eggs and caster sugar on medium speed for about 6 minutes until they become very thick and pale. Shake the flour mixture into this and gently fold the two together. When most of the flour is incorporated (it doesn't matter if there are still streaks of flour in the batter), give the butter mixture another good stir and carefully fold it into the batter too. It takes a little while for the butter to blend in, but it will eventually fold in to form a fairly sloppy batter.
- Pour the batter into the prepared tin, shake it gently to even it out, then pop it into the oven. Bake the cake for about 30 minutes, or until it is only just set and the top springs back when gently pressed in the middle.
- About 5 minutes before you think the cake will be ready, make the topping. To do this, melt the butter in a smallish frying pan over medium heat. Add the sugar and

cream and cook, stirring regularly, until the sugar dissolves. Once it has, stop stirring and bring the mixture to the boil. Let it bubble rapidly for 2½ minutes, then take it off the heat.

- All being equal, the cake should be cooked by now. Carefully lift it out of the oven and pour the hot caramel mixture over the top – it may well pool a bit at the sides, but that's fine. Scatter the almonds evenly over the caramel. Return the cake to the oven for 12–15 minutes (it may take a bit less than this if your tin is quite shallow), or until the topping is golden brown and bubbling. Remove and place on a wire rack.
- If the topping has pooled a bit at the sides, while the cake is still hot use a small blunt knife to gently press some of the almond mixture from around the sides onto the top, to fill any sparse areas.
- Let the cake cool in the tin for 15 minutes, then gently loosen it around the sides and remove from the tin. Leave the cake to cool, almond-side up. Serve barely warm or at room temperature, with cream and caramel sauce, if using.

A NOTE ON FLAKED ALMONDS

The trouble with writing a book like this is that you inevitably have to air your foibles, and this is certainly one of mine. I hate those really finely cut flaked almonds – they look pretty in the packet, but are as frustrating as all-get-out to use, as they are so fragile that they crumble and break when you handle them. I invariably find myself hunting through the various packets in the supermarket to find the thickest-cut ones I can, as they are easier to use and look so much better too. Nothing perfectionist about me!

Homemade Caramel Sauce

MAKES ABOUT 2 CUPS (500 ML)

My mum was always mad about caramel and anything that had caramel in it. As kids if we were 'in town' for the day, she would take us to a Cahill's Brass Rail restaurant for afternoon tea as a very special treat. That was where I first tasted their justly famous caramel sauce, which they sold in little brown and white cartons to take home. We would invariably buy some and then eke it out for months until our next visit to the city. I know Mum tried to replicate it at home, as I have done since, and this recipe is probably the closest I've got to the real McCoy. It's remarkably good and wonderful trickled over vanilla or coffee ice-cream. One thing before you start, though: you will need a sugar thermometer for this recipe. I know this is not your usual, everyday piece of kitchen paraphernalia, but they are relatively inexpensive – and a good investment if you have a sweet tooth!

1 cup (250 ml) cream
1 cup (220 g) brown sugar
⅓ cup (75 g) caster sugar
¼ cup (60 ml) pure maple syrup
¼ cup (60 ml) golden syrup
1 teaspoon vanilla extract

- Put all the ingredients into a smallish, heavy-based saucepan and clip a sugar thermometer onto the side. Sit the pan over high heat and stir the mixture just until the sugar dissolves, then stop stirring and bring it to the boil. Let it bubble rapidly until the thermometer registers 108°C (this should only take a few minutes). Keep an eye on it, though, as it can bubble over really quickly. Take off the heat and leave to cool for at least 20 minutes. You can use it warm, or store it in the fridge in a tightly sealed container for up to 2 weeks. It tends to separate a little when it's cold, but just give it a good stir and it comes back together.

NOVEMBER

7th November

Home again! Our trip went really well, and it was a real treat to be in France after an absence of too many years. I'm relieved to say that the cooking classes were successful. It was a hugely hectic week, but a lot of fun too.

It was such a special thing to be in the French countryside again – it was so beautiful, and blissfully quiet as most of the summer tourists had long departed. And Paris was divine!! What an exciting, exhilarating and utterly exhausting city it is. Oh, to have an apartment there and the time to absorb it all at leisure. We walked our legs off, stopping only for cups of coffee and numerous little fruit tartlets to keep us fuelled. The shops were exquisite: I had forgotten just how much style there is everywhere and the extraordinary detail in everything – clothes, shoes, furniture, buildings, not to mention the Parisians themselves. I could happily sit in a cafe all day just watching the passing parade.

That said, I have to admit that it's lovely to be home. It's hard to believe that three weeks have passed so quickly, and now here we are back again, with sweat prickling our backs and the thermometer (at 10 a.m.) already registering 32°C. It's far too hot for spring, and *so* far removed from the cool autumn days we were enjoying in Paris.

The first thing I noticed with quiet joy when I woke this morning was the sound of the birds singing their little hearts out. In the forests of the Dordogne, we had both been aware of a strange stillness and quietness. Although they were exceptionally lovely, with the trees decked in their red and gold autumn finery, the only sound we could hear when we walked through them was the papery rustle of leaves dropping from branches. Yet here, even in the wee small hours as I tossed and turned in a fitful sleep (what a pest jet-lag is), I could hear frogmouths and owls hooting, and the mournful calls of a koel. And when the dawn broke, a veritable chorus sprang up.

8th November

What's that saying about the best-laid plans of mice and men? Today I had planned to catch up with all the washing from our trip (a small mountain of winter woollies) and virtuously sit and sort out our accounts, but so far all I've done is wander around the garden to see how it has fared in our absence. I can see there is work to be done – the tomatoes I so carefully staked are now hanging at a crazy angle, and weeds have sprung up in all the places we didn't manage to mulch. However, I am pleased to say that despite this everything looks remarkably robust, if somewhat overgrown, and I'm itching to get my secateurs out and start tidying up.

Dinner tonight will be a real mish-mash as I'm rifling through the freezer and pantry to see what I can put together from what we have. So far I've unearthed a packet of puff pastry, some brown onions and olives, and I know there are some anchovies in the fridge, so I think a pissaladière is on the menu. It somehow seems fitting after our time in France.

Pissaladière

SERVES 4

I readily admit that I'm inordinately fond of salty foods. In my family I'm known as the queen of the anchovy-eaters, for ever since I was little I've been able to open a can of anchovies and happily eat them all, one after another. So, as you can imagine, any recipe even remotely related to anchovies has my undivided attention and potential devotion. It will come as no surprise then that this pissaladière, with its luscious, buttery puff pastry, generous layer of sweet, slow-cooked onions and salty anchovies and olives, is right up my alley! If you're one of those people who flinches at the very mention of the word 'anchovy', please bear with me, for this tart is easily adapted to suit non-anchovy-eaters. All you need do is to leave off the anchovies and dot the top with soft goat's cheese instead. Easy-peasy.

If you're wondering what to have with it, try a platter of roast tomatoes and whatever greens happen to be on hand – for us, it's often spinach or chard in winter and a big green salad (preferably with a few slightly bitter greens to balance the tart's richness) in summer.

1 × 375 g packet ready-rolled puff pastry, thawed
60–80 g tapenade, purchased or homemade (see page 388)
2–3 teaspoons thyme leaves
freshly ground black pepper
18–20 anchovy fillets
18–20 small black niçoise or ligurian olives
1 egg yolk, beaten with 2 teaspoons water
tiny thyme sprigs, to garnish

ONION TOPPING

¼ cup (60 ml) extra virgin olive oil
about 1 kg brown onions, halved and thinly sliced
1½ tablespoons sun-dried tomato pesto
2 teaspoons white sugar
1–2 tablespoons wine vinegar
sea salt flakes and freshly ground black pepper

- To make the onion topping, heat the olive oil in a large frying pan over low heat. Add the onion, tomato pesto, sugar, 1 tablespoon of the vinegar and a little salt and pepper. Cook the mixture, stirring it every now and again, for about an hour until the onion is meltingly tender and becoming caramelised. Taste it and adjust the seasoning to make a nice balance – you may need to add a little more vinegar. Set it aside to cool. (This onion mixture can be made ahead and refrigerated overnight.)
- Preheat your oven to 200°C. Line a baking tray with baking paper.
- For the tart base, unroll the pastry onto a floured bench. If necessary, roll it out gently so you can cut out a rectangle 29 cm × 26 cm. Sit the pastry rectangle on the prepared tray. With a ruler as a guide, use the point of a sharp knife to score a 1.5 cm border all the way around the edge of the pastry. Chill the pastry in the fridge for 10 minutes.
- Now spread the tapenade evenly over the pastry, being careful to keep it within the scored border. Dollop the cooled onion mixture over the tapenade and use a fork to spread it out evenly, again keeping it within the border. Scatter thyme leaves over the top and grind on some black pepper. Criss-cross the anchovies over the onions, and sit an olive in each of the diamonds created by the anchovies.
- Brush the border of the pastry lightly with the egg wash, being careful not to let any drip down the sides. (If you are wondering why, it's because these drips can glue the layers of pastry together, and to the baking tray, so they don't puff up and rise as the tart cooks.) ›

- Put the pissaladière in the oven and bake it for 15 minutes, then reduce the temperature to 180°C and cook it for a further 5–10 minutes, or until it's cooked through and the pastry is a rich golden brown.
- Carefully slide the pissaladière off the baking tray onto a large platter or board. Scatter it with tiny thyme sprigs. Serve warm or at room temperature.

THE VERY BEST PASTRY . . .

I rarely mention brands but in this case I make an exception, as I tried the oft-written-about Carême hand-made butter puff pastry for this and it was absolutely fantastic – crisp and buttery. It's well worth tracking some down: look for it in the freezer section at specialist food shops.

10th November

When we were growing up, stewed rhubarb (I suspect we would call it poached now – it sounds a lot more appetising!) was standard fare for us. For however long rhubarb was in season my mum would cook a batch of it weekly and we would eat it for dessert drizzled with cream from the top of the milk. We always had something sweet to finish our dinner, but somehow we never seemed to put on weight. I guess it helped that we were children of the pre-computer era and spent as much time as possible tearing about outdoors.

The desserts Mum made were often as simple as an apple crumble or bowl of just-picked mulberries from our neighbour's tree with a dusting of icing sugar. Funnily enough, the thing I loved most about this was the beautiful cut-crystal and silver shaker that the icing sugar was kept in. The crystal would refract the light and send rainbows spinning around the room, and to me it was quite magical – still is, actually. But I digress, for I really wanted to write about rhubarb, as I bought some lovely stalks today and am about to bake a cake with them.

I love the wonderful sharp edge rhubarb adds to desserts so they never seem too sweet, however it doesn't pay to be too meagre with the sugar when you cook it, as tart rhubarb is a real disappointment. One of my treats – and a simple way to tell how sweet your rhubarb is – is to pick out a raw stalk, sprinkle a little caster sugar into a saucer, then take both outside and sit on the back step quietly munching my way through it, dipping the end of the stalk in sugar between each bite. It's surprisingly delicious, and it always reminds me of my childhood home, where we would sit out on our back terrace in the sunshine doing the self-same thing. (That terrace got a real work-out as it was set at the top of a rockery and had a small grassy patch with a table and chairs. As kids we would often be given slices of watermelon and told to go outside to eat it. We would sit at the table, the sticky watermelon juice trickling down our arms, taking turns to see who could spit the seeds furthest. There would be seeds everywhere, and I remember being thrilled one day when I discovered that some of them had germinated and tiny little watermelon vines were springing up under the table – to this day, I'm not convinced that Mum and Dad were quite so impressed!)

Rhubarb, Sour Cream & Cinnamon Sugar Cake

SERVES 10

- **2⅓ cups (350 g) self-raising flour**
- **½ teaspoon salt**
- **2 teaspoons ground cinnamon**
- **60 g unsalted butter, at room temperature**
- **1½ cups (330 g) firmly packed brown sugar**
- **1 egg**
- **3 teaspoons vanilla extract**
- **1 cup (240 g) sour cream**
- **4 cups (440 g) rhubarb chopped into 1 cm chunks (you may need 2 bunches for this amount)**
- **¼ teaspoon grated nutmeg**
- **½ cup (110 g) caster sugar**
- **⅓ cup (25 g) flaked almonds**
- **cream or vanilla bean ice-cream, to serve**

BY THE WAY . . .

If by any chance you have leftover cake (wishful thinking here, but I can always dream!), it tastes even better the next day, although the top loses a bit of its crunch. Individual slices freeze well too.

This is a lovely cake – simple and homely and all the more enjoyable for being so. Chunks of tangy rhubarb are studded through the gently spiced cake, with the sugar and almond topping providing just the right amount of crunch. It really is a cross between a pudding and a cake, and as such it makes a great dessert at this time of year when the weather can be so fickle, for you can serve it warm and scoop it straight out of the dish, or let it cool, turn it out and slice it like a cake.

- Preheat your oven to 180°C. Butter a 26 cm × 6 cm round ovenproof dish (I use a glass Pyrex one) – and, if you want to turn out the cake to serve it, line the base with buttered baking paper.
- Tip the flour, salt and 1½ teaspoons of the cinnamon into a bowl. Use a balloon whisk to mix them together until they are well combined, then set the bowl aside.
- Put the butter and brown sugar into a large bowl and beat them with a hand-held electric beater on medium speed for 2 minutes until the mixture looks like wet sand – it won't be creamy at this stage due to the proportion of sugar to butter. Add the egg and vanilla then beat the mixture again for a minute or so, stopping and scraping down the sides of the bowl once or twice, until the egg is thoroughly incorporated and the mixture looks creamy. Now mix in the sour cream – don't worry if the batter looks a bit curdled, it will come back together once you add the dry ingredients. Now add the flour mixture and mix it in on low speed until it is just combined. Finally, stir in the rhubarb: do this with a spatula as the batter becomes very stiff and you will need to use a bit of the proverbial elbow grease to mix everything together.
- Scrape the batter into the prepared dish and smooth it down as best you can. Mix the nutmeg and remaining cinnamon into the caster sugar. Sprinkle half this mixture evenly over the top of the batter, scatter the flaked almonds over this, then finish off with the remaining sugar mixture. Shake the pan gently to level out the almond mixture.
- Bake the cake for about 1 hour 10 minutes or until a fine skewer inserted in the middle comes out clean (or with just a few moist crumbs sticking to it). Remove the cake from the oven to a wire rack and leave it to cool in the dish until it is barely warm. At this stage you can serve it straight from the dish as a pudding – or, to turn it out, sit a flat plate on top then invert the cake onto this. Remove the baking paper, then invert the cake again onto a serving plate so the sugared top is uppermost. (You will find as you invert the cake that some of the sugary almond mixture will drop off, so watch that it doesn't go everywhere.)

11th November

Since we arrived home we've been hit by a series of violent thunderstorms that more than once have threatened to lift the roof off the house. Their arrival is heralded by low rumbles that send us diving under the office desk to unplug the computers – it's not uncommon for lightning to hit close by and, having fried the motherboard of our main computer once, we really don't want a repeat performance.

As our house sits up quite high we can watch the thunderheads as they swing out over the mountain and roll their way along the valley. Of late there have been roiling banks of bruised clouds too, with that eerie green tinge that promises hail.

And the power and noise of them! The thunder is so loud and the lightning so ferocious that last night I really did think the sky would split in two. Poor Gus the labrador, who was visiting us at the time, dived for cover under the nearest bed and lay quivering, head facing the wall, until the last peal receded into the distance.

Speaking of power, inevitably that goes off too, however I've become quite adept at cooking by candlelight. Our gas stovetop is a blessing and that, along with an old transistor radio and stock of batteries, means we pass the time happily, and actually rather enjoy 'camping out' at home.

It rained cats and dogs after the storm passed and we're nearly ankle-deep in water today. I had to wear gumboots to hang out the washing as the water has transformed the compacted earth by the clothes line into a miniature lake, which, by the sounds of things, the frogs are loving!

A torrent of water also swept down the side of the house and has washed away some of my new plantings. I found a few rather dejected-looking coriander plants hanging onto the soil for grim death and, even more surprisingly, the tomatoes still clinging tenaciously to their patch of earth. Although they were somewhat battered about and have a few broken stems, I've managed to salvage enough to roast for dinner tonight. I'm trying to use up any odds and ends we have, as it's market day tomorrow and I like to start afresh.

Baked Ricotta & Goat's Cheese Rolls with Agrodolce Tomatoes

SERVES 4

I can happily make a meal of this dish with just some good sourdough bread to sop up the lovely oily juices from the tomatoes and onions. It's a lovely vegetarian dish – substantial enough for dinner and wonderfully flavourful.

- Preheat your oven to 180°C.
- For the ricotta rolls, put the cheeses, egg, garlic and sea salt into a food processor and whiz them until they are thoroughly mixed, stopping and scraping down the sides occasionally.
- Lay a large sheet of foil on your bench and sit a similar-sized sheet of baking paper on top. Spoon half the ricotta mixture into a compact, rough log shape about 4 cm in from the edge of the baking paper nearest you. With damp fingers, shape it as best you can into a log about 5 cm in diameter. Using the baking paper to help, roll the mixture up in the paper. Next roll it in the foil, then twist the ends tightly in opposite directions so you end up with something that looks like a long bonbon. Sit it on a baking sheet, then repeat with the remaining ricotta mixture.
- Bake the logs for 25–30 minutes, or until they feel firm when gently pressed. When they're ready, remove them from the oven and reduce the temperature to 155°C. Leave the logs to cool, still wrapped, while you cook the tomatoes and onions.
- To make the agrodolce tomatoes, sit the tomatoes in a single layer in a shallow baking dish that will just hold them comfortably. Drizzle with the oil, and roll the tomatoes so they're well coated, then sprinkle with the remaining ingredients.
- Put the onions into a small roasting tin and lightly coat them with olive oil too.
- Pop both dishes in the oven. Cook the tomatoes for about 30 minutes, carefully turning them every so often, until they're tender when you prod them gently. Remove from the oven and leave to cool in the dish. Increase the oven temperature to 200°C, give the onions a shake, and continue to cook until they're tender and a lovely deep brown – another 15 minutes or so.
- Before serving, it's a good idea to taste the juices from the tomatoes and adjust the flavour if necessary with a bit more salt, sugar or vinegar so you end up with a good sharp–sweet (agrodolce) balance. Once that's done, spoon some tomatoes and their juices into the middle of each plate. Unwrap the ricotta rolls and slice them on the diagonal into thickish medallions and sit these on the tomatoes. Spoon over a few onions and scatter the thyme sprigs on top.

500 g firm ricotta
60 g firm mild goat's cheese, grated
50 g goat's cheese marinated in olive oil
1 × 70 g egg
½ small clove garlic, finely chopped
sea salt flakes, to taste
16 pickling or very small brown onions (or golden shallots), peeled
extra virgin olive oil, for cooking
small thyme or lemon thyme sprigs, to garnish

AGRODOLCE TOMATOES

700 g just-ripe, small roma tomatoes (vine-ripened with stalks, if possible)
¼ cup (60 ml) extra virgin olive oil
2–3 teaspoons balsamic vinegar, or more to taste
1 scant tablespoon caster sugar
3 teaspoons thyme leaves
1 teaspoon sea salt flakes, or more to taste

12th November

I heard on the radio that it has been the wettest spring for years, and I can well believe it, as we all literally had to splash our way around the farmers' market this morning. But it was worth it, for I've come back with fat bundles of beetroot, the leaves so fresh and green that we shall eat them as a vegetable; loops of buttercup-yellow crookneck squash that have become an absolute favourite of ours; and a bagful of small golden tomatoes that are sweet as sweet. I know exactly what I'm going to do with the tomatoes, as I have some yellow capsicums in the fridge and the two should make a rather special salad.

Golden Tomato, Yellow Capsicum & Fresh Mozzarella Salad

SERVES 6–8

This simple salad, with its clear flavours and brilliant colours, just says spring to me. I do a number of variations on it – sometimes adding up to a dozen anchovies and a handful of niçoise olives; or using red capsicums and red tomatoes instead.

- 5–6 medium-sized yellow capsicums (peppers)
- ⅓ cup (65 g) capers
- 1 clove garlic (or more to taste), very finely sliced
- extra virgin olive oil, to taste
- balsamic or good wine vinegar, to taste
- sea salt flakes, to taste
- 5 medium-sized golden tomatoes, cored and each sliced into 6 wedges
- handful of basil leaves, torn into small pieces
- 9 bocconcini (or use 4–5 balls buffalo mozzarella), torn into bite-sized pieces
- small basil leaves, to garnish

- Line a baking sheet with foil. Slice the capsicums along their natural contour lines into large, flattish pieces. Remove any pieces of core, along with the seeds and white ribs. Sit as many pieces as you can fit on the prepared sheet, skin-side up, then run them under a hot grill until the skins blister and blacken. Transfer them to a plate and cover them with a clean tea towel or plastic film – this helps to loosen the skins. Grill any remaining pieces of capsicum the same way.
- It's best to peel the capsicum pieces while they are still quite hot, as the blackened skin tends to stain the capsicum flesh brown if it is in contact for too long (more often than not, I wear prep gloves for this, to provide some protection from the residual heat). Slice the peeled capsicums into nice wide strips – I usually make mine about 2 cm wide, as the bigger they are, the more luscious they seem to look and taste (don't ask me why!).
- Put the capsicum strips in a serving bowl that will offset the lovely gold, deep green and creamy white tones of the salad, and sprinkle the capers and garlic slivers over the top. Add rather a lot of olive oil and a good splash of vinegar then gently mix everything together. Cover and set aside for an hour or two. Half an hour before you want to eat the salad, gently mix in the salt, tomato and basil. Cover it again.
- Just before serving, add the bocconcini and mix everything gently one last time. Taste the juices that have accumulated in the bowl and add more oil, vinegar or salt to suit your taste (the capsicum strips should be lush with oil). Wipe the sides of the bowl free of any splotches and scatter a few small basil leaves on top.

13th November

Oh no, I can feel my time running out writing this book and yet there is still so much I want to share with you. Goodness knows how I shall fit it all in by the end of the month!

After a disgustingly humid day yesterday, this morning dawned with a drier, if not cooler, wind blowing and it was such a joy to walk early and not feel clammy within minutes. I wish you could have been with me – the melaleucas have flowered into creamy pink powder-puffs and their gentle honey scent was attracting every bee within cooee. The trees were vibrating with their Zen-like hum (or should that be 'om') as they worked their way along the blossoms. And there was a mist hanging softly in the fields, the shadowy forms of the cows nudging their way through it and in the distance I could hear a chorus of butcher birds and magpies competing with each other. Best of all, the toasty aroma of molasses grass filled the air – it's the fragrance of home for me, and I absolutely adore it.

Mushrooms were popping up everywhere too, and I was sorely tempted to pick some that were growing on the verge of the road. However, I decided it's probably wiser to buy them at the market than risk a culinary version of Russian roulette!

14th November

Our small prostrate gardenias have burst into flower – one day they were covered in buds and the next they erupted in a starburst of creamy blossoms. Although not as beautiful as their larger sisters, they have the most exquisite perfume, just like the sweetest, ripest apricots ever. I keep thinking that I must try and capture it by infusing some apricots with the flowers . . .

But it's cherries that are on my mind at the moment – or, I should say more accurately, all over my fingers, which are stained purple from pitting them. And, for every one that goes in the bowl, one goes in my mouth too! As you have probably realised, the cherries are not a local crop, but we're rather spoilt as the farmers' market committee invites a guest grower to attend the markets every few months, and the current guest is a cherry orchardist from Young. His cherries are the biggest, fattest ones I have seen for a long time, with the most satisfying crunch when you bite into them. We invariably arrive home with about half the amount we actually bought, and the bottom of the bag littered with cherry pits – you would think I would have learnt to buy double by now, wouldn't you? Thank goodness, I have managed to save enough to decorate some little tartlets for dessert tonight.

Almond-Sugar Filo Tartlets with Cherries & Lemon Cream

SERVES 4

These pretty little tarts are so easy to make as the tartlet shells are formed from squares of filo pastry sandwiched together with an almond and sugar mixture which bakes to form a lovely crisp crust to hold the lemon filling. The cherries look particularly gorgeous in them, but I've used all sorts of seasonal fruit – slivers of mango (nice), sliced peaches and nectarines (especially nice) and raspberries with tiny clusters of redcurrants (best of all!).

30 g flaked almonds
¼ cup (55 g) caster sugar
4 sheets filo pastry
40–50 g unsalted butter, melted and cooled
500 g medium-sized cherries
pure icing sugar, for dusting

LEMON CREAM

200 g mascarpone
1 cup (250 ml) thickened cream
¼ cup (40 g) icing sugar, sifted (or more to taste)
very, very finely grated zest of 1 large lemon
¼ teaspoon vanilla extract

- Very lightly butter four 11 cm (or thereabouts) non-stick tartlet tins and sit them on a baking tray.
- Put the almonds and caster sugar into a food processor and whiz together until the almonds are fairly finely ground. Set aside.
- Stack the sheets of filo on top of each other. Cut the pile into quarters then trim the stacked sheets into roughly 12 cm squares, discarding the off-cuts. Remove one square and cover the remaining squares with a barely damp tea towel to stop them drying out. Brush the filo square with melted butter then gently press it, buttered-side down, into one of the tart tins. Brush it again very lightly with butter and sprinkle 2 teaspoons of the almond mixture on top. Gently shake the tart tin, or use a spoon to spread the mixture evenly over the base and, if possible, a little way up the sides of the pastry too. Repeat this process with two more ›

squares of filo, sitting each one at a slight angle to the one below so you end up with a multi-pointed star effect around the edge. Finally, sit a fourth square on top, buttered-side down; brush it with butter but don't add the almond mixture. Repeat with the remaining tart tins, filo and almond mixture to make three more cases. Once they are all done, pop the tray in the fridge for about 30 minutes to firm up the butter in the shells.

- Preheat your oven to 180°C.
- Put the tray with the tart shells into the oven and bake them for 10–12 minutes or until they're crisp and golden. My oven cooks a bit unevenly so I usually rotate the tray halfway through the cooking time to help the shells cook evenly. When they're done, remove the tray from the oven and leave the tartlets to cool in their tins on a rack. (If you have room for them in your freezer, you can make these bases a few weeks ahead of time and freeze them – just make sure you store them in a container as the edges are very fragile.)
- An hour or two before you want to serve the tartlets, pit most of the cherries, reserving a few of the nicest ones with bright green stalks for garnishing. Set aside at room temperature.
- To make the lemon cream, put all the ingredients into a cool bowl and whisk them fairly gently with a balloon whisk for a minute or so until the mixture is softly thick, but not at all grainy. It's best not to use an electric beater as the mixture can go from being perfect to over-whipped in a trice. Cover the lemon cream and keep it cool.
- To serve the tartlets, sit a pastry shell on each plate and spoon in a quarter of the lemon cream, mounding it up slightly in the middle. Sit the cherries on top – you will notice when you pit them that one side looks better than the other so make this the side that is face-up. Dust the cherries and the edges of the tart shell with icing sugar. Sit a cherry with a stalk on top and scatter a few on the plate.

15th November

The compost queen is back in town! Oh dear, I do wonder about myself at times. One of the first things I did when we got back was check on the compost, and much to my joy it was looking and smelling wonderful. I can't wait to use it, as I'm sure whatever grows in it will flourish. And the first thing to be planted in it is a red papaya – they usually thrive here and I am hoping against hope that it will survive our treacherous clay soil.

16th November

It has been too hot to cook inside these past few days so the barbecue has been getting quite a work-out. Surprisingly, I didn't barbecue all that much until we moved here, yet now it's a constant source of pleasure. As much as anything I love cooking this way because it makes me feel as if I'm on holiday or that it's the weekend. I guess this feeling must go back to family picnics during my childhood. Once we were ensconced at the park or beach we kids would be sent off to collect firewood. My dad would then light a fire and we would wait impatiently until the embers were grey and he announced it was ready to use. More often than not we would have barbecued lamb chops – my favourite of all – and I remember snaffling them hot off the grill and burning my tongue on their salty goodness.

I still love a good plain barbecued lamb chop, however I've also become a fan of spice rubs and pastes and tend to use those a lot too. There is just something about the combination of spices and smoke that adds an exotic quality to whatever's being cooked: meat, fish, vegetables or, in the case of the following recipes, lamb and quail.

Butterflied Leg of Lamb with Chermoula

SERVES 6

1 × 2–2.5 kg leg of lamb, boned and butterflied (ask your butcher to do this)
mint sprigs and lime wedges, to garnish
cucumber, current and yoghurt relish (see page 406), to serve, optional

CHERMOULA

2 teaspoons ground cumin
2 teaspoons sweet Hungarian paprika
½ teaspoon smoked paprika, optional
2 teaspoons freshly ground black pepper
1½ teaspoons ground coriander
¼ teaspoon cayenne pepper
½ teaspoon ground turmeric
5 large cloves garlic, finely chopped
¼ cup (60 ml) extra virgin olive oil
¼ cup (60 ml) lemon juice
½ cup (25 g) finely chopped coriander

I don't know what it is about lamb and barbecues, but the two just seem made for each other, and never more so than in this easy dish where the chermoula forms an aromatic crust around the rosy-pink slices of lamb. I always try to leave the lamb to marinate for a day or two before cooking it, so it becomes imbued with the flavour of the spices. It's lovely served with cucumber, currant and yoghurt relish, and quite often while the lamb is resting I brush slices of eggplant, red capsicum and fennel with olive oil and barbecue them to go with it – they look striking tumbled onto a platter and the flavours go particularly well with the spicy meat.

I should warn you that this does make a bit of a mess on the barbecue as little fragments of the spicy coating can stick to the bars; however, for me it's a small price to pay for such a treat.

- To make the chermoula, put all the ingredients into a bowl and whisk them together until they're well combined.
- The next thing you need to do is a little messy, so you might want to wear prep gloves. Sit the lamb, skin-side down, on a chopping board and open it out. Spoon just over half the marinade onto the meat and work it in with your hands. Now turn the lamb over and rub the remaining marinade into this side. (You will immediately see why it's a good idea to wear gloves for this, as the turmeric and paprika tend to stain everything an amazing ochre colour.)
- Fold the lamb in on itself to form a bundle so it's easier to handle, then slip it into a large snap-lock bag. Squeeze as much air as possible from the bag then seal it. Now sit the bag in a container (preferably one with a tight-fitting lid or else your fridge will reek of garlic) and refrigerate it for 1–2 days. Occasionally I'll leave it an extra day, to allow the flavour of the chermoula to permeate the meat more thoroughly. Before cooking the lamb, return it to cool room temperature.
- Preheat your barbecue to high. When it's hot, sear the lamb for about 4 minutes each side, with the lid of the barbecue closed – it will look quite crusty and dark from the spicy coating. (If you don't have a cover for your barbecue you can improvise by covering the lamb with a large upended stainless steel bowl.) Now reduce the heat to medium, and cook the lamb, still covered, for 12–15 minutes, then turn it over and cook it for a further 12–15 minutes.

- When the lamb is done it will look charred on the outside, but don't worry – it will be moist and rosy pink in the thickest parts of the meat, while the thinner parts will be slightly more well done. Transfer the lamb to a small baking tray or platter, cover it tightly with foil and leave it to rest in a warm place for at least 15 minutes before carving. This resting time is important as it allows the juices to flow back into the centre of the meat so it's moist when you slice it.
- To carve the meat, I usually cut it along its natural contours into largish pieces then slice these across the grain. Because of the different thicknesses of the meat you will have slices of pink meat, not-so pink bits and a few cooked-through slices too – this comes in rather handy, as invariably there seems to be takers for all three. To serve the lamb, sit it on a platter and garnish it with mint sprigs and lime wedges. Serve it with a bowlful of cucumber, currant and yoghurt relish, if you like.

RARE OR WELL DONE?

I know that working out when lamb or beef is cooked can be a vexing business: the only way I can really tell is to give the thickest part a good prod – it should still have some give in it, but be a little resistant. If it feels soft, the meat will still be very rare; if it feels bouncy, it will be well done. I know it's a bit hit and miss when you first do this, but the more you practise, the better you'll be able to tell when meat is done to your liking.

Spicy Barbecued Quails with Cucumber & Yoghurt

SERVES 2–4 (DEPENDING ON HOW HUNGRY YOU ARE)

Quails are not something I cook very often, however I was given some recently which I barbecued and I must say they were perfectly delicious. We sat outside in the cool of the evening eating them with our fingers – the only way to go really as they're far too fiddly to tackle with a knife and fork. I had floated frangipani blossoms in our finger bowls and had delicate paper lanterns glowing softly in the tree above. What with the spicy smoke from the barbecue wafting on the breeze and some haunting Arabic oud music playing gently in the background, it was all quite dreamy.

4 good-sized quails, trimmed of neck and wing tips
1 cup (280 g) plain yoghurt
1 large clove garlic, finely chopped
2 tablespoons finely shredded mint, or more to taste
sea salt flakes, to taste
550 g Lebanese or other small cucumbers
tiny mint leaves and lime cheeks, to garnish

MARINADE

6 large cloves garlic, finely chopped
1½ tablespoons freshly ground cumin seeds
2½ teaspoons freshly ground coriander seeds
¾ teaspoon sweet Hungarian paprika
½ teaspoon smoked paprika
big pinch of dried chilli flakes
sea salt flakes, to taste
½ cup (125 ml) extra virgin olive oil

- To make the marinade, put all the ingredients into a large bowl and whisk together.
- Next the quails need to be butterflied. To do this, use kitchen shears to cut along the backbone of each one from top to tail. Open out the quails as best you can then sit them, skin-side up, on your chopping board. With the palm of your hand, press down firmly on each one to flatten it out.
- Pat the quails dry, then add them to the bowl of marinade and turn them about until they're well coated. Line an airtight container with a clean plastic bag then scrape the quail and their marinade into it. Squeeze out as much air from the bag as possible and seal it. Cover tightly with a lid and refrigerate for at least 4 hours (or, better still, overnight), squishing the quails about in the marinade occasionally.
- When you're ready to cook the quails, remove them from the marinade. Make a small slit in the web of skin between the body and the drumstick on each side of the quails just near the parson's nose. Push the tips of the drumsticks through the slits to secure them so they don't spread out while the quails cook.
- Heat your barbecue to medium–high (you could also cook the quails in a non-stick frying pan or chargrill pan, if preferred). Put the quails on the barbecue and cook them for 4 minutes each side. (If they don't want to stay flat, sit a large heavy frying pan or baking tray on top of them.) When they're ready, transfer them from the barbecue to a warm plate and leave them to settle for 5 minutes.
- While the quails are cooking, mix together the yoghurt, garlic, mint and salt in a medium-sized bowl. Halve the cucumbers lengthways and use a teaspoon to scrape out the seeds. Slice each half on the diagonal into fine crescents and gently fold them into the yoghurt mixture.
- To serve the quails, sit one or two on each plate and scoop some of the cucumber mixture on the side. Sprinkle some tiny mint leaves over the cucumber and serve the quails with lime cheeks and any leftover cucumber mixture.

19th November

I had to go to Ballina early today and, whenever I'm there, I can't leave without popping into my favourite fish shop on the coast: Northern Rivers Seafood. It doesn't look much from the outside, but inside it's like a Neptune's treasure chest of sparkling seafood – everything looks so fresh that it seems to have leapt straight out of the ocean into the tubs of ice.

It may sound a bit odd, but the display is such a feast for the eyes that I always have a great urge to pick up a brush and paint. The blue swimmer crabs are so carefully arranged on their icy bed, that from a distance they look like some sort of exquisite dot painting; plump scallops glisten in their fluted shells; and a tangle of local squid are piled next to the biggest, fattest Brunswick River prawns I've seen for ages. At every turn there is a still-life painting in the making. However, I am well aware that my cooking skills are somewhat better than my artistic ones, so I've contented myself with buying some of those glorious prawns (which we shall have for lunch with a dab of dill mayonnaise) and a clutch of beautifully fresh flathead fillets.

Off on a tangent for a moment, those flathead fillets bring back such memories for me. Growing up by Pittwater, much of my childhood was spent mucking about in, on or around the water. The tidal flats were just below where we lived and I well remember playing and fishing there when we were young. One of the first fish I caught was a flathead, and it was a beauty. I absolutely fluked it, as I was just trailing my hook along the bottom in very shallow water, and the next second I felt this tremendous pull on the line. Inadvertently, I'd somehow managed to hook a really big fella. I don't think I actually brought it in – it was far too powerful for me, and I suspect my brother took over. However, I do remember being ever so chuffed and feeling great pride in having caught dinner. It was quickly dispatched (I do come from a family of keen anglers!), and the snowy fillets turned up that evening simply cooked in butter with a big squeeze of lemon juice. The fillets I bought today are going to get a slightly more exotic treatment as I shall coat them in a fiery spice rub, which will give them a terrific flavour (see page 453). They're wonderful served on olive-oil mashed potatoes with a few leaves of rocket on the side.

I realise that I've mentioned olive-oil mashed potatoes numerous times throughout this book but have not actually given you a recipe for them, so it's high time I did. You can pretty much cook a potato any way and I will happily eat it – baked, boiled, roasted, fried, made into a salad (speaking of which, why is it so hard to get a decent potato salad these days?) – but for me the pinnacle of potato cooking is mashed potato. It's my comfort food when the world is just too big, or when I'm feeling a bit below par; the perfect partner to just about anything with sauce; and I'm sure what nature had in mind for potatoes from Day One. Like breakfast toast, it's also a very personal thing: it can be smooth, lumpy, mashed with the skins on, made with cream, milk, butter, have chives mixed through (not for this purist!) or be beaten into a rich golden mash by the addition of a liberal dose of good olive oil.

Olive-Oil Mashed Potatoes

SERVES 6 OR SO

I use this recipe all through the year as it goes with so many dishes – winter casseroles, grilled lamb chops, sausages and pot roasts, to name a few. But what I really like about it most is the way it goes so beautifully with spicy dishes like the flathead fillets overleaf. I think it's the intriguing fruity back-note from the olive oil that works the magic and blends so well with chilli and spices. I have that wonderful British chef Simon Hopkinson to thank for this particular version – I've altered it slightly, but it's well and truly based on his original. Just be aware that the mash is rather rich, so a little goes a long way.

900 g good floury potatoes, peeled and cut into similar-sized chunks
150 ml milk
1 large clove garlic, lightly crushed
1 rosemary sprig
1 cup (250 ml) extra virgin olive oil
sea salt flakes and freshly ground black or white pepper

- Bring a large saucepan of water to the boil. Salt it, then add the potatoes and boil them until they're tender when prodded with a fine skewer.
- While the potatoes are cooking, put the milk, garlic and rosemary into a small saucepan. Warm them gently over low heat until the milk is hot but not boiling (don't let it scald, as it alters the taste). Turn off the heat, then cover the pan and leave the milk to infuse.
- When the potatoes are ready, drain them, then briefly return the pan to the heat to dry them out. Now you need to mash them, and this is where your preferences may come in. I usually crush mine in a potato ricer – it looks rather like a giant garlic press, and operates in much the same way, as you press the potatoes through fine holes in the base. This method makes for very smooth mash; however, you can use a regular masher if you like your mash to have a bit more texture. Put the mashed potatoes into a bowl and cover to keep them warm.
- Strain the infused milk through a fine sieve into a jug. Rinse out the saucepan in cold water, then pour the milk back in, along with the olive oil. Put the pan over gentle heat and warm it up until the mixture is very hot but not boiling. Now pour it into the mashed potato in a steady stream, whisking all the while as you do – it takes a bit of elbow grease, but it's not for long and you should end up with a fine, glossy purée. Now add salt and pepper to taste, scoop the mash onto warm plates or into a serving bowl and serve it straight away.

ON HOLD . . .

It is possible to keep these mashed potatoes warm for a while. Scoop the mash into a heatproof bowl, cover the bowl tightly with foil, then sit it over a saucepan of barely simmering water. You can leave it for up to an hour like this, stirring it from time to time.

Spice-Coated Flathead

SERVES 4

Flathead is such a lovely eating fish – sweet, white, moist and not at all 'fishy' – but many other fish would be fine here too, such as snapper, bream or cobia. Just don't use anything too delicate, as the peppery heat of the rub will overwhelm it.

- Put all the ingredients for the spice rub into a bowl and thoroughly mix them together. Spread the rub out in a shallow dish that's large enough to comfortably dunk the fillets and set it aside.
- Pat the fillets dry. If they're really large, cut them in half so they're easier to handle. Press one fillet at a time firmly into the spice rub and turn it so it's well coated in the mixture – use your fingers to pat it on too. Give the fillet a gentle shake to dislodge any excess rub, then pop it onto a sheet of greaseproof paper (be careful not to overlap the fillets or the coating may become a bit soggy where they do). Repeat this with the remaining fillets.
- Pour enough olive oil into a large frying pan to come about 4 mm up the sides. Warm the oil over medium heat. Once it's hot add as many fillets as will fit comfortably in the pan without crowding it. Cook them for 1–2 minutes each side, depending on their thickness, then transfer them to a plate lined with greaseproof paper. Cook the rest of the fillets in the same way.
- When they're all done, either serve the fillets on individual plates or on a platter with a good pile of lemon or lime cheeks to squeeze over the top. Garnish with a few herb sprigs, if liked.

about 800 g flathead fillets, skin off
olive oil, for pan-frying
lemon or lime cheeks, to serve
herb sprigs, to garnish, optional

SPICE RUB

2 teaspoons finely grated lime or lemon zest
1 tablespoon freshly ground cumin seeds
1 tablespoon freshly ground coriander seeds
1 tablespoon finely chopped ginger
2 teaspoons mild chilli powder
1–1½ teaspoons freshly ground black pepper (more if you like things fiery)
1 teaspoon ground turmeric
1 teaspoon ground cinnamon
1 teaspoon sea salt flakes
1 teaspoon sugar
1 teaspoon curry powder

COOKING FISH FILLETS

It's nigh on impossible to give exact timing for cooking fish fillets because every piece is just a little thicker or thinner than the next. The most important thing though is not to overcook the fish – because it has little fat, there's nothing to protect it from drying out. To check if it's ready, carefully insert the tip of a fine knife into one of the fillets, use it to separate the flesh a little and take a look – it should be moist, barely flaking and only just cooked through, as it will continue to cook from the residual heat once it's out of the pan.

CURRY POWDER

I have a bit of a 'thing' for curried egg sandwiches so I always keep a tub of curry powder in the pantry as they just don't taste at all right made with curry paste. I've tried a number of brands but can't go past good old Clive of India – it is just so much nicer than most. I only mention this because I've been really disappointed by the taste of some and it would be a shame to spoil the flavour of the rub by using one that's a bit dodgy.

24th November

On my morning ramble, I pass beneath a massive old Coolamon tree. I didn't even realise that these beautiful rainforest trees flowered until a year or two ago, when a blush of flowers seemed to appear from nowhere. I have since surmised that they must need particular weather conditions to flower, including lots of rain – so it looks as though we are in for a bumper year!

It's funny what you *don't* notice, isn't it? I've obviously been deep in thought about goodness knows what these past few days, totally oblivious to what's happening overhead. But today I finally looked up, to see the Coolamon's enormous woody branches swathed in a mass of watermelon-pink blossoms like an elaborate carpet. And it would appear that I'm not the only one to have discovered them, for as I watched a screeching flock of rainbow lorikeets let out a delighted whoop before dropping down onto the branches to feed on the nectar. By the time I had picked up the newspapers and was walking back home, the ground was carpeted with flowers that had been dislodged during their feeding frenzy.

Hooray, I have grown my first bunch of celery! It's not very large, but it is wonderfully crunchy and sweet, and I feel ever so chuffed with it. A friend gave me an antique, etched-glass celery holder some years ago, and we used it last night – the delicate green tops of the celery stalks peeping over the rim looked very beautiful. I served this first flush of my celery crop with a wedge of local blue cheese and oat biscuits: classic, lovely stuff. However, tonight is a different story, for the rest of the stalks are going into a zingy squid salad, along with a good peppering of fresh chillies, garlic, red onions and capers.

Warm Squid, Celery & Chilli Salad

SERVES 4

This is a lovely salad – light and zesty, with tender squid, crunchy celery slivers, the mild, sweet bite of the onions and little bursts of heat from fire-engine-red chillies.

- Put the chilli strips into a small bowl of iced water. Cover it tightly and put it in the fridge. (The soaking takes a bit of the heat out of the chillies, so they make a more subtle garnish.)
- For the marinade, whisk together the oil, chilli and garlic in a medium-sized bowl. Cut down one side of each squid hood and open it out. Run your fingers over the squid to check that no little bits of the quill are still attached – the quill feels hard and looks rather like a shard of fine, clear perspex. Halve each piece lengthways and use a sharp knife to score a diamond cross-hatch pattern on the inside, taking care not to cut all the way through. Put the squid pieces into the marinade and swish them about so they're well coated. Cover the bowl and put it in the fridge while you make the dressing.
- Whisk together all the dressing ingredients in a large bowl, then set it aside.
- There is a bit of an art to cooking squid, and much of it is in the timing. In general, it should either be cooked very, very rapidly or slowly and gently – anywhere in the middle and it becomes incredibly tough. In this particular dish it's cooked quickly. Heat a large, heavy-based frying pan (or barbecue plate) until it's very, very hot – almost smoking. Add the squid pieces, scored-side down, and cook them for 1½ minutes, pressing down on them occasionally with a fish slice or wide spatula. Now turn them over. As you do this they may start to curl, but don't worry – as you turn each piece, press it flat for about 10 seconds then let it roll, by which time it will be cooked. (If you are cooking the squid in a frying pan, you may have to do this in batches.)
- Remove the squid pieces, place them on a chopping board and slice the rolls into rounds about 1 cm thick. Toss the rounds in the dressing until they're well coated – you can leave them in it for up to 30 minutes if you like. Just before serving the salad, add most of the finely sliced onion, celery and parsley to the squid and mix it in gently.
- I sometimes just pile this up in bowls, sprinkling it with the reserved onion strips, celery, parsley and chilli shreds. However, to make it a bit more substantial, sit a slice of garlic-rubbed toast on each plate, drizzle it with a little olive oil, then top it with some parsley sprigs. Divide the salad evenly among the four slices of toast. Garnish each one with a little of the reserved onion, celery and parsley, then sprinkle the chilled chilli shreds on top. Serve with lime wedges.

2 small red chillies, seeded and sliced into very fine strips
4 large squid hoods, cleaned (they should be nice and white)
½ red onion, very finely sliced (or more to taste)
3–4 celery stalks, finely sliced on the diagonal
generous handful of chopped flat-leaf parsley
4 slices garlic-rubbed toast, to serve, optional
extra virgin olive oil, for drizzling, optional
flat-leaf parsley sprigs, to serve, optional
lime wedges, to serve

MARINADE

90 ml extra virgin olive oil
2 small red chillies, finely chopped
4 large cloves garlic, finely chopped

DRESSING

⅓ cup (80 ml) lemon juice, strained
¼–⅓ cup (60–80 ml) extra virgin olive oil
1 tablespoon capers, rinsed and drained
1 clove garlic, crushed
sea salt flakes, to taste

28th November

We had the storm to beat all storms last night. In fact, tempest is probably a better word as I don't think I have ever sat through a more violent and spectacular show of nature's raw power. The noise alone was an assault on the senses: great bolts of lightning, three or four at a time, streaked to earth – and the thunder that followed was ear-splitting! The skies were illuminated by the most extraordinary light show, and the rain was almost horizontal as it lashed against the windows. At times I wondered if the roof would take off, snatched by one of the tremendous gusts of wind that hammered at it and pushed up under the eaves. Unfortunately, Clive was away, so I sat myself in the middle of the house, well away from the windows, and tried to think brave thoughts!

And, as happens so often here, when I woke this morning it was as though it had never been – everything was clear and still and peaceful. It was only as I walked into town that the devastation of the night before became apparent: branches and debris were strewn everywhere, some trees and power lines were down, the creek had overflowed its banks; and there was water, water, everywhere.

It was while I was absorbing all this that I heard a deep thrum above me and, when I looked up, two majestic white-headed pigeons, their wings folded like angels, were looking serenely around as if to say: 'Don't worry, all will be well now.' It was strangely comforting.

30th November

Well, what a way to end this book! Yesterday, when I was reaching up to get a jar down from the top shelf of the pantry, I managed to knock an even bigger jar off balance. Unfortunately, it fell and smashed, and a piece of the glass slashed my foot to the bone. Ouch! There followed one of those terrible moments when you don't want to look at the damage, but know you have to. I took one quick peek (one was more than enough, believe me) and realised it wasn't something that my usual band-aid and cup of tea would fix. To cut a long story short, I'm now sitting here, my foot neatly stitched up and swaddled in bandages, contemplating the prospect of having to stay off my feet as much as possible for a while. With Christmas coming and a garden that seems to have grown like Topsy over the past week, something tells me that this is going to be an interesting exercise in letting go! Still, it could have been so much worse and, in a funny way, I suspect that it was time for me to stop – and now I have no choice.

On a much happier note, we've just been sitting having breakfast outside in the cool of the early morning and it struck me just how much the garden has changed since we moved in. Back then it was pretty, but far more formal, whereas now it's a positive tangle of flowers, bushes and shrubs alive with all sorts of birds, bees, frogs, lizards and goodness knows what other creatures. Gussie lay at my feet, in the hope that a crust from my breakfast toast might find its way to him, and all in all a general air of contentment reigned.

I can't tell you how blessed I feel to be part of all this. It quite takes my breath away. The year has had its ups and downs, as life does for us all (what's that truism about wherever you go, there you are!) – but to be safe, healthy and able to enjoy this beautiful place is a privilege that's beyond compare, and I am truly grateful for it.

But enough of my reverie, I must be off: for despite my injury there are still dogs to feed, weeds to pull, veggies to plant – and, of course, much to cook!

ACKNOWLEDGEMENTS

There have been so many special people who have helped make this book a reality that it's hard to know where to begin. That said, perhaps the most important place to start is with my wonderful publisher, Julie Gibbs, without whom this book would still be a jumble of words and ideas sitting on my computer. I can't thank you enough for your unfailing wisdom, patience and friendship, and for encouraging Rodney and me to potter along in our own somewhat unusual way of doing things.

To Alison Cowan – I feel so very blessed to have had you as my editor. It has been a joy working with you and I know this book is so much the better for your discerning and caring eye. Thank you too to Rachel Carter who picked up this book in the final stages and ran with it to get it over the line – it has been such a pleasure working with you.

I could never imagine that the hundreds (if not thousands!) of photos Rodney and I took, and the reams of journal entries I made could have ended up as such a lovely, simple and inviting book. It is thanks to the great talent of designer Allison Colpoys that this has been possible – I think you deserve a medal!

Rodney, my dear old friend, where to begin? Your exquisite photos have brought my words to life. Thank you for the many years of friendship and collaboration that have resulted in this beautiful book, and the happy hours we spent shooting it. Do you think we have another one in us?!

To my sister, Cass, a very big and heartfelt thank you – firstly just for being you, the best sister I could ever wish for, and secondly for hunting out so many of the quirky and delightful props that pepper the pages of this book.

To my family both here and overseas, thank you for your unfailing support and encouraging words – you mean the world to me. As do the members of my 'other' family – my treasured friends and unofficial taste-testing team of Lizi Beadman, Nick Edmond, Abigail Lewis, Sue and Mark Kelly, Michelle Hartnett (and little Holly blossom), Barb Jeffery, Richard Kidby, Chris Moss, Don Drinkwater and Dean Shawcross. You are all so dear to my heart. Thank you for your love and faith in what I do, and for your patience when I had my 'busy writing' sign up!

There are two special people I would also like to thank: Helen Nott and Kate Llewellyn. I think you vie with Clive to be my number one supporters! I don't know what I would do without your infectious enthusiasm and care.

Not one of my books could ever have come about if it hadn't been for my beautiful mum, Cooee, and the love of cooking she instilled in me. Mum, thank you.

I'm also hugely grateful to the generous-spirited farmers and producers from the Mullumbimby and Byron Bay farmers' markets who fuel my love of cooking with their terrific produce and knowledge.

There are also a number of people who generously loaned me their treasured bits and pieces to use. Long-time friend and colleague Sue Jenkins and the lovely staff at Accoutrement, who are always so helpful and obliging. Old friends Kim and Chris Taylor, who generously loaned whatever we wanted from their amazing collections. Thanks to Carol Crennan for trusting me with her grandmother's beautiful bowls, which had spent many years on a sheep station at Brewarrina, and to photographer Andrew Payne, who allowed us to raid his weird and wonderful props cupboards.

Special thanks too to Lizzie at Honey Bee, who let us borrow so many of her gorgeous imports; Shelley Simpson and James Kirton of Mud for their generosity with such beautiful hand-made ceramics; and Anna and Cathy from Clay & Flax for their exquisite linens and pottery.

And last, the biggest and most heartfelt thank you of all to my darling Clive. None of this would have been possible without your unflagging encouragement and love.

INDEX

Q

R

S

LANTERN

Published by the Penguin Group
Penguin Group (Australia)
250 Camberwell Road, Camberwell, Victoria 3124, Australia
(a division of Pearson Australia Group Pty Ltd)
Penguin Group (USA) Inc.
375 Hudson Street, New York, New York 10014, USA
Penguin Group (Canada)
90 Eglinton Avenue East, Suite 700, Toronto, Canada ON M4P 2Y3
(a division of Pearson Penguin Canada Inc.)
Penguin Books Ltd
80 Strand, London WC2R 0RL England
Penguin Ireland
25 St Stephen's Green, Dublin 2, Ireland
(a division of Penguin Books Ltd)
Penguin Books India Pvt Ltd
11 Community Centre, Panchsheel Park, New Delhi – 110 017, India
Penguin Group (NZ)
67 Apollo Drive, Rosedale, North Shore 0632, New Zealand
(a division of Pearson New Zealand Ltd)
Penguin Books (South Africa) (Pty) Ltd
24 Sturdee Avenue, Rosebank, Johannesburg 2196, South Africa

Penguin Books Ltd, Registered Offices: 80 Strand,
London WC2R 0RL, England

First published by Penguin Group (Australia), 2010

10 9 8 7 6 5 4 3 2 1

Design by Allison Colpoys © Penguin Group (Australia)
Photography by Rodney Weidland
Props styling by Cass Stokes
Illustrations by James Gordon
Knitting for spine by Felicity Dawson

Typeset in Avenir book 9.25/13.8pt by Post Pre-Press Group, Brisbane, Queensland
Colour reproduction by Splitting Image Colour Studio Pty Ltd, Clayton, Victoria
Printed and bound in China by 1010 Printing International Limited

National Library of Australia
Cataloguing-in-Publication data:

Jeffery, Belinda.
The country cookbook / Belinda Jeffery.
ISBN 9781920989965 (hbk.)
Includes index.
Cookery--Australia.

641.5994

penguin.com.au/lantern

Thank you to the following stockists for providing props for our photo shoot.

Accoutrement
611 Military Road, Mosman NSW 2088
02 9969 1031

Clay & Flax
469A Pacific Highway, Crows Nest NSW 2065
02 9460 7511

Honey Bee Homewares
178 Sydney Road, Fairlight NSW 2094
02 9948 9908

Mud Australia
134 Edgecliffe Road, Woollahra NSW 2025
02 9389 5580

Front cover: Almond & Lemon Syrup Cake (page 186)